THE CHINESE ESSAY

古今散文英譯集

The Chinese Essay

TRANSLATED, EDITED AND WITH AN
INTRODUCTION BY

DAVID POLLARD

Columbia University Press
New York

Columbia University Press
Publishers since 1893
New York
Copyright © 2000 by David Pollard

First published in 2000 by
C. Hurst & Co. (Publishers) Ltd., London

All rights reserved

Library of Congress Cataloging-in-Publication Data

The Chinese Essay = [Ku chin san wen Ying i chi] / translated and edited by David Pollard.
   p. cm
   Parallel title in Chinese characters.
   ISBN: 978-0-231-12119-4

   I. Chinese essays—Translations into English. 1. Title: [Ku chin san wen Ying i chi]. II. Pollard, David.

PL2658.E8 C475 2000
895.1'4008—dc21

                                                                               99–089425

Contents

Preface   xi
Acknowledgements   xv
Skeleton Chronology   xvi

Introduction   1
Zhuge Liang 諸葛亮 (181–234)   25
    To Lead out the Army 出師表
Tao Qian 陶潛 (365–427)   28
    Requiem for Myself 自祭文
Han Yu 韓愈 (768–824)   31
    Address to the Crocodiles of Chaozhou 祭鱷魚文
    Goodbye to Penury 送窮文
Liu Zongyuan 柳宗元 (773–819)   38
    The Whip Vendor 鞭賈
    My First Excursion to West Mountain 始得西山宴游記
    The Small Rock Pool West of the Hillock 至小丘西小石潭記
Lu Guimeng 陸龜蒙 (? – ca. 881)   44
    A Monument to Rustic Temples 野廟碑
Ouyang Xiu 歐陽修 (1007–1072)   48
    The Old Toper's Pavilion 醉翁亭記
Su Shi 蘇軾 (1037–1101)   52
    The Terrace over the Void 凌虛台記
    Master Table Mountain 方山子傳
    Red Cliff: One 前赤壁賦
    Inscription for the Temple of Han Yu at Chaozhou 潮洲韓文公廟碑
Su Che 蘇轍 (1039–1112)   64
    The Pavilion of Elation 黃州快哉亭記

Fang Xiaoru 方孝儒 (1357–1402)   67
   The Mosquito Dialogue 蚊對

Gui Youguang 歸有光 (1506–1571)   71
   My Mother: A Brief Life 先妣事略
   The Xiangji Studio 項脊軒志

Yuan Hongdao 袁宏道 (1568–1610)   78
   Tiger Hill 虎丘記
   The Rewards of Stupidity 拙效傳

Zhang Dai 張岱 (1597–1684)   84
   The Full Moon Festival at the West Lake 西湖七月半
   Wang Yuesheng 王月生
   Liu Jingting: Storyteller 柳敬亭說書
   The Jades of Yangzhou 揚州瘦馬

Li Yu 李漁 (1611–1680)   93
   Pleasant Diversions: Judging Beauty 閑情偶記・選姿
   Pleasant Diversions: Accomplishments 閑情偶記・習技
   Pleasant Diversions: Literacy 閑情偶記・文藝
   Pleasant Diversions: Clothes 閑情偶記・衣衫

Fang Bao 方苞 (1668–1749)   100
   Life in Prison 獄中雜記

Yuan Mei 袁枚 (1716–1797)   106
   Thoughts on Master Huang's Book Borrowing 黃生借書說

Lu Xun 魯迅 (1881–1936)   108
   Three Summer Pests 夏三蟲
   The Evolution of the Male Sex 男人的進化
   Ah Jin 阿金
   Confucius in Modern China 在現代中國的孔夫子

Zhou Zuoren 周作人 (1885–1967)   129
   Relentless Rain 苦雨
   Reading in the Lavatory 入廁讀書
   On 'Passing the Itch' 談過癩

The Ageing of Ghosts 鬼的生長
In Praise of Mutes 啞巴禮讚

Xia Mianzun 夏丏尊 (1886–1946)   160
  The Ornamental Iron Mountain 鋼鐵假山
  Winter at White Horse Lake 白馬湖之冬

Ye Shengtao 葉聖陶 (1894–1988)   166
  Three Kinds of Boat 三種船
  My Own Patch of Green 天井裡的種植
  Intellectuals 知識份子

Feng Zikai 豐子愷 (1898–1975)   188
  Eating Melon Seeds 吃瓜子
  Autumn 秋
  Bombs in Yishan 宜山遇炸記

Yu Dafu 郁達夫 (1896–1945)   206
  Village School and Academy 書塾與學堂
  The Winter Scene in Jiangnan 江南的冬景

Zhu Ziqing 朱自清 (1898–1948)   216
  The View from the Rear 背影
  Traces of Wenzhou 溫州的蹤跡
  The Lotus Pond by Moonlight 荷塘月色

Liang Shih-ch'iu 梁實秋 (1902–1987)   225
  Sickness 病
  Haircut 理髮
  Listening to Plays 聽戲

Liang Yuchun 梁遇春 (1906–1932)   238
  On the Road 途中
  Well-meant Words 善言

Lu Li 陸蠡 (1908–1942)   247
  A Temple Lodging 廟宿

Yang Jiang 楊絳 (1911–)   259
  The Art of Listening 聽話的藝術

Cloak of Invisibility 隱身衣
He Qifang 何其芳 (1912–1979) ... 270
Elegy 哀歌
Ch'i Chun 琦君 (1917–) ... 276
Chignon 髻
Eileen Chang 張愛玲 (1920–1995) ... 282
The Religion of the Chinese 中國人的宗教
A Beating 打人
Wang Ting-chün 王鼎鈞 (1925–) ... 294
The Last Word in Beauty and Ugliness 最美和最醜
Footprints 腳印
Yu Kwang-chung 余光中 (1928–) ... 304
Thus Friends Absent Speak 尺素寸心
My Four Hypothetical Enemies 我的四個假想敵
Zongpu 宗璞 (1928–) ... 316
The Call of the Ruins 廢墟的召喚
Koarnhak Tarn 陳冠學 (1934–) ... 321
The Countryside of the Past 昔日的田園
Today's Countryside 今日的田園
Huang Chunming 黃春明 (1939–) ... 339
We Can't Bring Back the Past 往事只能回味
Waiting for a Flower's Name 等待一朵花的名字
Yu Qiuyu 余秋雨 (1946–) ... 350
Shanghai People 上海人
Zhang Xingjian 張行健 (1959–) ... 362
Goodwives 婆娘們
References ... 369

Illustrations

between pages 108 and 109

Han Yu's calligraphy
A letter by Ouyang Xiu
A letter by Fang Bao

Li Yu's calligraphy on a fan
'Ref Cliff', calligraphy by Su Shi
Yuan Hongdao's calligraphy

Calligraphy by Gui Youguang
A couplet by Yuan Mei aged 80
'Silent Studio', calligraphy by Fang Xiaoru

Calligraphy by Lu Xun
Lu Xun in 1933
Ye Shengtao
A couplet by Ye Shengtao

Feng Zikai in 1961
A drawing by Feng Zikai
Calligraphy by Yu Dafu, written in 1936
Yu Dafu in 1934

Calligraphy by He Qifang
He Qifang
Zhu Ziqing in 1931
Calligraphy by Zhu Ziqing

A letter by Liang Yuchun
A poem by Li Qingzhao in Xia Mianzun's calligraphy

Zhou Zuoren aged 78
A letter from Zhou Zuoren to Liang Shih-ch'iu
Calligraphy by Liang Shih-ch'iu
Liang Shih-ch'iu in 1975

Illustrations

The manuscript of 'Footprints' by Wang Ting-chün
Wang Ting-chün
Yu Kwang-chung
'Thus Friends Absent Speak' by Yu Kwang-chung

A manuscript by Zongpu
Zongpu
Yang Jiang
'Cloak of Invisibility' by Yang Jiang

Huang Chunming
'We Can't Bring Back the Past' by Huang Chunming
The manuscript of 'Chignon' by Ch'i Chun
Ch'i Chun

'The Countryside of the Past' by Koarnhak Tarn
Koarnhak Tarn
Zhang Xingjian
'Goodwives' by Zhang Xingjian

Preface

On Essays in General and this Anthology in Particular

When English essays were first translated into Chinese on any scale in the 1920s and 30s, there was no agreement on what to call them. The most favoured options were *xiaopinwen* (minor works, or short pieces) and *suibi* (occasional jottings), terms which applied to classes of classical literature. Presently the most commonly used term is *sanwen* (prose). *Sanwen* is also what the Chinese now call their own current prose compositions—or essays. So a correspondence has been established between *sanwen* and 'essay', and any modern collection published in Chinese under the title of *sanwen* will consist of essays and nothing else. But anthologies of classical writing entitled *sanwen* will draw on the wider (and sole original) meaning of *sanwen*, which is anything not written in verse. So they will include official memorials and rescripts, prefaces, letters, obituaries, prose poems, biographies, excerpts from historical and philosophical works, and more besides. That is because particular works in all those categories have been the most admired examples of prose composition down the ages, and it is they which comprise the prose heritage. About the only non-metrical prose traditionally excluded from *sanwen* is prose fiction.

The beginning of the problem for the anthologist who wishes to round up some of the best Chinese essays for the Western reader to enjoy can now be seen. Modern compositions only present the difficulty of choice, as they conform to the notion of the Western essay, and so are able to meet the expectations of the readers who see that word on the book's cover. Classical compositions, on the other hand, do not for the most part fit people's notions of the essay. They cannot, however, be ignored, partly because the last 2,000 years produced, as must be expected, some very fine writing, partly because their survival in the school curriculum has ensured their contribution to the education of every modern Chinese essayist. Given, then, the place of classical compositions in this anthology, I feel I should prepare the reader for what to expect and what not to expect of them. We will start with the negatives. Needless to say, we will deal in gross generalities. There will be some slight overlap with what is said in the Introduction, but some things can bear repeating.

China had no Montaigne, no background to produce a Montaigne, and no inclination to celebrate a Montaigne had he arrived as a freak of history. Neither his mindset nor the language he used had a place in China until the 20th century. Taking language first, Montaigne published his *Essais* in French in 1580, Bacon his *Essayes* in English 1597–1625. The European vernacular languages established themselves as the medium for educated discourse in the 16th and 17th centuries, replacing Latin, while in China the classical language remained the only respectable medium until the end of empire. The choice of language affects not only how something is said, but what is said: being dignified in itself, a classical language will naturally discourage discourse on undignified matters. Absence of dignity was a very important factor in the life of the European essay.

Along with the adoption of the national vernaculars in Europe went the development of a new national consciousness and a broad range of subject matter. Essayists in Europe, and later in America, played their part, some consciously, some not, in refining and directing thoughts and sensibilities to create a polity that was new and particular. From the early 1700s they spread their word through magazines that circulated nationwide and were read by newly literate classes. In China by contrast, dynasty succeeded dynasty after the initial phase with no significant change in ideology or modification to the ideal polity laid down in the Han dynasty as state Confucianism, and there was no free press until near the end of the 19th century (under the protection of the foreign enclaves). Thus there was no mission, no charge of energy, to make writers and intellectuals in classical China see the world afresh.

Literacy in imperial China was confined to an elite that was tiny in proportion to the population. Almost all the intellectually able among that elite aspired to a place in the bureaucracy, and their way to a career lay in an education in the classics, which were unchallengeable. In that respect a great deal of their own writing resembled that of the medieval European priesthood who took as sacred the Holy Bible and the works of the early church fathers. Here we come to mindset. Because of the great weight of authority, there was very little soul-searching or disinterested enquiry in classical prose. We rarely see impartial attempts to balance one view against another, or cases of thinking-in-progress: that is, the author wrestling with a problem as he goes along, as opposed to producing a pat answer. The classical author tended to make pronouncements *ex cathedra*, in a hollow voice. Hence one has to look far to find the personalized reasoning based on experience that was the trademark of the European discursive essay.

A further deficiency was the Chinese scholar's knowledge of the world beyond his frontiers. Such knowledge remained abysmal until the late 19th century, by which time Western books on world history and geography had been translated in large numbers. The Chinese empire previously regarded itself as self-sufficient, unlike the European states which sent their sailors and scientists all over the globe, and brought back knowledge along with commodities from those expeditions. Of course, Chinese culture was rich enough to provide much food for thought and much to write about despite its containment and those limitations, but a practical consideration bearing on this anthology intervenes here: since Chinese scholars wrote for their fellows who had the same education as themselves, they presumed a great deal of shared knowledge that is no longer shared by present-day Chinese readers, and certainly not shared by foreign readers. The most brilliantly argued essays on historical and cultural matters will therefore have to be sacrificed, as we work on the principle that essays should be read as essays and not as academic papers distended by annotation.

On the lighter side, all cultures worthy of the name have their entertainments. Entertainment value ranked very high in English essays in consequence of their publication in magazines that had to sell well, hence the prominence of wit and humour. The very exceptional Chinese writer who had to sell his writings to earn a living did seek to entertain, and of those few Li Yu in particular is consistently amusing. Men of letters otherwise received payment only for writing flattering obituaries and the like, whose entertainment value was not designed to be high. On the whole classical prose sought to *please* rather than entertain, by appeal to aesthetic tastes. Born wits, however, occasionally gave way to their nature.

Having, I hope, said enough to forestall incorrect anticipation of what Chinese classical prose compositions have to offer, brought about by my lumping them together with modern ones as 'essays', I need to say a word about their positive qualities. Here I may be brief, as they will shortly speak for themselves. The qualities are on the one hand common to mankind, on the other particular to Chinese literary arts. The first kind includes the expression of character in the writer, either impressively strong or appealingly weak; the expression of sentiment, usually to commemorate friends and relatives; nostalgia for past times; appeals for justice and compassion;

pleasure in diversions. The second kind concerns the musicality of the language, a prime and often, regrettably, *the* prime requirement for approval. It immediately poses the question of translatability. Musicality involves both the harmonies of words and the overall structure or architecture of a composition. The latter can be reproduced without loss in translation, as long as the translator is aware what the architecture is. The former obviously cannot be reproduced, as different words must be used. The tenor of the piece may be imitated, with matching of sonorities and dulcet tones, but the harmonies will be different in translation, and almost inevitably inferior. One has to face the both depressing and cheering fact that compositions that have survived for hundreds of years will be better written than the translator of today can manage.

In the Introduction that follows I will attempt to describe the historical development of Chinese prose, including this time the modern essay. In the main body of the book I preface each selection with a commentary to explain who the author was or is, what certain pieces are about if that is not clear, and the odd important reference that may be obscure. From some living writers I have been able to get clarification of points I did not understand myself, and I thank them sincerely for their collaboration. There will no doubt remain other points I thought I understood but did not. With classical authors, deaf to requests, I have relied heavily on the elucidations provided by modern editors of their works, unfortunately too many to acknowledge.

Perhaps it would be as well, in conclusion, to anticipate misunderstandings about my criteria for selection. The first thing to say is that it would be neither practicable nor desirable to follow one invariable principle. A variety of considerations, both personal and general, compete for preference. The personal one is that selflessness can only go so far: translators cannot translate well things they positively dislike, however high their prestige, and conversely may be excused for translating things that appeal to them more than to others. On the other hand, personal taste could not be allowed to call the tune, because the idea was to represent *the* Chinese essay in its past and present manifestations, as comprehensively as space allowed and ready intelligibility permitted. Some old favourites had to be translated yet again because of their centrality; at the same time, existing translations could be taken into account to avoid repetition in more marginal cases. What obviously had to be ruled out was attempting to fill the gaps in the existing stock of English translations, as that would have driven this anthology from the centre to the periphery.

We expect that some readers or users of this book will be able to read Chinese. For their convenience, Chinese characters have been inserted in the commentary sections to facilitate identification of certain names and titles. Other readers and users who do not know Chinese should regard the Chinese characters merely as decoration. They should not be alarmed into thinking that this must be a book for specialists. On the contrary, my aim has been to make its matter accessible to those who know little about China and nothing of the Chinese language.

Acknowledgements

Thanks should go first to Christopher Hurst, who has been prodding me to write another book for him ever since he published my first one, *A Chinese Look at Literature*, in 1973, despite the fact that it set a record for slow sales. In our present old age there are better things to look forward to than slow sales, so I hope his constancy will be more suitably rewarded with this anthology.

Next, Eva Hung subtly promoted the anthology enterprise by encouraging me to translate bits and pieces of Chinese prose for *Renditions* while we co-edited the magazine (1989–97). She and her team at the Research Centre for Translation, Chinese University of Hong Kong, have also undertaken the editing work for this book, which is to be a joint publication with Hurst.

Thirdly, the City University of Hong Kong very kindly offered me a research professorship for one year (1998–99), which enabled me to finish the job. Chen Shu Yee, my research assistant there, was very helpful, not only in typing my longhand drafts and dealing with correspondence, but also in finding material and on occasion disputing my reading.

Finally, the Bogliasco Foundation granted me generous hospitality in its villa on the Ligurian coast for me to acquire and apply a certain polish to my translations.

Chinese University of Hong Kong　　　　　　　　　　DAVID POLLARD
October 1999

Skeleton Chronology

Warring States	475 BC–221 BC
Qin Dynasty	221 BC–206 BC
Western (or Former) Han Dynasty	206 BC–23 AD
Eastern (or Latter) Han Dynasty	25–220
Three Kingdoms (Wei, Shu, and Wu)	220–280
Western Jin Dynasty	265–316
Eastern Jin Dynasty	317–420
Southern and Northern Dynasties	420–589
Sui Dynasty	581–618
Tang Dynasty	618–907
Five Dynasties	907–960
Northern Song Dynasty	960–1127
Southern Song Dynasty	1127–1279
Yuan (Mongol) Dynasty	1279–1368
Ming Dynasty	1368–1644
Qing (Manchu) Dynasty	1644–1911
Republic of China	1912–1949
May Fourth Movement	1919
People's Republic of China	1949–
Republic of China on Taiwan	1949–
Hundred Flowers Campaign	1956
Anti-Rightist Campaign	1957
Cultural Revolution	1966–1976
Fall of the 'Gang of Four'	1976

Introduction

The European prose tradition had two starts, the Chinese only one. In Europe, ancient Greece and Rome founded all the elements of European civilization and developed a prose literature that encompassed both high eloquence and modest ease. That heritage eventually passed to the European kingdoms which by then used their native tongues, and the same range of prose styles evolved in those divers languages, some suited to the highly educated, others attuned to common burghers. In China the elements of civilization were similarly established in the first millennium BC. Thereafter the Chinese empire went through periods of disunion, but always reknit, and the cultural tradition was unbroken. The written language remained essentially the same classical variety for some 2,000 years, becoming more and more remote from the spoken language and not being ousted until the 20th century. Popular literature designed to entertain the masses was the exception: that was written in the vernacular of the day. Educated written discourse was always conducted in the classical language, which was maintained at a high level by the ancient classics forming the syllabus for the state examinations that had to be passed for entry into the bureaucracy, the goal of every aspiring intellectual. All the pre-modern essayists in this anthology from the Tang dynasty onwards are noted as having passed at least two and usually all three of the examinations, which were from the district level (*xiucai*) to the provincial (*juren*) to the capital (*jinshi*).

Although they were mined for allusions, the more ancient classics did not provide the working written language for late ages. The actual models would have started with the philosophers of the Warring States period, prior to unification in 221 BC, and in practice been predominantly the outstanding literati of the Han dynasty. As each age produced its great writers, they in turn became models for succeeding generations. Emulation of predecessors helped continuity.

Two characteristics common to all periods of classical Chinese were conciseness and symmetry. Symmetry served the purposes both of euphony and of clause division, the latter because vocabulary consisted of single-character words incapable of grammatical inflexion, and there was no punctuation. Conciseness was achieved, leaving monosyllabicity aside, by severe economy with linking phrases and an absence of parentheticals. The fact that they had all had the same education also made it unnecessary for scholars to spell things out to each other.

By education and inclination, the scholar of old was more likely to write for pleasure in verse than in prose. Entirely quotidian experiences and unremarkable occasions were so celebrated, let alone the stirring of powerful emotions. Consequently there was an ever present risk of a prose composition breaking into verse. Indeed, an intermediate form between verse and prose, later known as *pianwen*, emerged after the fall of the Han dynasty; this consisted entirely of parallel units composed of four or six characters. Somewhat bizarrely, it was used for all purposes, including official communications, discourses and treatises, and even private letters. Thus the natural tendency towards symmetry was let loose to overwhelm the medium. From the Tang dynasty onwards *pianwen* and free prose (known as *guwen* or 'ancient style') competed for ascendancy.

Those general dispositions largely account for the complaint made by Lin Yutang 林語堂 in his book *My Country and My People* (1935) that 'There was very little good prose in the classical literature'. By 'good' he meant good by modern standards, that is having a broad sweep and wide canvas, substantial intellectual content, the rhythms of speech, and a familiar, personal tone. Classical Chinese prose, by contrast, was typically euphuistic and poetic, impersonal and stereotyped, economical with words, and cast in a dead language. Broadly correct though Lin's summary was, we will see it was not the whole story when we consider the history of prose literature in China.

The early philosophers and historians wrote as intelligent, closely reasoned, and stylistically versatile prose as any found in later ages. It would be possible to extract chapters and sections from their works and present them as fine discursive, or in the case of Zhuang Zi 莊子 as fantastically inventive, 'essays'. That however, would take us too far afield. To keep a grasp on our subject, we here limit our scope to the free-standing, self-contained, relatively short composition, though in order not to be too consistent we allow one exception from a later period. Such independent compositions surfaced in the stable empire of the Han dynasty. Stability, secured by the effectiveness of a strong central government, had its good side and its bad side. From the point of view of prose composition, it emboldened those who held orthodox opinions to write with ringing confidence. It severely hampered those who wished to think for themselves. It should never be forgotten in this connection that the Chinese empire was a despotism. Punishment for suspected heresy was arbitrary and terrible. It could bring about not only the death of the sometimes inadvertent perpetrator, but also the extermination of his whole family.

Jia Yi 賈誼 (200–168 BC) and Chao Cuo 晁錯 (200–154 BC) in laying down the law for the new empire founded the short political treatise. Jia Yi's style was commanding and magisterial, Chao Cuo's sober and relentless in building up an argument. Both were models for putting a case convincingly. At the same time, a powerful reign has to have its celebrants, hence an ornate kind of prose prospered alongside the forceful kind, written by courtiers. It was elaborately crafted, metrical, allusive, and florid in vocabulary. The really earth-shattering event in the Han dynasty, however, was the publication of a historical work, the *Shi ji* 史記 (Records of the Grand Historian) by Sima Qian 司馬遷 (145–87? BC), revered to this day for its supreme art without artifice. This compendious work of over half a million characters covered more or less all that was known and alleged of the Chinese world up to the author's own day. It was an inexhaustible source for later advisers on policy (as all the emperor's men aspired to be) because of the detailed pleadings of statesmen it recorded, and it included a wealth of material on the economy and applied sciences in separate treatises. Because of the prominence it gave to biography, fleshed out with reconstructed long speeches and dialogues, it exhibited a full gallery of personalities and the whole human range of ambitions and motivations. In that way it could be said to have defined human character in the Chinese setting. It even had, in the section on court jesters, examples of jokes that went down well with the Chinese.

The language of the *Shi ji* is rich and expressive, but in no way ornate or patterned. It suits itself flexibly to the matter, so may be dignified and decorous in one person's mouth, blunt and down-to-earth in another's, or urgent and impassioned in a third's. Despite this vividness, and its easy embrace of common sayings, the language was still the written language of the day, not the spoken language (whatever that was). Hence, no stigma of vulgarity attached to it, and as its antiquity accrued, later stylists who wished to return to healthy, robust, 'attic' prose found in the *Shi ji* what they wanted. Being a work of objective history, however, or at least attempting to be such, the author's own comments are minimal, so I have not been tempted to translate any excerpts. In any case, the bulk of the work has already been excellently translated by Burton Watson.

Potentially the first good candidate for inclusion as an essayist is Wang Chong 王充 (27–101? AD), especially as his *magnum opus* was entitled *Lunheng* 論衡, which roughly translates as 'critiques'. These eighty-five pieces very much presented a personal view, and not only expressed the truth as he saw it, but professed to do so, which is a good sign. He set out to refute accepted myths, falsehoods and superstitions, using plain words, common sense and the evidence of experience. For instance, he daringly argued that the births of the most eminent Han emperors were no divine nativities, but the unintended consequence of their parents coupling for no other reason than carnal desire. While that and other views of his were refreshingly sensible, he had his own blind sides, and overall his 'essays' would not now be found very impressive intellectually, or of any interest stylistically.

Wang Chong's critiques were a sign of the loosening of ideological bondage following the usurpation of Wang Mang 王莽 (9–23 AD) and the diminished authority of the restored house of Han. Views on a wide variety of topics were published in increasing numbers, mostly in the form of letters (*shu*) intended for circulation. At the same time there was a further trend in prose style towards the measured footfall of advancing battalions; even the fulminations of Wang Fu 王符 (?85–?162 AD) against social ills and moral depravity were locked into short segments of even length.

Complete freedom from ideological bondage was achieved in the period of disunity following the fall of the Han dynasty. Personal salvation and satisfaction replaced service to the state as the goal of the educated minority; Taoism ousted Confucianism, and Buddhism received a ready welcome, as both condoned retreat into protective cocoons and neither offered threat to life and limb. Literature ceased to rely on moral justifications for its existence, and declared independence as an aesthetic pursuit, in recognition of which treatises began to be written on the *art* of *belles-lettres*. It is a striking fact that Cao Pi 曹丕(187–226), son of Cao Cao 曹操 and the first emperor of the Wei, himself proclaimed that great literature was the supreme attainment of both state and person, for states will be overturned and graves dug up, but the literature will never decay. Cao Pi was also the first person known to have applied the notion of *qi* (in this context meaning something like 'generative energy') directly to literature. In his formulation, *qi* was elemental in all literary composition, and it varied according to the individual. Hence one can say that it was the physical underpinning of the distinctive character, or personal stamp, that an author's writing is imprinted with. From this notion flowed the ever more elaborate and particularized descriptions of past and present writers' personal styles that later critics were to produce, ornamented with colour and flavour terms.

More broadly, the conscious aestheticism of this period strengthened conceptions of the various literary forms and the styles appropriate to them. The recognized prose forms were those that had been established for official ceremonial and commemorative purposes. Lu Ji's 陸機 *Wenfu* 文賦 (On Style, ca. 300) attributed ideal characteristics to each genre, (the *shuo*, or plea, for instance, being 'dazzlingly bright and extravagantly bizarre') and Liu Xie's 劉勰 *Wenxin diaolong* 文心雕龍 (The Convolutions of the Literary Mind, ca. 500) concluded the process by extending discussions of each genre to chapter length.

The looser, occasional forms of prose, like *shu* (epistle), *lun* (discussion) and *ji* (account), though more difficult to describe, were also analysed and assigned their tone colouring. The general directive was that literature should 'give pleasure to the ear, delight to the eye' (*Wenfu*).

A negative result of this aestheticism was the promotion of form at the expense of content. Concretely this was manifest in the practically complete monopolization of the written word in the 5th and 6th centuries by *pianwen* (parallel prose). To explain a little further, *pian* means to harness a pair of horses alongside each other; applied to writing it designated antithetical pairs of clauses or phrases that exactly kept in step with each other. The units were either consistently of four characters or alternatively of four and six characters. Discourse in this form proceeded with two feet together, as it were, in a series of hops, which led to associated thoughts being merely juxtaposed, sometimes inconsistently, without the close binding of unilinear prose. So this form was pretty to look at and pleasant to hear when read out loud, but destructive of logical thinking. Both the theoretical works we have referred to, the *Wenfu* and *Wenxin diaolong*, were composed in *pianwen*.

More abstractly, the aestheticism of this period focused attention on the sensual experience of reader reception; thought content or mental power was downgraded, or barely mentioned. Criticism emphasized performance rather than content, as in a concert where the score is taken as given, and the interest is in the way the virtuoso plays. This order of priorities was unfortunately to persist in Chinese culture, no doubt reinforced by the assumption that the important things had been said in the ancient classics, and all that could be expected of later works was adumbration.

A landmark in literary history was recorded in the 6th century by the compilation of the *Wenxuan* 文選 (Anthology of Literature), under the supervision of Xiao Tong 蕭統 (501–531), crown prince of the Liang dynasty. Embracing both poetry and short prose compositions and excluding only living writers, this anthology arranged the works according to genre. On the whole the choice of pieces has been endorsed by later anthologies; in any case the *Wenxuan* became essential reading for later literati.

My own first choice for translation, Zhuge Liang's 諸葛亮 'Chu shi biao' (To lead out the army) appears in the *Wenxuan*. On the face of it it is an unpromising candidate, as it is a functional memorial presented by a first minister to his emperor, making arrangements for governance in his absence, but actually it exemplifies better than any other composition in Chinese literature what Cao Pi meant by *qi*, that is, the stamp of strong character. My second selection, Tao Yuanming's self-obituary, is included, apart from its intrinsic interest, as a piece of rhythmic prose, which is the nearest I approach *pianwen*.

At the end of the period of disunity there appeared a work that ran against the trend of ornamentalism. *Yan shi jiaxun* 顏氏家訓

(Family Instructions of Mr Yan) by Yan Zhitui 顏之推 (529?–591) was written in elegant but simple prose, and spoke, as its title indicates, of homely matters. Though it has runs of parallel clauses, they are well broken up, and overall it gives the impression of naturalness. In substance and manner it was a harbinger of things to come in the Tang dynasty.

Faith in the empire and the value system of Confucianism was restored in the Tang dynasty. The civil service was reformed as a meritocracy, with entry based on state-wide examinations, which meant that relatively disadvantaged individuals could rise to prominence by virtue of intelligence alone. As beneficiaries of the system, they supported it with force and conviction, though aware of its failings, and this accounts for the vigour and vitality of their writing. At the same time, as self-made men confident of their own talent, they were prepared to strike out on their own and create new kinds of prose compositions, albeit under the same old genre names. In addition to its utilitarian functions of narrative, exposition and argumentation, prose writing became an alternative vehicle to poetry for the expression of sentiment and emotional experience, and distinctively a vehicle for allegory, satire and sportiveness.

In terms of style and diction, prose writing in the Tang dynasty gradually divested itself of *pianwen*, whose mellifluity and euphuisms were associated with decadence, and returned to the plain, flexible, unilinear style of the classical period, which, by that time could properly be called *guwen* (ancient prose). The *guwen* school's view of prose style was close to that taken in the West, that a good style consisted of no more and no less than putting in the best order the words that could best express the author's thoughts. Along with disdain for ornament naturally went esteem for substantial content. On the other hand, the emphasis on restoring ancient virtues, summed up in the word *dao* (the Confucian Way), entailed reference to the authority of ancient scripture, and so was not conducive to the independence of thought that we associate with the prose essay—perhaps the ruminative essay truly comes into its own when there is no authority, or at least only lax authority, to refer to. Sharpness of thought, however, evinced in forceful argument, skilful reasoning, vehemence and subtlety of expression, is to be found in quantity in Tang prose, as it should be, considering that the

Introduction

Quan Tang wen 全唐文(Complete Tang Prose) includes 18,000 pieces by 3,042 authors. That the authors tended to deliver their discourses on serious subjects from an imaginary pulpit was just inherent in their situation.

As all scholars were perforce students of Chinese history, historical essays featured prominently among their occasional pieces, highlighting things they admired or censured or found a reinterpretation for. In the works of the two acknowledged *guwen* masters of the Tang dynasty, Han Yu and Liu Zongyuan, can be found many examples. As the intention was to prove a point, their focus was on clear and cogent reasoning, with no frills attached. Relaxed discussion of familiar matters had to find a home in letters (as mentioned), and of cultural matters in prefaces, neither of which allowed much expansiveness. In three respects, however, Han and Liu pushed forward the frontiers of prose composition. First, they used the *zhuan* (biography) to write of humble tradesmen (masons, nurserymen, snake-catchers), not so much for themselves as spokesmen for ways of life or healthy, common-sense attitudes that they, the authors, endorsed; in other words, the subjects were hardly any more than borrowed voices. Second, they developed the parable, Han Yu with his 'Maoying zhuan' (Biography of Mr Furpoint) and Liu Zongyuan with his animal parables, which were very like Aesop's fables. Third, Liu Zongyuan established the landscape essay as an art form. His 'Yongzhou ba ji' (Eight descriptions of Yongzhou, 809), each taking up on average no more than half a page in a modern edition, are like panels of a painting which put together form a broad vista. Yongzhou was on the remote southwest fringe of Hunan province, a wild region to which Liu had been demoted. There for the first time he apprehended Nature as an overwhelming presence that made his mind 'congeal' and his body 'dissolve'. From this communion derived the sketches that would inform the consciousness of nearly all subsequent practitioners of this genre.

The next high point in the history of Chinese prose came in the 11th century with the revival of *guwen*, which had in the interim been overshadowed again by *pianwen*. Compositions on matters of historical, philosophical and general interest, previously the province of the disembodied intellect, became personalized in the hands of Ouyang

Xiu, Su Shi and their like, and the taut and compact, heavily freighted language of Tang prose loosened and lightened. The sophistication and civility of the Song dynasty (960–1279) brought relatively ordinary and routine aspects of life into the ambit of prose composition, there to be celebrated precisely because they represented sophistication and civility. Ouyang Xiu's best remembered pieces are those about pavilions constructed in beauty spots—civilization brought to the wilderness. They gave occasion to talk about the surroundings, local history, and local personages, the author included. 'Zuiweng ting ji' (The old toper's pavilion, 1046), the most famous of all, pictures a scene of perfect rural harmony under the benevolent rule of the prefect, himself. Despite relaxing some tensions, though, Ouyang was still constrained by vehicles: his thoughts on retirement had to be framed as *zizhuan* (autobiography), and his thoughts on autumn framed as a dialogue and called a *fu* (description).

His protégé Su Shi went further than Ouyang in shaping what one might call the occasional essay, combining the elements of narrative, description and reflection. Persuaded of his own genius, justifiably it must be admitted, Su was the first writer in the pantheon of Chinese prose whom modern essayists were willing to recognize as a precursor, on account of his free thinking and uninhibitedness. Though Han Yu could be very witty, Su Shi's writing was unprecedented in its liberal display of humour, not to say jokiness. His sense of superiority, in being attuned to the true harmonies of the creation, led him to take his own view of everything, so he is almost always entertaining. On the other hand, his angle of vision is too elevated for modern tastes, that is, he as author places himself far above what he writes about. This characteristic is general among classical scholar-essayists, but is particularly salient in his case. His occasional essays typically set a scene, introduce someone else's responses to it, then cap that response with his own wiser view, leading to a serene resolution. They are faultlessly written, but they leave the impression that with Su Shi the magic of words takes precedence over truthfulness to experience.

The Tang-Song period is generally regarded as the golden age of Chinese classical prose, a view attested by the fact that to this day the 'Eight Masters of Tang-Song' (who include all those mentioned by name above) figure in every Chinese school syllabus. More information on them will be found in the commentaries attached to my translations of their works.

The mainstream of classical prose after the Eight Masters flowed along a smooth bed for several hundred years, too placidly for most tastes. Most general histories of Chinese literature give relatively little space to prose writing in the Ming and Qing dynasties (14th to 19th century), taking the view that creative energies were channelled into fiction and drama. However, only a very few of the literati actively participated in those fields. The rest carried on with their *guwen* compositions (the writing of *pianwen* having receded to the status of a minor occupation). That they were not more exciting than they were was no doubt connected with the fact that Ming-Qing literati were more earnestly backward-looking than their predecessors: they not only wrote in the manner of past masters, but also wrote extensively about how to write in the manner of past masters. And that mentality was no doubt connected with the fact of heavier pressure for orthodoxy and vigilance against dissent from above. The terrible fate of Fang Xiaoru who dared to oppose the will of one of the early Ming emperors (see relevant commentary) was a plain enough lesson to the scholar-offical class, and the rigid prescription for the state examination essay (popularly known as *baguwen*, the 'eight-legged essay') must have had the effect, as intended, of imposing conformity of thought, much as the selection of texts from the Marxist-Leninist canon for endless study did in the 20th century.

Domestic matters could of course be written about without restrictions. The delicate portraits of his home and family from the hand of Gui Youguang (1506–1571) stand out in his period, and indeed are unique in Chinese prose history. They did not meet the approval of Lin Yutang, who criticized Gui's most famous piece, in memory of his mother, for having only a purely literary craftsmanship, 'laid over a paucity of characterization, a vacuity of facts, and a baldness of sentiment'. There Lin erred. Granted the brevity (that and similar pieces are only about a page long) and baldness of statement, more sympathetic readers have still found that piece extremely vivid and unbearably moving. Though facts are few, they are tellingly chosen; and as for sentiment, Lin did not seem to realize that things half said or unsaid may be more powerfully affective than things said at length. Classical Chinese prose in fact made as much use of empty spaces as Chinese painting.

A surge of highwater disturbed the placid flow of prose at the end of the 16th century, when the Ming dynasty was nearing its end. Carried by the movement in philosophy towards individualism, it threw up the Gongan school of writers, headed by Yuan Hongdao (1568–1610) and his brothers. Like Su Shi, this school believed in genius, but unlike him they thought of genius not as a superior endowment but rather as innate in all individuals. As individuals live in the present and are not the same as people of past ages, so the literature of the present should be different from that of past ages; that position they openly maintained. The Gongan school's detestation of imitation and conventional learning and converse espousal of spontaneity and innocence (the 'child-like mind' was a kind of totem for their mentor, Li Zhuowu 李卓吾), made them prize the songs of village women and children and rejoice in popular entertainments, along with all interests pursued with gusto. Those inclinations are reflected in the topics of their little essays. Consistent with this attitude, the language they used, while till basically classical—for who would wish to relinquish such a rich inheritance?—straddled the boundary between the refined and vulgar, making raids in both directions, and frequently echoed the rhythms of speech.

The Gongan school were influential in their own day, but when another authoritarian dynasty, the alien Manchu one, succeeded the Ming, their business was closed down. That was not the end of their story, though. They enjoyed a revival in the late 1920s and 1930s, because they represented the body of past opinion closest to the ideas of the New Literature movement. The so-called 'late Ming *xiaopinwen*' (short essays) were reprinted and much discussed. Reading them today, one is certainly impressed by their freshness and zest, not so much impressed by their cleverness and facileness. Zhou Zuoren, their chief promoter in the 1920s, praised the works of the Gongan school for their natural charm, freedom from pretence, and their coining of striking phrases, but conceded that they were too transparent and lacked depth. That is a fair judgement.

Introduction

Zhou Zuoren had no reservations, however, in recommending Zhang Dai (1597–1684) who carried on their good work. The pictures in his exhibition have got much more going for them. The world he set out to capture in a series of miniatures had vanished with the Manchu conquest; memory lent it deeper colouring and finer texture. Besides which, it has to be said that he was wiser and more learned than the members of the Gongan school, though he could write as exuberantly as they did. Some examples from his collection *Tao'an mengyi* 陶庵夢憶 (Dream Memories) are translated here.

Other survivors into the Qing dynasty, like Gu Yanwu 顧炎武 (1613–1682) and Huang Zongxi 黃宗羲 (1610–1695), are still well known and respected for their integrity and independence of thought, which translated into an admirably direct and forthright mode of expression. If this was an anthology of historical and political essays, they would figure prominently. When the Qing dynasty settled firmly in the driving seat, however, ominous signs were not slow in coming. Dai Mingshi 戴名世, a compiler in the Imperial Academy, was executed in 1713 for ideological transgressions, and punishment extended far beyond him personally. Intellectuals wisely retreated into textual scholarship.

The literary scene came to be dominated by the Tongcheng school, which took its name from the place of origin of its leading lights. The founder of the Tongcheng school, Fang Bao (1668–1749), having come within a hair's breadth of execution himself because of his friendship with Dai Mingshi, spent the rest of his life demonstrating his loyalty. The written word, or the practice of letters, according to him, looked to two aspects: purport (*yi*) and method (*fa*). The purport had to conform unimpeachably with Confucian philosophy and morality, but also be substantial, and not just parroting; the method required the words to 'have sequence', the structure to have clean, clear lines. In addition, vocabulary had to be purged of decoration, colloquialisms and neologisms. The saving grace of the 'purport' aspect is that Confucian rectitude could make for uncomfortable reading, as Fang Bao's own piece on his experience in prison shows.

Fang Bao's severities were appreciably softened in the hands of two succeeding theorists of the Tongcheng school, Liu Dakui 劉大櫆 (1698–1779) and Yao Nai 姚鼐 (1731–1815). They restored the '*belles*' to '*lettres*', and included occasional, less sententious pieces in their field of vision. They took up the notion of *qi* (generative energy) that Cao Pi had said 'could not be had by striving for it', and used it to track the shifts in pace, strength and mood in compositions. By intoning the venerable works of antiquity to themselves, men of the present could, as it were, imprint their rhythms and cadences on their own vocal organs, and so capture their mechanics, though the source of the *qi*, in their view, remained ineffable. For descriptive purposes, *qi* was also useful in differentiating individual styles. Between the polar opposites of *yanggang* (masculine hardness) and *yinrou* (feminine softness) that Yao Nai posited, there was an infinite range of gradation.

In another approach, Yao Nai picked out eight elements that make up a work of literature, namely *shen* (presiding spirit), *li* (moral principle), *qi*, *wei* (taste), *ge* (structure), *lü* (measure), *sheng* (sound) and *se* (colour), which all formed bases for analysis. Committed as they were by conviction or *force majeure* to be backward looking culturally, the endeavours of the Tongcheng school were a creditable attempt to make current prose literature both readable and sophisticated. They did not deserve the uniformly bad press they got from the 20th century moderns, but considering that the latter were forward looking and populist in outlook, their repudiation was inevitable.

In the over two-and-a-half centuries of the Qing dynasty, there were, of course, non-conformists who appealed more to modern tastes, characters who were either dilettantes, drop-outs, pleasure seekers, or simply private persons. They are represented in token fashion in this anthology by Li Yu, from the beginning of the dynasty, and Yuan Mei, from the middle period.

The shift from classical to modern in China was precipitated by the penetration of foreign ideas following a series of military defeats from 1840 onwards. It was slowly recognized that the survival of China rested on an educated citizenry, as opposed to a very small governing elite, and a means to popular education was the newspapers and magazines founded in the foreign enclaves, with the highest concentration in Shanghai. Although the aims were utilitarian, at last the stage was set for the type of essay that the West had been familiar with since similar conditions pertained there: generous space to expatiate in, a readership of middle-class citizens eager to expand their horizons, and financial rewards adequate to make writing for journals a valuable source of income. A new kind of written language, popularized by journalists, became the standard medium for practical purposes. This still employed classical syntax, but of a limited kind; more positively, it opened its doors wide to the vocabulary of the social sciences that was introduced by translations of Western works. In the space of a few decades there was a revolution in the way thoughts were formulated, and the values of the Tongcheng school ceased to operate.

In 1906 the state examination system with its classical curriculum was finally abolished. The Qing empire itself was overturned in 1911. The simplified literary language adopted by the reformers carried over for another decade as the normal medium of educated discourse, but the argument that survival in the 20th century required that the written and spoken languages be unified gained strength, and the scales were tipped by the energetic support of the flower of Chinese youth who returned from studying abroad. The New Literature that took off around 1920 was all written in the vernacular (*baihua*).

For the first few years when the New Literature was fighting its factional wars, the polemical essay reigned supreme. In that genre the Chinese writer needed no instruction. But when the dust settled, and what we might call the civil essay asked for its place at the table again, foreign models had to be looked to in order to sustain the claim of newness. In the forefront was the English essay. British and American examples and discussions of the essay came in for close study in the Republican period.

The underpinning of Anglo-American literary criticism in the early part of the 20th century was liberal humanism. Awareness of that outlook was either filtered to the Chinese through Western interpreters like Lafcadio Hearn (who was based in Japan) or Japanese scholars, or directly apprehended—almost all prominent Chinese writers and critics in the Republican period (1912–49) knew one European language. The American critic Wilson Follett, with whose views Zhou Zuoren for one showed himself accquainted, wrote the following on the general proposition that the purpose of art is to give pleasure:

> The highest pleasures are the social emotions which came from a rational and truthful view of our status as fellow mortals—pity, compassion, fellow feeling, fraternity, solidarity; the pleasure of 'truth of intercourse'.

That quotation is chosen from hundreds in the same vein because of its brevity. The title of the book from which it is taken is *The Modern Novel* (1923). Obviously, the 'truth of intercourse' between fellow mortals finds an equally good, if not better, medium in the essay. This social doctrine was well received by the young Chinese intellectuals of the day, who were eager to be accepted as 'fellow mortals' in the world at large, rather than looked upon as strange or suspicious Chinamen, and also eager within their own country to tear down the barriers of class and status. So in writing their essays the more politically inclined explicitly expressed their solidarity, and the writers for pleasure implicitly expressed their common humanity, on level terms with the reader, in the shared plain language of *baihua*.

The polemical or contentious essay in Chinese needed to have its technique, the civil essay had to have its aesthetic. The latter was the more debatable. Granted the common humanity, the source of expression was still the individual writer, and writers were encouraged to express their individuality, without which they were not fully human. In the first tentative call (1921) for essays that were artistic in character (*meiwen*, or '*belles-lettres*', was the title of the piece), Zhou Zuoren put 'genuineness' as the first requirement, and added, 'we must use our own words and thoughts'. Such modesty had no place in the much quoted theoretical work of the Japanese critic Kuriyagawa Hakuson translated by Zhou's brother Lu Xun and entitled in Chinese *Chule xiangya zhi ta* 出了象牙之塔 (Out of the Ivory Tower, 1925). The background to Kuriyagawa's remarks on the essay is the view that 'literature as a whole is the only sphere, removed from the external pressures and compulsions of life, where one's individuality can be expressed on the basis of absolute freedom. The uninhibited expression of the life force, which cannot be looked for in political, social or working life, can be found in literature.' The 'life force' or 'élan vital' betrays the European origin of Kuriyagawa's ideas. Applied to the essay, the following description results:

> The ingredient more important than any other in the essay is the rich and full expression of the colouring of the author's own individual personality. . . . The newspaper report should be impersonal; it must at all costs avoid the individual, subjective note of the reporter. The essay is just

the opposite: it is something which enlarges and exaggerates to the limit the author's self; its interest lies in its personal note. A scholar has therefore characterized this form as a lyrical poem rendered in prose. If not activated by the spirit of the author it is uninteresting.

The higher notes here were echoed only by the more lyrically inclined writers, but toned down a bit the description would have met with general recognition and approval.

To revert to Zhou Zuoren's 1921 proposal, the English speaking essayists he commended by name were Addison, Lamb, Irving and Hawthorne, who he said were well-known in China, and of more recent date, Galsworthy, Gissing and Chesterton. Though one might take leave to doubt that the essayists Zhou named were really 'well-known', the cultural climate at the time decreed that they, as representing the Western pantheon, should be given pride of place over the Chinese classical 'prefaces, descriptions, discourses, etc.' that Zhou also mentions. Significantly, however, Zhou Zuoren never later enlarged on the virtues of the English essay, and never translated any, active translator though he was. From the mid-1920s he reversed the priorities expressed in his *'belles-lettres'* proposal, taking the view that the new kind of essay being written in Chinese was 'the product of literary revival rather than literary revolution', as it had a closer affinity, particularly in 'emotional ambience' and manner, to the informal prose literature of the Chinese past than to the Western essay. He started himself to mine the Chinese tradition for works that freely 'gave vent to the feelings' and 'revealed the inmost self', which as we have seen was a universal requirement, but also stood for native tastes, interests, sense of humour, and literary values.

Support for the English type of essay remained strong elsewhere, however. Kuriyagawa Hakuson's further prescription for the essay which attracted great attention in China was in fact describing the English familiar essay (despite the bathrobe). It read:

> If it were winter, seated in an armchair by the fire, if summer, sipping tea draped in a bathrobe; altogether casual, chatting freely with good friends: if these words were transferred just as they were onto paper, this would be an 'essay'. If the mood takes one, there can also be some serious discussion, short of the kind that gives one a headache.

Introduction

The same atmosphere of slippered ease where talk can be unconstrained was cherished by Lin Yutang, who balanced 'the self as the centre' with 'relaxedness as the tone'. Lin Yutang was very influential in the 1930s both for his own writing and for the magazines he published or edited in Shanghai. It is true that he followed Zhou Zuoren's lead in encouraging interest also in the freewheeling school of Ming-Qing prose writers, but his own essays were wholly Western in the effects they aimed at and the kind of things they discussed.

Lin Yutang wished the essays he published in his magazines to range in their scope from 'the magnitude of the universe to the minuteness of the fly'; 'to see the world in a grain of sand' was also a phrase much bandied about. In practice grains of sand most often stayed grains of sand, though none the worse for that. Among the modern Chinese essayists who did discuss universals were Liang Yuchun, the most enthusiastic devotee of the English essay, who put his heart and soul into his compositions, and Liang Shiqiu, whose touch was lighter. Both followed the English model in taking a topic and discussing it intelligently and entertainingly from a variety of angles. Examples of their work are included in this anthology.

While Zhou Zuoren's interests veered away from the English essay, he still appreciated it, and his own essays took up some of its civilized mannerisms. Other prominent writers positively disliked it, for being too philosophical, too unctuous, too prolix or too humorous. Argument, whether or not alleviated with wit or energized by histrionics, they preferred to assign to the category known as *zawen*, or contentious essays. Pure prose, in their book, should aim at other qualities, like refinement, soulfulness and intricate description. Loosely speaking, they preferred the elements of fire and air to the water and earth of the English informal essay. In that way, knowingly or not, they inclined towards traditional literary values.

Yu Dafu, for instance, maintained that the three most desirable qualities were fine detail, freshness and true feeling. The subject matter best suited for displaying them was the description of nature, usually in the form of accounts of trips the author had made, and sketches of episodes from the author's life. With Yu Dafu and others of the romantic Creation School (*Chuangzao she*), it was sometimes difficult to classify their pieces, because though told in the first person they included interludes they could not have personally witnessed, thus blurring the lines between fact and fiction. As Chinese classical writers set little store by truth to fact, they were in this respect too following an old path, one that led through the mixed shrubbery of 'prose' in the broad sense.

Success in the descriptive essay depends in the first place on the refinement of the senses of perception, and second on language resources able both to make subtle distinctions in the observed and convey the delicate sensibilities of the observer. In the Chinese context the second requirement prompted recourse to the vast storehouse of the classical language, which entailed moving away from the original objective of exclusive use of the common vernacular. Alternatively it led to coining new compound words that translated European (mostly English) vocabulary. Either way, the sense of listening to the spoken voice was lost. So a further bifurcation between plain language and a new written language opened up, which corresponded in part to Hazlitt's distinction between the 'familiar' and 'florid' styles, that is, between 'nature's own sweet and cunning hand laid on' and 'piles of precious stones . . . and all the blazenry of art'. Probably the most florid essayist in the Republican period was Xu Zhimo 徐志摩 (1897–1931), who was principally a poet. He has some strikingly good passages, but no essays that are very satisfactory overall, so I have not translated his work.

The same phenomenon of evolution to a written language not wholly intelligible to the ear took place in the discursive essay, alienation being compounded by grammatical constructions borrowed from European languages. This was most strongly deplored by left-wing writers and theorists, for obvious ideological reasons, but ironically the same people were among the worst perpetrators of 'Europeanization' because of stylistic contamination from the Marxist texts they conned and translated. However, like the human body, languages are able to protect their own health if left to their own devices. In time, hostile invasive elements were rejected and helpful new vocabulary and turns of phrase absorbed, becoming natural to new generations. In any age there will be individuals who write impenetrably, but certainly by the middle of the 20th century the *baihua* vernacular language had become Standard Modern Chinese, as flexible and versatile as any other national language, and with a wider range of register than most.

The short topical essay, commonly polemical in tone, was in at the beginning of the New Literature movement, as we have said. Feeding on dissent and fuelled by indignation, there was always enough cause in subsequent history to keep this type of essay alive. On the political level the targets were the acts of government, warlords and foreign powers; among society, backwardness, brutality and other weaknesses in the national character. The *zawen*, as this essay came to be called, had its heyday in the Republican period, when censorship was ineffective. It retreated when the Communist Party assumed power on the mainland and the Nationalist Party took over in Taiwan.

Daily newspaper supplements and little magazines provided ample space for *zawen* to proliferate: editors were delighted to accommodate controversy. Some contributors put a point of view earnestly and without frills, while others made polemics an art. Chief among the latter was Lu Xun. Being old enough to have completed his formal education under the empire (he was born in 1881), Lu Xun was well versed in classical rhetoric. Though his opponents denigrated his *zawen* as 'cold sarcasm and hot abuse', Lu Xun drew upon the entire range of classical debating techniques, and added new tricks besides. Apart from such techniques as mild, even ingratiating, openings leading to the springing of steely traps, repetition of mocking or menacing phrases, sudden changes of register, and so on, Lu Xun was noted for using analogues from the animal kingdom to carry part or whole of his message: dogs of diverse breeds, wasps, flies and other creatures are interspersed among the human population; this he no doubt also learned from classical literature.

The degree of vehemence that one finds in Lu Xun's *zawen* was condoned by the open political and military warfare that went on in the Republican period. After 1949 and particularly after the fake promise of the Hundred Flowers Campaign (1956–57) no one was foolish enough to attempt to emulate him, although he was canonized by the Party for his political exertions. The only independent stand that saw publication in newspaper columns was so indirect and patiently expressed that it took some time for it to be recognized as a threat to Party propaganda. I refer to the articles of Deng Tuo 登拓, Wu Han 吳晗 and Liao Mosha 廖沫沙

in 1961 and 1962. On the other side of the Taiwan Strait Li Ao 李敖, Bo Yang 柏楊 and Chen Yingzhen 陳映真 served terms of imprisonment for more forceful criticism. Thus quiet descended on the *zawen* front for three decades.

In Communist China the problem for writers was not, in the words of the song, 'how shall we extol thee?' but 'how shall we not extol thee?' Given that extolling the new society was the order of the day, a form lay to hand, namely reportage, or in Chinese, *baogao wenxue* (report literature). Reportage as a literary form developed during the war with Japan essentially for the purpose of internal propaganda to encourage the nation with uplifting stories and by presenting the people to the people to bind them together as a nation. The same purpose remained to be served after the Communist victory in 1949, and was served, initially with a will. Since the heroes of these reports were invariably peasants and workers from all over the country, and their words were quoted, regional and demotic expressions were absorbed into the common national language more rapidly than before. At the same time, the reporters were affected by the doctrine of Revolutionary Romanticism, and so tended to work themselves up into a lather, raising the pitch of their commentary to the rhetorical level of a hymn of praise. Consequently, reportage carried little credibility; considered as prose literature, it was hardly more than an exercise on the instrument of language. Interestingly, though, when a measure of independence of thought was allowed after the fall of the 'Gang of Four' in 1976, emotional outbursts and embarrassingly high-pitched perorations continued in the newly critical reportage, whether it was to do with historical ills, current corruption, or environmental protection.

Over the last twenty years, normality has been restored to prose literature in mainland China, except in the field of *zawen*, where remaining ideological restrictions and a far from free press have cramped writers' style. Coincidentally, the focus of interest in the population at large has shifted back to private lives and cultural matters. Here the values essential to the essay of truthfulness and subjectivity enjoy free play once more. Private lives had to be rebuilt, and the present enriched by memory of the past, hence the abundance of retrospective essays. Greater knowledge of the outside world, gained either through the media or travel abroad, has also broadened perspectives. In short, reason and humanity have been restored.

National anonymity is not helpful to personal identity: essayists set out to rediscover the cultural heritage. They found it in monuments, ruins, places, books, myth and history. This kind of essay had a reflective and philosophical bent that had lain dormant for several decades. Yu Qiuyu's 'cultural journeys', collected in 1992, won him the most enthusiastic following, but many other essayists who wrote less flamboyantly had the same agenda, and also had an appreciative readership. Completing the line-up of contemporary prose is the 'impromptu' essay—a stone thrown into a still pond that makes widening ripples. In the hands of novelists like Jia Pingwa 賈平凹 and poets like Shu Ting 舒婷, the impromptu essay has gained in sophistication, compared with the same type in the Republican period, but lost in innocence.

In post-war Taiwan there were, as we have noted, political restrictions on what could be written, but in most other respects the situation was the opposite to that in the mainland. American support for the island ensured a steady flow of students to the United States, Western books were prominent in all subjects in university curricula, and access to Western news media was open. At the same time Taiwan saw itself as the preserver and defender of the Chinese culture that was being destroyed on the mainland. Hence in Taiwan the traditional was fused with the modern, the native with the foreign, and the process that started with the New Literature of the 1920s continued unhampered.

Critics writing in the West about literature in Taiwan (a lot of them from Taiwan themselves) have concentrated on fiction and poetry, but at home prose writing has the larger following and enjoys greater esteem. Skilful use of language gives pleasure even when content is pretty vapid, as it often is, since 'sketches' bulk large in the output, and 'think pieces' are comparatively few; narrative and dialogue are more in evidence than reflection. One reason for this is simply that people are able to get around and do more things than they ever did before, and they write about what they do. More abstractly, agitation and dramatization is more characteristic of the present age than cogitation. Perhaps the feeling is that there are few great issues left to think about to any purpose, with the exception of the degradation of the environment, which has been especially rapid and severe in Taiwan. That concern is reflected in this anthology.

Impressions of foreign parts, gained from travel or residence abroad, have greatly increased in number in the last two decades, and the incursion of many liberated professional women into the writers' ranks, speaking of their experiences in confident voices, has in another way brought more life and colour to the essay. Academics, both men and women, also contribute heavily to the output of essays, as everywhere in the Chinese world. Unlike those of the pre-war period, who tended to write down, they tend to write up, playing all the notes on the instrument of the Chinese language they can produce, though some do adopt the looser, gossipy, socializing style of the newspaper column.

The essay in Taiwan having maintained the prestige as an art form that it once had in the West, writers of quality have directed their best efforts to its composition. Among the older ones who came to Taiwan as refugees from the mainland, the retrospective essay naturally looms large. Like Zhang Dai's re-creation of his life under the previous dynasty, it has served the function of safe-guarding the personal past against total loss, and in addition served the social function of reinforcing the sense of the Chinese identity (Taiwan having been under Japanese occupation from 1895 to 1945). Predictably, women writers write with more intensity of domestic life, men have the broader feeling for the homeland. Native Taiwanese authors, for their part, also recall with vividness the sights and sounds of the predominantly rural surroundings they grew up in.

Since the waves of modernist world literature broke on Taiwan shores in the 1950s, there have been innovations in the essay form that break the standard mould of the heart-to-heart with the reader. As we have noted, pre-war writers sometimes wrote essays as fiction, but that was because they made no distinction between the two. The post-war Taiwan writers have consciously made use of the conventions and devices of other forms of literature—the short story, the poem and the play. Wang Ting-chün stands out as a pioneer in this regard.

The essay scene in Taiwan is far more varied than that I have been able to represent in this summary. In compensation, some sidelight is shed in the commentaries on individual authors. The Hong Kong scene I have had to leave out altogether. There also the essay is alive and well. It shares several characteristics with Taiwan, in fact it shares some writers with Taiwan, there having been much coming and going between the two. What is different is that the 'no holds barred' spirit of Hong Kong enterprise has long applied too to the literature. Freedom of speech was guaranteed under British rule, which let in sharp criticism, not to mention downright irreverence. Quirkiness and humour are also very evident among local essayists, probably also owing to the influence of British culture. My regret at leaving out Hong Kong is somewhat alleviated by the fact that *Renditions* has published two special editions on Hong Kong literature, one in 1988 (Nos. 29 & 30) and the other in 1997 (Nos. 47 & 48). They contain a fair number of essays in English translation.

Finally, a word on whether what I have done is worth doing. Considering that no general anthology of Chinese prose has, to my knowledge, been produced in over a century of Western sinology, there must be some doubt about that. Herbert Giles' *Gems of Chinese Literature*, first published in 1884, has had no successor. Anthologies of poetry and fiction, by contrast, abound. There have, of course, been studies of particular prose writers and translations of their works (indeed, in the case of some 'gems' I have only embarrassingly added to the large number of existing translations), but exclusive attention to the essay form has been lacking. For that there appear to have been two main causes.

The first cause is that it is inherently difficult to talk about essay writing if the writing is in another language. Chinese critics are able to talk till the cows come home about characteristics and idiosyncrasies of style, and be at least partly understood, but to those who have no, or only superficial, knowledge of the Chinese language, such talk is no more than 'wind around the ears'. Given that personal style is so important to the essay, that is a major obstacle. If the commentator's intention is to commend the compositional merit of how an argument is put, that too is normally very difficult: there is nothing drier than a description of logical progression.

The second, probably more basic, cause is the decline in the prestige of the essay in the Western world, a perception that it belongs more to journalism than literature. Journalism has the drawbacks of having a limited 'shelf life' and being in over-supply. Yet it is surely true, as Robert Lynd pointed out in 1925, that 'the only important distinction between journalism and literature is that literature lasts. Journalism that lasts is literature.' Despite being related for the most part to issues of the day which fade very rapidly, more so than imaginative literature which tends to relate to the human condition, essays, whether published in journals or not, can and do last. There have, thankfully, been signs of a revival of interest, the chief of which was the publication of *The Encyclopedia of the Essay* by Fitzroy Dearborn in 1997, a thousand-page volume edited by Tracy Chevalier. It would be gratifying if this anthology of Chinese essays helped that trend.

Zhuge Liang 諸葛亮 (181–234)

COMMENTARY

Zhuge Liang is a figure of both history and legend. Historically he was the brains behind Liu Bei 劉備, the counsellor who helped Liu set up the kingdom of Shu in the west of China in rivalry with the kingdoms of Wei (founded by Cao Cao 曹操) and Wu (founded by Sun Quan 孫權) after the Han dynasty fell apart. Legendarily he was the possessor of preternatural intelligence. In later ages his name became a byword for wisdom. His extant writings are few, but the memorial here translated, addressed to his sovereign, the son of Liu Bei, is such a powerful piece of prose that it became required reading for all Chinese students right up to, and even including, the present generation.

Zhuge Liang's forefathers had been eminent servants of the state, but he was orphaned in youth, and although confident of his ability and knowledge of statecraft, chose to farm his land in obscurity rather than place himself in the hands of tyrants. Liu Bei, however, won him over, and Zhuge Liang served him with unswerving devotion to the end of Liu's life and into the next, in the person of Liu's son, Liu Chan 劉禪. As prime minister to Liu Chan, Zhuge led a successful expedition to subjugate the native tribes to the south, but in the end failed to realize Liu Bei's ambition as a descendant of the house of Han to reconquer the homeland occupied by the kingdom of Wei. He died on campaign.

The 'subtext' of Zhuge Liang's memorial (written in AD 227) is that he himself was a man of high intelligence and wide vision, and his sovereign was close to being an imbecile. That implication is evident in his every word, and was true in fact. Loyalty was the principle he lived by: no loyalty, no Zhuge Liang. Yet it must have been impossible for him to persuade himself that the object of his loyalty was worthy of it. The wording of his memorial suggests that he had found the way out of his dilemma: it reads like the last words of a veteran of many wars going out to battle expecting to meet his end. As it turned out, he led his armies for another seven years before he died in his tent. We read out of the text a life and a will that makes us feel humble, which is a rare and valuable experience.

To Lead out the Army
出師表

Your servant Liang advises:
The late Emperor passed away leaving his great enterprise less than

half completed. The world is still divided into three, and our base in Shu is beleaguered. At this time our very survival hangs in the balance. Yet the ministers who serve and protect you do not slacken their efforts at court, and loyal and principled officers act selflessly in the field: they will requite Your Majesty for the uncommon kindness of the late Emperor. Your Majesty should be truly openminded and attentive if he is to build upon the late Emperor's legacy and put heart into men of honour; he should not demean himself and draw on false analogies in order to put a stop to loyal remonstration.

The palace and the Chief Minister's office are one body: there should be no difference between them over promotions and demotions, favour and disgrace. If there be cases of trickery and misdemeanour on the one hand, and good and loyal service on the other, the matter of punishment and reward should be left to the responsible department of state, in order to demonstrate Your Majesty's fairness and impartiality. No favouritism should be shown, no different rules for the palace and the ministries.

Your Majesty has Guo Youzhi, Fei Yi and Dong Yun to advise him at court. They are all sound men, honest and true in their thoughts and purposes, which is why the late Emperor raised them up to be at your side. In my humble opinion, if they are consulted on all matters at court, great and small, before action is taken, there will be no oversights or shortcomings, and it will be for the greater good.

General Xiang Chong is good in character and just in deed. He has a thorough understanding of military affairs. When he was assigned tasks in the past, the late Emperor commended him as 'capable'. Therefore he was promoted to be commander-in-chief by common accord. In my humble opinion, if he is consulted on all matters concerning the garrison there will be harmony among the ranks, and the able and less able officers will be assigned their proper place.

The Former Han dynasty prospered because wise and moral counsellors were made welcome and mean and petty men kept at a distance. The Latter Han fell because mean and petty men were made welcome and wise and moral counsellors kept at a distance. Whenever the late Emperor discussed this thing with me, he expressed his exasperation and disgust with the last Han emperors, Huan and Ling, for that reason. Your present chief civil and military officers Guo Youzhi, Fei Yi, Chen Zhen, Zhang Yi and Jiang Wan, are all men willing to lay down their lives in the line of duty. If, as I could wish, Your Majesty made them welcome and trusted them, then we could count the days to the rise of the house of Han.

I, your servant, was formerly a commoner who tilled his own fields in Nanyang. I sought only to stay alive in troublous times, and had no ambition to make myself known to our dukes and earls. The late Emperor took no account of my lowly station; he condescended to pay three visits to my rustic dwelling, to ask my opinion on current affairs. Out of gratitude I promised to serve the late Emperor unflaggingly. Subsequently his fortunes were reversed, and I was given responsibility in the aftermath of defeat, at a time of peril and disarray. There has been my place for twenty-one years.

The late Emperor, aware of my caution and prudence, entrusted me on his deathbed with a heavy burden. After I received my orders, my nights were all sleepless, from worry that I could not fulfil my trust, and fear that I would tarnish the late Emperor's glory. Hence in the fifth month I crossed the Lu River and led an expedition deep into the wilderness. Now the southern tribes are pacified, our weapons and armour are adequate; the time is ripe to lead our armies north to pacify the Central Plains. I will exhaust my poor skill as a soldier to expel their cruel and traitorous overlords, thus to restore the house of Han and reclaim the ancient capital. In this way I shall do my duty to repay the late Emperor and loyally serve Your Majesty. As to the weighing of the wisdom of policies at home and offering honest counsel, that is the task of Youzhi, Yi and Yun.

I request Your Majesty to place the job of suppressing the bandits and restoring the dynasty in my hands; if I fail to execute my commission, I will suffer due punishment, to be reported to the spirit of the late Emperor. If beneficial counsel is not forthcoming, Yunzhi, Yi and Yun should be blamed for being remiss, and their fault proclaimed. Your Majesty for your part should also take thought for the future, enquire into the principles of good statecraft, judiciously admit good advice, and deeply study the late Emperor's last testament. Your servant would then be eternally beholden to you.

I shall soon be gone afar. As I write this report I cannot hold back my tears, and I hardly know what I write.

Tao Qian 陶潛 (365–427)

COMMENTARY

Tao Qian, also known as Tao Yuanming, was regarded in China as the supreme poet not of nature but of naturalness, the poet everyone loved to love, for his simplicity, for his closeness to the soil, his classlessness, his unpretentious pleasure in reading books and playing music, and above all for his election of poverty in preference to the corruption of office. Of his prose compositions, 'Taohua yuan ji' (The Peachblossom Fountain) quickly became proverbial as the classic Chinese statement of Shangri-la (around 1,500 years before Shangri-la). Of his 'Requiem' we will have more to say below.

Tao's great-grandfather had been a general who helped to found the Eastern Jin state, which had present-day Nanjing as its capital. Little of the family wealth remained for him to inherit, but he still belonged to the educated elite who were eligible for office. Indigence compelled him to seek such employment in his middle years, between the ages of thirty to forty, despite his aversion. It was with relief that he retired finally in 405 to till his land. In those last twenty years of his life he was known as one of the 'three recluses of Shunyang', Shunyang in Jiangxi province being his home district.

Tao's 'Requiem for Myself' is best seen against a network of relationships. The 'requiem' was an established genre, written in four-character units like his, and of course mournful in tone like his. In content Tao's 'Requiem' largely recapitulates an earlier composition, 'Wan'ge shi' (Funeral Songs), picturing his own deathbed, his wake, and his burial, but has in addition a summing up of his life. The funeral songs are written in five-character lines, Tao's standard verse form. The word *wen* in the title of the 'Requiem' suggests it is prose. It is included in some anthologies of prose, and J. R. Hightower translates it as prose. On the other hand, Roland Fang translates it as verse, with a few breaks for prose. I think the case illustrates the difficulty of the literati of Tao's period to write anything except narratives and straight biographies in any but regular lines. Besides its four-character units, the 'Requiem' also employs rhyme and tonal consonance, yet its lines do not have the easy flow of the funeral songs. Probably most readers would agree that it is on the borderline between verse and prose.

The 'Requiem' has its fascination, particularly in the dark shadows (absent in the funeral songs) that threaten Tao's habitual assertion of equanimity, and has some fine lines. However, the regularity of the four-character units patterned in couplets makes for severe limitations. His subjects shift and his sentiments vary, but the form remains the same: as in ballroom dancing, the same step is repeated time and again. Where are the peaks and the troughs? The form does not map them. If there are only peaks, then they induce the monotony that Su Shi's prefect suffered in 'The Terrace over the Void' (translated *infra*, p. 53). The four-character unit also admits only rarely of connectives, which makes it difficult to see how one group follows from the last—and also explains why able scholars come up with different interpretations.

The 'Requiem' has some similarities to the meditations on death of 17th century English writers like Robert Burton, Jeremy Taylor, Thomas Browne and Thomas Traherne. But because they wrote true prose we see in their writing 'the self thinking'; in Tao Yuanming we see only 'the self expressing'.

Requiem for Myself
自祭文

The year is the fourth in the cycle, the season the dying fall. The weather is cold and the nights long, the air is chill and the landscape bleak. Wild geese are on the wing, plants yellow and die. I am about to leave my temporary lodging and go to my permanent rest. My kith and kin, come to grieve, are gathered this night to perform my last rites. They present the sacramental food, pour the sacramental wine. Too late to look upon my features—they are blurred; too late to hear my voice—it has faded. Mercy on us!

The great earth and high heaven, unfathomable in their reaches, gave birth to the natural world; even so was I made man. My place in life was humble: my scoop and ladle dipped and often came up empty, my plain hempen weave had to withstand the winter. Still I joyously drew water from the stream, and sang to myself as I bore firewood from the hills; behind my wattle door I tended to my chores in winter gloom, springs and summers I laboured in the fields; my hoeing and ridging bore fruit in sturdy crops. In happy mood I turned to my books, in peaceful moments I played my zither. I basked in the winter sun and bathed in summer streams. Strenuous though my work was, I did not overtax myself. Knowing peace and serenity, I was happy with my lot, and so saw out my span of years.

Men cherish their life on earth. Fearful that it will pass without achievement, they seize upon the passing days, wishing to be valued in their lifetime and remembered after their death. Yet I trod my own path, which was not that of other men. Since I did not prize their favour, how could I be blackened by their dye? Aloof in my poor dwelling, I drank my fill and wrote my poems. Though I knew my destiny, who can be free from attachments? Yet I pass away today with no regrets. My life has run its full course, spent as I wished in obscurity: to come to one's end in old age leaves no yearnings unfulfilled.

Seasons change, time marches on, the dead are divided from the living. My relatives pay their last respects in the morning, my friends come to mourn at night. I am to be buried in the wild, so that my soul will have peace. Long and dark will be my journey, mournful the wind over my grave. Why fear the empty plain? I will no longer exist. Why give way to emotion? I will have gone far away. I despise ostentatious funerals, I scorn miserly burials. Build me no mound, plant me no trees, let the days and months roll by regardless. He who never harkened after fame in his lifetime will not miss psalms after death. It is life that is hard—what is death in comparison? Mercy on us!

Han Yu 韓愈 (768–824)

COMMENTARY

Han Yu, together with Liu Zongyuan, brought to fruition the *guwen* (ancient prose) movement, which aimed at moral regeneration as much as stylistic restoration. Ever since the revival of *guwen* in the Song dynasty he has been regarded as a kind of high priest in the realm of letters.

Han Yu's family home was in Heyang, Henan province. He came of a noble line, but his father was only a minor official. Han Yu was still in infancy when his father died; thereafter he was supported by his elder brother, Han Hui 韓會. Han Hui himself died while serving as prefect in Guangdong province, when Han Yu was aged twelve. Han Yu then returned to Heyang with his brother's widow. In 786 Han Yu went to the capital, Chang'an, to prepare for the highest academic examination (*jinshi*). He passed in 792, after three failed attempts. To secure an appointment in the civil service he had to pass a further ministry examination, which he again failed to do; his appeals to prime ministers fell on deaf ears. He left the capital in frustration after nearly ten years there to take secretarial posts with provincial military governors. On the recommendation of one of them he returned to the capital in 802 to be a tutor at the Imperial Academy. In 803 he was made Examining Censor, with Liu Zongyuan as a colleague. Han Yu was openly ambitious for promotion, but obstinately courted danger over matters of principle and justice. Thus he was rusticated for implied criticism of the prime minister. In 806 he returned to the centre, where he was academician, historian and administrator. He got into the hottest water over his protest against the emperor admitting a relic of Sakyamuni Buddha into the palace (in 819). He was lucky to be only banished to Chaozhou on the southern coast. In 820 he was back in the capital under a new emperor, as head of the Imperial Academy. While serving later in the War Office he undertook a dangerous mission to persuade a rebellious military commander to return to the fold. His success earned him more high office. He died in harness.

Amateur psychology might attribute the steeliness in Han Yu's character to the losses of his father in infancy and his brother-protector in early adolescence, and his fractiousness and discontent to his frustrations in his twenties. However that may be, his published work shows him to have been at times rigidly orthodox, at times erratically wayward. Both tendencies were very good for him as a writer: he could get on his high horse and write with compelling conviction, and he could break all the rules and shock with his inventions.

For centuries Chinese pupils have been introduced to Han Yu only in his first guise, summed up by Su Shi in his hyperbole, 'His writing lifted the debility of the eight ages, his Way roused the empire from its stupor.' The common impression of Han Yu is, accordingly, of intimidating rectitude. His own statements certainly support that view. He claimed not to read anything written after the Han Dynasty, that is after Confucian orthodoxy gave way to heterodox philosophies and euphuistic styles (the qualifying 'to begin with' is usually omitted in quotation); and he often insisted that good writing (*wen*) necessarily went hand in hand with moral correctness (the Confucian *dao*), *wen* in fact being only the outer clothing of *dao*. It is not so well known that he valued and drew upon the works of rival schools to Confucianism and learned from the styles of euphuistic writers. Everyone is familiar with the fact that he used abstruse expressions from ancient texts, but it is not so well known that he abhorred imitation of any predecessors, and believed that words fell into place on their own when the impulsion to write took hold.

Song Confucians criticized Han Yu for being a much more dedicated stylist than a moralist, which is correct, and a very good thing for the health of Chinese literature. His great achievement as a stylist was to beat the euphuists at their own game: that is to say, to show that unvarnished prose, as irregular in form as speech, could be more effective aesthetically and energetically than the rival media akin to verse that had been favoured after the Han dynasty. In short, he restored virility to the Chinese written language.

Han Yu's voluminous writings covered the whole gamut of literary forms. His serious prose works included memorials on moral, philosophical, political and practical matters, historical essays, and obituaries (those on his nephew and on Liu Zongyuan being most famous). If we look for uniqueness, however, we will find it most strikingly in his playful compositions. His wit and intelligence was later rivalled by Su Shi, but their comedy was of a different kind, Han Yu keeping a straight face, Su Shi signalling that he was being funny. Perhaps his closest kindred spirit was the modern writer, Lu Xun. Han Yu's most inventive comic piece was his 'Biography of Mr Furpoint', which treated the personified writing brush to the full biographical works, tracing his remote ancestry, praising his obedient service in office, recording his retirement on going bald, and concluding with the comment of the 'Grand Historian', in imitation of Sima Qian's practice in his monumental *Records of the Grand Historian*. Unfortunately Han Yu's jokes are too recondite to be appreciated without a lot of explanation. I have translated instead two more accessible pieces.

Address to the Crocodiles of Chaozhou
祭鱷魚文

TRANSLATOR'S NOTE

Han Yu was relegated to Chaozhou, at the farthest reaches of the Tang empire, in AD 819, as a result of incurring the emperor's wrath with his memorial reproving the emperor for condoning the superstition of the 'Buddha's bone'. Han Yu served for only one year in Chaozhou before being transferred back to civilization in Jiangxi province.

The account of the crocodile incident in the official *Tang History* 舊唐書 · 韓愈傳 says that on the night the address was given there was a thunderstorm, and some days later the waters where the crocodiles lurked dried up; the crocodiles never returned to Chaozhou. Although the *Tang History* was written when Han Yu was already venerated, it is still remarkable that the 'Address' was taken at face value. The very idea of the commissioner acting as the emperor's champion to challenge the crocodiles to do battle is an indication that this is a burlesque; the assumption is confirmed by the heroic rhetoric; and the final proof is the humour of the commissioner being willing to postpone the date of execution if the crocodiles cannot manage to pack up and leave very quickly. It is, of course, quite possible that Han Yu did effect the removal of the crocodiles by practical measures, like diverting water courses, but that would be a different story.

It must have been a relief to Han Yu to take a holiday from writing on matters of great moment and employ his very considerable talent for high sententiousness for burlesque purposes. Though it took some effort to find a way through the labyrinths of his long sentences, it was in turn a pleasure for the translator to follow where he led—in fact, it was a privilege.

On such and such a day, month and year, I, Han Yu, the Commissioner for Chaozhou, ordered my adjutant Qin Ji to cast one pig and one sheep into the deep waters of the Baneful River for the crocodiles to eat, and addressed the creatures thus:

When the kings of antiquity ruled the empire, they cleansed with fire the hills and swamps and used nets and spears to dispose of the creeping things and nasty creatures which did people harm, driving them beyond the frontiers of the realm. In later ages kingly power declined, and could not hold far sway; hence even the region between the Yangtze and Han rivers was given over to native tribes, let alone this southern littoral between the mountains and the sea, thousands of miles from the capital. It is understandable that the crocodile should have skulked and bred in these waters. But now the present Son of Heaven has succeeded to the throne of Tang, his saintly compassion and awesome majesty have imposed his authority over all within the four seas and all quarters of the known world. How then could his writ not run in this territory, where Great Yu left his footprints when in subduing the flood he included it in the circuit of Yangzhou and which, now administered by a commissioner and magistrates, sends tribute and taxes to provide sacrifices in the Temple to Heaven and Earth, to our liege's ancestors, and to the hosts of spirits? Let the crocodiles not think that they can share this territory with the commissioner!

The commissioner has been ordered by the Son of Heaven to govern this district, and keep its people in order. Yet the crocodiles truculently refuse to keep to their rivers and ponds, but instead encroach on the land and eat people's livestock, as well as bears, boar and deer, to bloat their bodies and nurture their progeny. They set themselves up against the commissioner, and strive to gain dominion. How could the commissioner, a nonentity though he may be, be willing to bow his head and bend his knee, be afraid to look them in the eye, and bring shame on subjects and officials alike, just to seek an ignominious survival here! Moreover, I have come to officiate at the behest of his majesty, in which position I have no choice but to lay down the law to the crocodiles. If the crocodiles have understanding, they should pay heed to the commissioner's words, as follows:

To the south of Chaozhou is the sea, whither creatures as huge as the whale and the roc, and as small as shrimps and crabs, resort to feed and procreate. If the crocodiles set out in the morning, they may reach it by evening. I now state my terms to the crocodiles. I set them a limit of three days to take their ugly selves south to the sea, if they wish to escape the wrath of the emperor's appointed. If three days are not enough, I will allow five days; if five days are not enough, I will allow seven. If after seven days they do not remove themselves, it will be proof of their recalcitrance and a clear sign of their unwillingness. They will be showing contempt for the commissioner and disregarding his orders. On the other hand, supposing that the crocodiles are obtuse and dull of sense, though the commissioner has spoken they will be unaware of it. Regardless of whether they brazenly defy the orders of the emperor's appointed and refuse to migrate to avoid his wrath, or whether they destroy the lives and property of his majesty's subjects out of simple obtuseness and dullness of sense, in either case they should be destroyed. The commissioner will select hardy and able officers and subjects and arm them with sturdy bows and poisoned arrows, and have it out with the crocodiles, not resting until all their kind are dead. Do not repent when it is too late!

Goodbye to Penury
送窮文

TRANSLATOR'S NOTE

This composition was apparently prompted by the custom prevalent among the common people to set outside their houses bowls of gruel and cast-off clothes on the last day of the first lunar month to tempt the demon of poverty to leave them. The demon was believed to be the ghost of a son of the legendary ruler Gao Xin 高辛 who despised rich food and good clothes. At the same time it has a literary ancestor in the 'Banishment of Poverty' 逐貧賦 of Yang Xiong 揚雄 (53 BC–AD 18), which established the pattern of the author's address to the spirit of poverty to persuade it to leave him, the spirit's reply, and the author's consent to its staying. In comparison, Han Yu's piece is much more dramatic and imaginative: he obviously greatly enjoyed creating the ghostly atmospherics. The whole composition is an excellent illustration of how the Demon of Penmanship made him 'stray into the odd and absurd'. It is also an adroit exercise in self-praise, though not overdone: the demons were right in predicting that his name would 'survive for a hundred generations'.

On the last day of the first month of the 6th year of the Yuanhe reign period [811], I instructed my servant Xing to plait willow wands to make a cart, bind straw to make a boat, furnish them with cereals, and harness oxen to the cart and attach a sail to the boat. Then I bowed three times to the Demon of Penury, and addressed it, saying:

'I have heard that my noble friend is due to depart betimes. I am not so impertinent to ask your destination, but I have taken it upon myself to furnish and provision a boat and cart. The weather is fine and the day propitious: the world is at your feet. If you will first partake of a bowl of rice and a cup of wine, you may gather your companions about you, and leave for fresh pastures, travelling like the wind and with the speed of lightning. Thus you will no more resent being detained here indefinitely, and I will have done my part as kind host. May I ask if you are ready to leave?'

I held my breath and listened intently. I seemed to detect a sound, like whistling, like keening, faint fleeting scratchings of speech. My hair stood on end and my head shrank into my neck. I thought I might be imagining it, but after some time I was able to make out what seemed to be a voice saying:

'I have dwelt with you for more than forty years. When you were still a little tot I saw you were not stupid. Whether you were to study or farm, seek office or fame, I would follow you unswervingly. Though your household gods cursed and shouted at me, I endured the indignity out of unquestioning loyalty, and never thought of transferring my allegiance. When you were sent to the burning heat and steaming damp of the southern wilds, I was out of my element, and was tormented by the native sprites. In the four years you were collegian at the Imperial Academy, when you lived on a ration of salted vegetables, only I came to your defence, everyone else contemned you. From first to last I have never betrayed you. No thought of separation has entered my head, no word of travelling has come from my mouth. From where have you heard I am departing? You must have heeded malicious talk, which has alienated you from me. I am not a man but a spirit, what need have I of boat or cart? We only taste scents and odours: the provisions can be dispensed with. I am all by myself: who should be my companions? If you know all, can you enumerate them? Were you able to name them every one, you would have the wisdom of the saints. Supposing all were laid bare, I would feel obliged to withdraw.'

I replied, saying:

'You can't think I don't know! Your company comprises not six and not four. They number ten take away five, seven minus two. They each take a view, each has a name. They jog my hand to make me overturn the soup, they twist my throat to make me say the wrong thing; everything about my appearance that people find disgusting, everything about my speech that people find objectionable, is all due to your machinations. To name you individually, one is called Penury through Intellect: mightily sure of himself; hating the round and accommodating, liking the square and straight, scornful of lying and deceit, unwilling to sully others. The next is called Penury through Learning: scorning mechanical scholarship, delving into the minute and abstruse, drawing freely on any school of thought, grasping the motions of the divine. Next is Penury through Penmanship: not cultivating one skill, straying into the odd and absurd, ignoring relevance to current concerns, aiming only to amuse himself. Next is Penury of Fate: my outward appearance belies my real substance, my face is ugly though my heart fair; I am the last in the queue for benefits, first in the line for blame. Last is Penury through Friendship: one bruises and chastises oneself to speak with utter honesty and sincerity, and eagerly awaits the regard of others, only to succeed in making oneself an enemy. All these five demons are my nemeses, who keep me cold and keep me hungry. They tell lies and spread slanders, so I know not what to trust. No one can come between us: in the morning I repent my conduct, by the evening I repeat it. Like circling flies or barking dogs, though you drive them away they will be back.'

Before the master had come to an end of his recital, the five demons in concert goggled their eyes and stuck out their tongues, staggered and fell about, clapped their hands and stamped their feet, and burst out laughing. Eventually they spoke to the master:

'You know our names and all our doings. But to drive us away would be to outsmart yourself. Consider how short a man's life on earth is. We are creating a name for you that will survive for a hundred generations. Petty men and noble men are different in mind. It is by being at variance with his time that one is attuned to the Eternal. You would take your precious jade and exchange it for a sheep's skin; you who feast upon the finest fare envy the coarse porridge of others. No one on earth knows you as we do: though you would expel us, we could not bear to abandon you. If you do not believe us, please consult your scriptures for their lessons.'

Thereupon the master hung his head in defeat, clasped his hands together and offered his thanks, burned the cart and boat and invited them to take the seats of honour.

Liu Zongyuan 柳宗元 (773–819)

COMMENTARY

Liu Zongyuan is permanently linked with Han Yu as one of the twin pillars of the *guwen* (ancient prose) movement in the mid-Tang dynasty. Both were indeed very influential, by force of example and by way of attracting disciples, and they were firm friends, but they worked together only very briefly, and their careers were opposite in pattern, Liu Zongyuan enjoying early success but being demoted for the last fourteen years of his life to the backwoods, Han Yu suffering early frustration but ending his career in high office. In personality too they were different, Liu being steadfast and sincere, Han being abrasive but astute (perhaps that explains why Han was able to bounce back from adversity, Liu not). Their common achievement in literature was to restore, and in some ways enhance, the prestige of nonmetric prose as a vehicle for art.

Liu Zongyuan's family came from the present-day province of Shanxi, but he was born in the capital, where his father was an official. His precocious skill with words was recognized when he was invited to compose a memorial at the age of twelve congratulating the emperor on putting down a rebellion. He passed the *jinshi* examination at the age of twenty, and the higher civil service examination at the age of twenty-five. After filling a number of provincial posts he was called to Chang'an to serve as Examining Censor (803). There he joined the band of middle-ranking officials led by Wang Shuwen王叔文who planned reforms to curb the excesses of eunuchs at court and governors in the regions. The reformers were empowered by the Crown Prince when he succeeded to the throne in 805 as Shunzong 順宗, but within a year Shunzong ceded the throne because of illness, and the reformers were all downgraded by the new emperor, Xianzong 憲宗. Liu Zongyuan was banished to Yongzhou, in the backwoods of Hunan province. He remained there for ten years. He was promoted in 815 to the rank of prefect, but his posting was to the even more remote Liuzhou. He died in office there.

Like any other person of principle, Liu Zongyuan believed that literature should serve a moral purpose, should encourage the good and deplore the bad. Although the accepted 'good' was the Confucian Way, and that had Liu's principal loyalty, he was not particularly dogmatic; his church was a broad one. His most representative pronouncement on the function of prose literature was that it should either directly express value judgements ('praise and blame') in the form of topical discussions, or use figurative means to satirize and instruct. His own compositions did both, and something else besides.

Liu's critical essays attacked the abuse of power, social evils and malpractices, and superstitions (including the greatest of all superstitions, the 'mandate of Heaven'); they praised people for standing up to the rich and powerful, for personal integrity, and for alleviating the burdens of the poor. Though one could say this was standard fare for the Confucian moralist, one senses that in Liu Zongyuan those benevolent principles were deeply internalized. One only has to read his 'Letter to Han Yu Discussing the Duties of Official Historian' (translated by Denis Twitchett in *Renditions* Nos. 41 & 42, 1994), in which he takes Han Yu to task for his fear of doing his job honestly, to be persuaded that his virtue was genuine, and incidentally be impressed by the cogency of his reasoning.

More interesting from the point of view of innovation was the second function that Liu distinguished, the use of figurative means to satirize and instruct. That function was carried out most obviously in his animal fables (featuring deer, donkey, rats, beetles, etc.). These were written after Liu's rustication to Yongzhou, when he had plenty of time to reflect on the world's vices and follies. Classical texts had used analogies from the animal kingdom to illustrate a point, but Liu's parables seem to be the first example of free-standing fables of the Aesop kind. Less obvious were his 'biographies' of working men he claimed to know, admirable characters every one. They included a tree planter, a builder, a herbalist, and most famously of all, a snake catcher who preferred snake venom to taxes. The pursuit of their trades all carried lessons for good government. While it would be excessively sceptical to doubt the existence of living prototypes for these characters, Liu Zongyuan plainly shaped his description of their callings to express his own views and principles.

'The Whip Vendor', which I translate here, belongs to the related category of metaphorical literature. The whip is the means by which a rider controls his horse, and it is used as a metaphor for the executive arm of government. There are some inherent implausibilities in Liu's story, but I imagine the author would have regarded any objection on those grounds as obtuse, the point for him being the aptness of the comparison between the overpriced whip and over-promoted officials, both being sure to fail in the event of a crisis.

The something else that Liu's formula did not mention was landscape descriptions. His fables became household reading, but his account of eight excursions made from his base in Yongzhou set a precedent that all later writers were aware of. It was not that previous literature had not noticed nature. Elaborate descriptions of landscape features had long been a topic for *fu* (rhyme-prose) compositions, but they were pleonastic, bookish, and usually inflated. Nature poetry had also made its appearance, but descriptions there were mostly generalized. Liu Zongyuan recorded his experience of specific locations, noting their unique features, and saying what effect they had on him and his companions. The accounts were not rhapsodic, they were written in sober prose, had much factual detail, yet also had emotional vibrations. The centrepiece of the series is the account of his excursion to Xishan (West Mountain). Its full title includes the word *de*, that is, 'getting hold of' Xishan: that word signifies not only climbing the mountain, but capturing the spirit of the place. That occasion was a revelation, a transcendental experience, which made him look with new eyes on the natural world. The other pieces all reflect his new sensitivity—including the sensitivity to not being very welcome, as in the piece on the small rock pool.

The 'eight Yongzhou excursions' were written in 809, four years after his demotion. We can accept that he was unhappy with his situation—as he says, he came to Yongzhou 'as a felon'—but it appears unwarranted to read into these descriptions of natural features analogies to pure and unblemished men (like himself) banished from sight and mind, as commentators have asserted. It is true that in his last piece (not translated here), Liu himself raises the question why the Creator should have hidden these marvels from the sight of civilized men, but since he dismisses the notion that it was 'to console worthy men relegated here', he appears to say that it had nothing to do with him. That is not to deny of course that his expulsion from the capital made him receptive to thoughts and intimations that would not have occurred to him otherwise.

The Whip Vendor
鞭賈

When you ask a hawker of whips in the market place the price of a whip that is worth fifty coppers, he will tell you fifty thousand. If you offer him fifty he will double up with laughter; if you offer five hundred he will be displeased; if five thousand he will be irate. He will not settle for less than fifty thousand.

There was a rich young man who went to the market and bought a whip for fifty thousand. He showed it to me to boast of his purchase. When I looked at its tip, it was knobbly and not pliable. When I looked at its stock, it was warped and not straight. The thongs were mismatched and loosely fitted. The joints were black with decay and had no marbling: when you pressed them with your thumbnail, your nail sank deep, without reaching solid wood. When you hefted the whip, it was weightless, as if you were brandishing nothing.

I asked: 'What attracted you so much that you did not begrudge the price of fifty thousand coppers?' He replied: 'I liked its yellowness and glossiness. Besides, the whip seller assured me . . .' I then told my servant to heat some water and soak the whip in it. It shrivelled and turned dry, aged and turned white. Its former yellowness was due to yellow jasmine dye, its glossiness due to waxing. The rich young man was downcast, but still used the whip for three years. Then on an outing in the eastern suburbs of Chang'an, he and another horseman disputed right of way going down Changle Rise. The horses jostled each other, and the young man made a mighty cut with his whip. The whip broke into five or six pieces. The horses continued their jostling, with the result that he fell to the ground and was injured. It turned out on inspection that the inside of the whip was hollow—its sinews turned to muck, so that it had no stiffening.

Now there are those who dye their skin and wax their words in order to peddle their virtues at court. If they are valued according to their worth, there is no harm done. If appointed above their competence they are delighted; if appointed at their competence, they are irate, and say, 'Why am I not made minister of state?' Yet many of their kind actually are given such high office. If times are peaceful, as long as three years may pass without ill consequences. But in times of need, if they are assigned demanding roles in order to deal with a crisis, and if, given that they are hollow inside and their sinews turned to muck, they are expected to achieve results from a mighty cut, will any not break that which they employ and bring about the calamity of fall and injury?

My First Excursion to West Mountain
始得西山宴游記

Since I came to this district under a cloud, as a felon, I have had no peace of mind. In my free time I have wandered about, travelling everywhere, aimlessly. Every day, with my companions, I have climbed mountains, plunged into forests, tracked twisting streams to their source, sought out hidden springs and strange-shaped rocks, however far away. Whenever we got to our goal we would sit down on the grass, pour out our wine, and get drunk. Having got drunk we would lie pillowed on each other, and once recumbent, dream. Where our imagination led, our dreams followed. On waking we rose, and on rising returned. We believed we had made all the remarkable features of the district's landscape our own, but we had not taken account of the singularity of West Mountain.

On the 28th day of the ninth month this year I sat in the Western Pavilion at the Fahua monastery, facing West Mountain. It was only then that it struck me how unusual it was, and I pointed in my excitement. I gave orders to my servants, and we crossed the Xiang river; following the Ran stream, we cut through thickets and burned off tangled undergrowth to make a way to the peak. When we sprawled on our mats at the summit, our roving eyes could take in the territory of several prefectures beneath us. The steep prominences and sunken marshlands of the terrain were like anthills and holes, hundreds of miles packed into feet and inches, with every detail exposed to our sight. The ribbons of green hills and the winding white waterways extended to the horizon, whichever way you looked. You realized then how eminent this mountain was: it put the molehills round it to shame. Ungraspable, it was equal with the cosmic breath, and its extent could not be measured; expansive, it consorted with the creator, and its end could not be known.

I drained my brimming cup, and felt myself go limp from the effects of the wine. The dusk gathered, approached, reached and enveloped me, yet I had no desire to leave. My mind was stilled, and my body was released; I was in harmony with the motions of the natural world. Then I knew that my previous excursions had not been real excursions: this was the beginning of my excursions. Hence I have committed this experience to writing.

This took place in the fourth year of the Yuanhe period [AD 809].

The Small Rock Pool West of the Hillock
至小丘西小石潭記

One hundred and twenty paces west of the Small Hill we heard the trickle of water coming from the other side of a thicket of bamboos, like the clinking of jade pendants. It was most appealing. We had a passage cut through the bamboos, and found a small pool below, its water pellucid. The bed of the pool was a whole slab of rock, which turned up around the edges and, breaking the surface, formed little islets and smooth and jagged outcrops. Tree canopies overhung the margins of the pool, trailing creepers formed a swaying, irregular weave, closing and parting.

There were some hundred fish in the pool, all as it seemed swimming in mid-air, without support. Where the sunlight penetrated the water, it cast their shadows on the basal rock, all motionless, as if transfixed; then suddenly they would dart away with amazing speed, as if playing a game with us visitors.

To the southwest, the pool snaked away like the Northern Dipper, its reaches now hidden, now visible. Its banks were as jagged as a hound's teeth, giving no clue to its source.

We sat by the pool, enclosed by bamboos and trees, cut off from humanity. The dead silence and utter seclusion cast a chill on our spirits and brought cold to our bones. The spot was too deserted for us to linger long, so I wrote down this description, and we left.

My travelling companions were Wu Wuling, Gong Gu and my younger cousin Zongxuan. The two sons of my sister, namely Shuji and Fengyi, came with us on this occasion.

Lu Guimeng 陸龜蒙 (?–881)

COMMENTARY

Luo Yin 羅隱, Pi Rixiu 皮日休 and Lu Guimeng were a group of late 9th century prose writers brought back out of limbo in the 20th century by Lu Xun to support his argument that the short classical 'essays' (*xiaopinwen*) that modern writers could regard as their heritage were not all light and frothy pieces written for entertainment, but also included hard-hitting social criticism (which was what Lu Xun himself wrote). Luo, Pi and Lu lived and wrote when the once powerful Tang empire was on its last legs (it ended in 907), and among the holders of office it was every man for himself. Their view of the state in which they found themselves was put most succinctly by Pi Rixiu: 'When men were given authority in ancient times, they used it to expel bandits; when men are given authority in present times, they use it to be bandits.' They all used parables and historical examples to satirize and attack current ills. Lu Guimeng's parable 'Rustic Temples' has found a place in the majority of recent anthologies.

Little is known about Lu Guimeng's life. He came from Suzhou, and is said to have inherited a small country estate, where he spent most of his time in seclusion. Distinctive features of his essays include expanding talk of country matters into general diatribes and adopting respectable forms of composition, like epitaphs, obituaries and reports, for satirical purposes. 'Rustic Temples' is an example of the latter practice. In the end it comes down to sympathizing with the common people for their hapless lot like many another humane essay, but it is a masterpiece of indirectness: at various way stations the reader is sent off in a different direction from that signposted.

The essay advertises itself as an epigraph, but the very first words show that it is not what it seems: the author promotes the homophone *bei* 悲, meaning 'mourn', over the generic term *bei* 碑 ('stone' inscription), by means of an exercise in etymology. The shift goes some way to achieving the author's purpose, but another twist is necessary to head the reader off to first base: it is not the temples themselves that are to be 'mourned', but the country folk who worship at them.

Everything in the next section confirms the reliability of the sign just posted. We are told in impressive particulars about the scale of these rustic temples: crude and tasteless they may be, but in local terms they are grand; and if the material burden of their construction and upkeep were not enough, the spiritual burden they impose is even more crushing. Truly cause for 'mourning'! And yet there are latent causes for the reader's unease: the vague names for those perhaps too life-like idols, and a lurking doubt that the rustics' subservience is too extreme to be wholly voluntary.

In the next section the reader is redirected from the ignorance of the rustics to consider the culpability of the idols—assuming now that they are active presences sustained by their worshippers. The new sign points two ways, to the past and to the present, and bears a question mark. The previous line of argument is continued a little way: yes, by the standards of the past it is perverse to worship these idols who have done nothing for the community, but—and here at last the true goal is revealed—their living counterparts hold much more baneful sway, and it is their conduct that is most to be lamented. The piece ends with the cancellation of the question mark.

One can assume that the author's motivation was to attack the pampered, cruel and cowardly local elite, and guess that the chance resemblance to the idols in the rustic temples gave him the structural analogy he was looking for, but he still had to cast his thoughts in a recognized form of composition. The 'monument inscription' was an inspired solution.

A Monument to Rustic Temples
野廟碑

The word for 'monument' (*bei*) comes from 'mourning' (*bei*). In olden days a wooden post was used in winching the coffin down into the grave pit; later on, inscriptions were written on these posts to make known the deeds and virtues of the deceased, so they came to be preserved for their sentimental value. This is the origin of the name *bei*.

From Qin and Han times monuments were also erected to honour the living for their deeds and virtues and services to the state, and stone replaced wood as the material, hence the derivation was obscured. In my erecting a monument now for rustic temples, it is not that there are any public services or private virtues to be recorded: my intention is simply to 'mourn' the way our country cousins waste their substance in the worship of nameless idols of wood and clay.

Along the course of the River Ou, in the region of Wenzhou, they are given to worshipping spirits and goblins. On the tops of mountains and banks of rivers many irregular services are held. In the temples there are idols called Generals which are martial and stern, black in colour and massive in proportion; others that are soft and gentle, young and pale of cast, and these are called such-and-such a Young Sir; dignified old ladies, who are known as Matron; and attractive females, yclept Missy.

Their place of abode is extended with courtyards and pavilions, elevated by means of steps, and surrounded by old trees that are densely planted and thick in girth; creepers form arches overhead, and owls nest in the branches. Models of coaches and horses and spirit attendants are strewn about grotesquely.

Our country cousins made these idols, and our country cousins fear them. For the major ones they slay an ox, for the next in rank they kill a pig, and even the minor ones rate a dog or hen. Failure to offer fish and pulse, or make sacrifices of animals and libations of wine to one's ancestors may be condoned, but not any neglect to these spirits. If ever there is slackness in their regard, calamity is bound to follow. Young and old go about their herding and husbandry in fear and trembling, for our country cousins, rather than looking on sickness and death as coming each in their due time, delude themselves as to the course of life, attributing everything to the agency of the gods.

All the same, while we may regard these practices as perverse in former times, in the present day the gods can hardly be blamed. For what reason? Because, while it is proper that those who in their lifetime fended off disasters and protected against calamities should after their death enjoy the sacrifices of the people, these anonymous artifacts of wood and clay should not be similarly entitled. Hence the perversity of the practice when measured against the standards of former times is clear to see. In the present day, however, the martial and stern and massive in bulk do indeed exist; the soft and youthful also do indeed exist; they are the kind who mount raised platforms, take their place in high halls, fill their ears with sweet music, dine off the best fare, ride in carriages and on horses, and possess servitors. Yet the obligation to save the people from peril, to relieve the people in their extremity, never enters their head. If the people are remiss in offering their tribute, they dispatch cruel lictors to inflict wanton punishment and press them into labour gangs. Compared with the good and ill that the gods bring, which is the lighter, which the heavier?

When everything is quiet and peaceful, they pretend to be sage and good, but should the safety of the nation be threatened and the time come when they should do their duty to the state, then they lose their wits and cower in fear, collapse in a heap or flee blindly; they cannot wait to supplicate to be taken prisoner. Such being the idols who wear bonnets and are gifted with speech, what cause do we have to disparage the real idols of wood and clay? Hence our conclusion: in the present day the gods can hardly be blamed.

I append a poem as an envoi:

> Of wood and clay their form and shaping,
> Our peasants' wine and meat their sinful taking;
> Yet we cannot give their crime a name.
>
> Of wood and clay their worthless brains,
> Our sovereign's pay their unearned gains;
> On them we pass what judgement, lay what blame?
>
> The pay and rank are huge and lofty,
> The wine and meat are scant and paltry.
> What the gods enjoy, who would trouble to denounce?
> This monument's erection does my true mourning pronounce.

Ouyang Xiu 歐陽修 (1007–1072)

COMMENTARY

The ancient prose movement that aimed to combine high thinking with plain writing, championed in the mid-Tang by Han Yu and Liu Zongyuan, fell into neglect when the centre lost control of the empire and high thinking ceased to be the order of the day. The Northern Song dynasty (960–1127) restored peace and unity, and conditions were once more favourable for *belles-lettres* to return to intrinsic quality, indissociable from the fineness of the thoughts expressed, and dispel extrinsic ornamentation. Ouyang Xiu belonged to the second wave of restorationists; he was, however, instrumental in turning the tide, and is therefore customarily placed at the head of the revival. He achieved that feat through a combination of patronage and example, in the latter respect producing a wide range of greatly admired prose compositions.

Ouyang Xiu belonged to the meritocratic class of officials whose chief concern was the good of the state and the welfare of the people. His family home was in Jiangxi province. Like Han Yu, he lost his father in childhood, and was educated initially by his widowed mother. He became an Advanced Scholar (*jinshi*) in 1030, and was given a post in Luoyang. In 1034 he was transferred to the capital, Kaifeng, but was demoted to a provincial post three years later for supporting Fan Zhongyan's 范仲淹 criticism of government affairs. The pattern repeated itself after 1040: recall to the capital, renewed support of Fan Zhongyan's reforms, and rustication again in 1045—to Chuzhou, where the piece I have translated was written. After filling a number of other provincial posts, he was recalled to Kaifeng to work on the *New Tang History* 新唐書. Momentously for the future of prose literature, while acting as Chief Examiner in 1057 he refused to pass any candidates who wrote in parallel prose; he did pass three young men who were later ranked with him as Masters of Tang-Song Prose, namely the brothers Su Shi and Su Che, and Zeng Gong. After that, again like Han Yu, his career at the capital progressed, and he retired loaded with honours.

Though Ouyang Xiu thought of himself ideologically as a follower of Han Yu, his personal style is very different from Han's. Han Yu lived after all in a still martial age, when large tracts of the empire were untamed. Ouyang Xiu lived in an age of civility, and his outlook was much more urbane. Ouyang was at least as outspoken in his criticism of his superiors—indeed of the emperor himself—as Han Yu, but his indignation was controlled, his attack remorseless yet calm. When he came to write his more leisurely pieces, he was as relaxed as could be.

Calmness and serenity pervade 'The Old Toper's Pavilion', Ouyang's most popular composition. Good order, the notion of things in their place, shapes the scene, and the persons in it. At the time of writing Ouyang was not quite forty years of age, but he pictures himself as a genuinely old buffer, presumably because that is what the scene needs.

Structurally this piece is famous for its twenty-one *ye* 也 particles. Almost every 'sentence' (the Chinese original did not mark sentence divisions) is concluded with *ye*, in most cases preceded by *zhe* 者. The *zhe* marks a noun construction, the *ye* marks a stative predicate, which normally identifies the semantic subject or agent of the sentence: crudely, 'what/who ... is ...', as in 'The one who has white hair is the prefect.' In other words, the whole composition is based on the one syntactical pattern of equation, X=Y. To avoid monotony, this is stretched and compressed like a musical phrase, and at times the *zhe* stop is removed; sometimes the semantic function of *ye* is also varied. We can call this technique 'layering'. Though there is incident and progression, the mode is not narrative, it is exposition: we have a demonstrator, pointing as it were to a succession of slides, explaining what it is that we are watching, and finally what it means.

The conceptual framework of the piece is a stratified order of existence in which those who belong to each stratum are quite content to get on with their own business, but where each stratum is in harmonious relationship with the neighbouring ones. In the case of Chuzhou, at least, under the benevolent rule of the prefect, the model works perfectly: all's right with the world. And the confident X=Y syntactical pattern underlines its stability. Overall the structure is pyramid shaped, representing an ascending hierarchy. The scheme is announced in terms of topography to begin with: the movement from the bland panorama through closer and closer focus to pick out the pavilion in the recesses of a mountain. It is reprised on the level of humanity with the vision of the common people out and about, the elect who participate in the feast, and the prefect at their centre. And it is summed up explicitly at the end in the hierarchy of (1) birds and beasts (2) sensual man (3) thinking man. So the layering of form matches the layering of content. The scheme is the theme.

It may be thought that for Ouyang Xiu to put himself in the centre of his picture of Chuzhou was excessively conceited. In fact there was simply no other place for him. It was inherent in Confucian thought that the consciousness that can comprehend—and by comprehending, maintain—the universal order was limited to a select few, and as the Son of Heaven's representative in the district he was the first of the few.

The Old Toper's Pavilion
醉翁亭記

On all sides of Chuzhou are mountains. The peaks to the south-west have the finest woods and gullies, and of these the one with the most thickly covered slopes and deepest ravines is Langya. Two or three miles up this mountain you begin to hear the plashing sound of water, and the spring that spills out from between two peaks is the Winebrew Spring. Further along the path that winds up over ridges and brows towards the summit there is a pavilion jutting out like a raised wing over the spring, and it is the Old Toper's Pavilion. Who built the pavilion? The priest of the mountain, Divine Sagacity. Who is it who named it? The Prefect, to refer to himself. The Prefect brings his guests to drink here. A little wine always makes him tipsy, and he is the most advanced in years, that is why he calls himself the Old Toper. The Old Toper's mind is not on wine, but on Nature. The pleasure of Nature he apprehends in his heart and simply vests in the wine.

The clearing of mists from the woods as the sun rises, the darkening of the caves in the cliffs as the vapours gather again, these changes of light and shade are what constitute morning and evening in the mountains. The wild flowers exuding their dreamy scent, the tall trees in leaf casting a profuse shade, the high winds and crisp frost, the rocks emerging as the waters recede, these mark the four seasons in the mountains. To go in the morning and come back in the evening is to discover views that alter with the seasons, and afford pleasures without end.

The carriers singing on their journeys, the walkers resting under trees, those in front calling, those behind answering, the old and stooped being helped, the young children being led, all the coming and going in endless procession, this is the people of Chuzhou out and about. The fish taken by anglers from where the stream is deep are plump, the wine made by others from the sweet waters of Winebrew Spring is fresh and clean; these are laid out, together with local game and wild greens, at the Prefect's feasts. As the feast grows merry, it is not the music of strings and flutes that provides the entertainment: it is the arrow pitched into the pot, the game of chess won, the score of cups downed as forfeit, the to-and-fro and hubbub of voices that the guests enjoy. The one with white hair and lined face to be seen legless in their midst is the Prefect in his cups.

By and by the sun sets over the mountains, people's shadows stretch and scatter; the Prefect sets out for home and his guests follow him. The woods grow dark and the birds start up their dusk chorus. This is the creatures of the wild making merry now that the men are gone. Yet the creatures of the wild, while they know the pleasures of woods and hills, do not know the pleasures of the men; the men know the pleasures of outings with the Prefect, but do not know the pleasure the Prefect takes in their pleasure. Able to share their pleasures when drunk, able to write an account of them when sober, this describes the Prefect. And who is the Prefect? Ouyang Xiu of Luling.

Su Shi 蘇軾 (1037–1101)

COMMENTARY

Better known as Su Dongpo, Su Shi is probably the most outstanding individual in the history of Chinese classical literature, celebrated equally for his poetry and prose, besides being unsurpassed as a calligrapher. His family was extraordinarily talented, both his father Su Xun 蘇洵 and his younger brother Su Che being later ranked along with him among the eight master prose writers of the Tang and Song period.

Since Su Shi's life has been so often told, most fully in English by Lin Yutang in *The Gay Genius* (1948), I will only summarize it briefly. He was born in Meishan, Sichuan province around the middle of the Northern Song dynasty and died twenty-six years before the north fell under 'barbarian' rule. In the relatively stable society of the time the civilized arts flourished as never before or since. In philosophy stern Confucianism was tempered with the relativism of Taoism and the compassion of Buddhism. At court, however, officials formed rival factions, and contention became acute when Wang Anshi 王安石 was appointed prime minister and instituted radical reforms in the 1070s. Su Shi, who had achieved office early and progressed from local administration to court appointments, was caught up in the factional strife and suffered a series of demotions and rustications alternately with restorations. He was unfortunate enough to displease in turn all factions that gained ascendancy. His last post was on Hainan Island, in those days considered the end of the earth. Against the worry and a certain amount of hardship that these postings to outlying places entailed must be set the wealth of experience they brought to Su Shi as a man and the material they provided for his literary genius to act on.

Genius is an attribution to be made with caution, but it can be made unhesitatingly in Su Shi's case. His fecundity and fluency bewildered even himself:

> My writing is like a mighty gusher that can break surface anywhere. On level ground it surges along, easily covering a hundred leagues in a day. When it meets heights and bends it takes its shape from the obstacles in an unforeseeable way. What can be foreseen is that it will go where it should go and stop where it has to stop. As for the rest, even I have no way of knowing.

If the speed of this simile's 'vehicle' is slowed somewhat, we will have another adjective suitable to describe Su's prose, namely 'mercurial'. Mercury shares with Su's gushing stream its fluid adaptability to the terrain, forming flows and pools where appropriate, but the adjective also has connotations of wit and mischief, of versatility and rapid recovery of high spirits. It is this mercurial quality which more endears him to modern readers, the flow and sweep of his rhetoric that more endeared him to earlier generations. Herbert Giles inherited the latter preference when he translated Su Shi and other Song prose writers for his *Gems of Chinese Literature* (1883). He wrote in his 'Note on Chinese Literature' in that book that the styles of the great Song writers are 'massive and grand, without grammatical flaw, exquisitely cadenced, and thrilling the readers with an inexpressible thrill. They exhibit to perfection what the Rev. Arthur Smith, a most accurate writer on Chinese topics, calls "an indescribable loftiness of style, which resembles expression in music".' Indeed, Su Shi could write sublimely. On the other hand, he could be provocative, irreverent, and very down to earth. That side of him is well represented in Eva Hung's selection from *Dongpo's Miscellaneous Records* (*Renditions* Nos. 33 & 34, 1990).

The four essays I have translated all call for a certain amount of commentary. For convenience I attach the commentary to the relevant pieces as Translator's Notes.

The Terrace over the Void
凌虛台記

TRANSLATOR'S NOTE

The terrace in question was constructed in 1063 by Chen Xiliang 陳希亮, prefect for the Fengxiang district in Shaanxi province. Su Shi was Chen's assistant and junior in generation, being friends with Chen's son, Chen Zao 陳慥. Because of the tenor of Su Shi's comment on the construction of the terrace, which is to point out the futility of building things in order to perpetuate the fair name of the builder, this composition has been taken as a mockery of the prefect. Such a view must be mistaken. Brash though Su Shi undoubtedly was, it is most unlikely that he would have so openly criticized his senior in position and the father of a friend. In fact he later wrote a laudatory biography of Chen Xiliang. Secondly, if Chen was to be mocked for building terraces and such, practically all local magistrates and prefects were to be similarly mocked, for they all did the same, including Su Shi when he had the chance. Thirdly, Chen had the terrace built only to get a better view of the mountains, not out of vainglory—except insofar as he ordered his deed to be recorded, but such celebratory pieces were also routine. Hence one has to assume a dislocation between the deed and the comment.

The standards of realism were not strictly applied to this kind of account. It is hard to believe that Su Shi really delivered himself of this lecture before doing as he was bidden, especially not as it is here put down. A great deal of tolerance was allowed to the author to take advantage of an occasion to express his own thoughts. After Su had done his duty by showing the prefect in a favourable light in the first half of his composition, he obviously felt he was licensed to break free from the immediate subject and expound his own philosophy in the second half. Very likely his train of thought was started by the word 'void' or 'emptiness' (*xu*) in the name of the pavilion. His fault lay in his eagerness for self-expression, not in any intention to snub the prefect.

Since its boundary walls nudge the foot of the Zhongnan range, the daily life of our town should be linked with the mountains. The Zhongnan range is the highest in these parts, and its nearest mountain to us is Fengxiang. Fengxiang's proximity should ensure for us sight of this highest prominence. Yet from the prefect's residence, one would never have known there were mountains at all. Though this did not affect the conduct of business for good or ill, it was foreign to the nature of things, hence the reason for the construction of the Terrace over the Void.

When the prefect, Master Chen, put on his walking shoes, took his stick and strolled beneath the range before the terrace was built, the mountains he glimpsed over the trees appeared to him like a procession of people passing by on the other side of a wall, of whom only their topknots were visible. 'There must be wonderful sights to be seen,' he said to himself. He set workmen to dig out a square pond over by the mountain, and with the soil excavated constructed a terrace rising to the height of the ridge of a roof. Thereafter those who ascended the terrace were deceived as to the height of the terrace: rather did it appear to them that the mountains had reared their heads and were bounding into sight. The prefect observed to his assistant, Su Shi, 'This should be called the Terrace over the Void,' and bade him write an account of the matter.

Su Shi addressed the prefect thus:

'Whether things form or fade, when they will rise or fall, is not for us to know. Formerly this was wild heathland, covered in hoarfrost, open to the dew, given over to burrowing foxes and lurking snakes; at that time, who could have predicted there would be a Terrace over the Void? Since rise and fall, forming and fading, succeed each other in an unfathomable way, we cannot tell when this terrace will revert to wild heathland. If we now ascend the terrace and look about us, to the east was the Qinian Palace which Duke Mu of Qin built, and the Tuoquan Palace where he was buried; to the south were the Changyang and Wuzuo palaces of Emperor Wu of the Han; and to the north were the Renshou Palace of the Sui and the Jiucheng Palace of the Tang. If we consider their one-time magnificence, their grandeur and splendour, their solidity and immovability, we would have to say they were in all these respects a hundred times and more superior to this terrace. Yet if after a few generations have passed we seek to discover their likeness, we will find that not even tile shards or dilapidated walls remain: where they once stood are now fields of grain, or briar patches on barren mounds. What other fate awaits this terrace? And if even this terrace cannot promise permanence, what other fate awaits the triumphs and failures of human affairs, and us who come in haste and go in haste? So if anyone were to congratulate himself on winning praise for his deeds, he would be deluded. There may be some things in this world that promise permanence, but the existence of a terrace is not one of them.'

So saying, he withdrew and wrote his account.

Master Table Mountain
方山子傳

TRANSLATOR'S NOTE

This essay was written while Su Shi was serving in Huangzhou, a small town some sixty miles downriver from Hankou, between 1080 and 1084. In fact his post was a nominal one, and carried no salary. He was relegated there after being tried for writing seditious poems while serving at court, a charge which could easily have cost him his life.

The subject of the essay is Chen Zao, familiarly known as Jichang 季常. He was the son of the prefect Chen Xiliang, under whom Su Shi served when he wrote 'The Terrace over the Void'. During that previous posting, roughly twenty years earlier, Su Shi and Chen Zao had become close friends, and after the chance encounter here recorded they resumed that friendship, visiting each other frequently. The extent of their intimacy is not revealed in this essay; Chen is, rather, treated as the seat of an enigma.

Chen Jichang is introduced as a mysterious character, known locally not by name but by his headgear. Su describes him as a 'recluse' (*yinren*), but as we see that term does not signify extreme solitariness: it means only that he lives a simple life as a commoner. In the modern vernacular he might be said to have dropped out of the rat race. Having started his essay in the manner of a conventional biography, Su then follows a typically wayward course, introducing himself into the story, and in fact allowing his personal preoccupations to take over. His own career, which up to that point had been spectacularly successful, had been dashed, and he had just been released from prison. He pictures Chen Jichang as another man of ability, who could have served the state either as a military man or as a civil official. In pondering why he chose not to do either, or indeed to enjoy his inherited wealth, Su is asking the general question of what a man should do with his life. Untypically, however, Su does not volunteer an answer: Chen becomes an empty space between contradictions.

Master Table Mountain is a recluse who is to be found in the Guangzhou-Huangzhou area. In his youth he admired the character of the intrepid knights Zhu Jia and Guo Jie, and in turn all the chivalrous gentlemen in his locality took their lead from him. When more mature he devoted himself instead to study, hoping thereby to make his mark in society, but that hope was not fulfilled. In his later years he retired to the small town of Qiting, on the borders of Guangzhou and Huangzhou, lived in a rustic dwelling, and confined his diet to vegetarian fare. He disposed of his carriages and horses, destroyed his fine clothes, and went about the hills on foot. People did not know who he was. Seeing the hat he wore, tall and with a square top, they said, 'Wouldn't that be the type of hat they wore in olden days, that they called a "table mountain" cap?' Consequently they gave him the nickname of Master Table Mountain.

When I was demoted to a post in Huangzhou I passed through Qiting, and happened to run into him. I exclaimed, 'If it isn't my old friend Chen Jichang! What are you doing here?' Master Table Mountain was equally surprised, and asked me the same question. When I told him the reason, he looked down, saying nothing; then he lifted his head and hooted with laughter. I accepted his invitation to spend the night at his place. His rooms were just bare walls, and his furnishings were rudimentary, yet his wife and children and maids all appeared happy and contented. I was quite astounded. I reflected on

Master Table Mountain's younger days, when he drank heavily and loved swordplay, and spent money like water. Nineteen years ago, when I was in Fengxiang county, I saw Master Table Mountain riding with two horsemen in the Western Hills, with two quivers of arrows strung from his shoulders. A magpie took flight in their path, and he ordered his horsemen to chase it and bring it down, but their arrows missed. Then he spurred his own horse forward, and hit the bird with his first arrow. Afterwards he talked with me as we rode of the use of troops and of military victories and defeats: he saw himself as a hero of the age.

To look at him today, you would think that only a few days had passed. The signs of ability and valour are still perceptible in his features. He can hardly have been cut out to be a 'man of the mountains', can he? And yet Master Table Mountain's forebears had rendered distinguished service to the state, and by virtue of that he was entitled to an official post. If he had been active in the administration, he would today enjoy prominence and fame. Furthermore, his family property in Luoyang boasts a lovely house and grounds, comparable to a ducal domain. He also has land in Hebei, which brings in an annual rent of one thousand bolts of silk, quite enough to keep him in luxury. All this he abandons, and comes to live a solitary life in these bare mountains. This resolve can hardly be put down to disappointment or inadequacy, can it?

I have heard that in this region there are numbers of eccentrics, who feign madness and smear themselves with dirt, and avoid all human contact. I wonder if Master Table Mountain might have contacted them?

Red Cliff: One
前赤壁賦

TRANSLATOR'S NOTE

This essay has a good claim to be the best known single composition in the history of Chinese literature. Like 'Master Table Mountain', it was written while Su Shi was in disgrace, living in Huangzhou. The Red Cliff in question was not the same Red Cliff where Cao Cao suffered his fabled defeat, despite the seeming identification of the two places in the essay. Cao Cao

(155–220) was the dominant figure in the Three Kingdoms period following the breakup of the Han empire.

Su Shi typically sets his scene, here quite lyrically, goes on to an incident, and rounds off with philosophy. We are not meant to believe that everything happened exactly as described. There is some confusion, for instance, over the number of people in the boat. Despite the absence of indication of number in Chinese nouns, it is clear from the description of the flautist as one 'among my companions' that Su Shi had more than one person with him, yet subsequently Su seems to forget about the others. The main thing for him was the resolution of the question, 'To what end do we strive?' Apparently Su Shi was worried that he might not have given a safe answer, because he kept this composition under wraps for some time. The emperor himself, nevertheless, should have been satisfied with his song, as the 'fair one' in it conventionally refers to this Sage Ruler.

In the autumn of the year 1082, on the 16th of the seventh lunar month, I took a boat trip with friends to the foot of the Red Cliff. The breeze was so mild that no wave ruffled the surface of the water. I raised my cup and toasted my companions. We recited the 'Bright Moon' ode from the *Book of Songs*, and sang the verse on 'graceful motion'. Before long the moon came up over the mountains to the east, and tarried between the constellations of the Dipper and Herdboy. A white dew spanned the river, the gleaming water was continuous with the sky. Letting our small craft take its own course, we scudded over the measureless flood, grandly as if harnessing the wind to ride on air, heedless of where it should take us; weightless, as if freed from the entails of the common world and borne on wings to sport with the immortals.

Thereupon we drank deeply, and at the height of my joy I beat time on the side of the boat and broke into song. The song went:

> Oars of cassia and sculls of magnolia
> strike the glittering air
> and ascend the stream of light.
> Far away in reverie, my gaze shifts
> to seek my fair one
> at the other end of the earth.

Among my companions was one who played the flute. He improvised an accompaniment to my song. The long drawn out notes were as if bitter and wistful, as if weeping and complaining; the song over, they fluctuated on the air, trailing out endlessly like silken threads. They were such as to make dance the dragons in their submarine grottoes and the widow in her lonely boat dissolve in tears.

Sober now in my mood, I sat up and composed myself. 'Why did you play as you did?' I asked. My companion replied:

'Bright the moon and faint the stars,
Southward wing the darkling birds.'

'Was not that the song composed by Cao Cao? With Xiakou to the west, Wuchang to the east, encompassed by mountains and rivers, hemmed in by impenetrable forests, was not Cao Cao caught here in Zhou Yu's trap? He had just razed Jingzhou and taken Jiangling, and now was pushing eastward down the Yangtze. Prow against stern, his war junks stretched a hundred miles, his banners blotted out the sky. He poured a cup of wine and composed that verse looking down over the river, his lance slung across his body. Truly he was the hero of his age. But where is he now?

'And what are we in comparison? You and I fish from the banks and gather fuel on the shoals, fish and shrimps our companions, deer and elk our mates. Cast off on our frail barque we raise our crude beakers and pledge each other, but we are as mayflies in our passage on earth, as insignificant as grains of corn floating in an ocean. I was saddened by the thought of the brevity of our lives, and envied the infinitude of the great Yangtze. I wanted to link arms with some immortal and fly with him into the blue beyond, clasp the moon to my bosom and last with her till the end of time. But knowing that was not easily done, I let my lingering notes confide my thoughts to the sad wind.'

I replied, 'I suppose you are aware, my friend, of the nature of the river and the moon? The water flows away like this you see, but never is gone; the moon waxes and wanes as you witness, but never is bigger or smaller. Seen from the perspective of change, heaven and earth cannot be held still for the blink of an eye; but seen from the perspective of constancy, we and the whole of creation are eternal. What is there to envy? Furthermore, every object under heaven has its owner: if it does not belong to us, we may not lay claim to the slightest thing. Not so the fresh breeze over the river, the bright moon over the peaks: they are mine in my ears as sounds heard, they are mine in my eyes as sights seen. There is no let to my possession of them or limit to my using them. This is the great bounty provided by the Creator, to be enjoyed by us both alike.'

My companion smiled in pleasure, rinsed out the winecups and offered another toast. By the time we finished our victuals, cups and plates were littered about the boat. Pillowed against each other in rest, we were unaware that day had dawned.

Inscription for the Temple of Han Yu at Chaozhou
潮州韓文公廟碑

TRANSLATOR'S NOTE

This inscription was written in 1092 on the completion of the new temple, at the request of the governor of Chaozhou, Wang Di 王滌. It set one literary giant to sum up the achievements of another. Yet it was no ordinary appraisal that Su Shi had to write. Han Yu was to be worshipped as a divinity. To support that belief, Su had to concentrate on the evidence of divine stature manifested by Han Yu in his lifetime. The attribution of divinity to a person was a tricky question for the intellectual. One source of the attribution was folklore, of the kind mentioned in the first paragraph; Su Shi does not seem comfortable with that. The other source was the more respectable one of traditional metaphysics, which viewed the physical and spiritual world as a continuum, both the concrete and palpable and the incorporeal and ethereal being composed of the same matter-energy (qi). This made it possible for living persons who were endowed with or who had cultivated a high concentration of qi to exercise remarkable dominion. Su Shi expounds this aspect of 'divinity' much more confidently in the second paragraph. But he has to go on to explain why, possessing this power, Han Yu nevertheless suffered frustration and setbacks: apparently the perversity of man could resist his authority.

Behind all this hagiography, however, lies Su Shi's genuine and steadfast admiration of Han Yu, put into words that have reverberated ever since. It requires no superstition and no mystification to hold that by force of personality and example, and above all by the persuasiveness of his writing, an individual can wield enormous influence.

Though there are a lot of allusions to persons in this inscription, I have not identified them where it is clear what qualities they are called upon to exemplify.

A commoner, yet a model for a hundred generations; a word from him and the whole world cleaves to it: thus are those who partake of the transforming power of heaven and earth, and command the tides of glory and decay. Their birth has its begetting, their passing has its effect. Thus Shen and Lü were born of a spirit sent down by the great mountains, and Fu Yue became a star on his decease.[1] The legends of past and present should not be decried.

Mencius said: 'I know how to cultivate my overwhelming energy.' This energy is immanent in the ordinary, and fills the space between heaven and earth. If they chance to encounter it, in comparison kings and princes lose their nobility, Jin and Chu lose their wealth, Zhang Liang and Chen Ping lose their wisdom, Meng Ben and Xia Yu lose their courage, Zhang Yi and Su Qin lose their eloquence. And what you ask makes it so? Of a surety not that which stands supported by a physical frame, nor relies on physical strength to move, not that which waits upon birth to exist, nor ceases upon death. This energy is manifest in heaven as the stars, on earth as rivers and mountains, in the shades it is ghosts and spirits, in this world it becomes men. This is simply the way things are, it is nothing extraordinary.

After the Eastern Han dynasty, the way was lost and letters were corrupted; heresies rose on all sides. All the vigour of the first two emperors of Tang, assisted though they were by the wise ministers Fang, Du, Yao and Song, could not save the situation. It was only when Han Yu came forth in commoner's clothes and took charge with easy confidence, and captivated the whole empire, that the right way was restored—now about three hundred years ago. His writing reversed the decline in letters of eight dynasties, and his rectitude lifted the empire from its stupor. His loyal reprimand provoked his sovereign to anger, his courage thwarted an army rebellion. How could one deny that he partook of the power of heaven and earth, commanded the tides of destiny, and towered alone in his greatness!

People have discussed before the difference between the powers of nature and man, arguing that men are capable of anything, but nature

---

[1] The origin of Shen and Lü, warrior lords who lived in the 9th century BC, was stated in the *Book of Songs*. Fu Yue, prime minister in the 14th century BC, was said to have an astral afterlife in the *Zhuangzi*. Su Shi knew both books backwards.

will not abide falsity. With their wits men can delude kings and princes, but cannot delude dumb animals; with their strength they can win the empire, but cannot win the hearts of humble men and women. Hence the pure earnestness of Han Yu could disperse the clouds of Mount Heng,[2] but could not save Emperor Xian from his delusions;[3] could tame the violence of crocodiles, but could not dispel the calumny of prime ministers Huangfu Bo and Li Fengji; could gain the faith of people on the southern seaboard, so that they would worship him for a hundred generations, but could never secure him a day of peace at court. The reason is that what Han Yu could achieve lay with nature; what he could not achieve lay with man.

To begin with the people of Chaozhou had no notion of learning. Han Yu appointed the scholar Zhao De to be their preceptor. Thereafter the Chaozhou gentry cultivated the arts and civilized behaviour, and this spread to the common people. To this day they are well known for being easy to govern. True indeed are the words of Confucius: 'The gentleman who learns the way cares for others; petty persons who learn the way are amenable to direction.' The respect of the people of Chaozhou for Han Yu is shown in the fact that at every meal they set aside an offering to him and at times of flood or drought, illness or pestilence, they are sure to address their prayers to him. Yet his temple is located behind the compound of the commissioner, and access to it by commoners is awkward. A previous chief official wished to petition the court to build a new temple but nothing came of it. In the fifth year of Yuanyou period [1090], Wang Di, a Gentleman of the Court, came to govern this territory. He followed in every particular the example of Han Yu in educating the gentry and governing the commoners. Seeing that the local people gladly complied, he issued an order: 'Those who wish to build a new temple may go ahead.' The people joyfully set about the task, and chose an auspicious site seven *li* south of the county town. In one year the building was completed.

It has been said: 'Han Yu was relegated to Chaozhou, far remote

---

[2]Han Yu refers in a poem to the sky clearing as he passed by Mount Heng in response to a silent prayer from him.

[3]Presumably a reference to Han Yu's 'Buddha's Bone' memorial of 819.

from the capital, and was reassigned before a year was up. If he retained consciousness after death, you may bank on it, he would feel no affection for Chaozhou.' But I say, 'Not so. The presence of Han Yu's spirit in the empire is like the spread of water in the ground. There is nowhere it does not extend to. And the people of Chaozhou especially have profound faith in him, and deeply miss him: so much so that they seem to see him in the mournful smoke of the incense they burn to him. To make a comparison, if when one sinks a well and strikes water one says that the water is just there and nowhere else, what kind of nonsense is that?'

In the seventh year of the Yuanfeng period [1084], the Emperor ennobled Han Yu, giving him the title of Lord Changli. Hence the nameboard on the temple reads: 'Temple of the Prince of Letters, Lord Han Changli.' The people of Chaozhou have asked me to write his memorial to be carved in stone, and I have also composed a poem for them to chant in their services to him.

(Poem omitted)

Su Che 蘇轍 (1039–1112)

COMMENTARY

Although also ranked among the Eight Masters, Su Che (also pronounced Su Zhe) was outshone by his elder brother Su Shi. Su Shi was the genius in the family, Su Che was the sobersides, measured in his thoughts and responses. While Su Shi was unable to account for his inspiration, Su Che was sure that a writer could grow to greatness by associating with the great, that is, essentially by pupillage, experience and accretion of knowledge. Appropriately, his forte was exposition.

Su Che took his responsibilities seriously. Having got off to a good start by passing the *jinshi* examination at the age of eighteen and being soon called to the capital to work in the central bureaucracy, he got into trouble on his own behalf for voicing his criticism too freely and frankly, and on account of being Su Shi's brother when the latter got into trouble. In his time there was a seesaw contest between the reformists and conservatives at court. Su Che thought that the evils of implementation exceeded the virtues in principle of the reformist schemes, and so gravitated to the conservative camp. His career peaked under the regency of the Dowager Empress Gao 高太后(1086–1094). On the Emperor Zhezong 哲宗 reaching his majority, however, political power reverted to the by then somewhat degenerate 'reformists', and Su Che was downgraded, along with all the prominent conservatives, to minor posts in the provinces. He served in Henan, Jiangxi, Guangdong and Hunan, before retiring to Xuzhou in Henan to spend his declining years in solitude.

Su Shi characterized his brother's work as unimpassioned on the surface, but with swelling depths. The piece I have translated is perhaps not the best calculated to bring out those qualities, being essentially celebratory, but Su Che's inclination to go deep is illustrated in his integration of a pavilion in a world view. It was written in 1083. The pavilion was built by Zhang Mengde 張夢得(Zhang Huaimin 張懷民), a good friend of Su Shi. At the time all three were out of favour, so joy in the view has to contend with the gloom of rejection. The stretch of the Yangtze that the pavilion overlooked was the locality of the battle between the mighty forces of Cao Cao and Sun Quan, immortalized in the popular novel *Sanguozhi yanyi* (The Romance of the Three Kingdoms). King Xiang of Chu reigned in the third century BC, and both Song Yu 宋玉 and Jing Cuo 景差 were prominent poets. The Orchid Palace was a royal resort in present-day Hubei province.

It is impossible to translate this essay well because the word *kuai* 快 runs through it like a connecting thread, and there is no one word in English to match it in all its uses. The translator therefore has to choose invidiously between varying the word according to context and thereby losing the thread, or sticking to one word at the expense of naturalness of expression (I chose the latter). The word *kuai* signifies the 'quickening' of satisfaction, and is used of states of elation, invigoration and exhilaration, or simply happiness. To complicate matters, the *kuai zai* in the name of the pavilion is an exclamation, making the name more exactly 'The "What a joy!" Pavilion'. Despite these difficulties, the essay is worth translating in order to illustrate the practice of using key words as a unifying device, which was not uncommon.

The Pavilion of Elation
黃州快哉亭記

The flow of the Yangtze reaches majestic proportions only after it passes through the Xiling gorge and reaches level ground. Its power is even greater expanded by the influx of the tributaries Yuan and Xiang from the south, and Han from the north. Downstream from the Red Cliff the river floods out, forming something like a lake. Master Zhang Mengde of Qinghe county, when demoted to a post in Qi'an, built a pavilion to the southwest of his dwelling to watch the spectacle of the river, and my brother Su Shi gave it the name 'Elation'.

From the pavilion you can see thirty miles north and south, and ten miles east and west. You can see the waves billowing and the wind-driven clouds merging and parting. In the daytime boats appear and disappear in front of you, at night-time scaly creatures bawl mournfully below you. The scene changes from moment to moment, moving the heart and startling the eye, such that one cannot look at it for long. Yet today I am well placed to observe it in comfort, seated in the pavilion, and can take everything in at a glance. To the west I can see the hills of Wuchang, their crests and ridges rising and falling, and their rows of trees and plants. As the morning mist clears and the sun comes up, the cottages of the fishermen and wood gatherers can be made out, every one. This is the reason for the name 'Elation'. As for the river shoals and the ruins of the one-time palace on the bank, this is where Cao Cao and Sun Quan gazed haughtily about them, where Zhou Yu and Lu Xun led headlong charges.[1] These memories

---

[1] Another reference to the Three Kingdoms wars. Zhou Yu's greatest victory was against Cao Cao at Red Cliff. Lu Xun's greatest victory was against Liu Bei at Yiling.

of great deeds also cause elation in common men.

In days of old, King Xiang of Chu took Song Yu and Jing Cuo to the Lantai Palace, where they were met by a howling wind.[2] The king bared his breast to it, saying, 'How elating this wind is! Is it not something that prince and subjects can enjoy alike?' Song Yu replied, 'This is a manly wind, fit for your majesty alone. Your subjects can hardly enjoy it with you!' Song Yu's words seemed to carry a hidden reproof. Winds allow of no distinction between manly and womanly, but men are truly exposed to differences in fortune. The cause of the king of Chu's elation and his subjects' anxiety was the differences between men: what had they to do with the wind? If a man in his progress in life feels frustrated, wherever he goes he will be out of humour. If in his progress in life he achieves peace of mind, and his good nature is not disturbed by conflict with external things, wherever he goes he will be elated. Now Master Zhang has not regarded demotion as a calamity; he has made use of the time he could spare from his duties to resite himself amidst mountains and rivers, and in this has proved more resourceful than others. Were he reduced to using bracken to stop up his door and a crock to serve as his window, he would not cease to be elated. So how much more elated is he, being able to cleanse himself in the clear currents of the Yangtze, to have for company the white clouds of the western hills, and divert himself by revelling in the most glorious sights and sounds! And yet it may be otherwise. These same chains of mountains, the plunging gorges, the spreading forests and ancient trees, stirred by a fresh breeze, lit by a bright moon, might afflict poetic and inward-looking souls with unbearable misery: how could they see cause for elation in contemplating them?

---

[2]Song Yu, 3rd century BC poet, refers to this incident in his 'Rhyme-Prose on the Wind' 風賦. The extravagant King Xiang will reappear in Li Yu's 'Judging Beauty' (p. 94).

Fang Xiaoru 方孝儒 (1357–1402)

COMMENTARY

Fang Xiaoru, a native of Zhejiang province, was an eminent scholar and stern moralist. In 1392 he secured an appointment at the court of the founding emperor of the Ming dynasty on the recommendation of Song Lian 宋濂, who played a major part in formulating the Confucian ideology of the new regime. Fang became tutor and chief adviser to Emperor Hui 惠帝, who succeeded in 1399. The succession was contested by the Prince of Yan, and battle was joined. In 1402 the Prince of Yan came out the victor. He demanded Fang Xiaoru's loyalty, and ordered him to draft a proclamation. According to legend, Fang wrote 'The bandit Yan has usurped the throne'. Fang was then put to death along with all his clan and associates, to the number of several hundred persons.

The occasional prose compositions of Fang Xiaoru that survive in modern anthologies are all moralizing parables. One is about a man who neglects a pustule that appears on his thumb until the infection spreads and threatens his life. The moral is then explicitly drawn, in terms of minor delinquencies that might grow to imperil the state. Another is about the dangers of empty bragging. 'The Mosquito Dialogue' is easily the best of these parables. It comes out of the same stable as Lu Guimeng's 'Rustic Temples', but its argument is easier to follow, being dramatized. To that end the author represents himself in the third person, as the 'Tiantai scholar' (the Tiantai mountains being located in his home district), and the moralizing is given over to the servant. The humble mosquito plays the same role here as the idols in 'Rustic Temples', standing as a comparator for the human parasites and pests that prey on the populace; again the human kind comes off worse in the comparison.

The composition has been prized in China chiefly for its rolling periods, and for its poetic description of the mosquito and its doings. The latter is indeed highly entertaining, but the modern reader may find some unintentional humour too in the mosquito apparently getting marks for good manners in tactfully going about its business in private, so causing the minimum of embarrassment to its host. The modern reader may also find the know-all servant amusing: having read P. G. Wodehouse, he will find it hard to suppress the thought that he is what Bertie Wooster's valet Jeeves must have been like as a brash youth, before he learned to be discreet.

The Mosquito Dialogue
蚊對

The scholar from Tiantai, made drowsy by the heat, reposed himself come evening behind his mosquito net. His servant boy stationed himself before the bed and manipulated a large fan, thereby inducing such pleasant coolness that he soon fell asleep. After some time the servant boy himself became sleepy; he put down the fan and propped himself against the bed. Before long he was snoring like thunder. The scholar awoke with a start, believing a storm was imminent. He sat up and clasped his arms round his knees.

After a while he heard the drone of things in flight past his ears, as if in song and in sorrow, as if in complaint and in courtship. They brushed against his arms and pricked his flesh, glanced off his legs and bit his face. His hair stood on end and his muscles twitched. Clapping his hands together, he felt on his palms a dampness as of sweat. When he drew his palms up to his nose to smell them, they gave off the stink of fresh blood. He was seized with great alarm, and his wits deserted him. He kicked the boy awake and shouted at him:

'I am plagued by invaders! Jump up and get a candle to give some light!'

When the candle was brought, the net was seen to be wide open. Thousands of mosquitoes were clustered against it. They scattered in all directions at the sight of the candle, like ants and like flies. Their mandibles were pointed and their bellies distended: shining, red, and rotund.

The Tiantai scholar berated his servant boy: 'Are these not the things that sucked my blood? It's all due to your carelessness, you dragged open the net and let them in! They are alien creatures; if you take proper precautions against them entering our preserve, how can they be of harm to people?'

The boy made a bundle of artemesia and lit the end, whereupon dense clouds of smoke belched forth. Rotating the bundle from side to side, he circled the bed a few times and drove the mosquitoes from the room. He then made reply to the scholar: 'You may retire now, the mosquitoes are all gone.'

The scholar smoothed his bedmat and lay down, sighing to Heaven as he did so: 'Why did Heaven have to inflict these beastly little creatures on mankind?' On hearing this, the boy suppressed a smile and said:

'How is it that you who are most favoured should be the most vehement in complaining against Heaven?

'In the beginning the *yin* and *yang* elements spread in clouds to fill the space between Heaven and Earth, bestowing shape and substance. Man and the myriad creatures were thus made different. Those made huge were the elephant and the rhinoceros, those made monstrous were the dragons, those made fierce were tigers and leopards, and those made docile were the deer and long-tailed monkeys. Those given feathers we know as birds, those given fur we know as beasts, while the hairless were variously men and insects. None of these kinds lacks the wherewithal to sustain itself. Though in size and stature they are different, they are the same in that each has been given its place in the order of things.

'From our point of view, man is noble and the rest of creation lowly; but which is noble and which lowly in the eyes of Heaven? As we see, men have promoted themselves to nobility, and entitle themselves the lords of creation. All the denizens of land and sea, all varieties of life, they trap on the surface or net in the water: the hills give up their tribute and the seas their offerings. No frog can escape with its life, no wild goose can hide from its trackers. Man's feeding off other creatures can be said to have no further to go.

'That being so, must we suppose that the rest of creation is debarred from seeking its nurture from man? This evening the mosquitoes had only to poise their proboscises for you to wail to Heaven and rail against them. Suppose the things that are eaten by men all howled and appealed to Heaven, what punishment would Heaven wreak on man?

'Now with regard to other creatures dining off man and man dining off other creatures, we are talking about different species, hence the practice may be justified. What is more, the mosquito is timid and cautious. It does not dare to reveal itself in daylight. It bides its time until it cannot be seen and takes advantage of fatigue to seek its satisfaction from men. Now there are among one's fellow men those who in eating cereals and drinking soup are the same as others; and in supporting a wife and raising a family are also the same as others. In their attire and manner there is nothing to distinguish them.

Yet in broad daylight they blatantly attack their fellow men where they are most vulnerable, suck their juices and feed on their marrow, so that they collapse from hunger in the wilderness and are made vagabonds on the roads. Their appeals to Heaven blend together in a continuous chorus, yet they are still shown no pity.

'In your case, at the first prick of a mosquito you are wakeful and restless, yet when you hear of your fellow humans battening on one another, you pretend it has nothing to do with you. Is this the way one should observe the duty of the gentleman to put others before himself?'

Thereupon the Tiantai scholar cast aside his pillow, examined his conscience, and sighed loud and long. Then he threw on his clothes and went outside to spend the rest of the night sitting in contemplation.

Gui Youguang 歸有光 (1506–1571)

COMMENTARY

Gui Youguang's career was a failure in terms of office held, but as a stylist he was renowned in his lifetime and promoted even higher after his death, being regarded as the most worthy successor in the Ming dynasty to the Eight Masters of Tang and Song in the sphere of unadorned classical prose (*guwen*).

Gui Youguang's immediate family was an undistinguished branch of the most powerful clan in Kunshan county, Jiangsu province. Neither his grandfather nor his father had attained office. Gui Youguang himself, however, showed early promise in the art of letters and he passed the provincial examination in 1540 with flying colours, but failed the highest state examination eight times before finally passing in 1565, his sixtieth year. In the meantime he lectured as a kind of private academician, and built up a high personal reputation. His first post after getting the *jinshi* degree was magistrate for Changxing county in Zhejiang province. Before his term was up he resigned, supposedly because he tried and failed to curb the privileges and excesses of the local gentry. In 1569 he was given charge of the postal service in Shunde county, but managed to transfer to the capital to work on historical projects. His death brought an early end to those endeavours.

Though he wrote serious tracts on matters of governance and composed according to the conventional categories, Gui Youguang's reputation as a prose writer rests on short essays of a personal nature. The shortest of those short pieces was only 112 characters long. It was written to mark the death of Hanhua 寒花, the bondmaid who at the age of ten accompanied his wife on her marriage to him in 1528, and survived her mistress, who died in 1533, by only four years. It recalls only two trivial incidents, yet those few words so typify the girl's behaviour and so vividly evoke her relationship with her kind mistress, that the rest does not need saying. The longer essays that are translated here employ the same art. 'My mother: a brief life', written when Gui Youguang was himself a husband and father, commemorates the mother who died when he was only seven (by Western reckoning). The portrait can hardly avoid being idealized: the mother so lost must have been well-nigh perfect in her son's eyes. So she is portrayed as a capable and fair manager of a large household, tireless herself in pursuing the traditional female occupations, thrifty and economical, and dutiful in educating her children. By implication she is also seen as a well-loved daughter. Yet she is not a stereotype: there is enough that is particular about her, the suggestion of obsessiveness for example, to make her real. What gives the essay a special dimension, however, derives from the guilt the author must have felt in contributing to her early death, in that he was one of the children whose births 'wore her out'; at least, one assumes that is the explanation for his unusually sensitive appreciation of the sorrow of the woman's lot as a breeder of children: not only does he feel her desperation at the frequency of her pregnancies (the reader senses it too with the relentless repetition of the word 'bore': in all she gave birth to seven children in ten years) but understands her struggle with her conscience in taking the contraceptive potion. The fact that his mother's memorial portrait could only be composed from her children's features pathetically underlines the point that she existed for her children and had no identity separate from them.

The second essay, 'The Xiangji Studio', invites more commentary. The main part was written in 1524, when Gui Youguang was only eighteen. The last two paragraphs were added it would seem twenty years or more later. Despite this gulf of years, and a noticeable difference of tone between the two sections, both are clearly from the same hand, which bespeaks a surprising maturity on the part of the young man.

Overtly a description of the room Gui made his study in his tender youth, the essay in reality tells the story of his family. The primary composition is so loosely constructed that it might give the impression that its parts are disconnected, but in fact they have a unity whose locus is the young man's sense of a coming encounter with destiny. Everything previously mentioned contributes to his final expression of high resolve. The destruction of the once idyllic environment by the division of the family property and the decline, we may presume, in family fortunes form the background to his resolve, the recollection of his late mother's solicitude for her children, the trust put in him by his grandmother, his retreat into watchful solitude, and his belief that his studio is divinely protected: all these prepare him to think that he is intended to reconstruct the idyll, and do more. To fortify himself against any disabling feeling of insignificance he recalls the historical precedents of the Widow Qing 清 who by her own skill and enterprise accrued impregnable wealth in the ancient kingdom of Shu (her story is told in *Shi ji*: 'Huozhi liezhuan' 史記・貨殖列傳), and Zhuge Liang, the fabulously clever strategist who came from obscurity to shape history at the end of the Han dynasty (see p. 25).

The supplement that updates the original essay reflects a sadder and wiser mind. Composed as a series of notes, it is even more emphatically disconnected and understated, so to speak, than the preceding section. Instead of openly expressing sentiment in conclusion, it deflects it into the object of the tree planted by his wife just before her death: the thoughts it gives rise to, as Wordsworth said in a later age and under different skies, 'lie too deep for tears'.

Wordsworth, by coincidence, promoted an aesthetic revolution that was similar to that which Gui Youguang was less determinedly engaged in in the later half of the Ming dynasty. Diffuseness was not part of it, but rejection of the artificial, the ostentatious, the grandiose and rhetorical was common to both movements. The idea was not to deny grandeur and power, profundity and even sublimity, but to relocate them in the humble and trivial, the plain and everyday. Gui Youguang's achievement in this respect did not go unappreciated. Lin Shu 林紓, one of the last great writers in the classical language, is quoted as saying: 'The old lady's words reported by Gui Youguang are extremely trivial and wholly immaterial, yet no one who has lost his mother in childhood can read them without shedding tears.' One might add that their power to move is not confined to those so orphaned.

At the same time, R. L. Stevenson's remark in another context is also pertinent: 'To show beauty in common things is the work of the rarest tact. It is not to be done by the wishing. It is easy to posit as a theory, but to bring it home to men's minds is the problem of literature, and is only accomplished by rare talent, and in comparatively rare instances.' *Mutatis mutandis*, this essay is one of those rare instances.

My Mother: A Brief Life
先妣事略

My late mother was Madam Zhou. She was born on the eleventh of the second month of the year 1488. She married into the Gui family at the age of sixteen. In the second year of her marriage she bore Shujing; Shujing is my elder sister. The following year she bore me, Youguang, and the year following that bore twins: one soon died, and the other did not survive into her second year. Two years later she bore Youshang, after a pregnancy of twelve months. In the second year thereafter she bore Shushun, and in another year she bore Yougong.

Though she was in more robust health when suckling Yougong than with the other children, she frequently knit her brows and complained to her maids: 'Having so many children has worn me out.' An older maid placed two snails in a cup of water and offered it to her, saying: 'After drinking this, your pregnancies will be fewer.' My mother drained the potion in one go, but she was so distressed she could not speak.

On the twenty-third of the fifth month, 1513, my mother died. Seeing all the other family members weeping, the children wept along with them, but they thought their mother was merely sleeping.

How cruelly they were deluded! Afterwards when the family engaged a painter to paint her portrait, they produced two of her children and ordered him: 'From the nose upwards paint Youguang, from the nose downwards paint Shujing.' For these two children favoured their mother.

My mother's personal name was Gui. Her grandfather's name was Zhou Ming. Her father Zhou Xing was a student at the Imperial Academy. Her mother's surname was He. The Zhou family had lived for generations at Wu Bridge, some ten miles southeast of the county town. From Qiandunpu southwards right up to the bridge, along the east side of the little port, all the settlers thereabouts belonged to the Zhou clan. My grandfather and his three brothers were looked up to as men of substance, but they valued simplicity and lived plainly. In mixing with their neighbours they unassumingly adopted the local patois, and they treated kindly all the junior members of the family, close and distant relatives alike.

When my mother went to stay at Wu Bridge she applied herself to spinning cotton; back in town she twisted hemp thread. She regularly worked until midnight by the flickering light of the lamp. Nearly every day her parents sent people with enquiries and presents, so mother had no cause to worry over the supply of necessities, but she still slaved and toiled as if she had not enough to get through the day. In spring she had the maids make briquets of the coal dust left over from burning the stoves in the winter, and piled them out of doors to dry. No litter was left in the house, nor were there idle hands at home. Her older children dragged at her skirts, her little ones fed at her breast. All the time she went on with her sewing and mending. Everything was kept spick and span. She treated the servants considerately, and even when she had them beaten, they did not have it in their hearts to murmur and complain. Every year fish, crabs, and pastries were sent from Wu Bridge, and everyone had their share: when the news spread that the man from Wu Bridge had arrived, there was general rejoicing.

I started school at the age of seven along with my cousin Youjia. Whenever the wind was cold, or it was drizzling, my cousin stayed at home. I longed to stay at home too, but was not allowed to. When my mother woke at night, she would make me recite from the *Classic of Filial Piety* in the dark. If I had got it by heart and did not stumble over a word, she was very pleased.

When my mother died, her mother Madam He also died. The Zhou family was laid low by a disease contracted from their animals: my uncle's wife died; then my mother's fourth sister died shortly after marrying into the Gu family; in all thirty people perished. Only my grandfather and two uncles survived.

Eleven years after my mother died, my elder sister married Wang Sanjie, a match that had been arranged by my mother. In the next year I got my bachelor's degree. In the sixteenth year after my mother's death I got married, also to a partner chosen by her long before. After another year I was blessed with a daughter. I was very attached to her, and my mother was more than ever in my thoughts. Waking in the night, I fell to weeping when I told my wife about my mother. Those few things I could recall were as fresh as yesterday, the rest was all a blur.

To lose one's mother in childhood, heavens, how painful it is!

The Xiangji Studio
項脊軒志

The Xiangji Studio is an old apartment giving onto the southern verandah. The living space is only ten feet square, just enough for one person. The structure is a hundred years old, so the dust filtered in, the rain poured through. When one wanted to shift the position of the table, one could find no other place to put it. Then too the studio faces north, which means it got no sun: by afternoon it was already dark.

I had some repairs made, which stopped the roof leaking. I had four windows cut in the front, and a wall built to encircle the courtyard, so as to catch the southern sun. Thanks to the light reflected by the wall, the interior was bright for the first time. I also had orchid, cassia, bamboos and trees planted here and there in the courtyard, which enhanced the aspect of the existing verandah. With borrowed books filling my shelves, I would lie back and intone and chant, or sit upright and meditate. Though the pipes of Nature played round about, it was quiet and still in the courtyard. Sometimes small birds came to feed there, and did not fly away when humans approached. On the night of the full moon, when the bright moonlight reached halfway down the walls and the cassias shed a dappled shade which moved when the wind stirred, one knew then what bliss was.

But while I enjoyed many pleasures residing there, I had my share of sadness too.

In the beginning my courtyard linked north and south compounds in one whole, but when my father's generation divided up the property, numbers of little gates and walls were installed internally and externally: wherever you went you came up against them. The dog that belonged to the household on the east went and barked at the people on the west; guests had to thread their way through the kitchen to get to their feast; and chickens even roosted in the reception rooms. At first fences were put up in the courtyards, then walls replaced them, and everything was changed round again.

There is an old lady still in our household who once lived here. She was maid to my grandmother, and nurse to two generations. My late mother treated her with great kindness and consideration. On the west side there is access to the mistress's bedchamber, and my mother had had occasion to come into this room. The old lady was fond of telling me, 'This is where your mother stood.' She once recalled: 'I was nursing your sister in my arms, and she was crying at the top of her lungs. The mistress tapped on the door with her fingers and asked, "Is the child cold? Does she want a feed?" And I answered her from this side of the partition.' Before the old lady had finished I burst into tears, and she was overcome also.

From the age of fifteen I used this annex as my study. One day my grandmother came by. 'Son, I have not set eyes on you since I can't remember when,' she said, 'Why do you hide away here from morn till night, just like a young lady?' As she was closing the door behind her, she said to herself: 'It is a long time since we have had a successful scholar in the family. Perhaps with this young man there is some hope?' In a moment she was back with an ivory tablet, saying: 'My grandfather, Director of the Court of Sacrificial Worship, held this when he attended court in the Xuande reign. In time to come you shall use it.'

When I look back, these memories of days gone by are as fresh to me as if they had been of yesterday. They make me cry my heart out.

There was formerly a kitchen to the east of the studio; people had to pass in front of the studio on their way there. I closed my windows and kept out of the way. In time I could tell who it was by their footsteps.

The studio caught fire four times in all. That it was not destroyed I put down to the protection of the gods.

The keeper of the Xiangji Studio says: The woman called Qing managed a cinnabar mine in the far west, and became so fabled for her wealth that after she died the Emperor of Qin built the Terrace in Memory of the Woman Qing to honour her. And Zhuge Liang emerged from the backwoods when Liu Bei and Cao Cao fought over the realm. How could the world recognize the merits of these two while they were hidden away in some obscure hole? I am a person of no importance, dwelling in an old shack, yet I look proudly about me, and my eyes glint as I perceive a remarkable future for myself. Were other people to know of this, no doubt they would think me no different from the frog at the bottom of a shallow well who has never seen the mighty sea.

Five years after I wrote this piece, I married, and my wife came to live in the family house. She would often come to my studio, and ask me about events in history, or practise calligraphy bent over the table. When she paid the customary return visit to her mother's home, she recounted these matters to her little sister, who asked: 'They say you have a studio in your new home. Could you tell me what they mean by "studio"?'

Six years later, my wife died. The studio went to rack and ruin, but I did nothing to repair it. Two more years on, I underwent a long illness, and out of boredom had the studio refurbished, making some small alterations to the layout in the process. But afterwards I was mostly away from home, and rarely used it.

There is a loquat tree in the courtyard that my wife planted with her own hands the year she died. Now its leaves make a dense canopy.

Yuan Hongdao 袁宏道 (1568–1610)

COMMENTARY

Yuan Hongdao, also known as Yuan Zhonglang, founded, with his brothers, the Gongan school of writers (Gongan in Hubei province being their native place) at the end of the 16th century, and enjoyed considerable fame—touched with notoriety—in his lifetime. He was restored to prominence in the early 1930s by modern prose writers who were seeking a native ancestry for their compositions, their sights having previously been set on foreign 'essays', 'sketches', *belles-lettres* and so on. His attraction was that he both advocated and exemplified individualism and contemporaneity in a culture that was basically conformist and backward looking. He is still well represented in recent anthologies of classical prose.

Yuan Hongdao came from the scholar-gentry class. He followed the conventional path to a career in government by taking the provincial degree in 1588 and the metropolitan degree in 1592. His first post was as magistrate of Wu county in Jiangsu, which embraced Suzhou, in 1595. He soon resigned, complaining of the excessive paperwork. Thereafter he held a number of posts in ministries in Peking, interspersed with long periods of rest and travel. He died shortly after retirement to his home province.

Yuan Hongdao was an effective communicator, and he played his part in propagating the Gongan school's philosophy of *xingling* (native sensibility). This derived from the doctrine of *tongxin* (the childlike mind) of their mentor, Li Zhi 李贽 (1527–1602), and stood for being one's own native unspoilt self, looking on the world with fresh eyes, unclouded by convention or tradition, and making one's own interests; correspondingly, one's words too were to be one's own, freed from the trammels of conventional rhetoric and breaking with habitual rhythms. As the school all agreed, they lived in their own times, so should write for their own times, and let the dead bury the dead. But Yuan Hongdao's great personal contribution to the development of Chinese prose was not in originality of thought but in showing the way: that is, translating an attitude to life and literature into practices that clearly worked and that others could learn from, through pouring new wine into old bottles (biographic and scenic sketches), and extending the range of what one could write about entertainingly (vulgar pursuits, riffraff, etc.).

Youji (travelogues, scenic descriptions) bulk largest in Yuan's prose, travel being a joy of his. From the great variety of these compositions one can see the virtue of the Gongan school's approach to literature, for they are all inspirational: you never know what to expect. You may indeed get a full description of the scene that met the travellers' eyes (Chinese scholars usually made these outings in a group), but equally the interest may be in a story that attached to the place, or what happened to the party, or even just focus on a joke someone made. In other words, the shaping force is subjectivism: whatever took the author's fancy, whatever made the deepest impression, is what went down on paper, to the disregard of any plan or overview.

To take, however, a standard scene description as an example of his work, 'Manjing youji' (An Excursion to the Brimful Well) records a visit to a famously big well about a mile outside the walled city of Peking, made in 1599 when Yuan had a post in the capital. The long view of the distant hills, the middle view of the surrounding fields and dykes, and the close-ups of the well itself are not given in any ordered way, but by abrupt switching, and are described either by elaborate similes or in highly condensed four-character phrases. The soft contours of the hills are likened to a woman's high coiffure, freshly combed into place; the shine on the surface of the well, from which the 'skin' of ice has just melted, is compared to the 'cold glint' that shoots from a silver mirror when its box is opened. Compactness is achieved by exploiting the grammatical flexibility of Chinese words, mostly by using nouns as verbs: so fellow trippers are classed as 'spring-and-tea-ists' (those who drink tea made with spring water), 'goblet-and-song-ers' (those who quaff wine and sing), and 'red-attire-and-hack-ers' (colourfully dressed women riding docile horses). This kind of freshness of conception and fluidity of language does indeed betoken a true liberation from convention, a release of the brakes on the mind.

More celebrated and much more exuberant is Yuan's 'Huqiu ji' (Tiger Hill, 1596). This describes the droves of people who stream out of the city of Suzhou on the night of the Mid-Autumn Festival to enjoy the full moon from Tiger Hill. Syntactically isolated strings of words are used like splashes of colour to convey the carnival atmosphere, and to plunge the writer from his normal elevation into the thick of the mêlée. The description of the amateur singing competition reaches the height of lyricism, the magical moment.

It is however typical of Yuan Hongdao that he will undercut his own lyricism, as in 'Tian Chi' (The Pool of Heaven), when after waxing enthusiastic about the beauties of nature he asks his pageboy 'Isn't that fine?', the pageboy answers 'I'm dog tired, what's fine about it?'. This kind of deflation was not calculated to startle the reader; it was inherent in his dedication to truthfulness to experience, and his complete open-mindedness about what should go into a composition. It was in that spirit that he wrote entertainingly about ant fights and spider fights, about beggars and drunkards, about dreams and uncanny happenings. Those things were to him objects of interest, not of amusement. Occasionally he did write purely to amuse. The second essay translated here is an example: everyone could be expected to find the stupid servants comical.

Tiger Hill
虎丘記

Tiger Hill is two or three miles from the city. It has no lofty crags or plunging ravines. The reason why it attracts the tall pleasure boats and resounds with fife and drum every day of the year is simply because of this proximity to the city. Every night of the full moon, every morning there are flowers in bloom, every snowy evening, the trippers thread back and forth like stitches in a tapestry. And the crowds reach their peak at Mid-Autumn Festival.

On this day, houses are shut up and the whole city empties. The citizens troop out shoulder to shoulder, all done up in their finest attire, from the cream of society down to the city dregs. They bring with them piles of mats, and stop for wine at every crossroad. From Thousand Mile Stone right up to the monastery gate they pack as dense as the teeth on a comb or the scales on a fish. You could pile their clappers up as high as a hill, the wine flows like clouds bursting. From the distance you would think it was a flock of wild geese landing on some river flats—or sunset clouds spreading over some great river—or rumbling thunder and flashing lightning: no words can describe it.

When they first take their place and spread their mats, the singers are numbered in thousands; they sound like a swarm of mosquitoes: individual voices cannot be distinguished. But when eventually they are organized into orderly teams, the singers compete against each other, and the sheep are soon separated from the goats. Before long those left swaying to the rhythm are no more than a few dozen. Then the moon floats up into the bare heavens, the rocks gleam like raw silk. The dull crocks fall silent and just three or four in a group are left to harmonize: one long flute, one short pipe, one man singing to the slow beat of his clappers. Bamboo flute and human vocal chords coincide, the pure notes are thrillingly clear, the listeners are enraptured. When the night grows late, and the moon casts long shadows that wave like fronds in water, the flutes and clappers too have served their turn. One man takes the stage, and there is a deathly hush. His voice is like a thin strand of hair. It cuts through the air and pierces the clouds. One syllable is drawn out for what seems a quarter of an hour. Birds are arrested in flight, and strong men break down in tears.

The Sword Pool is unfathomably deep, the jutting rocks around it are as if hewn out with a blade. The Mountain of a Thousand Acres of Cloud has the Heaven's Pool Hill as its pedestal; its sharp prominences and clefts are a fine sight, and it is most inviting as a place for a picnic; but in the afternoon it gets the full force of the sun, and one cannot sit for long. The Wenchang Pavilion is also a splendid building, its trees at dusk being especially delightful. Facing north from there you look out over the ruins of Pingyuan Hall, a totally empty vista, with Mount Yu the only point in view. The Hall has long been disused. Jiang Jinzhi and I planned to restore it, with the intention of setting up shrines to Wei Yingwu and Bai Juyi,[1] but I fell ill and sought leave from my post, and I'm afraid Jinzhi lost interest. There is a cycle of growth and decay, and all things surely have their season.

I was in office in Suzhou for two years, and climbed Tiger Hill six times. The last time I waited for the moon on Shenggong Rock with Jiang Jinzhi and Fang Zigong. When the word went round that the magistrate had come the singers melted away. So I said to Jinzhi: 'See how high and mighty we officials are, how boorish our lictors! But the time will come when I will take off this black cap and listen to the singing from this rock, may the moon be my witness!' Now I have happily retired and am only a sojourner in Suzhou. Oh moon of Tiger Hill, do you still remember my words?

The Rewards of Stupidity
拙效傳

The rabbit is of all creatures the slyest in making itself scarce, yet the hunter catches it. The cuttlefish puffs out ink to conceal itself, but that is the cause of its destruction. What is the use of cleverness? To talk of ruses of concealment, the sparrow is not as good as the swallow; to talk of the art of survival, the crane is not as good as the cuckoo. This

---

[1] Jiang Jinzhi 江進之 was a fellow member of the Gongan School. Wei Yingwu 韋應物 and Bai Juyi 白居易, both eminent Tang dynasty poets, had at one time governed Suzhou.

was noted of old. Now I offer to you 'The Rewards of Stupidity'.

There are four dense servants employed by my family. Their names are Dong, Tung, Qi and Kui.

Dong is my servant. He has a turned-up nose, blue eyes and a curly beard. His skin is the colour of rusty iron. He once went with me to Wuchang. I sent him on an errand to a scholar who lived nearby, and he could not find his way home. He wandered back and forth a score of times, and though he saw other servants passing by, he did not approach them for directions, despite being over forty years old. I happened to go out myself, and saw him peering about disconsolately, seemingly on the point of tears. He was overjoyed when I called out to him.

He is very fond of drinking. When we were heating a new pitcher of wine over the cooking range, Dong begged a cup. But then he was called away to do a chore, and he left it on the table. A woman servant drank it while nobody was looking. The one in charge of the wine heating took pity on him, and offered him another drink. Dong bent forward into the chimney piece in his eagerness, and was caught in the flame from the cooking fire, which singed his beard and eyebrows. Everybody laughed, and he was given a flask instead. Dong was delighted, and held the flask in the boiling water, ready to drink it as soon as it was warmed up, but in his carelessness he was splashed by the hot water and let go of the flask. In the end he got not a drop to drink, and went off in a huff.

Another time I told him to open a door whose hinges were rather stiff. He pushed with all his might, and was propelled forward when the door opened, tumbling head over heels. That caused great merriment.

This year he accompanied me to my posting in Peking. There he mixed with the servants of other households for half a year, but when I asked their names he hadn't a clue.

Tung is also old-fashioned in appearance, but is a bit of a joker too. He was indentured in boyhood to my elder brother Boxiu. When Boxiu contracted a new marriage after his wife died, he sent Tung to the city to buy cakes as required for the betrothal present. It was roughly thirty miles to the city, and the happy day was near. He was expected back in three days. On the afternoon of the third day, my father and Boxiu stationed themselves at our gate, but there was no sign of him. When evening came, a figure was seen approaching along the Willow Dyke, with a carrying pole over his shoulder. It was Tung. My father was very relieved. He urgently bade him to go inside. But when Tung's load was set down, he saw it consisted only of a large jar of honey. He asked where the cakes were. Tung replied, 'When I got to the city yesterday, I found the price of honey was cheap, so I bought some. The price of cakes was high, they weren't worth buying.' The betrothal presents had to be delivered the next day, so the thing fell through.

Qi and Kui are my younger brother's servants. Once Qi was sent to cut firewood. When he knelt down to tie the branches in a bundle, he pulled too hard on the rope and it broke. His clenched fist struck his chest with so much force that he collapsed in a faint. It took him a long while to come round.

Kui reminds one of a roebuck in appearance. He reached the age of thirty without being capped. His hair was twisted at the back into a knot, rather like a thick rope. Kui was given money to buy a hat, but he forgot about the knot. On his return he bound his hair and placed his hat on his head: it fell down right over his eyes and nose! He moaned and groaned the rest of the day.

On another occasion, he was chased by a dog when he went to a neighbour's house. He did battle with it with his bare hands, as if he was in a wrestling match—and got his fingers bitten. These are typical examples of his daftness.

Despite all that, it is our cunning and calculating servants who commit offences, whereas it is these four thick ones who keep to the rules. The clever ones are sent away one after the other, and having no means of livelihood, are on their beam-ends in a year or two. The four thick ones, on the other hand, are fed and clothed on account of not having transgressed. Out of regard for their loyalty alone, their masters assign them their rations, worried only that they might lose them. The case for the rewards of stupidity is thus demonstrated.

Zhang Dai 張岱 (1597–1684)

COMMENTARY

Zhang Dai was born in Shaoxing, Zhejiang province. He came from a prominent family, moved in the best circles, travelled between the rich cities of the Yangtze valley, and lived off the fat of the land. He can be thought of in his gilded youth as a kind of Baoyu (the hero of *The Dream of the Red Chamber*) let out from his mansion to do his own thing. Baoyu, too, had he not disappeared from the sight of the world, would probably have become in later life an equally novel and interesting writer. In fact, if we suppose that Cao Xueqin 曹雪芹, the author of the *The Dream*, was essentially portraying himself in Baoyu, we could say that is what Baoyu did indeed become, though in the medium of fiction, not prose.

To give a little substance to 'gilded youth', Zhang Dai indulged in such cultivated pursuits as book collecting, antique collecting, music and opera appreciation and tea tasting, and such uncultivated pursuits as street entertainments, drunkenness and debauchery. When youth began to wear off he took up more serious interests in addition to those. In 1618 he began on the ten-year task of compiling biographies of men and women who had died in the cause of justice. Interestingly, his martyrs came from all levels of society, and his choice favoured those unsung in official histories. The egalitarian outlook which that choice bespoke underlay the appeal of the later prose portraits for which he is now celebrated. After the biographies he embarked on a monumental history of the Ming dynasty which was to occupy him till the end of his life.

The cataclysm in Zhang Dai's life was the fall of the dynasty to the Manchu invaders. He was caught up in it through one of the imperial clan, the Prince of Lu 魯王, descending on Shaoxing and setting up court there in 1645, after the demise of the emperor in Peking. Resistance to the Manchus was, however, short-lived, and Zhang Dai fled to the mountains in 1646, there to live frugally till the end of his days, as far as is known. To this latter part of his life belong the collections of prose pieces that earned him a permanent place in Chinese literary history, the favourite with his readers being *Tao'an mengyi* (Dream-rememberings of Tao'an, ca. 1865—Tao'an being his pen-name), from which all the pieces here translated are taken. As is often the case, a man's loss is literature's gain. Zhang Dai's misspent youth accounts for the stock of interesting material he had to draw on, but without the fall of the dynasty and the vanishing of the world he looked back on, the scenes and personalities he depicts would not have been so vivid to his mind and so not been set down so vividly on paper—if indeed he had thought them worth recording at all.

At the same time these compositions would not have been conceivable in the literary sense without the precedence of the Gongan school of prose writing. Through its advocacy and example it taught writers to think about individuality, personality, the vital spark; to apprehend directly, without the mediation of philosophy and ethical judgement; and to use the language of the day, much as if writing was like speech. All these lessons Zhang Dai obviously learned, and practised better than his masters.

The *Tao'an mengyi* collection combines essays where the author is merely a seeing eye and others where he himself is a more of less prominent actor. If the latter kind are a little too self-regarding, it is an innocent kind of conceit that is displayed, and there is more than adequate compensation in the rare quality of the experience that is shared with the reader, or the interest of the matter itself. In our selection, the author puts in an appearance only in the 'West Lake' piece, in a similar, though less clever, role to that of Su Shi in the 'Red Cliff' essay (Cf pp. 57–60). Like him too he goes to sleep at the end of outing (a convenient way to end an essay). Very different, though, is the eruption of life independent of the author, which is comparable to that portrayed in Yuan Hongdao's 'Tiger Hill'. The animation is conveyed by even greater plastering than Yuan Hongdao's of isolated phrases without grammatical linkage. Over all, however, the essay is more thoughtfully structured than Yuan's, with alternation of mood and variation of pace being deliberately controlled.

A further comparison with Yuan Hongdao's essays can be made in regard to character portrayal. Word portraits of friends and acquaintances go back a long way in classical literature, as we have seen, and humble characters used as mouthpieces appeared quite often in the works of Han Yu and Liu Zongyuan. Yuan Hongdao, in his democratic way, showed interest in real people quite other than himself, if they were sufficiently amusing. Zhang Dai goes one better in seeking to capture the essence of a personality, as in these portraits of the chanteuse Wang Yuesheng and the storyteller Liu Jingting. He also goes out of his way to accord them dignity, despite the indignity of their professions.

'The Jades of Yangzhou' is different again, being a description of what could be called a social phenomenon, namely the selling of young women into concubinage. These young women were bought in girlhood and trained in none too pleasant charm schools to make themselves attractive to men. The Chinese expression for them is *shou ma* (skinny nags), presumably referring to the girls' state before they were 'fattened up'. By coincidence the English word 'jade' also has the double meaning of a 'nag' and a flirtatious girl or 'minx'. The ceremonials for the wedding are deliberately described as chaotic: stages that would normally be well spaced out are crammed into one forenoon, so closely that they overlap. To clarify a little, the steps required for taking a wife (and here, oddly, for taking a concubine) are the dispatch of presents of food, drink, etc. from the groom's house to the bride's house; the preparation at the groom's home of the provisions and trappings for the feast and ceremony; a procession from the groom's home to the bride's home with the bridal chair and other paraphernalia; the return of the bride and her attendants; and finally the wedding feast.

The Full Moon Festival at the West Lake
西湖七月半

There is nothing to watch at the moon festival on the West Lake save the people watching the moon festival. There are five classes of people to watch watching the moon festival.

The first kind: storeyed pleasure boats, orchestra playing; high hats and grand banquets; actors and servants, a blaze of lanterns. In this riot of light and sound they pretend to watch the moon but actually do not see the moon. These one watches.

The second kind: also pleasure boats, also storeyed; society belles and highborn ladies, pretty pageboys in tow; laughs and squeals at intervals. Seated in a circle on the poopdeck, looking left and peering right, they are physically under the moon but do not watch the moon. These one watches.

The third kind: also on boats and also with music and song; famous singing girls and unattached priests; sipping wine and crooning songs; subdued flutes and gentle strings; voices and instruments as one; also in the moonlight, they both watch the moon and want people to watch them watching the moon. These one watches.

The fourth kind: boatless and carriageless; coatless and hatless; well gorged and well grogged; hallooing to their mates, in threes and fours, barging through the crowd, congregating around the Zhaoqing Temple and Broken Bridge; making an unearthly din, pretending to be drunk and singing tuneless songs. They watch the moon, they watch those watching the moon, and also those not watching the moon, but actually they watch nothing. These one watches.

The fifth kind: small boats, net curtains; clean tables and hot stoves; tea quickly boiled, white china cups quietly passed; good friends and fine females, invited to enjoy the moon together; either seeking concealment under the trees or escaping the noise in the inner lake, they watch the moon but do not strike a pose of watching the moon, and make no matter of watching the moon. These one watches.

Hangzhou people normally go boating on the lake from late morning to early evening: they avoid the moon like poison. But this evening their reputation is at stake: there is a veritable battle to get out of town. Having generously tipped the soldiers at the city gates, their bearers light the way with burning brands, and they queue up at the jetties for a boat. Once embarked they press the boatman to make full speed to Broken Bridge, where the most action is. So by about nine o'clock the place is a bedlam of voices and music: aboil and aquake; nightmare ravings and delirious babblings; bellows of the deaf and mouthings of the dumb.

As the big boats and small boats pull in to the bank, they see absolutely nothing, except pole striking pole, boat butting boat, shoulder rubbing shoulder, face staring into face. Very soon enthusiasm wanes, the banquets of the officials break up and their lictors clear a way for their cavalcades to return. The chair bearers call out to the people on the boats, threatening them with city gates closed in their face if they delay, and then they depart pell-mell, their lanterns and torches like stars strung out across the sky. The people on the shore also join the crowd making for the city gate; the masses thin and very quickly are gone altogether.

Only then do we steer our boat to the shore. The steps of Broken Bridge are now cold. We spread our mats, toast our friends and drink freely. Now the moon is like a polished mirror, the hills have freshened their make-up, the face of the lake is cleansed again. Those who previously sipped their wine and crooned their songs emerge, those who sought shelter under the trees also emerge. We advance and make their acquaintance, and draw them into our circle. Joined by these gentlemen of taste and chanteuses of repute we sit down to our refreshments, and voice and flute make music together. We do not break up until the moon turns pale and chill and the sky whitens in the east. Then our little party casts off, and we fall asleep surrounded by acres of waterlilies, lapped by waves of heady scent, and content to dream our untroubled dreams.

Wang Yuesheng
王月生

The chanteuses in Nanjing are ashamed to be associated with the prostitutes of the Carmine Quarter. Wang Yuesheng started life in the Carmine Quarter, yet in all her thirty years as a chanteuse there has been absolutely no one to compare with her.

Her complexion is like the new bloom of a Fujian orchid, her person delicate and softly graceful. The upturned tip of her tiny slipper is like a red water-chestnut breaking the surface of the water. She holds herself aloof and is sparing with her words and smiles. When her younger sisters in the profession and local wags use all their arts and guile to pillory acquaintances, she is not amused. She writes a beautiful hand, paints orchids, bamboos and narcissi, and can sing the songs of Wu, though she will do so only to a select few.

The great and good of Nanjing may be pressing with their invitations; still she cannot afford them a full programme's entertainment. For the rich merchants and power brokers to get her to preside for any length of time, they must send her fee a day in advance, and it must be a handsome sum, no less than five gold pieces, perhaps ten: she is not to be casually hired. To enjoy connubial relations with her, she must be engaged at the start of the season, otherwise one may wait a whole year in vain.

She has a taste for tea, and is on good terms with Min Wenshui: though she be booked for a banquet, and a storm may rage besides, nothing will stop her going first to his house and drinking pots of tea with him. She will also take favoured acquaintances along to meet the old gentleman. One day a great merchant among his neighbours had got together a dozen or so singing girls. They were sitting in a circle, carousing and engaging in loose talk and persiflage. Yuesheng appeared on the balcony and paced to and fro along the railings, evidently abashed and discomfited. When the wenches saw her their spirits were deflated, and they moved to another room to avoid her.

Yuesheng is as cool and reserved as a 'single plum blossom in the cold moonlight': icily self-possessed, she is not daunted by the frost. She does not like to mix with vulgar fellows; if from time to time she finds herself in their company, she looks straight through them. Once a young aristocrat procured her services, and they shared bed and board for two weeks without him getting a word out of her. One day her lips made as if to speak, whereupon the hangers-on present were surprised and delighted, and rushed to relay the news to the young master: 'Yuesheng is about to break her silence!' Sure that this was a good sign, they were wild with excitement. He hastened to attend upon her. Her face was flushed; she started to speak but stopped. The young man entreated her time and again. At last she uttered three words through clenched teeth: 'I'm going home!'

Liu Jingting: Storyteller
柳敬亭說書

Pockmarked Liu of Nanjing has a swarthy complexion and his face is covered in craters and ridges. His manner is languid and detached, and he is just as nature made him. He is an excellent storyteller.

He tells one episode a day, and his fee is one ounce of silver. To engage him you have to make your booking, and forward his retainer, ten days in advance, and even then you may be out of luck. There are at present two entertainers in Nanjing in great demand: one is Wang Yuesheng, the chanteuse; the other is Pockmarked Liu.

I heard him tell the story of Wu Song killing the tiger on Jingyang Ridge.* His version diverged greatly from the original text. He will describe things in the minutest particular, but his choice of what to put in and leave out is nice and neat, and he is never wordy.

---

*Probably the most famous episode in the Ming novel *Shuihu zhuan* 水滸傳.

His bellow is like the boom of a mighty bell, and when he gets to some high point in the action he will let loose such a peal of thunder that the building will shake on its foundations. I remember that when Wu Song goes into the inn to get a drink and finds no one there to serve him, he suddenly gave such a roar as to set all the empty vessels humming and vibrating. To make dull patches come to life like this is typical of his passion for detail.

When he goes to perform in someone's house, he will not loosen his tongue until his hosts sit quietly, hold their breath, and give him their undivided attention. If he spots the servants whispering, or if his listeners yawn or show any signs of fatigue, he will come to an abrupt halt, and be impervious to persuasion to continue. He will often talk till past midnight, still keeping up an unhurried flow, while the servants wipe the tables, trim the lamp, and silently serve tea in cups of tasteful porcelain. His pacing and his inflexions, his articulation and his cadences, are exactly suited to the situation, and lay bare the very body and fibre of the matter. If one plucked all the other storytellers alive by the ear and made them listen to him, I do not doubt but they would be struck dumb with wonder and give up the ghost on the spot.

Pockmarked Liu is remarkably ugly, but his lips are puckish, his eyes animated, his dress quietly elegant: all of which effectively puts him on a par with Wang Yuesheng for comeliness, hence their equal drawing power as entertainers.

The Jades of Yangzhou
揚州瘦馬

The number of people in Yangzhou who live off the bodies of jades runs into scores and hundreds. Those who have it in mind to take a concubine had better not let it be known, for if even a breath of the news gets out, the go-betweens and dealers in flesh will besiege their gates like blowflies fastening on carrion; it will be no good hoping they can be shooed away.

At the crack of dawn they knock at your door to hurry you on your way. The first matchmaker in the queue wins the right to be the first to march you off; the rest tag after you, waiting their turn to attend on you. When you have got to the jade's house, taken your seat and been served with tea, the go-between takes the jade's arm and leads her out, saying: 'Greet the guest, miss,' she then curtsies. On the order 'Please to promenade, miss,' she walks forward. When she is told, 'Turn about, miss,' she turns to face the light, thereby revealing her face. Then in succession: 'Let us see your hand,' she rolls her sleeve right up: her hand is displayed, her arm is displayed, and her skin is displayed too. 'Look at the gentleman,' she shyly shoots him a sidelong glance: her eyes are displayed. 'How old are you?' she says how old she is: her voice is displayed. 'Walk some more,' she lifts her skirt to walk: her feet are displayed. Actually there are more canny ways of telling the size of the girl's feet: if the rustle of her skirts precedes her entrance, her feet must be big; if she has hitched up her skirts and enters best foot forward, they must be small. Finally she is told: 'Please to retire.' That girl retires and another comes out. At every house there will be five or six girls to be seen, all according to the same routine.

If a girl suits the man's taste, he fastens a gold clasp or pin in her hair; this is called 'pinning on the pledge'. If none suits him, he tips the matchmaker, or the servants of the house, a few strings of cash, and goes on to inspect the girls elsewhere. When the matchmaker tires, there is always a queue of others waiting to take over. One day, two days, as many as four to five days may be spent in this way, just depending on how long he can keep it up; but when he has seen fifty or sixty, all powdered faces and red dresses, each an exact duplicate of the last one, it comes to resemble an illiterate person copying out a character a hundred or a thousand times without ever learning its meaning: the mind confers with the eye, but they have no particulars to go on, so there is nothing for it but to make the best of a bad job and plump for one at random.

After the 'pledge' is made, the girl's establishment draws up a list on red paper: so much coloured silk, so much jewellery, so many wedding presents, so many bolts of cloth. A brush is loaded with ink and the list is handed to the client to check. If the client ticks a satisfactory number of items, he is entertained and escorted back home. Long before he reaches his abode, a band of musicians and the customary panniers of sweetmeats and dressed mutton and wine have preceded him. In very short order the presents, confectioneries, and so on are made ready and the little procession sets off to the bride's place, led by the musicians. Before they have gone half a league, the bridal sedan chair, the fancy lanterns, the torch bearers, astrologers, bridesmaids and groomsmen, and the ceremonial paraphernalia of candles, fruits, meats and wines are all in front of the man's gate, ready and waiting. With the arrival of the cook and his baskets all the equipage is complete and all the personnel assembled: fruit and vegetables, cooked meats, dumplings and cakes; altar trappings, canopies, mats, wine jugs, crockery, lucky signs, nuptial sash, and packets of cash; a string quire and singers. Without waiting to hear from the bride's end, and likewise anticipating the command of their employer, the bridal sedan and attendant sedans set off to collect the bride's party. Before long the musicians, lantern bearers, and the bride and her attendants in their sedan chairs come back together. The bride kowtows before the altar, the guests take their place at table, the musicians strike up, the singers sing, and all is noise and merriment. Before the hour of noon the hired hands have already collected their gratuities and are hurrying to another house, where the whole process will be repeated.

Li Yu 李漁 (1611–1680)

COMMENTARY

Li Yu came from a wealthy family but he lost his patrimony when the Ming empire fell to the Manchus. He resorted to providing entertainment, and eventually made a very good living from his pen, enjoying nationwide fame for his plays, fiction, essays and poems. Because he was an entertainer, his essays went where none had gone before.

Li Yu started life conventionally enough in his home province of Zhejiang, taking and passing the first degree examination in the classics with high honours at the age of twenty-four. By 1640, however, civil order was visibly collapsing, and between 1643 and 1645 he withdrew for safety to his small country estate. In 1647, when the Manchus had secured their hold on the south, he sold his estate and moved to the city of Hangzhou, where he started to sell his writings under the pen-name of 'The Old Fisherman of the Lake' 湖上笠翁; he is probably better known as Li Liweng 李笠翁 than as Li Yu. Apart from commissions for individuals, he turned out in the course of his career numerous light operas, short stories and various other saleable products like anthologies of poems and prose, historical snippets, and his own advice on how to live well. In 1657 he moved to Nanjing where he built a small estate and opened a bookshop. From his base in Nanjing he undertook tours with his domestic drama troupe all over the country, as far as Peking in the north and Gansu in the west. His leading ladies were his concubines. However large his income, Li Yu was constantly in debt. In 1677 he sold up everything in Nanjing and moved back to Hangzhou, where he died three years later, still writing.

Since Li Yu wrote to sell, his work was aimed at the general reading public, as opposed to the highly educated social elite. He was in bad odour with many of the latter on account of his clowning and vulgarity and bawdiness. If it had been widely known that he was the author of the pornographic *The Prayer Mat of Flesh* 肉蒲團, his name would have been muddier still. But if he betrayed his social class by his commercialism, his irrepressible wit recreated the by then stereotyped short story, and his original mind transformed the customarily dull notes on work and hobbies into essays that are a joy to read. Li Yu would never accept accepted wisdom, and while he was not alone in enjoying being contrary, he had the intelligence and inventiveness to avoid being tiresomely facetious in his contrariness.

The passages translated here are excerpts from his book *Pleasant Diversions*, published in 1671, which contains sections on the writing and acting of plays, female charms, house design, furniture and utensils, pastimes, food and drink, gardening—indeed everything in life that can be made an art of. Li Yu thought *Pleasant Diversions* his best book, and his opinion has generally been endorsed by scholars as far as the sections on drama go, but it has only been in liberal times in this century that his other observations have been well thought of. These excerpts, being taken from the section entitled 'Female Charms'聲容, will test the tolerance of the modern reader, but it should be remembered that his views on women were enlightened in his own age.

The quotations that begin the first excerpt are from *Mencius*.

Pleasant Diversions: Judging Beauty
閑情偶記・選姿

'To love good food and beautiful women is human nature.' 'Not to know how handsome Zidu is, is not to have eyes in one's head.' The sages of old chose their words carefully. The reason why they made this point repeatedly, yet without giving offence, is that they did not pretend that what is natural to man does not exist. If I lust after another man's beautiful wife or concubine, that offends his instincts; not only is the lusting immoral, it may get me killed. If I lust after my own beautiful wife or concubine, that conforms to my legitimate instincts: if the sages were to come back to life, they would find in my favour, and not regard it as a transgression. Confucius said, 'Those who enjoy wealth and honour should behave as befits their station in life.' If a man who is in a position to do so does not buy one or two concubines for his pleasure, that would be to enjoy wealth and honour but behave as befits the poor and humble. The way of the sages was based on human feelings; what need is there for such dissembling, such feigned purity and frugality? But if you have a harridan for a wife, it would be sensible to use this pretence to disguise your motives, otherwise your partiality for a beautiful concubine would in effect be cruelty, your tenderness might be the very cause of her death. If that happened, you could not plead in justification the belief that a beauty's fate is always sad, and act as the heartless agent of Heaven in bringing about her punishment.

I am a poor scholar, and have always been out of luck. I have not only never got near the nation's supreme beauties or come across heavenly perfection, even women of passable appearance and rough and ready quality I have rarely had the good fortune to meet. That being so, if I presume to rank women's qualities of voice, bearing and looks, and perorate on their singing and dancing, I will be laughed at by the veterans of the pleasure quarters. Yet, though my score has been low, my enthusiasm is high; though experience is lacking, the principles are easy to figure out. The wondrous pictures our minds conceive of are more appealing than the impressions of those who have personally trod the primrose path. If you don't believe me, you can test my claim against the record of history.

King Xiang of Chu was a ruler of men. His harem was packed full of shapely females, and what he didn't get up to with them isn't worth mentioning. Yet what has come down the ages to us is not his real exploits, but his dream of making love to the nymph of Mount Wu, and that is known to every soul. But where can we find the terrace where the tryst took place? Where is the nymph's dwelling? The legend says the nymph turned into a floating cloud in the morning, and into drifting rain at dusk: how can we account for that? Are there any clues we can trace, any facts we can set out? It was all an illusion. The force of an illusion is ten times that of fact; that is why that story lives on.

If I can write down in some sort of order things that are ten times superior to fact for people to go on, then the secret of pleasant diversions will be open to all. If my readers wish to investigate the source of my learning, I respectfully refer them to the story of the King of Chu's adventure with the nymph.

Pleasant Diversions: Accomplishments
閑情偶記・習技

'For a woman to be without talent makes for virtue.' Though this adage has some truth in it, it is not without bias. To say that intelligent women tend to go off the rails, and are therefore not to be as highly prized as those without ability, stems I do not doubt from some ancient animus, very similar to that of the man who gets into trouble in his administration, and as a result looks upon the way to officialdom through study as a perilous path, so leaves behind instructions to his posterity not to study and not to take office. Such advice is of the same kind as proposing to give up food for fear of choking, for after all can books all be thrown away, and office be completely abolished?

In my opinion, talent and virtue are in reality not at odds. Talented women are not all depraved in their conduct; equally, who can say that wanton women are all well-read? The main thing is that the husband concerned should be of a mind to encourage talent, but at the same time know of ways to harness talent, not forgetting that concubines and handmaids are to be treated differently from wives. Marrying a wife is like buying fields: nothing is to be grown there bar cereals, nothing is to be planted apart from mulberry and hemp; any plants that lean towards the ornamental are to be uprooted on sight. The reason is that the fields are there to produce food and clothing, and as space is limited, no other thing can be accommodated. Buying concubines is like managing a nursery garden: seed-bearing flowers should be grown, and non-seed-bearing flowers also grown; trees that provide shade should be planted, and trees that do not provide shade should also be planted. The reason is that the garden is designed for pleasure, and the emphasis is on the appeal to the senses. For physical needs are not always uppermost: appearance has to be catered for separately from substance.

Supposing that I have a house full of concubines, and all are brainless creatures, then I will find that when I want to talk, they will be silent; when I want peace and quiet, they will kick up a din; what they answer will not be what I ask; what they provide will not be what I seek. That would be no different from a vixen's den, where there is no occupation apart from free sex. Hence the learning of skills has to be discussed along with my main subject of cultivating appearance and dressing in suitable style.

The skills and arts of brush and ink should be foremost, followed by musical instruments, followed by singing and dancing. Needlework is every woman's business, so I need not go into it. However, for a woman to devote herself to men's refinements and neglect this women's work, despising weaving and sewing as drudgery, and regarding the needle and thread as an enemy, to the extent that she will not even stoop to make her own little slippers but will get some old dame or poor woman to be her stand-in, that must be condemned as disguising her own inadequacy and betraying the intention of the Creator! I maintain that needlework has to be the primary occupation of women. Other skills can follow after that has been mastered. The reason why in what follows I talk about learning skills but leave out needlework, is that the business of embroidering pretty designs is perfectly well known in the ladies' apartments, and my interference is not wanted. Yet I still mention needlework here to mark my concern for it, because I fear I might otherwise encourage later generations to put the cart before the horse and pay no heed to the making of silk and weaving of cloth. Though my subject is 'pleasant diversions', I intend no harm to our great way of life. This is my guiding principle in all I write.

Pleasant Diversions: Literacy
閑情偶記・文藝

Females find reading and writing difficult only at the point of entry. Once they have got their foot in the door, they are quicker to learn than males, because males lack concentration, while females pay undivided attention. It is best to show them across the threshold before they are initiated into sex, because once they are so initiated, their firmness of purpose suffers somewhat, and they are not as single-minded as before. The trouble is, concubines are installed at the age of fifteen or sixteen, usually, and how many of us can treat them as apprentices seeking instruction from us, instead of taking them to bed? We would never have a student all our lives if we had to wait for a virgin. The only thing is to lead them on gently and patiently, taking care not to blunt their initiative—the use of the stick as a teaching aid, as recommended in our *Book of History*, does not apply to female students.

A girl should be first taught to recognize characters, and only afterwards taught to write them. There is no virtue in quantity: just a few characters each day will do, teaching first those which have the fewest strokes, and which represent things near at hand. As the days and months pass she can progress from easy to hard, and from few to many. After six months or a year, you won't have to assign her any passages, she will know how to find things to read by herself. Before her interest in reading flags, you should look out some romances with a good plot, and some novels without obvious weaknesses, and let her leaf through them. In this way a book will not be a book, but a not-angry and not-forbidding teacher who will lead her into the inner halls of learning. Why do I say that? Because the language of romances and novels is the common talk of everyday, and when a woman reads it, it is like meeting with familiar things. For example, if in a sentence there are ten characters and she knows seven and doesn't know three, let her read it out naturally and there will be no mistake, because she can guess the three characters she does not know from the seven characters she does know. Thus those three characters were not taught by me, but by the romance or novel. By this means her wits are activated, and she can get the answer on her own by inference. If on top of that a man takes her well in hand and guides her progress from shallow to deep, his discourses on literacy while in bed with her will enter her mind like the timely rain, and will be infinitely easier to absorb than classroom lectures.

One or two out of ten concubines may be selected for their superior intelligence, and these you can talk to every day about poetry, and by and by make them understand tone and metre. As long as their speech has a ring to it, and they don't keep repeating themselves or use grating words, then they have the makings of a poet or prose-writer. The wife of Su Dongpo said, 'The moon on a spring night is better than the moon on an autumn night. The moon on an autumn night makes you feel cold and wretched, the moon on a spring night makes you feel good and glad.' This was not a poem, it was a casual remark. Yet Dongpo thought it had a good rhythm, and praised his wife for being able to make poetry. His words have since been much quoted, and go to prove what I said, that if a person's speech has a ring to it, and has no awkward repetitions or jarring sounds, then they have the makings of a poet. The other girls may not all reach this level, but if they can get the hang of books, they will have the key to the various arts of letters in their hands, and need not fear being locked out.

Pleasant Diversions: Clothes
閑情偶記・衣衫

The kind of clothing that offends against right and reason, and makes one fear for the state of the nation, is that made of odd pieces patched together, popularly known as 'paddy field dresses'.

Clothes have seams not because our forebears liked making them, but because there is no alternative. Given that people's bodies come in a variety of shapes and sizes, cloth cannot be woven to fit the figure, it has to be made in whole bolts, which are then cut up and the pieces tailored. Hence the one or two seams that result can be compared with outgrowths or swellings on the body: there is absolutely no way to remove them, so we have to put up with their existence. When people praise divine workmanship, they are sure to use the expression 'a seamless robe, made in heaven'. That shows that on earth, by contrast, we are stuck with the extra of a seam. But nowadays the one or two seams have been increased to dozens and scores, making clothes not only unlike heavenly robes but unrecognizable as human apparel. Yet the trend still goes from bad to worse: one shudders to think what the clothes will end up looking like.

If one traces the source of this trend, it seems it arose not by deliberate design, but from the crafty practices of tailors. They cut off bits of cloth allegedly for shaping purposes, but on the quiet for their own filching. Having stolen strip after strip and hidden them away, they invented this new product to get them off their hands, and make a killing from their duplicity. Oddly enough, people proved to prefer the bizarre over the usual: they not only did not criticize the abuse, they fell over themselves to take up and imitate the style. Whole cloth was ravaged to yield little bits and bobs. What sins had those whole bolts of cotton and silk committed that they should have suffered the punishment of a thousand cuts? When the scraps were sewn together they made a monk's habit of a hundred patches. What sins were those women guilty of, that they should look as if they had renounced the world?

Changes in fads and fashions are often related to the fortunes of the state. This fashion in clothing did not dawn in the present; its dawn was in the last years of the Ming dynasty. At the time I was astounded by it, and said, 'There must be dark forces at work for clothes to change their style without reason. Is the empire on the point of falling apart?' Before long generals rose in rebellion on all fronts, and the homeland was torn asunder. People said my prophecy had, alas, proved true. Now that a sage emperor wields the sceptre, the sundry principalities have submitted to his rule, and normality has been restored in the nation's manners and standards, this kind of outlandish apparel should by rights quietly fade from the scene.

If I am fortunate enough to encounter like-minded persons who do not scorn a country yokel's talk, but join in remonstrating with womanhood not to imitate the ugly sisters in their dress, then in writing this piece, though it may sound like cocks crowing and dogs barking, I will have made some slight contribution to the civilization of this our glorious age.

Fang Bao 方苞 (1668–1749)

COMMENTARY

Fang Bao found himself in prison in 1711, and consequently the author of this piece, as a result of implication in the inquisition of his friend Dai Mingshi 戴名世.

In his *Nanshan ji* 南山集, Dai had signified that the remnants of the Ming dynasty which held out in the southwest after the Manchu conquest in 1644 should be regarded as reigning legitimately. Dai was condemned to death for this treason. Fang Bao had written a preface to *Nanshan ji*, and kept a set of the blockprints. He went to prison for a year and a half. He was, however, a loyal subject of the new house, and was recognized as such. His career prospered after his release, and before he retired in 1742 he had held a number of high academic posts at court. One mark of favour was the imperial commission to edit a collection of examination essays (*baguwen*).

Fang Bao was a thoroughly orthodox Confucian, austere in his tastes and grave in his pronouncements. His place in literary history is somewhat higher than he deserves, because the Tongcheng school of prose, which was ascendant in the latter half of the Qing dynasty, looked back to him as its founding father. For him the perfect models were the early histories, *Zuo zhuan* 左傳 and *Shi ji* 史記, because they were lean and spare in diction, clear in ordering and exposition, and packed with meaning. After them came the works of the masters of the Tang-Song *guwen* school, who referred to the same models. He abhorred all ornamental rhetoric, bombast and vacuousness. These preferences are unexceptionable in principle, but if clung to too dogmatically they set uncomfortably narrow limits. Even his most interested promoter, Yao Nai 姚鼐, conceded that Fang lacked breadth of spirit. It is perhaps a token of his restricted vision that he aspired to elevate *baguwen* to parity with the best free composition. Wiser men realized that *baguwen* was ultimately sterile as a form of literature.

The present composition is an excellent vehicle for Fang's virtues. The chief aim is to present an irrefutable case, hence clear explanation, strong lines of argument, and impressive documentation are at a premium. The subject calls for balance and firm control, but allows overt expression of feeling at key points. One can regard it as an early example of 'reportage literature': the campaigning articles by people like Liu Binyan 劉賓雁 and Su Xiaokang 蘇曉康 in the 1980s show a remarkable family resemblance to it.

Life in Prison
獄中雜記

In the late spring of the year 1712, being at the time incarcerated in the Board of Punishments prison, I witnessed three or four persons expire each day and their corpses expelled through a chute. The honourable Mr Du, Prefect of Hongtong, offered this explanation:

'This is brought about by the plague. The number of deaths is in fact relatively low, thanks to the temperate weather; in past years a dozen or more a day have gone that way.'

I asked him to elaborate. Mr Du obliged:

'This disease is very contagious. One has to avoid proximity even with members of one's own family if they catch it. Now there are four cell blocks in the prison, each consisting of five chambers. The gaolers live in the middle one; it has windows in the front to admit light, and a shaft in the ceiling for ventilation. The four side chambers lack both, yet they normally house over two hundred prisoners. As the doors are locked at dusk, the prisoners have to relieve themselves inside, which contaminates their food and drink. In the depths of the winter the poor sleep on the floor; when spring brings its warm currents, it is only the odd one who does not succumb to disease. There is a firm rule that the doors are not to be unlocked until dawn. During the night the living lie head to toe with the dead: there is no way they can keep apart from them. That is why so many are infected. Remarkably, the bandits, hardened criminals and major offenders mostly enjoy rude health: scarcely one or two in ten go down with the disease, and some of these soon recover. The ones who die in droves are those charged with minor offences or as accomplices, or simply detained as witnesses, people not guilty of any crime.'

I asked: 'How is it that the Board of Punishments prison is so crowded, given that there is the Metropolitan prison in Peking, as well as all the district prisons?'

Mr Du replied: 'For one thing, in recent years the Metropolitan and the five city district courts have not dared to decide the more serious cases for themselves. For another thing, all suspects investigated and charged by the Garrison Police of the nine City Gates are tried by the Board of Punishments. On top of that, the more enterprising among the directors of the fourteen offices of the Board of Punishments, along with the secretaries, wardens and gaolers, all have to gain from a large number of prisoners: everyone remotely implicated is hauled in.

Once committed to prison, regardless of any guilt, they are all fettered, put in the cells, and subjected to intolerable ill-treatment. Then they are advised to offer surety so that they can get bail. The sum is set according to their means, and the officials and subordinates all take their cut. People of comfortable means and above secure bail at the cost of impoverishing themselves. The less wealthy can aspire to being freed of their fetters and being allowed to live in the wooden houses outside the cell blocks, but the charge will still be twenty or thirty pieces of gold. As for the very poor and unconnected, their fetters are kept screwed tight, as an example to intimidate the rest. So it happens that among fellow prisoners those charged with serious crimes are allowed their liberty, while minor offenders and the totally innocent suffer the worst excesses of the system. Given the fact that they labour under a sense of injustice, and do not get regular sleep or nourishment, once they fall ill they invariably die, there being no medical care.'

From my humble position I have observed the goodness of our gracious sovereign in seeking reasons to reprieve those condemned to death when he reviewed the verdicts of the courts, as previous emperors had done. Yet the innocent have to suffer like this. How many more lives could be saved if some man of honour were to put it to him directly that as distinct from the major criminals condemned to death or to exile on the frontier, those awaiting trial for minor offences or as accomplices should be confined in another place, and should not be fettered! Someone said, 'In the old days the prison had five buildings, called remand houses, where those charged but not yet sentenced were kept. If the old system were restored, that would be a help!' Mr. Du responded: 'By the grace of our sovereign, the officers in charge of the prison were to occupy the wooden houses. The grounds for the present practice of incarcerating the penniless in the cell blocks while the big villains live in the wooden houses should be looked into closely! Another place should be found for them, and that would go to the root of the problem.'

Old Mr Zhu and Master Yu, my fellow accused, died of the plague, as did a certain priest from Tongguan arrested on another charge: none of them was liable for severe punishment. Then there was a certain father who accused his son of unfilial conduct; their neighbours were put in chains and thrown into the cells [as witnesses], where they wailed and howled all the night long. I was moved by their plight to enquire widely if Mr Du's statements were true. As everyone confirmed them, I set them down here in writing.

When death sentences are confirmed, the executioners attend at the gate, and send their associates in to demand payment—a practice known as 'coming to an understanding'. If the condemned man is rich they approach his relatives, if poor they deal with him directly. If the sentence is dismemberment they say: 'You play along with us, and we will stab you first in the heart; if not, your limbs will all be cut off before your heart gives out.' If the sentence is strangulation, they say: 'You play along with us, and we will choke you to death at the first attempt; if not, we will half-choke you three times and apply instruments of torture before you are finally allowed to die.' Only if the sentence is decapitation do they have no means of exerting pressure on the condemned; even so, they keep back the head, for the family to redeem at a price. So it is that the rich pay out scores or hundreds of gold pieces in bribes, and the poor are stripped of their clothes; as for the utterly destitute, they receive the threatened treatment. The warders in charge of restraining the prisoners do likewise. If the prisoners do not fall in with their demands, they crush their limbs and break their bones when they first put on their shackles. At the annual Autumn Executions, three or four out of ten are marked for immediate execution; the remaining six or seven out of ten are taken in chains to the Western Market to await their fate. Those injured by their shackles, supposing their lives are spared, need several months to regain their health, if indeed they are not left permanently crippled.

I once questioned an old secretary on this point: 'It is not as if these people had any grudge against the prisoners to be punished or shackled; they merely expect to get something from them. If it turns out that they have nothing to give, would it not be humane to still exercise a little leniency?' The reply was: 'This is a case of laws being made as a warning to others and to deter future offenders. Otherwise people would delude themselves that they could get off lightly.' The warders in charge of manacling and bastinado responded in the same vein.

Among those arrested with me there were three who were interrogated under torture. The first gave twenty pieces of gold; his bones were bruised, and he was ill for a month. The second paid double; he suffered flesh wounds, and was well in twenty days. The third paid sixfold, and the same evening was walking about as normal. So I posed a further question: 'The prisoners differ in their ability to pay. Since something is got from all of them, why make a distinction according to the amount?' The reply was: 'If they were treated alike, who would offer more?' Mencius said: 'One has to be careful in the exercise of one's profession.' How true that is!

The secretaries of the Board keep forged seals at home. They often secretly alter documents for transmission to the provinces, adding or deleting vital clauses, the which changes go undetected by those who act on the directives. They would have to be very bold, however, to dare tamper with papers to be submitted to the throne, and those which are passed to other central government ministries. The law decrees that in cases of brigandage not involving murder, and other crimes where many conspire together, only one or two of the ringleaders should be summarily executed; after trial at the autumn assizes the rest routinely have their sentence reduced and are exiled to the frontier. When the court's verdict on such cases where summary execution is recommended is sent up for approval, the executioners wait in readiness outside the prison gate. As soon as the order comes down, the condemned are brought out in chains, and the sentence is carried out without a moment's delay.

Now there were two brothers who were facing summary execution for robbing a public granary; the sentence had already been recommended. A certain secretary told them: 'I can save your life for a thousand pieces of gold.' They asked what trick he would use. He replied: 'It is all very simple. I will just draw up another report, using all the same wording, except that I will substitute for your names those of two of your minor accomplices who are alone in the world. Then when the report is to be sealed and forwarded, I will secretly substitute my forgery for the original. This is all there is to it.' His colleague objected: 'Those who die might not learn of the deception in time, but you could not fool the judges. If they queried the names on the order that came back from the throne, all our heads would be on the block.' The secretary replied with a smile: 'If the names were queried, true, our heads would be on the block, but then the judges would be dismissed too for negligence. They would never exchange their posts for the lives of two men. Rest assured, our lives will not be at risk.'

His proposal was in fact carried out, and two of the minor accomplices were summarily executed. The judges were flabbergasted, but in the end did not dare pursue the matter. While I was in prison, I personally saw the two brothers concerned. The other inmates pointed them out, saying, 'These are the men who traded the lives of so-and-so for their own heads.' That certain secretary met with a violent death one night, and everybody said it was divine retribution.

In cases of homicide, culprits who are judged not to have premeditated murder are, after trial at the autumn assizes, assigned to the 'clemency' category, that is, the death penalty is lifted. Officials use this channel to subvert justice. A person named Guo murdered four people in a row, but had his sentence commuted on the grounds of mitigating circumstances, and was subsequently pardoned. As his release approached, he celebrated every day with his cronies, carousing and singing the live-long night. When someone asked him about his record, he recounted his murders in every last detail, without betraying the least sign of contrition, indeed as if very pleased with himself. Woe betide us! Base and corrupt officials stoop to sell verdicts, and get off without a reprimand. On the other hand, such is the ignorance of the principles of true justice that good officials often regard saving people from execution as meritorious, and do not seek out the true facts of a case. The wrong they do the people is also great, of that let there be no doubt!

Shifty individuals serving long sentences are known to enter into collusion with the secretaries and gaolers, and derive handsome profit from it. A Mr Li from Shaoxing, imprisoned for murder, amassed several hundred gold pieces a year. He was pardoned and released in the 48th year of the Kangxi reign [1709]. For months he was at a loose end. Then when a local person killed someone, he took the blame on himself. Because it was not premeditated murder, according to the code he had to be sentenced to long-term imprisonment, rather than death. In the fifty-first year there was a general amnesty, and following established precedent, his sentence was reduced and he was banished to the frontier. He lamented: 'I will never be lucky enough to come back here again!' It is normal practice to transfer prisoners intended for frontier service to the Shuntian District Prison to await onward dispatch. As it was winter, and the onward dispatch to the frontier would not take place until spring, Li drew up a petition to remain in the Board prison in the meantime. He submitted his petition time and again, but was not granted his request, and departed feeling very sorry for himself.

Yuan Mei 袁枚 (1716–1797)

COMMENTARY

There were close similarities between Yuan Mei and Li Yu. They both supported themselves for the greater part of their adult lives by selling their writings; they were both iconoclasts and freethinkers; they were both sensualists, Li Yu inclining towards epicureanism, Yuan Mei inclining towards hedonism; and both constructed estates for themselves in the environs of Nanjing, to which they were very attached. Yuan Mei was more of a poet, Li Yu more of a prose writer, but since they both lived by their wits, when they wrote they both wrote wittily.

Yuan Mei was born in Hangzhou. He was a child prodigy, passing the first degree (*xiucai*) examination at the age of eleven. In 1739 he passed the *jinshi* examination, and was employed in the Hanlin Academy. From 1742 to 1748 he served as magistrate in various districts. In 1749 he retired to his Suiyuan estate in Nanjing, and never resumed office. Such was his fame that in later life he was able to command very large sums for commissions like tomb inscriptions. Among his best-selling books was a collection of tales of the supernatural, entitled *Zi bu yu* 子不語 (What the Sage Did Not Talk About). He encouraged female literary talent (perhaps not entirely disinterestedly), at one time having a school of young women poets under his wing. In this century he has been esteemed principally for his notes on poetry (*Suiyuan shihua* 隨園詩話), in which he did his best to demolish conventional dogma and to assert the principle that native talent, being diverse, should flow into the channels and find the forms best suited to it, without reference to what was right and proper.

Yuan Mei's philosophy of enjoying life to the full led him to break taboos and offend against good taste. Inevitably, those who heard of his doings and read his impudent views were often scandalized, but those who met him seem to have been won over by his engaging personality. The short essay translated here gives a taste of his unconventionality, his cleverness, and that great redeeming factor, his kindness.

In the text 'the master of the Suiyuan' is Yuan Mei himself. The 'Seven Divisions' (七略) were devised by Liu Xin 劉歆 towards the end of the Western Han dynasty to classify the imperial book collection; the 'Four Libraries' (四庫) were created at the behest of the Qianlong 乾隆 emperor in 1772 to embrace all that was fit to read. Who Master Huang was remains obscure; perhaps he borrowed the wrong books.

Thoughts on Master Huang's Book Borrowing
黃生借書說

When Master Huang Yunxiu asked to borrow a book, the master of the Suiyuan handed it over, and tendered this piece of advice: if books are to be read, they must be borrowed.

You will have heard, sir, of the collecting of books. The Seven Divisions and the Four Libraries house the Emperor's books, but how many emperors have been readers? The mansions of the rich and noble are stacked to the ceilings with books, but how many of the rich and noble are readers? And the case of the forebears accumulating only for the descendants to dissipate speaks for itself.

This rule does not apply only to books, it applies to everything under the sun. If a thing is not one's own, but borrowed, and that importunately, the fear of its being demanded back must be constantly on one's mind, so one fondles it tirelessly, saying to oneself, 'Today I have it, tomorrow it may be gone, and then I will be able to look upon it no more.' But if a thing belongs to me, it will be parcelled up in my storeroom, or shelved in my gallery, with the promise that 'some time in the future I will take it out and look at it.'

When I was young, I loved books, but I was poor and they were hard to come by. I went to see a certain Mr Zhang, who had a vast collection, to borrow some, but he turned me down. I felt the refusal so keenly that after I got home it haunted my dreams. So when I did get my hands on a book, I read it intently and remembered it well. After I was appointed to office, my salary went out and books came in, until the whole place was heaped with them. In time the volumes became infested with bookworm and covered in dust and cobwebs. Then I bethought me how concentrated the mind of the borrower is, and how to be prized is the time of one's youth.

Now Master Huang is like me in his poverty, and like me too in his book borrowing. The only difference appears to be my liberality with my books compared to Mr Zhang's stinginess. Yet was it really my misfortune to encounter Zhang? And is it really your good fortune to encounter me? You will show you understand the distinction between good fortune and misfortune if you read the books intently, and return them quickly. I offer this advice, along with the books.

Lu Xun 魯迅 (1881–1936)

COMMENTARY

'Lu Xun' is a pen-name that supplanted the real name of Zhou Shuren 周樹人, a fact which was curiously apt in his case, as he was consumed with and by his writing. Four years after his death in middle age, Chairman Mao Zedong praised him in the highest terms, and his works became holy writ while Mao lived. Since we can be confident that Lu Xun would have been extremely unhappy with that situation, his essays are of interest to us.

When Lu Xun was born in Shaoxing, Zhejiang province, in 1881, his once prominent family was in decline and his country was in decline. The family resources still afforded him in boyhood a sound education in the classics, and he entered the first round of the state examinations that led to officialdom, only to change course and enrol in one of the new technical colleges set up to catch up with the West. He first went to the Naval Academy in Nanjing, in 1898, soon switched to the School of Mines, graduated in 1902, and proceeded, as was then customary, to Japan for further study. During his studenthood in Japan from 1902 to 1909 on a Chinese government grant, he made an abortive attempt to study medicine, but otherwise largely occupied himself with studying Western literature and thought in Japanese and Chinese translation. Among his own translations were two novels of Jules Verne and some short stories from eastern Europe. He also sat at the feet of Chinese dissidents in exile.

Two years after his return to China, the Qing dynasty was overthrown, and in 1912 Lu Xun was invited by Cai Yuanpei 蔡元培, the new Minister of Education, and a fellow provincial, to go to work in his ministry in Peking. There he stayed unnoticed until 1918, when he published 'Kuangren riji' (The diary of a madman), which was acclaimed as the first 'modern' Chinese work of fiction. He stopped writing fiction in 1926, by which time he had published two volumes of short stories, which were good enough to ensure his lasting literary fame. In the same period he established himself academically with a pioneering history of Chinese fiction (1923–24), and lectured at Peking University and elsewhere.

In 1927 Peking fell under warlord domination, and Lu Xun joined the exodus of liberal and left-wing intellectuals. After brief stops in Guangzhou and Xiamen he settled in Shanghai, to earn his living with his pen. Rather than repeat here what is very well known about his remaining years, I will incorporate some salient facts in the following consideration of his prose writing.

Han Yu's calligraphy.

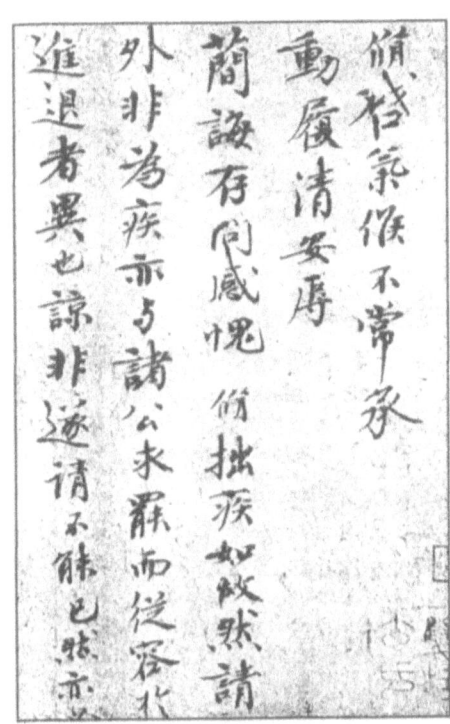

A letter by Ouyang Xiu.

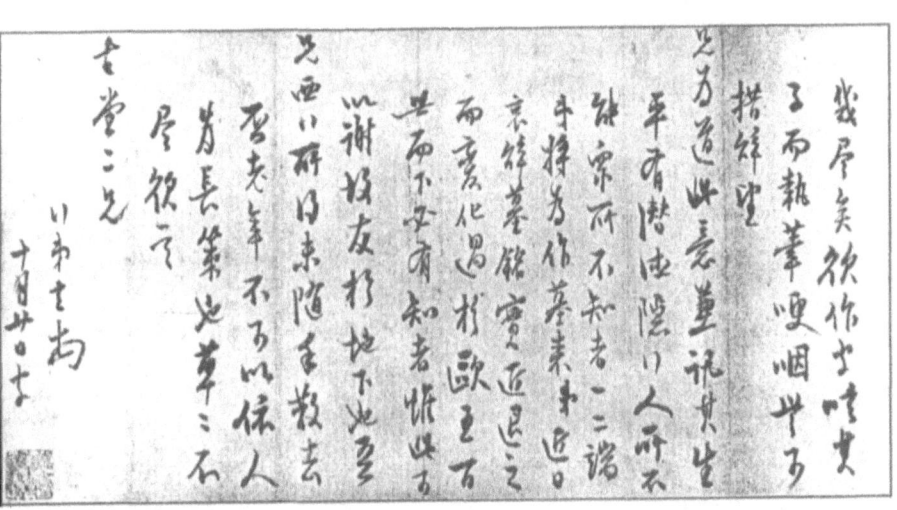

A letter by Fang Bao.

Li Yu's calligraphy on a fan.

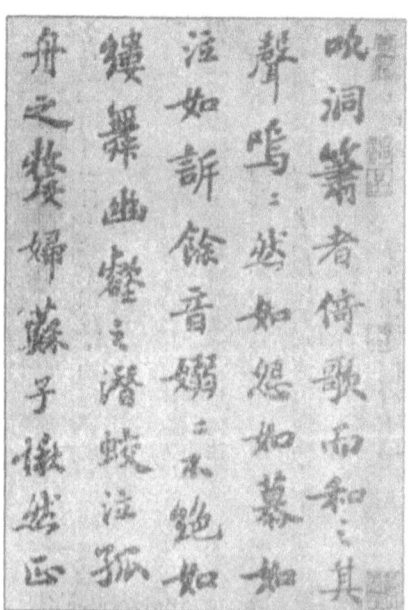

'Red Cliff', calligraphy by Su Shi.

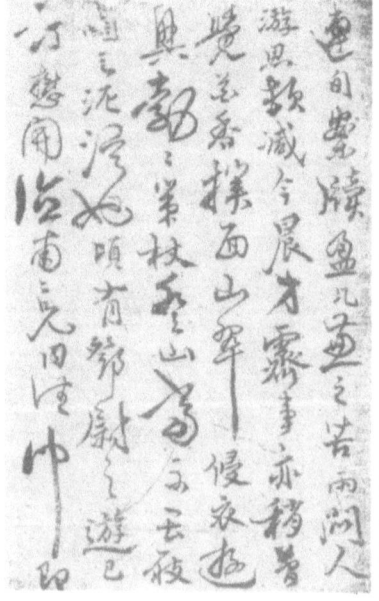

Yuan Hongdao's calligraphy.

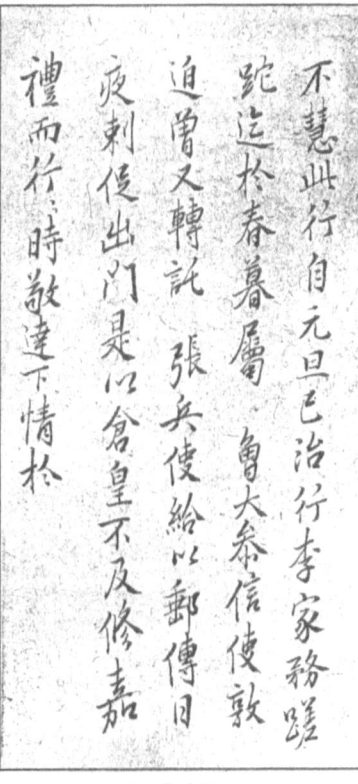
Calligraphy by Gui Youguang.

A couplet by Yuan Mei aged 80.

'Silent Studio', calligraphy by Fang Xiaoru.

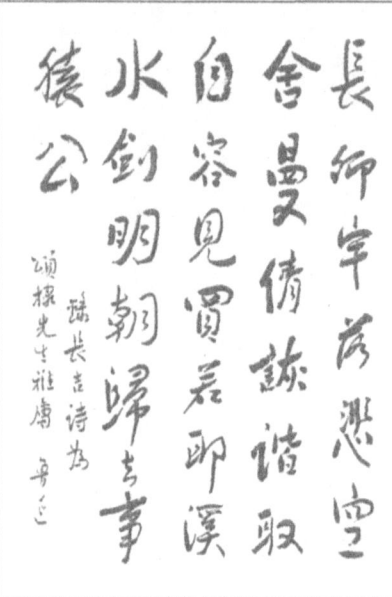

Calligraphy by Lu Xun.

Lu Xun in 1933.

Ye Shengtao.

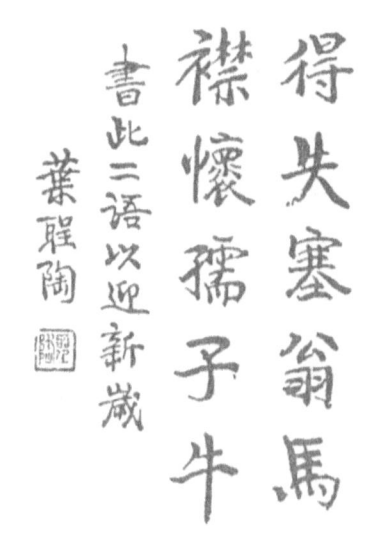

A couplet by Ye Shengtao.

Feng Zikai in 1961.

A drawing by Feng Zikai.

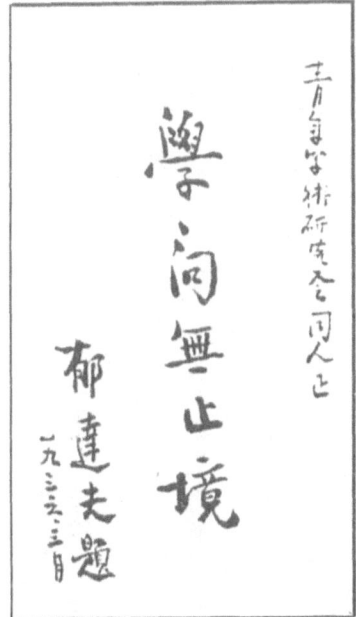
Calligraphy by Yu Dafu, written in 1936.

Yu Dafu in 1934.

Calligraphy by He Qifang.

He Qifang.

Zhu Ziqing in 1931.

Calligraphy by Zhu Ziqing.

A letter by Liang Yuchun.

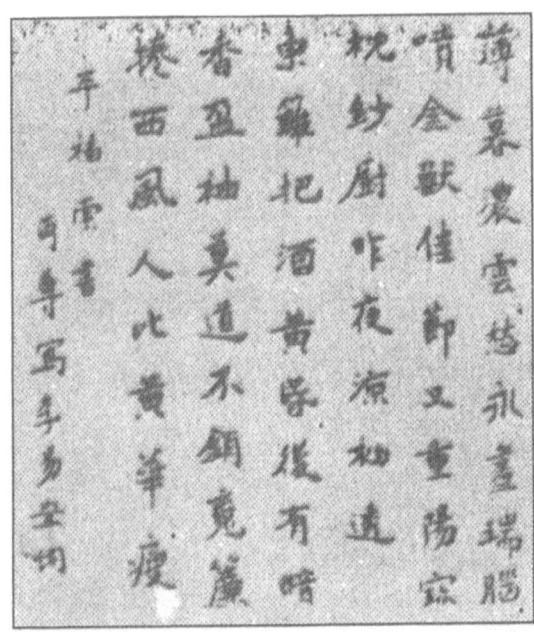

A poem by Li Qingzhao in Xia Mianzun's calligraphy.

Zhou Zuoren aged 78.

A letter from Zhou Zuoren to Liang Shih-ch'iu.

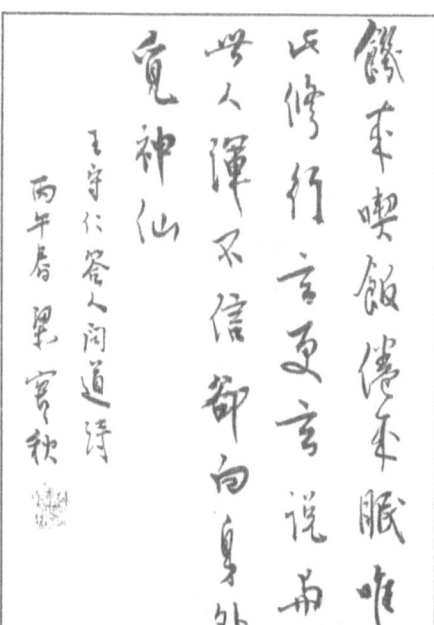

Calligraphy by Liang Shih-ch'iu.

Liang Shih-ch'iu in 1975.

想想看，有朝一日，我们要在密密的树林裡
，在黄叶底下，拾起自己的脚印，如同当年拾
坚果。花市灯如画，长街万头鑽动，我们去
分开密密的人腿揀起脚印，一如当年拾橡
的鞋子。想想那个湖！有一天，我们得砸破镜
面，撕裂天光云影，到水底去收拾脚印，一如
当年採集鹅卵石。

The manuscript of 'Footprints' by Wang Ting-chün.

Wang Ting-chün.

Yu Kwang-chung.

尺素寸心　余光中

接读朋友的来信，尤其是远自海外犹带
著异国风云的航空信，确是人生一天快事，如果
无须回信的话。回信，是读信之乐的一大代价。
不回信，虽不回信，接信之乐必然就相对减少，
以至於无。这时，友情便暫告中断了，直到有一天
在赎罪的心情下，你毅然起信来。蹉跎了这么
久，接信之樂早变成久信之苦，我一便是这么一個累
犯的罪人，交遊千百幾乎每一位朋友都数得出
我的前科来的。

'Thus Friends Absent Speak' by Yu Kwang-chung.

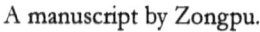

A manuscript by Zongpu.   Zongpu.

Yang Jiang.   'Cloak of Invisibility' by Yang Jiang.

Huang Chunming.

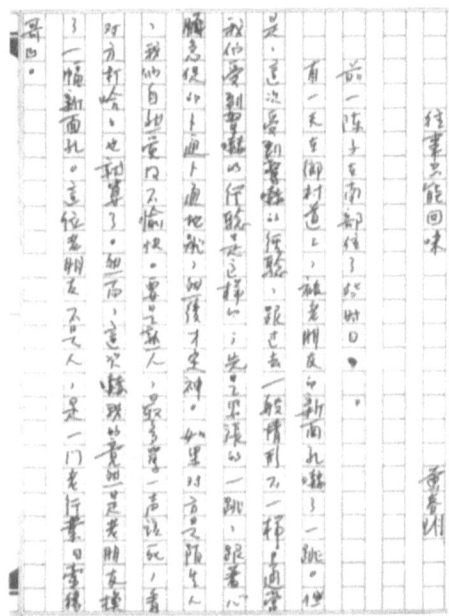

'We Can't Bring Back the Past' by Huang Chunming.

Ch'i Chun.

The manuscript of 'Chignon' by Ch'i Chun.

Koarnhark Tarn.

'The Countryside of the Past' by Koarnhak Tarn.

Zhang Xingjian.

'Goodwives' by Zhang Xingjian.

It was Lu Xun who introduced the best known description of the familiar essay to China when he published a translation of the Japanese scholar Kuriyagawa Hakuson's *Chule xiangya zhi ta* (Out from the Ivory Tower) in 1925. Using Western sources, this pictured the essay as a transcription of a good conversation round a winter fire among friends, in an atmosphere of slippered ease. Ironically, Lu Xun's own reputation as an essayist was of the opposite kind: that of a warlike, biting, often deadly polemicist.

Lu Xun had all the qualifications to be a good polemicist. On the personal level he easily imagined himself slighted or traduced, and bore long grudges; he had a brilliant mind, and never having had a job which kept him busy, had devoted many years to reading Chinese history and literature, and through Japanese to learning about the foreign experience, which gave him a superior stock of allusions and analogies; and under the imperial regime he had learned how to plan a composition and to use rhetorical devices. That he was able to mock and abuse the authorities without being arrested he owed to the relatively civilized regime in Peking up to 1926 and subsequently to the protection of the International Settlement in Shanghai, as well as latterly to his nationwide fame.

The May Fourth movement (1919) was a kind of revolution against the 'feudal' culture which the 1911 revolution had not seriously disturbed. As one of its pioneers, Lu Xun won his spurs as an essayist by laying into the establishment, and there was much in the conduct of national life to keep him embattled thereafter. When he joined the League of Left-Wing Writers, a communist front organization, in 1930 he committed himself to fight the Nationalist (Kuomintang) government until the end of his days. A great deal of his polemical output dealt of course with current affairs and need lengthy footnotes for the present-day reader to fully understand them, but his habit of relating current ills to perennial complaints and deep-rooted vices makes them appreciable without knowledge of the detail. Since China at that time was at the mercy of the colonial powers, especially Japan, the story that events told was one of weakness and subservience. This situation Lu Xun summed up in memorable words. Perhaps his most famous dictum was that China had only known two phases in its history, the one when its people were happy being slaves, the other when they were unhappy because they could not be slaves.

Lu Xun became known as dedicated to 'hot abuse' and 'cold sarcasm', but what raised his polemical essays above those of his contemporaries, aside from his powerful intellect, was his way of marshalling his words like troops on a battlefield, now feinting an attack, now feigning weakness, now holding, now retreating, finally springing a trap, all very much as the ancient manuals on the art of war recommended. The repetition of key phrases, with some variations (like Mark Antony's 'an honourable man') was one of his stand-bys, but patterns were rarely repeated. General characteristics of opponents were often subsumed in animal behaviour (Pekinese dogs, packhounds, wasps, etc), a trick he borrowed from traditional satirical parables. His most flexible and reliable resource, however, was a more or less total command of the Chinese language, classical and modern: the ability to mix and switch registers was used very effectively to mock and shock. There is no doubt that as a polemicist Lu Xun was world class.

Though the greater part of Lu Xun's some sixteen volumes of miscellaneous essays was *littérature engagée*, he had other sides to him. When in the mid twenties he went through his dark night of the soul, the experiences resulted in a collection of prose poems entitled *Ye cao* 野草 Wild Grass, 1927), which some regard as his finest work, others denigrate as derivative. The tone does seem to have been set by Nietzsche's *Also sprach Zarathustra*, to which Lu Xun was very attracted in early manhood. Stark and barren landscapes, symbolic figures and images, and strange encounters and cryptic speeches dominate the collection.

Of more normal human interest were the backward-looking essays of *Zhao hua xi shi* 朝花夕拾 (Morning Blossoms Picked at Eventide, 1928), which recalled the background of his early life, with some affection, and the more ruminative essays scattered throughout his collections, which are not without wit and humour. Though Lu Xun dissociated himself from the deliberate humour of the magazines that Lin Yutang was responsible for in the 1930s, he had a fund of wit which was used facetiously as well as cuttingly, as can be deduced merely from the title 'You Zhongguo nüren de jiao tuiding Zhongguo ren de fei zhongyong, you youci tuiding Kong fuzi you weibing' 由中國女人的腳推定中國人的非中庸又由此推定孔夫子有胃病 (To reach the conclusion from women's feet that Chinese people do not follow the golden mean, and thence further to conclude that Confucius suffered from his stomach, 1933). Humour of a generous kind can also be found in his work, though he was reluctant to admit it. A case in point is 'Ah Jin' (1935), which I translate here. The essay is one long complaint, but it is an index of its humanity that the reader not only does not feel that the author really regretted his encounter with that feisty lady, but also is sorry that he never had the opportunity to meet her himself.

Given that no one who writes as extensively as Lu Xun did can maintain consistent quality, the fact that so many of his essays bespeak a mind wound up to its maximum tension to give of its considerable best makes it very hard to dispute the claim common in his homeland that all round Lu Xun was 20th century China's most effective essayist.

Three Summer Pests
夏三蟲

TRANSLATOR'S NOTE

This is an example of Lu Xun speaking in figures, which was one of the distinguishing features of his *zawen*. The three pests obviously have symbolic status, representing types of humanity. As such they have general significance, and most of Lu Xun's diatribes had as their targets people who could variously be assigned to these classes of fleas, flies and mosquitoes. But at any one time they would have particular significance. At the time of writing (4 April 1925) Lu Xun was employed part-time as a lecturer at the Women's Normal University in Peking. In January 1925 student representatives petitioned the Ministry of Education for the removal of their woman principal. The conflict led to the expulsion of six student activists in May, which in turn led to a long-running dispute in the press between the supporters of the principal and the supporters of the students. Lu Xun was prominent among the latter. It seems likely that the 'mosquitoes' who come off worst in this piece most immediately represented the principal and her allies who claimed that the student rebels had to be punished for the good of the institution, to preserve academic and social discipline, and other worthy reasons. More widely 'mosquitoes' represented the 'proper men' who could be relied upon to justify and give a fair name to any wrongdoing. Lu Xun had a special hatred for 'proper men' who preached civic virtues, branding them as the front men for tyrants and bandits.

Summer approaches, and with it will come three pests: fleas, mosquitoes, and flies.

If someone proposes a question, asks me which of the three I like most, and insists that I like one, not letting me hand in a blank answer paper, as I did with 'Required Reading for Young People', then I would have to answer: fleas.

Although the sucking of blood by fleas is detestable, the way they go straight in for their bite without a sound is splendidly blunt and to the point. Mosquitoes are a different matter. The jab of their sting into the skin can of course be said to be rather thorough, but all the drone-drone palaver they go in for leading up to the sting is hard to put up with. If the droning is to explain why they should have human blood to alleviate their hunger, that would only make it worse. Fortunately I can't understand it.

When wild sparrows and deer fall into man's hands, their one and only thought is to get away. Actually, with birds of prey overhead and beasts of prey round about, their life in the forest is in no way safer than it is in man's hands. Why didn't they seek refuge with human kind in the first place, instead of now seeking refuge with birds and beasts of prey? Perhaps the relationship of birds and beasts of prey to them is like that of the flea to us. When their belly is empty, they make a grab, take a bite and are done with it: no question of justification or mystification. The ones to be eaten, for their part, do not, prior to being made a meal of, have to concede how right it is that they should be eaten, how willing they are to submit, and how they will be faithful unto death. Man, however, has made a specialty of drone-drone, so, choosing the lesser of two evils, they give him as wide a berth as they can, and in that they show remarkable intelligence.

Flies, when they come to land after making a long fuss with their buzz-buzzing, only lick up a little drop of sweat or grease. Naturally if there is a cut or sore there are more spoils to be had. Besides that, they take pleasure in depositing flyshit on anything that comes their way, however good, fine or clean it might be. But because they only lick up a little drop of sweat or grease, only leave behind a speck of dirt, and do not go as far as inflicting the pain of penetrating the skin on apathetic people, they are left to get on with it. The Chinese are not very aware that they can spread germs, and one cannot see the fly-killing movement really catching on. Their future is assured; in fact they will continue to multiply their kind.

Nonetheless, when they have left their droppings on good, fine and clean things, as far as we can tell they don't go to the length of gleefully turning round and mocking those things as tainted: one has to allow them a modicum of morality.

Superior people of all times have castigated others as beasts, blithely unaware that even insects can offer many models for emulation.

(1925)

The Evolution of the Male Sex
男人的進化

TRANSLATOR'S NOTE

This piece should be read in conjunction with 'Ah Jin', which follows. It represents Lu Xun's normal view of women. Like most or all progressive intellectuals of his day, Lu Xun was committed to regarding women—particularly Chinese women—as victims, and he habitually dwelt on their enslavement, physical degradation and mental suffering. Logically that left only one role for men, that of tyrants, but that was all right, as Lun Xun liked to write about tyrants even more than about victims: when he wrote about the occasional woman in authority, she became a tyrant. But I am slipping into the 'Lu Xun manner' myself, so back to objectivity. In 'The Evolution of the Male Sex', Lu Xun puts the beginning at the end, that is to say his starting point is evidently the appallingly complacent notion of 'scientific chastity' he finally turns to. Who proposed this idea the annotators of *The Complete Works of Lu Xun* do not say, and I do not recall coming across it myself, but we may presume that it had recently come to Lu Xun's notice. He interprets it as a piece of male humbug designed to deny women fulfilment and, now that social change had weakened the efficacy of external sanctions, dupe them into a self-imposed docility. Lu Xun counters this proposal not by argument but by ridicule: he pretends to accept the author's complacent claim, then extends his approbation to a series of outrages perpetrated against women in the past, thus damning by association. His cleverness is in reversing the order of his thought process, and first going back to primitive history to forge a chain of despicable practices, in which order 'scientific chastity' will seem merely the latest link. If on the contrary 'scientific chastity' had been highlighted as the object of his complaint, his readers might have been put on their guard against dubious historical comparisons.

Scrupulosity had no part to play in the ideological warfare Lu Xun was engaged in. So in his interpretation of the evils of traditional Chinese marriage, he, shall we say, 'telescopes' different things together. Jumping down a well was not actually regarded as an appropriate response to the sexual demands of a woman's legitimate spouse: it was to be reserved for a time when there were no further demands forthcoming from his quarter, namely when he neglected her or died; and otherwise to avoid, or as a penance for, violation by another man. Also, the bit about unclean thought being tantamount to adultery is a direct quotation from Matthew 5:28, which reads: 'Whosoever looketh on a woman to lust after her hath committed adultery with her in his heart.' (Lu Xun's wording follows the Chinese translation very closely.) The fact that this injunction was laid upon men is disregarded.

However, Lu Xun was fighting for the revolution, and as we have been told, revolution is no tea party. Literary mayhem has been practised with less excuse at periods in our own history. Alexander Smith in a *Dreamthorp* essay describes the 18th century as one such time: 'There were literary duels, fought out in grim hate to the very death. It was dangerous to interfere in the literary mêlée. Every now and then a fine gentleman was run through with a jest, or a foolish Maecenas was stabbed to death with an epigram, and his foolishness settled for ever.' The advocate of 'scientific chastity' probably knew how that felt.

To call the coupling of birds and beasts 'love' would verge on impious, one has to admit. But it cannot be denied that birds and beasts do have their sex life. When male and female come together in the mating season, we have to expect a bit of flirtation to go on. Indeed, the female does sometimes put on an act of coyness, running away and then looking back, even calling out, and may keep this up right until 'cohabitational love' is put into effect. Although there are many species of birds and beasts and their forms of 'love' are complex, one thing is beyond question: the male has no special rights to speak of.

That mankind is the lord of creation is evident in the first place in the capabilities of the male. To begin with nobody was very fussy, but owing to children 'knowing their mother but not their father',[1] the distaff side 'ruled' for a period; at that stage the matriarch was probably a more imposing figure than the clan head of later days. Afterward, for whatever reason, women ran out of luck: round their necks, on their hands and on their feet shackles were secured, rings and bands were fixed. Though several thousand years later the rings and bands were changed to gold and silver and set with pearls and gemstones, these necklaces, bangles, rings and so on are still today symbols of female subjugation. Since women had been turned into slaves, men no longer needed their consent to 'love' them. As a result of tribal wars in olden days, captives would become slaves, and

---

[1] The quotation is from a description of primitive communities in *The Spring and Autumn Annals of Lü* 呂氏春秋.

women captives would be raped. By then the mating season had long been 'abolished', and the male master could rape female captives and female slaves at any time and in any place. The practice of present-day bandits and toughs and their like not to regard women as human actually harks back to the warrior code of the tribal chiefs.

But although the capability of rape put mankind one step ahead of birds and beasts on the ladder of 'evolution', in the end it was still only half civilized. Imagine how off-putting all that women's crying and snivelling, wringing of hands and contortions of body must have been. It was after that wonderful thing called money made its appearance that the evolution of the male sex was really impressive. Everything on earth could be bought and sold, sexual gratification naturally being no exception. At the expense of a few coins men could get what they wanted of a woman. On top of that he could say to her, 'I'm not taking you by force, you are doing this of your own free will; if you want to earn some money, you have to do thus and thus, and submit to my every wish. This is a fair exchange between us!' Having debauched her, he required her to say 'Thank you, sir.' Are birds and beasts up to this? Whoring then marks quite a high stage in men's evolution.

At the same time, the old-style marriage made 'at the behest of the parents and after consultation between matchmakers' was superior even to whoring. Under this system, the man came into a piece of live property that was his to hold forever. From the time the bride was deposited on the bed of the bridegroom she had only duties and obligations to perform; even the freedom to haggle over a price was denied her, let alone love. Like it or not, in the name of the Duke of Zhou[2] and the sage Confucius, you had to cleave to one man for all your days, and you had to preserve your virtue. The man could use her whenever he pleased, yet she had to abide by the morality of the saintly fathers: even 'to conceive an unclean thought is to be guilty of adultery'. If the dog had used such ingenious and harsh measures against the bitch, you may be sure the bitch would have 'jumped the

---

[2]The Duke of Zhou 周公 is said to have been the author of the *Li ji* 禮記, which sets out rules of a marriage ceremony but in fact has little or nothing to say about the relations between husband and wife after the ceremony.

wall' in desperation.³ But the woman's only resort was to jump down a well and earn a reputation as a virtuous wife, a pure woman, or a martyr to chastity. The evolutionary significance of a marriage made according to religion needs no elaboration.

As to men's resorting to the 'most scientific' theory to make women willingly bind themselves to lifelong fidelity without the benefit of religion, and firmly believe that sexual desire is 'animal lust', not the precondition for love, thus inventing 'scientific chastity'—that of course is the acme of civilized progress.

Ah me, the difference between the ways of man—the male sex—and those of birds and beasts!⁴

(1933)

Ah Jin
阿金

TRANSLATOR'S NOTE

'Ah Jin' was written at the end of 1935 when Lu Xun was already plagued by illness, and within a year of his death. He refers in the essay to a decline in his writing. In one sense that was true and inevitable in view of his condition, but in another way he rose to new heights in that last phase, revealing—though not by any means in all that he wrote—a humanity that had only rarely been glimpsed previously. In 'Ah Jin' he divests himself of his armour and goes forth in cotton gown, unprotected even by his fame, for an encounter with the all too solid flesh of the neighbourhood menace. The essay is not written altogether 'straight': it does have some exaggeration of phrase and touches of irony, as well as passing sarcasms and aspersions that survive as tics induced by long habit; but his confession of frustration and self-doubt seems basically real and sincere. In themselves the incidents he has to tell of are described vividly and entertainingly enough, but of deeper interest and memorability is the perplexity of the commentator on the world's affairs who knows exactly what to think and say when he keeps

---

³This is a reference to the popular saying *gou ji tiao qiang* (the frantic dog jumps the wall), meaning anyone driven into a corner will risk injury in an attempt to escape.
⁴This is an unfinished quotation from *Mencius*.

his subject at arm's length, and can *imagine* how things must be or have been, but finds that when real human beings enter into the picture they do not obligingly conform to their expected roles. Because Ah Jin is one of these he does indeed 'detest' her. As a neighbour most of us would find her objectionable too, but Lu Xun's rueful retrospection is ultimately directed against himself; behind the animus against Ah Jin one senses a broader good humour, and perhaps a grudging admiration for his tormentor. In this ambivalence we discover his humanity.

For some time now I have detested Ah Jin.

She is a domestic; in Shanghai they call them 'aunties', while foreigners know them as 'amahs': her employer was in fact a foreigner.

She had a lot of women friends. As soon as dusk fell a succession of them would come and stand under her window and call up 'Ah Jin, Ah Jin!' in loud voices. This went on well into the night. She also seemed to have a string of paramours; she once proclaimed her philosophy from her back doorstep: what's the point of coming to Shanghai unless you're going to take a few lovers? . . .

But that did not concern me. The unfortunate thing was that the back door of her employer's house was across the street from my front door, so when the cry of 'Ah Jin, Ah Jin!' went up I could not help but be affected: sometimes I could not get on with my writing, at others the word 'Jin' would actually find its way into my manuscript. Even more unfortunately, in my comings and goings I had to pass under the balcony where she hung her washing; presumably she was averse to using the staircase, for bamboo poles, planks of wood, and other whatnots were liable to be just tossed over this balcony, which made me exercise extreme caution in passage. I would first look to see if the said Ah Jin was on the balcony; if she was, then I had to give the house a wide berth. Of course, this was mostly due to my own timidity, to my putting too high a price on my own life; but one had to take into consideration that her employer was a foreigner: if I got my head cut open that of course would have been neither here nor there, but even if I had been killed, nothing could have come of calling meetings of my fellow townsmen and sending telegrams of protest— leaving aside my doubt that I would have merited a meeting of my fellow townsmen being called.

The world is a different place after midnight, one where the humours of the day do not pertain. One night I was still sitting up translating something at half past three when I heard someone in the street softly calling somebody's name. Though the sound was muffled, I could tell it was not Ah Jin's name they were calling, and naturally it was not mine either. I thought to myself, who could be calling anyone so late at night? With that I got up and opened my upstairs window to take a look. In fact there was a man standing looking up at Ah Jin's lattice window. He had not noticed me. I regretted my impulsiveness, and was about to close my window and withdraw when the upper half of Ah Jin's body appeared in the opening of the little embrasure across the street. She spotted me immediately, and pointing in my direction said something to the man I did not catch. Another gesture from her, and the man made off at some speed. After that I could not get on with my translation, and I told myself: in future just mind your own business; you have to harden yourself to the point that you would not turn a hair were Mount Tai to crumble in front of you, and not flinch if bombs fell about your ears! . . .

But Ah Jin was apparently quite unperturbed, because she continued to laugh and joke as boisterously as before. However, I did not reach this conclusion until the next evening, so I suffered from my conscience for part of a night and a whole day. At that point I felt grateful to Ah Jin for her broadmindedness, but at the same time no less detested her loud conferences and boisterous laughter. Ever since she appeared on the scene, the whole neighbourhood had been thrown into a state of agitation, so great was her power. My warning intended to quell the disturbance proved entirely ineffectual: they did not even spare me a glance. Once a foreigner living nearby remonstrated with them in his own tongue, and they ignored him too; but he then rushed out and gave them all his boot, which did make them scatter and bring their conference to an end. The effect of his kicks lasted, as I remember, five or six nights.

Thereafter the former clamour was resumed, and the scope of the disturbance was enlarged. Ah Jin got into a row with the old woman who kept a small general store across the main road, and some men joined in on her side. Her voice was penetrating at the best of times; on this occasion it carried even further, being audible, I was sure, twenty houses away. In no time a crowd gathered. As the war of words drew to a close, inevitably there was reference to 'taking lovers' and the like. I did not catch what the old woman said, but Ah Jin's reply was:

'Nobody fancies you, you old bag! But people do fancy me!'

I am afraid this was the truth, and the spectators on the whole seemed to find in her favour; the 'unfancied old bag' was thus defeated. A foreign policeman strolled up hands behind his back, looked on for a while, then began to disperse the spectators. Ah Jin rushed over to him, and poured out a long story in his language. The foreign policeman heard her out attentively, then said with a smile:

'It seems to me you gave as good as you got!'

He made no move to arrest the 'old bag', just crossed his hands behind his back again and strolled on. So in a sense ended this backstreet battle. But the altercations of this world are never so neatly settled: it seems that the 'old bag' still had some forces in reserve. The next morning the 'boy' who worked for another foreigner a few doors along from Ah Jin fled to her place for refuge. Three hulking men were pursuing him. His shirt was torn. It seems that he had been lured out of his house, and then had his retreat blocked, so all he could do was to flee to his lover's. Men have always sought a safe haven at the side of their beloved: Per Gynt, in Ibsen's play, was one great personage who in defeat ended up hiding under the skirts of his lover listening to her lullabies. But I fear Ah Jin could not match up to Norwegian girls: she had no heart, and no spirit. She was alive only to her instincts. When the man was within a few strides of her back door, she slammed it in his face. With his escape cut off, he simply came to a halt. This turn of events seemed to take those hulking men by surprise too, for they visibly hesitated; but eventually they put up their fists, and two of them punched him about the body—only three blows in all, and apparently not very heavy ones—while the other gave him one in the face, which did immediately leave a red mark. This backstreet battle was over in a flash, and as it was morning too, there were very few people on the sidelines. The victorious and the defeated left the field, and the world was temporarily at peace. Nevertheless, I was still uneasy, for I have heard it said: so-called peace is no more than a lull between two wars.

Yet a few days later Ah Jin disappeared, presumably discharged by her employer.

Her replacement is a fat maidservant whose countenance bears some marks of felicity and refinement. Twenty days have passed and all is yet peaceful; she has only hired a pair of poor balladeers to sing some rollicking songs like 'The Eighteen Gropes'.[5] No one could object to her taking such harmless pleasure after having 'earned her keep'. The only worrying thing was that it attracted a motley crowd, including even Ah Jin's lover, thus posing the threat that backstreet warfare might erupt again at any time. But for myself I was grateful, for it was a pleasure to listen to a natural baritone voice, so infinitely preferable to the strangled cat of 'Drizzling Rain'.[6]

Ah Jin was very ordinary in appearance. What I mean by ordinary is that she was like a multitude of others, quite unmemorable. After less than a month, I can no longer describe her looks. But I still detest her; the mere recollection of her name is repugnant to me. That she caused an uproar in the neighbourhood is of course no reason for deep-seated malice; I detest her because in the space of a few days she shook the beliefs I have held and the stands I have taken for thirty years.

I have never credited the old stories about Wang Zhaojun bringing peace to the Han dynasty by marrying the barbarian khan, and the nomad girl Hua Mulan preserving the Sui by going to war, nor believed that the temptress Da Ji brought about the downfall of Yin, the fabulous beauty Xi Shi ruined Wu, or the emperor's concubine Yang Guifei plunged the Tang into chaos. In a male dominated society, women could not exercise such power: the responsibilities for the fortunes of the state must rest on men's shoulders. All along male authors had put the blame on the heads of women, but that just showed what worthless and pathetic men they were, I thought. I had not bargained for Ah Jin, a domestic nondescript in appearance and of no striking ability, turning our little neighbourhood upside down in just a few weeks. If she had

---

[5] 'Eighteen Gropes' 十八摸 is a vulgar song sung by blind balladeers. It must have been very popular in the 1930s, as it figured in the repertory of the vulgar boatman in Shen Congwen's 沈從文 story 'Baizi' 柏子, set in far-off West Hunan.

[6] 'Drizzling Rain' 毛毛雨 is a song composed by Li Jinhui 黎錦暉, popular ca. 1930.

been a queen, an empress, a dowager empress, one shudders to think what an effect she would have had: enough to wreak awful havoc, certainly.

In olden days Confucius 'on reaching the age of fifty understood the will of Heaven', yet I am thrown back on doubt and uncertainty even about human affairs, all because of a nobody like Ah Jin. Though one cannot rightly compare the Sage with ordinary men, it shows the degree of her potency, and my utter uselessness. I do not wish to blame the decline in my writing on Ah Jin's kicking up a row, and what is more, the above discussion verges on spitefulness, but it is a fact that lately I have detested Ah Jin, for as it were blocking one of my pathways.

I just hope that Ah Jin does not rank as a specimen of Chinese womanhood.

(1935)

Confucius in Modern China
在現代中國的孔夫子

TRANSLATOR'S NOTE

This essay was originally composed in Japanese for publication in the June 1935 edition of *Kaizo* 改造 magazine. It was translated into Chinese by Yiguang 亦光 and appeared in *Zawen* 雜文 in July. This translation is from the version revised by the author that was printed in *Qiejieting zawen erji* 且介亭雜文二集, 1935.

Despite its textually muddied history, which might have diminished it stylistically, and left behind some untidiness, the essay has the attraction for readers fifty years on of being largely self-explanatory. Intrinsically it has the merit of showing Lu Xun's humour to advantage. Without some deliberate distortions it would hardly qualify as a *zawen*, but on the whole it is also remarkable for its fair-mindedness.

It was reported in a recent Shanghai paper that to mark the occasion of the completion of a temple to Confucius in Yushima, Japan, General He Jian, Governor of Hunan Province, has donated a hitherto jealously treasured portrait of Confucius.[7] One has to point out that the Chinese man in the street has practically no idea what Confucius looked like. From time immemorial every county without exception has had a Confucian temple, or as it is known, a Temple of Culture, but they have hardly ever contained a likeness of the sage. Whenever portraits or statues of venerable personages are made, the rule is that they should be made to look very grand, but when it comes to the most venerable personages, saintly people like Confucius, it would seem that even images are a form of profanation, and it is really better to do without them. As a matter of fact, this is not unreasonable. Confucius left behind no photograph of himself, so naturally we cannot know his true appearance: though in the literature there are references to it, they may be just bunkum. If a figure were to be sculpted from scratch, then one would have even less confidence in it, as it would have no other basis than the unfettered imagination of the sculptor. This being so, Confucianists are in the end thrown back on adopting the attitude of Brand: 'All or nothing'.[8]

Still if we are talking about portraits, those may indeed be occasionally encountered. I have seen three such: the first was an illustration in *Kongzi jiayu*;[9] the second was a frontispiece to *The China Discussion*, published by Liang Qichao after he took refuge in Japan, and imported back into China;[10] and another was a relief of Confucius meeting Laozi carved on a Han dynasty tomb. As regards the impression I got of Confucius' appearance from these pictures, it was that this gentleman was a very thin old boy who wore a long gown with loose sleeves and had a sword stuck in his belt, or a staff under his arm, but had never a trace of a smile, and was extremely intimidating. Seated at his feet one would have had to have kept one's

---

[7]The Yushima Temple in Tokyo burned down in 1923. Rebuilding was completed in April 1935.

[8]Brand is the eponymous hero of Ibsen's play. Ibsen's plays are mentioned several times in essays Lu Xun wrote while in Japan.

[9]A collection of writings on Confucius' deeds and sayings compiled and annotated during the Three Kingdoms period (220–265).

[10]Liang Qichao 梁啟超 (1873–1929) fled to Japan after the failure of the Hundred Days' Reform in 1898. *The China Discussion*, or *Qingyibao* 清議報, advocated constitutional monarchy.

back as straight as a ramrod; after a couple of hours the pain in one's joints would have been killing, and any ordinary person could hardly have been anything other than desperate in his desire for deliverance.

Afterwards I went travelling in Shandong. As I was suffering misery from the bumpiness of the roads, Confucius suddenly came into my mind. At the thought of the sage wearing his sanctimonious expression sitting in olden days in a rudimentary cart, jolting and lurching along as he hurried about his business thereabouts, I was struck by the comicality of it. Naturally this feeling was not a proper one; to put it bluntly, it was nigh on irreverent. Had I been a follower of Confucius I suppose it should never have occurred to me, but at that time there were lots of young people who were of the same impertinent mind as myself.

I came into the world in the last years of the Qing dynasty, when Confucius had already acquired the frighteningly imposing title of Perfect and Saintly King of Letters: needless to say, this was an age when the Saintly Way held sway over the whole country. The government required that all educated people should study certain books, that is the 'Four Books' and 'Five Classics'; should abide by a certain exegesis of them; should write a certain kind of composition, that is the so-called 'eight-legged essay', and should produce a certain kind of disquisition. However, these Confucians, all stamped in the same mould, while very much at home with a square world, were quite at sea with a round one; consequently when they waged war against France and England, countries which went unrecorded in the Four Books, they were defeated. I don't know if it was because they thought that to die in the service of Confucius was not as masterly a strategy as self-preservation, or what, but the long and the short of it is that this government and these bureaucrats who were so dead set on venerating Confucius were the first to break ranks. Out of government funds they paid for heaps of books of the foreign devils to be translated. Such scientific classics as Herschel's *Outlines of Astronomy*, Lyell's *Principles of Geology*, and Dana's *Manual of Mineralogy* still survive as relics of that era: from time to time they may be found lying around in some second-hand bookshop.

However, there was bound to be a reaction. Grand Secretary Xu Tong, described as the epitome and apostle of Confucianism at the end of the Qing dynasty, emerged. His dismissal of mathematics as the learning of the foreign devils was not the worst of it: though he acknowledged that there were states like France and England on earth, he adamantly refused to believe in the existence of Spain and Portugal, maintaining that these were countries dreamed up by France and England out of embarrassment at their own appetite for spoils. He was also a covert instigator and director of the famous Boxer Rebellion in 1900. But the Boxers were completely routed, and Xu Tong committed suicide. The government then once more took the view that there was quite a lot in the politics, law, learning and skills of foreign countries. It was at that time that I had the yearning to go to Japan to study. This objective attained, the place where I started my schooling was the Kobun Academy in Tokyo founded by Mr Kano.[11] There Mr Mitsu Rikitaro taught me that water was made up of oxygen and hydrogen and Mr Yamauchi taught me that some spot on a shell was named a 'mantle'. Then it happened one day that the Dean of Students, Mr Okubo, gathered everyone together and said: 'As you are all disciples of Confucius, today you shall go and make your obeisances at the Confucian temple in Ochanomizu.'[12] To this day I still remember thinking to myself then that it was precisely because I despaired of Confucius and his disciples that I came to Japan; was it nevertheless to 'bow down' all over again? For a while I was quite perturbed. I think I was far from the only one who had this feeling.

But Confucius' being without honour in his own country did not begin in the 20th century. Mencius judged him 'the sage whose actions were timely'.[13] There is really no other way of translating this into present-day language except as 'fashionable guru'. From his own point of view, this is no doubt a harmless honorific, though as a title it is not a wholly welcome one. But perhaps it was not like this in reality. Confucius' establishment as a 'fashionable guru' was something that happened after his death; in his lifetime he had a

---

[11]The Kobun Academy was a Japanese language preparatory school set up in Tokyo for Chinese students.
[12]Ochanomizu refers to the Yushima Temple above.
[13]Quotation from *Mencius*, Book 5B. The translation is from D. C. Lau, *Mencius*, Penguin Books, 1970, p. 150.

pretty rough ride. Always running from pillar to post, he did once achieve eminence as Commissioner of Police, but in no time he was out in the cold again and unemployed. Furthermore he was despised by the high and mighty ministers, ridiculed by the common folk, even menaced by a pack of ruffians; and his belly went empty. Though he collected 3,000 disciples, only seventy-two were of any use, and there was only one of them he could really trust. One day Confucius cried out in exasperation: 'If the Way were proved unviable, and I were to put to sea on a raft, I suspect only Zilu would be with me.'[14] From this forlorn conclusion we may deduce such intelligence. Yet this same Zilu later on had his hatstring cut in a fight for his life, and being the estimable Zilu that he was, still mindful even at this pass of the precept learned from Confucius, he declared, 'The gentleman does not doff his cap when he meets his end,'[15] and as he set about retying his hatstring was chopped up into little pieces. At the loss of this one and only trustworthy disciple, Confucius was naturally grief-stricken; it is said that when he got the news he ordered the mincemeat in the kitchen to be tipped away.[16]

I think one can fairly say that Confucius' fortune after his death was somewhat better. As his tiresome wrangling was buried with him, all kinds of wielders of power used all kinds of whiting to make him up, and raised him all the way to awesome heights. But compare him with the later import, Sakyamuni, and you can't help being sorry for him. True, every county had its temple of the Sage, or Temple of Culture, as we have said, but what cheerless and depressing places they are: the average commoner would never dream of going to offer prayers there; if he went anywhere it would be to the Buddhist temple, or some local shrine. If you asked the ordinary person who Confucius was, he would naturally answer that he was a sage, but in that way he would only be acting as a gramophone for the wielders of power. The ordinary person also treasures the written word, but that is because of the superstition that if he did not treasure the written word he would be struck dead by the Thunder God. Admittedly, the Temple of Confucius in Nanjing is a very lively place, but that is because of the

---

[14] The quotation is from Confucian *Analects*, Book 4.
[15] The quotation is from 'Duke Ai 15th Year', *Zuozhuan*.
[16] This anecdote appears in 'Zigong wen' 子貢問, *Kongzi jiayu*.

other attractions—the entertainers and tea houses. Though Mencius said turbulent ministers and treacherous sons were sore afraid when Confucius wrote *The Spring and Autumn Annals*,[17] nowadays there is practically nobody who could tell you the names of those turbulent ministers and treacherous sons who fell to that verbal foray. Mention of 'turbulent ministers and treacherous sons' would probably suggest Cao Cao to most people, but that view of him was formed by anonymous authors of novels and plays, not by the Sage.

To sum up, Confucius owes his exalted position in China to the wielders of power, he is the sage of the wielders of power or those who would be wielders of power; it has nothing to do with the mass of common people. But with regard to the temples to the Sage, the enthusiasm of the wielders of power has been a passing one. As they already had other aims in mind when they did reverence to the sage, once the aims were attained this instrument ceased to be useful, and if they were not attained it was even less useful. Thirty or forty years ago, all those intent upon achieving power—that is those who wanted to become officials—all studied the Four Books and Five Classics, and wrote 'eight-legged essays'. A separate few gave these books and compositions the general name of 'bricks to bang at the door'. That is to say, as soon as success in the examination for civil officials was gained, from that moment these things were forgotten, just like the brick that is used to bang on the door: when the door is opened, the brick is thrown away. In fact from the time he died and ever after old Confucius served this office of a 'brick to bang on the door'.

A look at some recent examples makes the case even more apparent. From the beginning of the 20th century, Confucius' fortune had been very bad, but in Yuan Shikai's time he was remembered again: not only were the sacrifices restored, weird sacrificial robes were also created for those offering the sacrifices.[18] What appeared in the wake of these exercises was an imperial order. However, in the end that door resisted banging, and Yuan died on the outside. He left behind the Northern Warlords. When they felt they were nearing the

---

[17]*Mencius*, Book 3B.

[18]Yuan Shikai 袁世凱 was the first president of the Republic; he proclaimed himself Hongxian 洪憲 Emperor in January 1916, but was forced to abdicate in March. He died the same year, in June.

end of their road, they used this brick to bang on other doors to fortune. Entrenched in Jiangsu and Zhejiang, General Sun Chuanfang, who slaughtered common citizens by the roadside without a second thought, restored the 'arrow tossing' ceremony.[19] Holed up in Shandong, General Zhang Zongchang, who couldn't even count the money or soldiers or concubines he had, for his part printed the Thirteen Classics;[20] and looking on Confucianism as something akin to syphilis that can be transmitted through physical relations, he made one or other descendant of Confucius his son-in-law. Still the door to fortune opened to neither of them.

All these three used Confucius as a brick, but times had changed, and they failed conspicuously. Not only did they meet with failure themselves, indeed they also reduced Confucius to an even sorrier state. The perversity of these barely literate characters holding forth on the Thirteen Classics and so on people found a joke; the blatant discrepancy between their deeds and words people viewed with greater loathing. Revulsion for the monk leads to distaste for the habit, and the exploitation of Confucius as an instrument to gain a certain end becoming once more transparently obvious, the desire to dethrone him grew the more potent. Therefore when Confucius is dressed in perfect dignity, articles and works exposing his flaws are bound to appear. Confucius though he be, he must have his flaws. In normal times no one would pay them any heed, because a sage is still a man, and as such they may be forgiven him. Yet if the disciples of the Sage come forth and start prating, telling us that the Sage was this and was that, therefore you must be likewise, people will not be able to keep from laughing out loud.

Five or six years ago the staging of the play *Confucius Saw Nancy* caused some trouble.[21] In that play Confucius appears on stage in

---

[19]Sun Chuanfang 孫傳芳(1885–1935) revived the ceremony of tossing arrows into a pot—originally a drinking game (Cf. Ouyang Xiu, 'The Old Toper's Pavilion', p. 50)—in Nanjing in 1926.

[20]Zhang Zongchang 張宗昌 (1881–1932) led a campaign to promote Confucianism in Shandong province in 1925.

[21]'Zi jian Nanzi'子見南子 was published in 1928 in the *Benliu* 奔流 magazine; its author was Lin Yutang. While the play was in rehearsal at the Qufu Second Normal School, the Kong clan objected to the Ministry of Education that it was a 'public insult' to Confucius. Lu Xun published documents relating to the case in 1929.

person: viewed as a sage, one must admit that in some respects he is somewhat lacking in gravity and rather slow-witted, but seen as a human being he is actually a likeable sort of cove. Nevertheless the descendants of the Sage got very hot under the collar, and in the upset took the dispute right up to the courts, the reason being that the place where the play was put on happened to be Confucius' birthplace. There the descendants of the Sage had multiplied exceedingly, forming a privileged class that would make Sakyamuni and Socrates blush from inferiority. However, that might be precisely the reason why the local youths who were not descendants of Confucius were driven to put on *Confucius Saw Nancy*.

The mass of ordinary folk in China, especially the so-called 'ignorant commoners', may call Confucius a Sage, but they do not believe he is a sage. They show respect for him, but do not feel close to him. I think, though, there is no one in the world for understanding Confucius like the ignorant Chinese commoners. True, Confucius did devise an outstanding scheme for ruling the state, but that was a scheme made in the interests of those who ruled the masses, that is those who wielded power; it gave no thought to the interests of the masses themselves. This is summed up in the sentence, 'The rites do not extend to the common people'.[22] That he became the sage of the wielders of power, and finally 'a brick for banging on doors', should give Confucius no ground for complaint. One cannot say he had nothing to do with the masses, but I would have thought that to say he was in no way close to the masses would have been the politest way of putting it. It is only natural that they should not approach the wholly unapproachable sage. You can put the matter to the test any time you like; try going barefoot and in rags into the Grand Hall of a Confucian temple to look round; in just the same way as if you had strayed into a posh Shanghai cinema or the first class compartment of a tram, I'm afraid in no time at all you'd be out on your neck. Everyone knows that is the domain of the bigshots: the masses may be 'ignorant', but they aren't ignorant to that extent.

(29th April 1935)

---

[22]The quotation is from 'Quli'曲禮, *Li ji*.

Zhou Zuoren 周作人 (1885–1967)

COMMENTARY

Born into a once distinguished family, then in decline, Zhou Zuoren and his elder brother Lu Xun were to restore the family's fortunes: they became the best known men of letters in China in the first part of the 20th century.

After private education in the classics, both brothers enrolled in vocational colleges set up by the Qing government to train Chinese students in Western military and civil technology. Zhou Zuoren studied at the Jiangnan Naval Academy in Nanjing from 1901 to 1906, where he learned some English, and proceeded to further study in Japan, from 1906 to 1911. Like most other students he lived on a government grant, but took little interest in his formal studies. Instead he gave himself a general education in the humanities. In particular he was very impressed with the Western savants who wrote on man as a social animal, people like J. G. Frazer, Andrew Lang, Jane Harrison, and above all Havelock Ellis. While in Japan he married a Japanese girl, one Hata Nobuku.

In 1912 Zhou Zuoren found work in his home province of Zhejiang as an inspector of schools and teacher of English. In 1917 he moved to Peking, where his brother was already established, and was taken on to teach the history of European literature at Peking University, which was undergoing rejuvenation. Having previously published only translations, Zhou now launched himself as an essayist. Wedded to Western humanism, and equipped with a knowledge of English, as well as easy access to Japanese scholarship, which was the first to channel knowledge of Western trends to the orient, his was a voice that his compatriots, especially the younger ones, wanted to hear, and he spoke of many things. His 1918 essay 'Ren de wenxue' (A literature of man) was seminal in the development of a new Chinese literature to replace the classical model.

In the first half of the 1920s Zhou was very prominent as a leader of progressive opinion in the capital, but following the taking over of Peking by a warlord in 1927 and the swing to the right of the Guomindang (Kuomintang), he drew in his horns, and wrote on 'harmless' subjects, switching in his own words from 'rebel' to 'recluse'. After the Japanese occupied Peking in 1937, Zhou was a natural target for recruitment to the puppet administration set up by them, as he had a Japanese wife and was a lover of Japanese culture. Eventually he succumbed to pressure and accepted a post in the Bureau of Education. For this act of 'treachery' he was sentenced to ten years' imprisonment after the war, but was pardoned as the communist armies neared Nanjing. Thereafter he lived quietly in

Peking, supporting himself by translating and writing reminiscences under pen-names. Some twenty years after his death in 1967 his essays began to be reprinted in China, and by now he is fully restored to his position as one of the very best of 20th-century China's essayists.

Besides writing over twenty books of essays himself, Zhou guided his compatriots' conceptions of the genre. His first important pronouncement on the essay emphasized the aesthetic aspect, in order to point out that the essay could be an art form to stand alongside poetry and fiction, rather than simply a medium for controversy, which it then chiefly was. In 'Mei wen' (*Belles lettres*, 1922) Zhou looked to Western paragons, especially English essayists whose work was an extension of their personality. He commended particularly their 'genuineness', a quality sadly lacking in contemporary Chinese compositions. 'Genuineness' was to remain for Zhou a *sine qua non*, but from roughly 1930 onwards his attention was focused practically exclusively on the compositions of his own Chinese tradition known as *xiaopinwen*, a free form that the educated elite had used down the ages to express their private thoughts and feelings and record their own experiences, released from the obligation to speak 'on behalf of the sages'. For most of Chinese history this kind of essay had been regarded only as a diversion, at certain times as the authentic voice of literature. Yuan Hongdao and Zhang Dai represented the latter standpoint, and Zhou was responsible in no small measure for their revival. But whether English or Chinese, and whatever name you gave to it, in Zhou's view the true essay excluded service to any cause. To be written by individuals for individuals, it displayed man in all his humours and in all his diversity, but since it put a premium on 'naturalness' and 'sincerity', in this diversity there was community; it was the ideal medium for a 'literature of humanity'. This did not mean, of course, that the essay was limited to talking about man and his works: it extended to the world of creation in which man found himself.

As to Zhou's own essays, they naturally changed in content and colouring over the years. From initially applying 'scientific common sense' (largely derived from Western sociology, psychology and anthropology) to issues of the day and his own country's habits and practices, he tended more and more towards bookishness and remoteness from the fray, having persuaded himself—perhaps for his own safety—that literature was 'useless' and that any attempt to prove otherwise would only cause pointless 'vexation of spirit'. Perhaps unwittingly, Zhou described what was to become his typical manner as early as 1923, when he distinguished two types of writer produced by his home province of Zhejiang, the one magisterial, trenchant in judgement and pungent in expression (which fitted Lu Xun), the other mild and gentlemanly, easy and unaffected, given to mixing the amusing and serious (which fitted himself). The 'amusing' element in Zhou's writing was a thin and rueful kind of humour, neither silly and frivolous nor strained after, as with Lin Yutang and his school. By the end of the 1930s his style became excessively dry, too many of his essays consisting of quotations with linking commentary, which catered to the reader's education but not much to his enjoyment.

Zhou Zuoren's typical essay does indeed give the impression of being 'easy and unaffected', but its 'gentlemanliness' is in fact subtly mannered. One soon notices the professions of ignorance, the elaborately unassuming tone and the polite disclaimers. In their interests too his essays often recall the pursuits of the traditional scholar-gentry. Yet as his 'conversation' with his reader progresses, he enters into a closer and closer relationship with him and sheds the mannerisms, sharing his knowledge and thoughts on equal terms, and sometimes expressing himself with painful frankness and directness. The 'rebel' may have been officially banished, but in fact never left. Leaving aside their educative value, which is considerable, the edge that Zhou's essays have is this tension between rebel and recluse, or as he also put it, between gentleman and ruffian. You can never quite plumb the author's depths.

Relentless Rain
苦雨

TRANSLATOR'S NOTE

This relatively early essay of Zhou Zuoren displays several characteristics of its time. First, it is framed as a letter, according to the belief that letters, along with diaries, are the most 'genuine' form of literature, though the pretence is not consistently maintained. Second, it implicitly asserts the view that 'human interest', even on the smallest scale of one person's affairs, is sufficient matter for literature. The otiose rejection of criticism on this account towards the end of the 'letter' shows how sensitive this issue was. Thirdly the composition is deliberately casual: it is not meant to display fine writing, but as a vehicle for the personality of the writer. It is his scholarly bent, for example, which makes the monotonous racket of the frogs seem tolerable by attempting to fit it into the eight classes of sound established by the ancients, and it is his quietist live-and-let-live attitude that makes one see a cacophony as a joyous thing. The personality of the unworldly bookman is of course exaggerated for humorous purposes, but if there is no sense of humour in the author, there is none in the writing.

The addressee of this 'letter' was Sun Fuyuan孫伏園(1894–1966), a young associate of Zhou Zuoren. Chuandao川島(Zhang Tingqian章廷謙1902–1981) was another such young associate. The last phrase, 'outside of expectation' might be puzzling: it is brought in because of a contemporary controversy over the correctness of the formulation *yi biao zhi wai*; my translation hints at the doubtfulness of the phrase.

Dear Fuyuan,

We have had a lot of rain in Peking in the last few days. I don't know if you have run into it on your way to Chang'an; if so, it must have added considerably to the pleasure of your journey. I don't mean to say it is always a pleasure to travel with rain. It often rained when I took the train between Hangzhou and Shanghai, and I found it depressing, so I can't feel excited by the thought of rain in trains, but lying back in our Shaoxing 'black awning' boats, listening quietly to the sound of rain beating on the awning, together with the slapping sound of the oar and the calls of 'Pull over to the bank, keep in to the bank', is a dreamlike scene from a poem. If you are bolder, and lie on your back in a little foot-pedalled boat, braving the rain on a night crossing, it brings out even more the exhilaration of living on the waterways—though it is rather dangerous: if you're not careful and turn over awkwardly, you'll tip the boat upside down. More than twenty years ago when we went to Dongpu for the funeral of my late father's nurse, we ran into a squall on the way back, and the shallow barque careered through Big Tree Creek, tossing on the foaming waves; it was extremely dangerous and at the same time great fun. I have probably inherited something from the 'piscine', or at least the painted savage, stage of evolution, and so feel a positive affinity with water. Not that the many 'lakes' like mud ponds of Peking give me much satisfaction: if there was no water of that kind it would not be much of a loss.

On your way to the uplands of Shaanxi, you will have a good two days in semi-desert. If you run into a storm then it should be a great relief. I can imagine you lounging in your mule cart, the desert sands underneath, the pelting rain above, quaffing large quantities of soda pop as you proceed serenely on your way: that would be really living it up. But that is only my fancy, no more reliable than the poet's daydreams. It might be that a downpour would just be a nuisance to you, and you might at this very moment be complaining to high heaven. I shall have to wait till you return to Peking to find out.

As for me in Peking, these several days of rain have been quite a trial. Peking normally gets very little rain, so not only are people not well provided with rain gear, the houses are not well constructed to keep out the rain, either. Leaving aside the really rich, they don't use solid bricks for their walls, they make do with mud walls rendered with a coat of plaster. Recently the weather has reversed itself, with the south being bitter cold and the north drenched with rain; consequently the defects in the buildings both north and south have been revealed. A week ago the rain caused the west wall of our back garden to collapse, and the next night we had a visit from gentlemen of the burglar fraternity to test the steel mesh over our north wing windows. The day after discovering that we hurriedly hired seven or eight building workers, and in two days they had the wall practically rebuilt, after which we could sleep soundly. But another downfall the night before last brought down twenty or thirty feet of the south wall next to the main gate. This time it wasn't us who had the wind up, but Chuandao and his wife, because if the burglar gentlemen patronized us again, it was their windows they would hide under to spy out the land. To dispel the Chuandaos' disquiet we will have to put major repairs in hand as soon as the weather clears up, which I hope will not be very long. In the meantime we will need to put Chuandao's younger brother to the trouble of acting as watchman for them.

The night before last it rained the whole night through, waking me up I don't know how many times. Apart from when someone in high spirits sets off a few fire crackers, Peking is always quiet at night, so I was unused to the drumming sound of the rain. Even when I did fall asleep, it was as if something like strings of noodles was sticking to my ears, and I did not sleep very soundly. For another thing, the children had reported in the evening that the water lying in the front courtyard was less than an inch from the top of the step. Listening to the rain in the night I kept thinking in a befuddled kind of way that the water must have come over the step and invaded the study in the west wing. At long last five o'clock came round, and holding an umbrella I ran to the west wing in my bare feet to take a look. Indeed it was as I had thought, there was water all over the floor, to a depth of about an inch. Only then did I give a sigh, out of relief. If I had rushed over there so keyed up and found there wasn't any water, I fear I would have been disappointed, or perhaps not as satisfied as I was. Luckily none of the books had got wet. Although they are of no value, for them to be sodden together into cakes of paper pulp would have been very unpleasant. Now the water has receded, but it has left behind the stink usual after flooding. I certainly can't invite people there for a talk, in fact I can't sit there myself to write, so this letter is written at the table in the back room of the house.

There are only two kinds of people who really like this heavy rain. The first is the children. They love water, but they have great difficulty in finding any. Seeing that the front yard had now turned into a river, they all queued up to 'go for a wade'. When you dipped your bare foot into the water it really was rather cold, but they weren't afraid. Once they stepped into the water, they wouldn't come out again. Since the children were obviously having such good fun, some of the adults joined in, but their record was not spectacularly good. Of the three people who slipped over, two were adults, they being my younger brother and Chuandao.

The second category of those who like rain is not exactly people, but frogs. Some time ago I took the children to Gaoliang Bridge to fish. We didn't catch any fish, only a lot of frogs, green ones and striped ones. We brought them back and put them in the yard. Normally they just give the odd croak, but these last few days they have been croaking all day long. It may be a bad omen for the harvest, but it makes it seem quite like the country. Now, there are quite a number of people with sensitive eardrums who hate noise; all things which keep them from sleeping peacefuly, like the sounds of sparrows, frogs and cicadas, they profoundly abhor and detest, and would lief exterminate these enemies for the sake of their siesta. I think that is all quite unnecessary. There isn't anything you can't incline a casual ear to without pleasure: not only those things that have long been the subject of poetry, all animal calls are in fact worth listening to.

When you hear frogs croaking in chorus in the paddy fields at dead of night, it very often takes on a kind of metallic sound—really most peculiar. At other times you could mistake them for dogs. The habit in classical texts of describing the croaking of frogs as 'barking' probably came from practical experience. The frogs remaining in our yard are only of the striped variety, and their call is even less attractive:

they simply go 'ge ge ge', which might be put in the timpanic class of sounds. They normally range from one to three calls, never more. Only on rainy mornings can you hear them call up to a dozen times at one go, which shows they must be loving it.

This spell of heavy rain is no doubt a great misfortune for the poor farmers in the country, but I haven't personally seen how things are for them, and it is no use relying on imagination, so I will not utter hypocritical laments on their behalf. If I am accused of writing solely of individual concerns and ignoring the greater good, I admit that is so. It was never my intention to speak of anything but my personal affairs.

Today the sun has come out, and as dusk is falling I will go out for a spot of relaxation. So I will bring this letter to a close.

I had originally intended not to write until I had received your account of travels in the ancient territory of Qin, but I find I have anticipated. An example of 'outside of expectation', I suppose.

(1924)

Reading in the Lavatory
入廁讀書

In chapter four of Hao Yixing's *Notes from the Studio of Sun-dried Books*, there is an item on reading in the lavatory:

> Legend tells of a pious Buddhist lady who chanted the sutras without cease, even in the lavatory. Though she reaped the reward for her piety in other ways, it was in the lavatory that she expired. The idea is to warn against such behaviour. Though the source of the story is the Buddha's object lessons for humanity, and it is not necessarily factual, yet we may take the point that unclean places are not suitable for chanting holy script. Ouyang Xiu's 'Return to My Fields' records Qian Sigong's saying that he had been a lifelong reader: when sitting up he read the classics and histories, when lying down he read novels, and while in the lavatory he read folksongs. Xie Xishen is also quoted as saying that Song Gongchui invariably took a book with him when he went to the lavatory, and his voice resounded far and near as he read from it.
>
> I can't help laughing at all this. When you go to the lavatory you have to pull down your trousers, and if you have a book in your hand, it is not only mucky, it is also very hard to manage. A person may be devoted to study, but need he go to such lengths?

As for Xie Xishen's reference, quoted by Ouyang Xiu, to the three 'on's' he most utilized for composing pieces, namely on horseback, on the pillow and on the lavatory, being the three places most conducive to thought, that is in contrast a very good crack: it is neither insincere nor superficial.

Master Hou writes a very good essay, but I can't entirely agree with him, because I am inclined to go along with reading in the lavatory. When I was small my grandfather told me the footmen in Peking had a saying: 'The old masters make fast work of their food, the young masters make fast work of their crap.' Though there is an element of calculated interest in the footmen's words, I'm afraid they tell the truth. Granted that it is hard to be definite about the time spent in the lavatory, yet at all events it is unlikely to be very short. Moreover—which is not the case with a meal—however short it is, you can't help feeling it is time wasted, and want to find some way of utilizing it.

For instance, the country folk where I come from like to take along a pipe when they go to the privy, and if there are people rinsing rice or washing clothes on the stone steps by the river, or someone passes by carrying a load, they can also engage in loud conversation, asking how many coppers the rice costs or where he is going to. Reading serves the same purpose, I would have thought, as smoking a pipe.

Having said that, one has to admit that some places are not terribly convenient for reading, and smoking a pipe is the only option. The privies by the river in a certain part of Zhejiang just mentioned are one example.

Long ago, I once stayed in a bookshop in Nanjing kept by a friend from Hunan, called Liu. I was introduced to him by Zhao Boxian. The provincial examinations were being held that year, and he had opened a bookshop near the Floral Arch. I found it very uncomfortable living in the academy dormitory because I was unwell, so he invited me to stay with him. What with preparing medicine and making congee for me, catering to the book requirements of the gentlemen candidates for the examination, and on top of that secretly working for the revolution, he expended enormous energy, and I greatly admired him for it. I slept behind the bookcase at the rear of the shop, and took my medicine and consumed my congee there too. The trouble was, the convenience was outside. I had to go out of the shop and past two other shopfronts to an empty lot where there was a pile of rubbish against a wall. It was quite an ordeal for me to go there, partly it is true because my illness made walking difficult, but even if I had been in good health I suspect I wouldn't have been too keen. This is my second example.

When I was in Japan in the summer of 1919, I went to visit a friend, and stayed in a mountain village called Kijo. Although the privy there was like most others in that it had a roof over the top, wooden sides, a door and a window, the disadvantage was that it was some fifty yards from the house, stuck out in the middle of a field. At night you needed a lantern to light your way, and an umbrella if it was raining. Unfortunately it seemed to be a particularly wet place: it rained for at least four out of the five days I was there. This is my third example.

Lastly there are the latrines in Peking that consist only of a brick either side of a hole, and you just have to get on with it regardless of pouring rain, howling wind, or baking sun. Last year I went to Dingzhou to visit Fuyuan. The privies there are of the kind you find in the Ryukyus, where you perch over the edge of a pit with pigs grunting away beneath you. If you are not used to it, it is very unsettling, and you are hardly in the right frame of mind to read. This is my fourth example.

According to the 4th-century *Book of Anecdotes*, Shi Chong's toilet had a bed in it with silk drapes and beautiful cushions, and two maidservants standing by with sachets of perfume. This is too extravagant, and unsuitable too. Actually my point is a very simple one. All I require is a roof over my head, and walls, window and door, and a light to turn on at night, or a candle if there is no electricity. I would have no objection to it being twenty or thirty steps from the house: that would require an umbrella, but fortunately it does not rain much in Peking. Given this kind of lavatory, I wouldn't have thought there could be any harm in taking a book along for a bit of a read.

Tanizaki Junichiro's book *Setsuyo Zuihitsu* has a chapter called 'In Praise of Shade'. The second section is on the good points of Japanese lavatories. In the monasteries of Nara and Kyoto, all the lavatories are old-fashioned. Situated in clumps of trees where you get the smell of green leaves and moss, they are dark but kept very clean. There are covered walkways joining them with the living quarters. To squat in the semi darkness, illuminated by the pale light from the paper screens, and lose oneself in thought, or to look through the window onto the temple gardens, is a wonderful experience. He goes on:

I repeat, there must be a certain degree of obscurity, immaculate cleanliness, and a quietness in which you can hear even the whine of a mosquito clearly. Those are necessary conditions. I love to listen to the patter of rain in these lavatories. In Kanto especially, the lavatories have a long narrow slot at floor level for sweeping out the dust, which enables you to hear from right next to you the rain which drips from the eaves or tree leaves seep softly into the ground after washing the feet of the stone lanterns and moistening the moss on the stepping stones. These lavatories are truly the best places for the sound of insects, the song of birds, as well as moonlit nights, best indeed for appreciating the character of all four seasons. I suspect that from ancient days our haiku poets have derived countless material from these places. In this regard, it would be no exaggeration to say that the most romantic constructs of Japanese architecture are the lavatories.

Tanizaki is at bottom a poet, which explains why he writes so well, perhaps to the extent of dressing things up, but that is only in his wording: his viewpoint is sound enough. In the Warring States period of the late middle ages, the preservation and furtherance of culture in Japan rested entirely on the Gozan monasteries. That brought about a change in style and temper, seen for example in ink and wash paintings of dead trees, bamboos and stones replacing the finely detailed academy style. Architecture naturally followed the same trend, represented in the tea houses. The romantic transformation of lavatories was an after-thought.

Buddhists seem to have always been very particular about the use of toilets. From my occasional dipping into the rules of conduct of both the Mahayana and Hinayana schools, I have been extremely impressed by the close attention of the old Indian sages to every aspect of life. In respect of toilet practices, the *Two Thousand Observances of the Bhiksu*, translated in the Han dynasty, lists 'Twenty-five practices in the ablutions'; chapter 6 of *Sarvastivada Vinaya Matrka* (the Song dynasty translation) from 'How to keep downwind' to 'How to prepare toilet paper' consists of thirteen items; the Tang text by Yijing called *Report on Buddhism in the Southern Seas*, 2:18, has a chapter on 'The Convenience'. They all contain very precise instructions, some extremely solemn and at the same time funny. They really bowl you over when you read them. Then when we consider how the monk Lu Zhishen in the *Shuihu zhuan* was promoted from being in charge of growing vegetables to be in charge of ablutions, we can see that in Chinese monasteries they also used to take such matters seriously. But times have changed: it is no longer so. In 1921 I spent six months convalescing in the Western Hills, and stayed in the Ten Directions Hall of the Azure Clouds Temple. In all my walks I never discovered a halfway decent lavatory. It was as I wrote in my 'Letters from the Hills':

> My peregrinations have recently been extended to the springs east of here. It really is very nice there. I go there first thing in the morning before the daytrippers get there and linger a while, enjoying the beauty of living waters. Sadly, though, it is not very clean. The path there is very smelly, because of the large quantities of what the *Pharmocopoeia* calls 'human brown matter' spread about. China is a strange country: on the one hand people have a hard time finding nourishment, and on the other have no way of disposing of their waste products.

In this situation, to find an ordinary sort of lavatory in Chinese temples is a great good fortune; to hope to find somewhere you can lose yourself in thought or read a book is asking for the moon. Since the monks foul things up themselves, you can hardly blame the common folk.

But given a clean lavatory, it is still all right to read a book, though we can put writing out of our mind. And we needn't be particular about the kind of book—anything suited for dipping into is fine. My own rule is not to take rare books or hard-to-read books, though grammars are among my regulars. In my experience essays are best, and novels worst. As to declaiming, now that we no longer study the Eight Prose Masters there is of course no call for that.

(1935)

On 'Passing the Itch'
談過癩

The other day the papers carried a report from Guangdong saying the Police Bureau was detailing officers to arrest lepers: they were to be taken in chains and locked away. I was rather busy at the time, and though I felt this item of news was very entertaining, I did not cut it out and keep it. Now I have no means of tracing it, which strikes me as a great pity. Later I heard that some people had sent telegrams of protest, which indicates there was perhaps some truth to the report. But at the same time it was also reported that plans are afoot to raise 140,000 yuan to build a leper hospice, so we are left guessing again. What the true state of affairs is we have no means of knowing, but our society is always getting worked up about one thing or another, and now we are all provided with the makings for a discussion, what harm is there in me having my say?

The Chinese do not seem to have displayed very sound sense with regard to disease and doctoring, but they do keep quite a good record of peculiar stories on these subjects. Our present topic of leprosy is a case in point. So let us look for now at that favourite subject of conversation, the transmission of leprosy. In the 'Heartening News' column of the *Shi bao* (True News) of 27 April there was an article entitled 'Leprosy epidemic in Guangdong province'. It ran:

> Just lately in Guangdong province leprosy has been spreading like wildfire. Some propose the Western method of controlling inferior races and shooting the lot of them. The lawyer Ye Xiasheng has sent a telegram in protest: he askes hypothetically, if a father or mother were to contract this disease, would their child stand idly by while they were executed? Controversy rages among the citizenry in Guangdong, the cities are as if swept by storms. The Chairman of the province, Wu Tiecheng, newly in office, argues that they should proceed on a humanitarian basis, in the scientific spirit, to make prudent provisions and take conscientious curative measures; he was at that moment engaged in inviting experts to draw up a plan of action.
>
> It is said that the reason why leprosy is so rife in Guangdong is that it arises from the heat and humidity of the climate, and the mugginess of hill vapours and miasma. Fujian province also has this disease, only it is not as widespread as in Guangdong. This sickness is common to both men and women. When it reaches the critical stage the whole body swells up, it itches unbearably, and the patient gradually succumbs. As to the way it is passed on, food and drink have nothing to do with it. Yet men do not infect other men, women do not infect other women; it is only transmitted to the opposite sex, and then only through sexual intercourse. If a woman with leprosy has contact with ten or more uninfected men, the woman will be completely cured. There is an old Cantonese saying 'a leper-woman does not end up on the river' (the river being the Pearl River). Organized prostitutes in Guangdong mostly ply their trade on boats, as alluded to in the lines, 'Charming spring beauty fills the Pearl River, nubile young sirens as gorgeous as flowers.' A girl suffering from

leprosy is not allowed on the boats by their owners, but supposing a client with leprosy had intercourse with an uninfected prostitute, then inevitably the latter would become a leper. In that Wu Tiecheng is now in the process of setting up a lepers' clinic, we must praise his charity and wisdom: his mercy falleth as the gentle dew on all alike.

I just want to take up one thing in this article, passing over the rest—which is the statement that leprosy can only be transmitted to the opposite sex and that a woman leper can cure herself by passing on the disease to men. There is a special term for this: 'passing the itch'. Legends about 'passing the itch' have no doubt existed since time immemorial, but my learning is scant and my memory poor. I cannot draw up an extensive catalogue, I can only quote a few items in illustration from books at hand. In chapter 7, entitled 'On Men' of Qu Wengshan's book, *New Notes on Guangdong* (published in 1700), there are two passages to do with lepers. The first runs:

> There are numerous lepers in Guangdong. In the city of Xiancheng large numbers of men and women suffering from leprosy beg by the roadside. It is very easy to catch the disease from the foul air or from their urinating in the streets. In the Gaolei district it is borne in high summer on wind and waves, by miasma and hill vapours. The inhabitants are particularly susceptible to leprosy, to the extent that they regard it as a hereditary affliction and make little to-do about it. The serving women in inns all wear an embroidered bag at their waist, mostly filled with fruits. They offer them to customers as they dismount, and regardless of age, they address all customers familiarly and laugh and joke with them. There is a local ditty from Wulan which would seem to allude to this:
>
> > Low hang the embroidered bags below the waist
> > In them areca flowers most odiferous
> > Greeted with smiles the travellers all dismount
> > Plied with purple crabs and wine right royal
>
> In these parts lepers account for five or six out of ten of the population. Before the signs of leprosy appear on the face, a reddish glow can be seen under the skin when a candle is held up to it. This is the stage at which they 'sell leprosy'. No male leper can 'sell' it to a woman, but a female leper can 'sell' it to a man. When the transaction takes place the microbe leaves its host, and the woman is made whole again. For the 100 leagues between Yangchun and Haikang, the charms sold for a few groats by rustic bridges and in country inns should be shunned at all costs: this is the business known vulgarly as 'passing the

itch'. Though leprosy is bred by humidity, it is contagious, therefore those who contract it are placed by their family in a small boat, amply provided with food and clothing and cast adrift on the waves—or otherwise exiled to some lonely place and deprived of human contact. Sometimes people are kidnapped by lepers and only a heavy outlay can secure their release.

To the north of the city of Canton there was formerly a lazaretto, but over the years it has fallen into ruins. If the authorities were to once more buy land and build a home, take in all the lepers and care for them, put them in charge of a head man from among their number, and not allow any of them to leave without permission, then this pestilence would in time be removed. This would be an act of charity which would earn the gratitude of a hundred generations.

In the Qianlong period [1736–1796] Li Yucun compiled *Notes on the Kingdom of Nanyue* in sixteen fascicles out of extracts from the *New Notes on Guangdong*, and printed them in his *Hanhai* collection. In fascicle 7 there is a section headed 'Lepers' which is identical with that quoted above, except that the last sentence has been cut.

In 1850 Chen Jiongzhai wrote *A Nanyue Travelogue* in three fascicles. In fascicle 2 there is a section headed 'The Transmission of the Mange', which is also to do with leprosy. It reads:

In the southeast the land is low and the climate moist. The inhabitants are plagued with the mange, which beyond the mountains is called leprosy. This disease is contagious, and cripples whole families. Those who get it are abominated by others and ostracized from their own kind. In their condition distress and helplessness reach their ultimate. In Canton and Chaozhou there were formerly leper colonies where they came together like with like, and lived in a community. They were led by a leper chief. In their ranks were lepers of the second and third generations. The leper chief arranged their marriages in strict order, ensuring no miscegenation. With the children of the third generation the disease had run its course, and they were allowed to leave the colony—hence the saying 'leprosy lasts only three generations'.

The face of a leper is swollen, his hands and feet ulcerated; the sight is nauseating. Women lepers, on the other hand, are transfigured: their complexion takes on a bloom, and there are no outward signs. They often deck themselves in finery and slip out to tempt men to fornication. When some stupid young ne'er-do-well falls into the trap, he contracts the disease. It attacks his vitals, and in no time his limbs itch unbearably. He takes over her disease entirely, while the woman's chronic condition vanishes, and she is restored to normal.

In 1841 when the English barbarians invaded Canton, troops were assembled from various provinces. Those from Hunan were violent and undisciplined, and the Cantonese ground their teeth and secretly sent women lepers to lead them into debauch. Subsequently their bodies were covered with running sores, and death followed closely for the majority of them. Of the remainder most were killed in battle. Those spared to return home numbered only a few dozen.

In 1876 Chen Zihou compiled *An Anthology of Poems on Cantonese Matters* in eight fascicles. In fascicle 5 there is a poem called 'Marketing the Mange':

> Do not mistake the vernal bloom for arcadian charms
> When they have 'marketed the mange' their curse is lifted
> Being slaves to pleasure brings inescapable consequences
> When you come to your senses your issue is doomed.

The footnote reads:

> In Guangdong province leprosy is handed down for three generations. Women with this disease are always on the lookout for the opportunity to fornicate, so as to transfer the poison to someone else. This is called 'marketing the mange'. Liang Shaoren's *Essays from the Autumn Rain Hut* reports that east of the Pearl River there is a habitation called 'Leper Mound', set up to gather lepers together. One girl inmate of entrancing aspect used to put out in her dinghy every day, vending sweetmeats to support her mother. A whoremaster took a fancy to her, and inveigled her mother with heavy bribes into forcing her daughter into prostitution. A certain young man of Shunde established a mutual bond with the girl, but on the night when they were to consummate their love the girl peremptorily rejected the young man's advances, on the grounds that he was the only surviving scion of an old family, and had been adopted to carry on the line of an uncle. She then told him of her disease and they wept in each other's arms. When the young man came to revisit her after a week or two, he discovered that the girl had drowned herself in the river some days previously. He was grief-stricken, and performed the ceremony of heaping earth on her grave, just as if they had been a married couple. Huang Rongshi (styled Yujie), a provincial graduate from Panyu, wrote a song to commemorate the incident.

Out of all these commentators, the palm must go Xu Renhu. In 1883 he wrote *Traceries with a Coral Tongue: First Versions* in eight fascicles. In fascicle 1 there is a section entitled 'Passing the Itch':

In the middle of the Daoguang period [1821–1851], Assistant District Magistrate Lin Yangshan, styled Guanguang, from Guangdong province visited this district. Collegian Fan called on him on business at that time, and pressed him on the question of whether the story about 'passing the itch' (in Guangdong) was true or not. Li strenuously denied it, and condemned the whole thing as a pack of lies. Then someone suggested to Fan he could prove the point by adducing the cast-iron evidence of Wu Qingtan's *Miscellaneous Notes on Guangdong*. Now these *Notes* say:

'Leprosy is extremely common in Chaozhou. The authorities have set up a leper colony on Phoenix Mountain. There the lepers are grouped together and supplied with rations. A leper chief is appointed to govern them, Yahu by name. He wears full regalia and is very comfortably off. When there is a wedding or a funeral in a family, queues of lepers form at the door, demanding money and food. If they are given short measure they let out a stream of abuse. People have to slip Yahu some cash in exchange for a strip of paper to paste on the door, and then the lepers do not dare to create any commotion. In the colony they have a well called Phoenix Well; its water is sweet and has curative powers. When lepers drink from it, it keeps their disease in check and their flesh in normal condition. If they leave the colony, however, their disease will break out again. For visitors to the colony the leper chief provides clean quarters and clean utensils. When the boys and girls in the colony grow up they are naturally paired in marriage. Their progeny are normal healthy specimens. The beauty of the leper women is doubled by drinking this well water. If any young rake should have congress with her, the next day the leper woman's malady disappears as if it had been a dream, and she leaves the colony without a care in the world. This is what is popularly known as "passing the itch". Within a few days of being contaminated, the rake loses his facial hair, his joints erupt, and he dies.'

Such being the case, why did Mr Lin have to cover up? Perhaps he was in ignorance himself. For my part, I judge that Lin and Fan were both at fault; Fan for displaying no tact with his superior, and Lin for not mildly rebuking him for his lack of respect, so to avoid the taint of vulgarity himself.

Afterwards I came across a note on 'passing the itch' in *City Tales*,[1] as follows:

---

[1] *Shuofu* 說郛 is a collection of anecdotes compiled by Tao Zongyi 陶宗儀, who lived towards the end of the Yuan dynasty. The original has not survived, but a reconstruction was made in the early Qing period.

'The leprosy microbe is carried in the seminal fluid of both sexes, hence it is very easy for it to pass from one to the other. If the man wishes to expel the microbe, he wraps his penis in a lotus leaf before inserting it into the vagina. As soon as he ejaculates he withdraws the leaf, the microbe and semen both enclosed in it, and discards it. In this way the semen does not enter the vagina and the woman is protected from harm. In the case of the woman wanting to rid herself of the microbe, the situation is unclear.'

I surmise that neither Assistant District Magistrate Lin nor Collegian Fan was acquainted with such accounts.

The material I have found is really too scanty, though when I copy it out it seems a good deal. From these gleanings we can see for a start that there is quite a long tradition here. From the 39th year of the Kangxi era [1701] to the 26th year of the Republic [1937] a full 236 years have elapsed, but the legend of 'passing the itch' has survived unscathed. Though there are discrepancies in the telling of it, its versions are united in their fabulousness. Two hundred years ago there was some excuse for it; and in 1898 there was after all the campaign of the Heavenly Soldiers of Righteous Harmony [the Boxers] belonging to the White Lotus sect, so one's expectations of that time could not be high on any front, but in the last thirty years it does seem rather unwarranted. Is it not true that in these times China is undergoing a renaissance, and is in the process of reforming its old culture in order to adapt to modern needs? Well then, we should at any rate make some progress in the matters that most critically affect our lives, medicine being one.

I have no connection with the Chinese or foreign medical professions, but on this subject I cannot help giving way to lamentations. The development of China's medical profession differs from that of Japan. Unlike their Japanese counterparts our native doctors did not initiate their own research which would have turned them from the old ways of occultism to the new ways of science, thus leaving a simple distinction between earlier and later periods, rather than between Eastern and Western schools. Instead the scientific methods are propagated and taught by foreign doctors, with the result that to Chinese occult medicine was added Western scientific medicine, and the opposition between them persists to this day. And as for the ordinary person the fees for Western treatment are too high, and the lore of Chinese medicine is fascinating, the thieving quack is enthroned as our national physician: he not only has dominion over the lives of our people, he exerts an influence in the cultural sphere into the bargain, directly or indirectly fostering preposterous notions and legends. The so-called 'passing the itch' is a good example. Since Hansen discovered the leprosy bacillus in 1879, the nature and condition of leprosy have been quite clear. Though it is still a terrible thing, it has completely lost its mystery. I have heard that in Japan public and private leprosariums now number fourteen, which shows that its incidence is quite considerable there too, but I have never seen in print or heard in conversation the kind of preposterous story just quoted. Granted I am unlettered, but I do not know of any reference to 'passing the itch' in ancient times either. So this seems unique to China, which makes it all the weirder.

I am a complete outsider when it comes to medicine, but I feel that of our poor stock of common knowledge the part relating to medicine—including both physiology and pathology—is really vital: whatever happens it cannot be skimped. This thing leprosy is like the mango: you rarely see it in the market, and ignorance of it would not affect life's great matters, but it is as well to know a bit about it if you want to discuss the question of 'passing the itch', for then you could judge whether the story was true or false. The medical books say that leprosy belongs to the class of skin diseases; the bacillus has been discovered; its onset is brought about by direct contagion, not through heredity. Therefore the claim about 'three generations' is unfounded. The incubation period for the leprosy bacillus is quite long—some say several months, some say several years, one cannot be definite. Before abnormal sensations are felt in the skin, up to the point when a red rash appears, there is no means of knowing that one has contracted it, so though Qu Wengshan's description of 'charms sold for a few groats' is very deftly phrased, its facts are open to doubt. The bacillus stays under the skin, but it also spreads through the body to mucous membranes and such places. Intercourse naturally rates as a capital means of transmission, though it is not necessarily limited to the heterosexual kind (the same applies to syphilis). To transmit one's disease to another through intercourse only results in one more sufferer, that is all: one is not thereby cured oneself. Syphilis could serve as an example here too: leprosy cannot be the sole exception to the rule.

It is popularly believed that illness can be cured by magic. People write 'Influenza for sale' on a piece of paper, wrap it round a coin, and leave it by the roadside, or write a notice 'Cold for sale' and stick it on a wall. I have personally met with such things. For my part, I did not necessarily come away with my purchase, while the vendor probably still suffered from his influenza—or it might even have got better by itself: both magic and illness go their own sweet ways. In the case of a person who has a contagious disease being willing to sacrifice her body to sell it, the purchaser should naturally not go away empty-handed; for the vendor, however, nothing will have changed. Germs are rather like a cornucopia, you can never use them up; or again, as the popular jingle goes, 'The thing has been sold, yet there it still is.'

In sum, leprosy is just a malignant infectious disease. Though as no cure has yet been found, it is felt to be particularly repugnant. When the ancients called it an evil malady they hit the nail right on the head. The route by which it is transmitted is through direct contact, also exactly the same as with other infectious diseases. Likewise it is an invariable rule that the contagion can enter but not leave. There can be no two ways about that.

As for those strange stories, though they might come from the mighty pens of the ancients, or have a superficial interest in themselves, and therefore appeal to the general taste, they are pure hogwash, and have no basis in fact. In the interest of truth they should be rectified. Even judged as anecdotal literature there is nothing to recommend them. Perhaps their only use is to provide me with the material for an essay, no more.

A few years ago a foreigner wrote a book on the Chinese national character, saying the Chinese were obsessed with sex.[2] Even the eating of bamboo shoots was for their symbolic value, and so on. Quips like this, all very diverting, were taken as a sign of mental derangement: they at

---

[2]This probably refers to the book *The Chinese National Character as Seen in the Novel* by the Japanese author Yasuoka Hideo that Lu Xun wrote about in his essay 'Mashang zhiriji'馬上支日記(A sub-diary written in haste), collected in *Huagai jixubian* 華蓋集續編 (Bad omens, sequel). The relevant passage may be found in Yang Hsien-yi and Gladys Yang tr., *Selected Works of Lu Hsun* (Beijing: Foreign Languages Press, 1957) vol. II, p. 280.

once became a laughing-stock. I would not dare to subscribe to that person's theory about bamboo shoots; however to say that the Chinese get somewhat overwrought about sex would not seem to be entirely groundless. The legend of 'passing the itch' illustrates the point. Why is this story told with so much relish? The list extends from the native Cantonese Qu Wengshan to outsiders from other provinces, the time span from Kangxi to the present. According to Xu Renhu it already figured in *City Tales*, but as we cannot examine the original work, we will leave that aside for now—are we to believe that Tao Zongyi invented the story himself? The reason why is twofold: salaciousness and eccentricity. It is said that with the exception of the works of R. L. Stevenson, all good stories need some feminine interest, so this is actually nothing out of the ordinary, only the Chinese practice undeniably tends to excess: descriptions routinely start with wasp waists and end with tiny feet. It is also ordinary human nature to tell tales of outlandish things, only the Chinese invariably end up by discarding the truth: truly a case of 'eating scabs without regard to the flow of blood'.[3]

On the subject of 'winter insect, summer grass',[4] I have seen people quote the recently published *Dictionary of Chinese Pharmacology*, and adduce learned terms from botanical science, yet still maintain that the westerners are mistaken. In fascicle 2 of *Unorthodox Observations from Liu Ya*, published in 1791, Xu Houshan writes: 'With the onset of winter the grasses gradually wither. The insect then pulls itself out of the ground and wriggles along, its tail still swishing the grass attached to it.' He thought the summer grass really did spring from the winter insect. As a story, Liu Ya tells it entertainingly, in all conscience, but in terms of fact it has not only been shown conclusively that the 'grass' is a parasite, even on a common sense basis one wonders how an insect with its head stuck in the ground and its tail growing grass could ever dig itself out again. That an insect in the maggot stage could be

---

[3]The story is told of Liu Yong 劉邕 of the Southern Song dynasty (420–479) that on a visit to his friend Meng Lingxiu 孟靈休 he picked up a dried scab that had fallen from a moxibustion point and ate it. Meng then peeled off scabs that had formed on other moxibustion points for him, leaving himself bleeding. 'Eating scabs' thereafter became a by-word for inclinations that are taken to unreasonable or disgusting lengths.

[4]Cordyceps Robertli, a fungus which grows as a parasite on small insects.

wriggling about in the winter when the grasses are dying is equally illogical. The reason why present-day Chinese pharmacologists disavow fungology and only put their trust in a romancer who lived more than a century ago is none other than that they are captivated by the marvellous nature of his explanations.

Reading the notes and jottings of recent times I have come to the reluctant conclusion that those which recount anecdotes and praise meritorious service are the best of the bunch. Over the generality which delight in the bizarre and tell of retribution I can only sigh. I sense they are of no small consequence, but have no antidote to prescribe. Over the last twenty years general education has progressed, but common sense and discrimination seem not to have advanced correspondingly, doubtless because the old stain is dyed too deep. A few years ago there was a sudden clamour for scientific essays. This was indeed a good sign: at least it would have let in a breath of fresh air. But later the clamour subsided for some unknown reason, and whether any volumes of scientific essays came out or not I cannot ascertain. If it was not that the fashion passed and there was another signboard to be hung up, then probably it was because the masses did not need them. All in all, it seems to be decreed by fate that there will be no such scientific essays in China. In not coming forward to write articles about leprosy and like matters, let us face it, the medical men show more insight and wisdom than my humble self.

(April 1937)

The Ageing of Ghosts
鬼的生長

I am as a rule quite eager to learn about the business of ghosts, but what, you might ask, is the use of such knowledge once gained? Probably none: at bottom it may be mere curiosity. The Ancients said, only the sages can know the condition of ghosts and spirits, which shows it is hardly an easy matter. I repent myself that in my youth I did not meddle with metaphysics: now that avenue is closed, all that is left to me is to make good use of a passion for digging for textual evidence, and seek material in chronicles ancient and modern; perhaps in that way one can get a hint or two, one never knows. But the hundreds and thousands of years they go back is an unconscionable time, the records have multiplied endlessly, and the uninitiated are unlikely to stumble on the scent. What is more, the world of ghosts seems absolutely full of conundrums, quite enough to occupy the gentlemen of the academies of science for a lifetime. Here I raise only one question, namely that mentioned above, the ageing of ghosts. If I may be allowed, I will make light work of a heavy task, and sketchily set out my myopic view, all the time 'respectfully awaiting the favour of instruction'.

After a person dies and becomes a ghost, does the ghost in the shades or some other place actually continue to grow older year by year as before? That one would like to know. There are two approaches possible. One would be in accordance with our unregenerate theory that ghosts do not exist, but that would scarcely be to the point, and would moreover be too unsporting. The other would follow the common line that ghosts do exist, so when you come down to it, we are stuck with this single approach. However, though the existence of ghosts is an article of faith for all believers, whether they age or not is a question on which different people have different views, and on which there is no hallowed doctrine.

Ji Yun of the Qing dynasty says in chapter 4 of his *Thus Have I Heard It Said*:

> Ren Zitian reports that someone out at night in his locality saw in the moonlight two people sitting together on a cemetery path amid the cypresses. One was a young man of sixteen or seventeen, of pleasing and handsome aspect, the other a woman whose white hair hung down to her shoulders, whose back was stooped and who carried a stick: she appeared to be in her seventies or eighties. They were billing and cooing, apparently delighting in each other's company. Wondering to himself of what provenance this old hussy could be that she was so saucy with the youth, he went nearer to them, whereupon the figures melted away. The next day he enquired whose grave they were from, and only then discovered that this certain person had died in his youth, and his wife survived to maintain a virtuous widowhood for another fifty years. When she died she was interred with him in this place.

One must suppose from this that ghosts never grow old: their appearance and age are tied to the time of their death. But when you reflect on the implications of this, you discover many awkwardnesses. The young husband and old wife is one such. Then, too, there is the eventuality of the son being old and the father being young: according to etiquette, the duties of keeping the parent warm in winter and cool in summer, of tucking up at night and enquiring after comfort in the morning, may not be neglected, but they would impose a crippling burden on the son, and he would deserve all our pity. Again, as our mundane law permits remarriage, consider the poor scholar who takes a new wife when widowed in order to continue his line: after death he would then be responsible for supporting quite a few households, and this old fellow too would have to command our sympathy. On the other hand, the wife who remarries is according to popular belief sawn in half: when the former husbands come in for their share of an old body, what are they supposed to do with it?

Shao Bowen of the Song dynasty writes in chapter 18 of his *Records of Things Seen and Heard*:

> When Madam Li gave birth to Master Kangjie, a girl twin was still-born. Over ten years later, the mother saw in the moonlight from her sickbed a girl curtseying to her from the doorstep. The girl said, weeping: 'Unbeknown to you, mother, the ignorant doctor poisoned me with his drugs. Woe is me.' Madam Li replied: 'It was fate.' The daughter said: 'If it was fate, how is it that my brother survived and I did not?' Madam Li answered: 'That is just what was fated, that you should die and your brother survive.' The girl departed, still in tears. Another ten years or so passed, and Madam Li again saw the girl come to her, weeping. She said, 'Having missed my chance because of an ignorant doctor, I have had to wait these twenty long years before being born into the world. Mindful of the maternal bond, I am come to say goodbye.' Then she left, once more in tears.

Mr Quyuan[5] quotes this passage in chapter 8 of his *Commonplace Book of the House of Tea Fragrance*, Series Three, and comments:

> This matter is most peculiar. Since the girl died in her mother's womb, she was just a lump of flesh quite without consciousness. But after ten years or so she could both curtsey and speak. How could it be that after dying she could still mature with the passing years, as in normal life?

---

[5]Quyuan is the assumed name of Yu Yue 俞樾(1821–1906), a favourite author of Zhou Zuoren.

As I see it, going by what Mr Shao says in *Records of Things Seen and Heard*, it is indeed indisputable that ghosts do mature with the passing years. If you apply this assumption to Ji Yun's account, the young man of sixteen or seventeen ought to have become an old gent of seventy-odd, in which case the story would not get off the ground, as a pair in their seventies or eighties canoodling in the moonlight, though one would have to reckon it a case of 'long in the tooth but young at heart', is not particularly outlandish. And there is another thing: ghosts can observe people, but people cannot observe ghosts. When at last they met among the cypresses, the man-ghost would be sure to recognize his wife, but I fear the wife-ghost, assuming no one re-introduced them, could by that time have hardly recognized her spouse of half a century before.

The viewpoints of Shao and Ji both have their strengths and weaknesses. We ordinary people would find it extremely difficult to choose between them. Probably we can only allow them to co-exist: whether in the underworld the ghosts are divided into warring camps, each choosing to grow old or not grow old as they wish, that we have no means of knowing. The theory that ghosts do not grow old seems to be the common one, the theory that they do grow old is slightly eccentric, but I have turned up some other supporting evidence. The one-volume *Supplement to The Trials of the Wangxinglou*, printed in 1899, was written by Qian Hecen of Wuxi to commemorate his son Xingbao. The main volume is unfortunately unobtainable. The supplement contains a *Diary of Conversations via the Planchette* which records Qian's written communications with his children. His third son Dingbao was born in 1879 and died within forty days; his fourth son Xingbao was born in 1881 and died at the age of twelve; his third daughter Ezhen was born in 1887 and died five days after birth. They all responded at the seances. The diary reads:

> 21st of 12th month, 1896, evening: Xingbao came at last. I asked: 'When you left us you were twelve. Have you grown physically since then?' He replied: 'I have.'
>
> 17th, 1st month, 1897: I rose early and took my place at the planchette. My late brother Yunsheng and my sister Run and Xingbao were all in attendance. I asked my brother: 'You were only twenty-seven when you passed over, now you are over fifty. Have you grown older in appearance?' He replied: 'I have.' 'Have you grown whiskers?' He replied: 'I have.'

From this it can be seen that ghosts are no different from the living in ageing with the passing of the years. There are several other entries:

> 29th, 1st month: Question: 'At what age did you achieve consciousness?' Answer: 'At three.' Question: 'For how many years did you take suck?' Answer: 'Three.' (This to Dingbao)
>
> 21st, 3rd month: My sister Run came. Question: 'Was there something?' Answer: 'Glad tidings.' Question: 'What glad tidings?' Answer: 'On the fourth of the fourth month Xingbao is taking a wife.' Question: 'How old is his bride?' Answer: 'Thirteen.' Question: 'Are we invited to wish them happiness?' Answer: 'No.' Question: 'Are you going?' Answer: 'Yes.' Question: 'Are wedding presents required?' Answer: 'They are.' Question: 'Is Dingbao married?' Answer: 'Yes.' Question: 'Has he any children?' Answer: 'Two sons, one daughter.'
>
> 29th, 5th month: I asked Xing: 'Is your wife Shannan well?' Answer: 'There is to be a happy event.' This meant she was pregnant. 'When did she become pregnant?' Answer: 'The fifth month.' 'What month is she due to give birth?' Answer: 'The seventh month.' Subsequently I asked my departed brother: 'People give birth after ten months. Do ghosts all give birth after three months?' He replied: 'Yes. Such are the differences between people and ghosts. Girls are ready for marriage at the age of eleven.'
>
> 12th, 6th month: I asked my second daughter Yingke: 'How many children have come with you?' Xingbao replied for her: 'Ten.' I was greatly surprised, and thought there must have been a mistake. I repeated the question over and over again, but the answer was as before. I called on my sister Run and asked her, but she replied in the same terms as Xingbao. I asked how it could come about that she could have produced so many children after having been married only five years. Did it mean she gave birth more than once in a year? The answer came: 'Yes.' Only then did it come home to me how wide the gulf is between ghosts and people—they seem in this respect to be practically the same as cats and dogs. When I had heard previously that Xingbao had married a wife eleven years old, I had thought it make-believe, but now when I piece it all together, I realize that the ways of ghosts are not to be fathomed by the reasoning of men.
>
> 19th: I asked Xingbao: 'Is your great-uncle Shouchun still with you?' He replied: 'He is dead.' 'How long has he been dead?' Answer: 'Three years.' 'When someone dies, are they buried in coffins, as here?' Answer: 'Yes.' Till now it had not dawned on me that ghosts also die. The ancients used a special word for the death of ghosts, evidently not without reason. No doubt the children born in the shades receive their souls from those who die there.

The above excerpts all contain discoveries about the nuptials, obsequies, birth and death of ghosts, and as material for a treatise on the life of ghosts is very precious. I discovered this volume in the spring of 1933 on a bookseller's pitch in Changdian.[6] It was printed with wooden movable type on white paper, with corrections made in ink: a pleasingly elegant production. The *Diary of Conversations via the Planchette* and *Supplement* are most interesting; their account of conditions down below is quite detailed, but lack of space prevents me from quoting more. Though it is a matter of regret that I was not able to get hold of the main volume, it would not appear to contain any record of planchette sessions, so its value is not as great as it might have been otherwise. My reaction on reading this compilation was that Mr Shao's theory had received endorsement, and the case that ghosts grow up thus could not be denied.

I do not believe in ghosts, yet I like to hear tell of the affairs of ghosts: this is a great contradiction. Nevertheless, though I do not believe people turn into ghosts after death, I do believe that there is a human being behind every ghost. I do not understand what the 'natural function of *yin* and *yang*'[7] is all about, but the idea that ghosts are the projections of the hopes and fears of living people is surely sound.

Tao Yuanming is one of the great free spirits in history. His 'Going Back to Live on My Land' says 'Human life is like a passing pageant / In the end we return to nothingness', and 'Spirit Explains' has, 'When the time comes you have to make an end / There's no point in making too much fuss.' Yet in his 'Dirge for myself' it says, 'I want to speak but my mouth utters no sound / I want to see but my eyes have no sight / Formerly I slept on high couches / Now my nights are passed in the wild grassland.' One would not expect Master Tao to cling to illusions about life and death, yet he does write in this vein with great strength of feeling. However, to deduce the nature of life after death from the sensibilities of one's lifetime is after all the inclination of humankind, and is quite natural.

The average person is more bent on survival, and neither can nor will believe that he or his loved ones will simply fade into oblivion, so he

[6]A seasonal street market in Peking.
[7]This is the formula of Zhang Zai 張載(1020–1077), devised to account for the phenomena of ghosts and spirits.

comes up with all sorts of conjectures, on the assumption that existence must continue. The conditions of this existence differ slightly with the race, the locality, and even individual likes and dislikes. These are revealed not deliberately, but unwittingly, in fact listening to people talking about ghosts is tantamount to listening to people discussing their most private thoughts. It would seem that the view that ghosts exist is the opium for a life of trouble and care, a form of comfort for those helpless in the face of the greatest sorrow and fear: 'Amorous young men and women can continue unfinished romances; of dauntless heroes it is said, "in another twenty years they'll be back again as other brave fellows" .' It is those who hold to materialism who are in for a hard time: as with those of powerful wills for whom anaesthetics are ineffective, they have to look on wide awake as their flesh is cut into. Guan Yu's 'scraping of his bones'[8] certainly counts as heroic, but really involved uncalled-for suffering, and is not something the ordinary person could stand up to; so it is not surprising that the majority turn to anaesthetics for deliverance.

The *Diary of Conversations via the Planchette* says:

> 1st, 8th month: A stray ghost responded to the planchette. He announced that Ezhen had been reborn into the human world. I asked where, and the answer came, 'In the city.' I asked her name, but the stylus wrote, 'Not known.' All of my kith and kin who have awaiting rebirth for so long have departed one after another in the space of a few months. Am I to presume that mortal births have been exceptionally numerous this year, and so they have all gone to make up the quota? It really passes understanding. If this report is true, then henceforward my dealings with the planchette are over and done with.

When I read this section I could not help my spirits drooping. The Supplement to *The Trials of the Wangxinglou* is one of the saddest books I have read, and I have this sensation every time I leaf through it. It is as if one were suffering agony from a wound and found relief in taking morphia, but that morphia was actually brewed from home-made fudge: the passer-by observing this would not know whether to laugh or cry.

I myself do not believe in ghosts, but like to hear about ghosts, and have great sympathy with the superstitions of the old way of life.

---

[8] In the novel *Sanguo yanyi* (Romance of the Three Kingdoms), Guan Yu 關羽 carries on with a game of chess while a surgeon cuts his arm open to the bone to draw the poison from an arrow wound.

This shows that I am already an old man, for those with one foot in the grave tend either towards harshness, or towards tolerance.

(April 1934)

In Praise of Mutes
啞巴禮讚

There is a proverb which runs: 'The dumb man chews on yellow rue',[9] the point of which lies in the matching line, 'Bitter as gall, but he can't tell you.' But another proverb says, 'Under the rue bush strumming a tune', which indicates that making merry when things look black is common enough too. Though the mute is afflicted by not being able to express himself, doubtless he has his own private pleasures, which may be superior to those of us who can wag our tongues; how are we to say?

It is commonly held that dumbness is a form of disability, on a par with being eyeless or having one leg. This is very unfair. A dumb person's mouth is neither unformed nor infirm, he just cannot speak, that is all. The *Shuowen*[10] says, 'Dumbness: the ailment of not being able to speak.' Even accepting, as Mr Xu would have it, that inability to speak is an ailment, it is quite an unimportant one, which does not much detract from the main uses of the mouth. When we look into the uses of the mouth, roughly speaking we find them to be the following: 1. eating; 2. kissing; 3. speaking. Actually the mouth of a mute is perfectly all right: it is not short of a tongue, neither are the upper and lower lips joined together. So if he wants to eat and drink, no matter if it is foreign fare or 'Chinese menu', he can indulge himself to his heart's content, without the slightest inconvenience. Therefore we can take it as read that dumbness does not cause the least impairment to a person's constitution.

What about kissing? Given a mouth which, as explained above, can drink and munch at will, it will of course meet no difficulty with this line of work, for as the Dutchman, Dr Van de Velde, says in chapter 8

---

[9]'Yellow rue': the plant *huanglian* is not actually rue, but to English speakers, rue is about the only plant proverbially associated with bitterness.

[10]*Shuowen jiezi* 說文解字, compiled by Xu Shen 許慎 of the Han dynasty is the first dictionary of the Chinese language.

of *Ideal Marriage*, the business of kissing is confined to the three senses of smell, taste and touch, and has no connection with sound, which shows that the mute's inability to speak by no means stands in the way.

When all's said and done, the so-called ailment of dumbness is still only in respect of 'not being able to speak'. As I see it, that is neither here nor there. That mankind can speak is in fact surplus to requirements. Consider the teeming life on this earth, all sentient beings. None does not act out its destiny, each fulfils its nature. When have they ever spoken a word? It was said of old, 'The chimpanzee can speak, yet it remains a beast; the parrot can speak, yet it remains a bird.' How sad that these creatures, having painfully learned a few of somebody else's catchphrases, are still the same creatures they ever were, and have become the butt of the sage's jibe to boot. Honestly, has it been worth it?

When in time past the four-eyed Mr Cang Jie[11] officiously invented script, it set the kindly ghosts howling a whole night through, and I fear that when among the ape-men the first one stretched his larynx and learned to speak it might well have made the primitive gods heave a profound sigh. To what end do we toil and scheme in life? 'Drinking, eating and sex: men's great desires reside in these.'[12] Assuming that they do not encroach upon these great desires, may not other matters then be allowed to look after themselves? The most important clause in the Chinese philosophy of practical living is, 'The less you get involved in, the better.' With regard to the mute, you might say he is able to dispense with one involvement.

The saying goes, 'Sickness enters through the mouth, calamity issues from the mouth.' That speech is not only of no advantage to people, but on the contrary is harmful, is here plain to see. Once you utter something, your words imply a judgement, which is dangerous, these days. People cannot always be saying 'I love you' and such sweet nothings; what is more, when you look into it carefully, 'I love you' carries implications like 'I do not love her', or 'I won't let him love you', and so might sow the seed of ruin. It is not for nothing that your wise man in chatting to visitors will only say, 'The weather today . . . ha ha ha', without elaborating further, for though the

---

[11] The legendary being accredited with the invention of Chinese characters to replace knotted string. His four eyes betoken discernment.

[12] 'Drinking, eating, sex': a quotation from the *Li ji*.

weather is insensible, yet to call it good or bad is ultimately rather imprudent; hence he passes the matter off with a laugh.

Years ago, I read Yang Yun's letter to Sun Huizong.[13] I only remember a few sentences like, 'I planted a field of beans and was left with acres of stalks.' I was privately much taken by it, little suspecting that Mr Yang was actually cut in half for writing these words. It is as beyond comprehension as fifteen- or sixteen-year-old girl students in Hunan being shot for reading *Fallen Leaves* [Guo Moruo's, not Xu Zhimo's].[14] But this world is beyond comprehension, and we, alas, are at its mercy. Our forefathers who were subjected to these experiences over the last few thousand years have left us this parting advice: 'The man of foresight practises self-preservation.' The tea-houses which have grown accustomed to this situation over the last few decades are plastered with slogans saying 'Do not discuss national affairs'. The gold statue in our family's history had its lips thrice sealed,[15] and for 2,500 years has been an example to the world, his reputation second to none. Now, should we not suppose the mute is the gold statue of our time?

Ordinary people regard the ability to speak as a virtue, but there are those who have achieved renown through pretending dumbness. I might add that high and low, past and present, people of this kind have been very few, which very fact goes to show what a rare and estimable thing dumbness is. Pride of place goes to the illustrious Lady Xi.[16] By virtue of her looks which were of a kind to 'cause kingdoms to fall', she was twice made consort. She bore the King of Chu two sons, but never spoke a word to him. The litterateurs of China who like to give the glad eye to dead and gone beauties of olden times then went to town writing poems about her; some said she was good, some said she

---

[13]Yang Yun 楊惲 (d. 54 BC) was an official at the court of the Han emperor Xuan 宣帝. He was elevated to the nobility for exposing a plot, but was later schemed against in turn, and reduced to commoner status. His letter to his friend Sun Huizong 孫會宗 stating his grievances was the cause of his execution. It survives in the *Wenxuan* 文選.

[14]*Fallen Leaves* 落葉 is the title of an autobiographical novel by the left-wing Guo Moruo 郭沫若, and a poem by the right-wing Xu Zhimo 徐志摩.

[15]According to the *Kongzi jiayu* 孔子家語, Confucius encountered a gold statue on a visit to the state temple of Zhou; three times he stopped its mouth, and inscribed on its back the motto, 'The man of antiquity most chary of words.'

[16]Lady Xi 息 was the wife of the ruler of Xi in the Spring and Autumn period (770 BC–476 BC). When Xi was conquered by Chu, King Wen 文王 took her as part of his booty.

was bad, all flaunted their frowzy finery. But still Lady Xi's fame thereby grew great. Quite frankly, hers was truly a tragedy in a woman's life: it did not simply concern one person in one place at one time, you could almost say it symbolized the fate of all women. Nora, the heroine of Ibsen's play, *A Doll's House*, says she had never imagined she could have born two children to a man who was a stranger to her: this was precisely the fate of Lady Xi. In fact, could one deny that it is the fate of all women under capitalism?[17]

There is another non-talker. I mean the hermit at the end of the Han dynasty called Jiao Xian.[18] My fellow provincial Jin Guliang [fl. 1661] included this hermit in his *Register of the Peerless*; he also wrote this judicious encomium:

Xiaoran lives alone
Seals his lips, does not speak
Quietly hidden till the end
A joke to creatures of the wild

Moreover, as was said, 'In this wise he lived out his days, and passed the hundred ere he died'. In which case, by pretending dumbness you can both gain a reputation for high integrity and enjoy the fortune of long life. The praiseworthiness of dumbness is this blindingly clear.

Manners are in decline, men's hearts are not as pure as of yore. Nowadays the dumb have actually affected certain gestures and begun to speak. However, these still cannot be used in the dark: they cannot speak then. Confucius said, 'When the state has lost the way, actions may be bold but words should be modest.'[19] Could it not be that the mute is conforming to the ancient ways?

(1929)

---

[17]By 'capitalism', Zhou seems to mean a form of social organization that is not communist, specifically a system based on the notion of property. In relation to women, he is thinking of them as being treated as their husband's chattels, as opposed to companions or equals. Zhou restated his long-held grievance against 'capitalism' in this regard in his 1951 letter to 'the responsible member of the Central Committee', published in *Xin wenxue shiliao* 新文學史料, 1987 No. 2, pp. 214–215.

[18]Jiao Xian 焦先(styled Xiaoran 孝然) went into voluntary seclusion in the age of turmoil following the fall of the Han dynasty. He lived in the barest poverty, but nevertheless observed the nicest proprieties. His story is told in the *Sanguo zhi* 三國志 (History of the Three Kingdoms).

[19]This passage is in Book XIV of the *Analects*.

Xia Mianzun 夏丏尊 (1886–1946)

COMMENTARY

Xia Mianzun came from what we would call a middle-class family in Zhejiang province. His father had passed the first degree in the old examination system, as he did in turn while still in his teens, shortly before the system was abolished. With his father's support, the young Xia made several starts on a formal education in the 'new learning' from the West, but they were cut short for financial reasons. He had to return also from study in Japan, in 1907. However, he made use of the Japanese language he had learned to read Western literature in Japanese translation. His subsequent career in China consisted of teaching in middle schools and teacher training colleges, editing for publishers, running magazines, and writing and translating. He died of consumption in Shanghai.

Xia Mianzun was highly respected for his work in education and appears to have been universally thought a good man: decent, right thinking, honourable. If that description implies that one should not look for the flash of brilliance in his writing, the implication would be correct. And the 'humour' he detected in certain things he treated seriously, not amusingly. For instance, the essay entitled 'Humorous Vending Cries' (幽默的叫賣聲, 1935) refers to two examples. The first is the street vendors of preserved beancurd, the malodour of which is matched only by the durian fruit: their honest cries of 'smelly beancurd!' are a challenge to the hypocrisy and deceit of society. The second example is the shouts of the vendors of evening newspapers: their practice of first calling out the price of the newspaper ('two coppers') and then giving the main items of national news to be read about, suggests that such news is worth practically nothing.

The two essays translated here are his best known pieces: they crop up in most modern prose anthologies. They do not appeal to a taste for humour, nor do they impress by their stylishness. But they do embody qualities much appreciated by Chinese readers. Though the display of sensitivity of soul, nay even overt sentimentality, is found quite palatable, the opposite is also welcomed. That is to say, solidity and sober-mindedness is also a virtue. The impression of a plain man, not given to but driven to tell of his experiences or express some emotion, can touch the reader deep.

Both essays practise strict reduction. The winter at White Horse Lake is reduced to the wind, and memories of the Japanese attack on Shanghai are reduced to a bomb fragment. Expression is freer in the first, as the purpose is to describe an experience that most readers will not have had. The author even allows himself some mild fancies, though we are not told what they were: it is enough that along with the description of the nature and effects of the wind we have one touch of subjectivity, namely the sense of the 'poetry of desolation', which, we may note, is more or less imposed on him. Expression is more noticeably constrained in the second essay. The plodding pace of the narrative, the ponderousness of the language, the repetitions (which the translator has to resist varying elegantly) are in a way a restraint and discipline, a protection against stridency, which would have ruined the impression of swirling undercurrents of emotion forcibly held in check. In any Chinese readership, but especially the people of Shanghai where the essay was published, the subject of Japanese aggression aroused a response that needed no prompting. Those emotions, which the author obviously fully shares, are held and crystallized—and perpetuated—in an inanimate lump of iron. At the same time, there is lightening and elevating in the painterly associations of the metal's shape, which match the 'poetry' of the cold nights at White Horse Lake.

In essence, then, these essays project the personality of an honest man. But their art is also self-conscious. Xia once recommended to budding writers the virtues of economy and reticence, the latter meaning to hold back or veil from the reader the nub of what you want to say, so that he has room to exercise his imagination. Just so does Xia hold back from telling us what words he intends to write on the lump of iron.

The Ornamental Iron Mountain
鋼鐵假山

On my desk I have a miniature ornamental mountain made of iron. I got it without spending a penny, but it means more to me than any other object I have in my room.

It is an ornamental mountain because that is the way it serves my use. In itself it is just a crude lump of iron. It is none of your lucky talismans, in fact to say what it is will only evoke outrage, for it is a fragment of a bomb dropped by the Japanese when they attacked the Chinese City of Shanghai in 1932.

The thing happened three years ago now. Shortly after the Japanese troops withdrew, I went to Lida School in Jiangwan to inspect the damage, and lingered over that mournful scene for some hours. On the way back I picked up this lump of iron. The ground roundabout Lida School was littered with lumps of iron, some big, some small. I was told they were bomb fragments. The one I picked up was a small one, measuring roughly six inches across, three inches high and two inches thick. Its weight was about a catty. One side retained the curve of the cylinder, and judging by the roundness of the curve, the diameter of the original cylinder must have been about a foot. I don't know how heavy a bomb that would have made it. The other side was the fragmented side, all jagged and uneven, some part of it like a cliff face, others like proud rocks, the edges as sharp as a knife.

Many houses in the Jiangwan district were destroyed by bombs, and many people killed the same way. To mention only the Lida School grounds, more than half the school buildings were destroyed. Corpses could still be seen among the rubble when I was there. That small bomb fragment must have taken part in the murderous work: like the executioner's sword it carried the reek of blood. In terms of the reliability of evidence, this was indeed 'ironclad'.

All kinds of associations rose in my mind when I placed that ironclad evidence on my desk. Because of its angularity it would not rest stably, and every time I moved it round, its sharp edges left scratches. At first I thought of having a stand made for it, so that it could be displayed like an ornamental mountain, but then I felt that this evidence of painful history should not be mounted like an antique. It is true that many of the antiques that have come down to us bear witness to history, but once clothed in the garments of antiques they lose their historical sting, and are just played with as curios.

I fairly soon removed this crude lump of iron from my desk and put it away, only occasionally taking it out thereafter when I remembered its existence. Recently we moved house, and when sorting things out one of my family threw it in the rubbish basket. It took me a lot of searching to discover it. I devoted a lot of thought to its long-term preservation. Suppose I were to put it out on my desk, it would not sit properly, and would scratch the surface. Suppose I were to put it away in a clothes chest, I would have to watch out for it rusting and spoiling the clothes, and it would not be easy to dig out. Eventually I concluded it would be better to have a frame made and set it on my desk as an ornament. So I got someone to go to the City Temple district and have one of the redwood shops make a frame for me.

Now this lump of iron rests on a little redwood base and sits on my desk as an ornamental mountain. After three years it is covered with a coat of brownish rust, particularly thick in the depressions. The surfaces that are broken off cleanly are like the cliffs in Shen

Shitian's Ming dynasty landscape paintings, the irregular surfaces are like the veining effect in Huang Zijiu's Yuan dynasty landscapes, while the peaks and valleys remind me of Ni Yunlin's contours. When visitors see this ornamental mountain for the first time, they all praise it for its resemblance to a painting, and ask me where I got it. My family also have come to respect it, and will not throw it in the rubbish basket again.

So after all that, this lump of iron has now found a place and a means of preservation, but unfortunately has at the same time taken on the garb of an antique. To minimize the antique aspect and emphasize the historical aspect, I intend to write some inscription on it, to make it something more than an ornamental mountain with a strong resemblance to a painting in people's eyes.

What kind of inscription should I write? A poem or an admonition in classical style? I do not wish to go in for frivolous wordplay on this grave relic of history: I would prefer to record a few facts in a plain and simple way. What should I use to write the words? Black ink would not show up on the iron. By rights blood should be used, but a practical alternative would be blood-coloured red lacquer. Today is the 10th of January; in another eighteen days it will be the anniversary of the Japanese attack. I will write the words on that day.

(1935)

Winter at White Horse Lake
白馬湖之冬

The deepest sense of winter I have experienced in my forty-odd years of life was ten years ago when I first went to live at White Horse Lake. In the intervening ten years White Horse Lake has become a small settlement, but at that time it was still wilderness. The new buildings of the Chunhui Middle School rose grandly on the other side of the lake, while all there was on this side was a couple of newly built bungalows at the foot of the mountain. They were occupied by my and Mr Liu Xinru's families. There was no other sign of human habitation for a mile around. When towards the end of the 11th month of the lunar calendar my family had moved from the teeming city of Hangzhou to this mountainous barren fastness, it seemed to us that we were pioneering the polar regions.

The wind blew practically every day there, booming and roaring like a tiger. Though the buildings were new, they were crudely constructed and the draught that came through the cracks round the door and windows nearly cut you in two. After we had pasted layers of paper over these cracks, the wind still came in through gaps around the rafters. When the wind was strong we shut ourselves in before dark and all the family took to their beds after supper and lay there listening to the angry howl of the wind and the waves of the lake washing on the shore. A little rear annexe facing the mountain which served as my study was the room most sheltered from the wind. I used to pull my Russian hat down over my ears and work till the small hours by the light of a kerosene lamp. The wind roared down from the pineclad hills like a wild beast, frosty moonlight framed the window, hungry mice scurried squeaking over the ceiling. It was at times like these that I most keenly appreciated the poetry of desolation: all by myself, I would frequently stir the embers in the stove and prolong my vigil. Casting myself as the tiny figure we often see in landscape paintings, I gave myself up to fanciful musings.

Now trees are everywhere around the shores of White Horse Lake; at that time not one had been planted. Neither the moon nor sun met any obstruction, they both shone full on us from the time they came up to the time they went down. When the skies were clear, and the wind dropped, the sun made it so warm that we couldn't believe it was winter. The whole family would sit sunning themselves in the yard, and even take lunch outdoors, in the same way as we had supper in summer. Chairs and stools were moved around to catch the best of the sunlight. But then if the wind blew up we were forced to beat a hasty retreat indoors, carrying our chairs with us like a lot of refugees. Normally the wind would get up towards dusk and die down again about midnight, though when a winter monsoon set in, it would rage all day and night, and not let up for two or three days. When the cold was most extreme, the earth would be blanched grey like cement, the mountains would purple into sombreness, and the waves of the lake be shot with deep blue.

I have actually nothing against snow. When snow fell it was extremely bright indoors, so bright you hardly needed to light a lamp in the evening. The snow-covered hills in the distance would provide a sight worth contemplating for weeks on end, and were always visible from our windows. But we were after all in the south, and it snowed only once or twice a winter. The sense of winter I customarily imbibed there almost all derived from the wind. The reason why White Horse Lake was so windy can be put down to geographical causes. It is ringed around with mountains, all except for the northern rim where there is a gap a few hundred yards wide, as if deliberately left as a funnel for the wind. In its natural features White Horse Lake has little to distinguish it from other places, it is only special in its wind, whose strength and prevalence is familiar to all who have been there. From ancient times the wind has always played an important part in the feeling of winter, and the wind of White Horse Lake excels in that respect.

We have now been living in Shanghai for quite a time. When we occasionally hear the sound of the wind at the dead of night, we all think of White Horse Lake, and say 'It must be blowing a gale over White Horse Lake tonight'.

(1933)

Ye Shengtao 葉聖陶 (1894-1988)

COMMENTARY

Ye Shengtao (also known as Ye Shaojun 葉紹鈞) seems to me the most stalwart of the New Literature stalwarts. He produced a continuous stream of works for publication, covering all the chief categories of fiction, essays, poems, children's stories, criticism, even plays. He was also responsible for launching, managing and editing a vast number of magazines and books. All of them were progressive. He was a man to rely on. The quality one expects from his prose is precisely that, reliability.

Ye Shengtao was born and spent most of his early life in and around Suzhou, the city of canals, known humanly for its soft-spoken people and comely women. His father was literate but relatively poor, a rent collector for a big landlord. Ye Shengtao was sent to 'modern' primary and secondary schools, but was unable to continue his education due to lack of funds. He went straight into teaching primary school, and remained a school teacher for over a decade, until his publishing activities took precedence. His wife, whom he married in 1916 by arrangement, was also a school teacher.

Ye was in on the beginning of the New Literature movement. He joined the Xinchao She (New Tide Society), based at Peking University, in 1919 on the recommendation of his school friend Gu Jiegang 顧頡剛, who was a student there, and in 1921 became a founder member of the Wenxue Yanjiuhui (The Literary Research Society) which was the leading campaigner for literature with a social conscience. Ye's involvement in publishing came about through his membership of the Literary Research Society, when he went to work part-time at the Commercial Press in Shanghai on the society's journals and books. His own reputation as a writer was founded on short stories, including children's stories. Eventually he built up to a full-length novel, said to be the first in the New Literature, called after the principal character Ni Huanzhi 倪煥之, perhaps not surprisingly a school teacher. That was published in 1929.

In the 1930s the Chinese literary world became increasingly politicized. Ye's sympathies were left-wing, but he was advised he would be more useful if he did not join the communist backed League of Left-wing Writers. He continued to write for and edit publications of a left-liberal hue. As a refugee in the interior during the war against Japan (1937–45), Ye was active organizationally in the cultural war effort while working for the Kaiming Press. After 1949 he held a number of responsible posts, the highest being Vice Minister of Education. Though over eighty when the Cultural Revolution ended, he took up his pen again and wrote a regular column for one of the national newspapers.

Ye Shengtao wrote various kinds of prose pieces, including some passionately patriotic ones, some polemical, some portraits of people he knew, some of 'the world in a grain of sand' type. The style in which he excelled, and which he made unmistakably his own, could be called 'steady as you go'. It was said to have 'the beauty of plainness'. His words, being indeed of the plainest kind, did not draw attention to themselves: they directed all the reader's attention to the matter. The matter was substantial, concrete, factual, informative. If one of the virtues of the essay is to tell the reader of modes of living, working, travelling, and diversion that they do not know at first hand, Ye Shengtao, educator that he was, knew how to exemplify that virtue. He inspired trust as a reliable scribe and chronicler, for as well as stating things plainly, he also seemed to see things plainly, his steady gaze unaffected by common prejudice.

Yet if that were all that his essays consisted of, they would be no different from entries in an encyclopaedia. In fact, even at his most objective, Ye Shengtao tells not only the way it was, but also the way it felt. Nor is the broad social background very far away. The description of objective conditions is blended with the personal and the historical. His account of the Shanghai 'alley houses' and his own concrete yard that he tried to turn into a garden would have fallen fairly flat without the focal event of the Japanese attack on the Chinese part of the city, though it is not allowed to interrupt the gardening saga long. The personal element is not intimately or confessionally personal, except for humorous effect. For the most part, the things that happen to him could have happened to anybody. Disclosure of his private feelings comes where it will do most good compositionally: a brief show at the end of an essay.

Other ways that Ye Shengtao had of leavening his bread will be apparent from reading on.

Three Kinds of Boat
三種船

I had not gone back to Suzhou for three years in a row to tend the graves. This autumn I had some spare time, so I did go. 'Tend the graves' in practice means no more than to give the grave attendants some money, to let them know that your family grave has not reached the stage of neglect when it can be robbed. To get to my family grave I had to take a boat. In fact most Suzhou people do take a boat to go and tend their graves. If the weather is good it is indeed a great pleasure to get out of the city's confines and fill one's lungs with the fresh air that is in ample supply on the river.

For this trip I hired a boat that I was used to. Its paint had practically all peeled off, the window frames were warped, the deck planks cracked; in general it was a sorry sight. The boatman confirmed, on being questioned, that the boat had not been out of the water for several years. In this summer's drought it was stuck in the mud by the river bank: obviously there was no business for it, and still more obviously there was no money to haul it up into the bank for repairs. Even in years past, apart from spring trips to tend graves, the boat had been relegated to the pierside, where its only duty was to welcome the day and say goodbye to the setting sun. It would have been as hard to get it onto the bank as for an old beggar to throw a birthday party. Times had changed: for short distances the rickshaw could replace the feet; for longer distances to outlying villages and towns there were river steamboats, or alternatively the Shaoxing 'dang-dang' boats, which actually were no slower than the steamboats, and were very cheap at that. If it were not for the custom of tending the graves, I fear the Suzhou city boats would be chopped up for firewood. And the custom of tending the graves seemed to be falling off: I, for example, had changed to going once every three years.

Suzhou city boats are called 'fast boats'. They really are no faster than other boats. As they aren't meant to navigate major rivers or big lakes, their draught is shallow, and their hulls are broad and flat. Apart from the open bow, their decks are divided into front cabin, middle cabin, and stern shelter. The roof of the front cabin can be raised to allow people to stand up straight without bumping their heads. On either side are arranged two or three little armchairs, with neat little tea tables in between. Horn lanterns with red tassels are suspended from the front eaves. Underfoot are varnished floor panels, six of them usually, which are supported by transverse and upright struts. When the floor panels are removed, the boatman's storage space is revealed.

The middle cabin also has a number of floor panels, but they are placed more or less directly on the boat's bottom, so there is a step of one foot or so down from the front cabin. There are two rows of small windows on each side of the middle cabin; the upper row can be hooked up, the lower row removed, to allow passengers to lean over the boat's sides to get a good view. Formerly the windows were made of translucent shell, or they had little squares of glass set between the shell tiles, but afterwards when glass became more available, the whole window was made of glass.

Dividing the middle cabin from the front cabin and the stern shelter are partitions constructed of six decorated screen doors, which fit into grooves top and bottom; to open and close them you just have to push on their sides. The painting and calligraphy on the doors is all in gold lacquer, and the themes are 'Cold rain spans the river as the boat enters the lower Yangtze at night', 'Frost blankets the land as the moon goes down and the birds call' and suchlike, and there are the usual plum blossoms, orchids, bamboos and chrysanthemums. To the right and rear of the middle cabin are placed long planks for the passengers to sit on. If they spend the night on the boat, one or two more planks can be added at the rear, and bedding laid out on them. Below the windows on the left is placed a small square table, with four stools around it. Ten or so people can eat at the table if a round table top is laid over the square table. The long planks to the right and the rear and the floor panels from the front cabin are all used for seating and the little stools are placed in the corner to make up the number.

Finally, the stern shelter. This is the whole domain of the boatman. Like the front cabin, the rear shelter has storage space under the floor panels, which holds a cooking stove and crockery as well as bedding, clothes chests and the like. The boatmen remove a panel and squat down to prepare their food and do their cooking. There is also a space for the oarsmen to stand and work their oars. There is one oar to port and starboard, each oar manned by two persons, one pulling the oar handle, the other pulling the oar rope. If there is a baby who cannot walk it lies in a cradle on the raised stern; if it is mobile, it is allowed to crawl about, only a rope is tied round its waist and attached to a shelter support, to stop it falling into the water. Four rounded staves protrude from the stern, arranged in sequence: presumably these were originally weapons to defend the boat with, but later they became ornamentation. Besides the parts of the boat that are in contact with the water, the rest of it, that is the windows, doors, flooring and posts, are all protected with natural varnish, so there is not that unpleasant smell of tung oil that other boats often have. Varnished things can easily be wiped clean, and there is no shortage of water around the boat, so as long as the boatman is not lazy, the boat can be made to look spick and span at a moment's notice.

In the old days when a married daughter went home to see her parents or an old lady went to see her daughter, they called for a boat if it was too strenuous to be carried in a sedan chair. To sit or lie in a boat was very comfortable, and at the same time they could have tea, or smoke a hookah, or even smoke opium. The only trouble was that the city's waterways were extremely dirty. People tipped their domestic rubbish in them, the dyeworks ran their coloured effluent into them, and the water was also used for washing rice and vegetables, laundering clothes, and cleaning commodes, with the result that the water's colour and smell were simply indescribable. Sometimes the corpses of cats and dogs with bloated bellies also floated in them, and in summer the red, white and yellow melon rinds were even more picturesque. Suzhou is a city of many waterways, which has led it to be called the Venice of the East. If Venice is like that, what has it to brag about?

Yet such things the married daughters, old ladies and their kind did not concern themselves with. As long as their own little domain was comfortable, what was outside it could be as sloppy as it liked. And with acclimatization, even the effort to raise a hand to cover the nose was unnecessary. The waterways outside the cities are a lot wider and cleaner, so to hire a fast boat to go to nearby villages and towns, or for an outing on a nice spring or autumn day, or to go to tend the graves—an important duty in our patriarchal society—could of course be most enjoyable.

The meals prepared on the boat are in a different class from meals in restaurants, and have earned the special name of 'boat fare'. Proper boat meals include a wide variety of dishes, plus all sorts of snacks: there is always more than one can finish. Occasionally ordered dishes will still be good, for the cook will have had long training, and will not produce anything that is not in the authentic boat fare style. To expose their secret, the reason why boat fare is good is that they cater for one table at a time: with their little pans and woks, they cook the dishes one by one, each in its own juice, and with picked ingredients. Naturally every dish will have its true taste, and will make you greedy for more. Supposing the boat cooks were to operate in a restaurant kitchen, frying big woks of shrimps and stewing big pans of chicken, they would certainly be taken down a peg. To get back to our subject, since the boat fare was good, and travelling was comfortable, allowing you to look out on the scenery, laugh and talk, and play mahjong or amuse yourself with girls, the fast boats used to be in great demand, more than they could meet. At that time the idle rich in Suzhou had not come across the word 'slump', and there was no notion corresponding to 'slump' in their minds, therefore the fast boats suited the mood of the time and place, and were well favoured.

Besides their cooking, boatmen have another remarkable skill, and that is in cursing. If cursing can only be used defensively, not aggressively, that is nothing special. If cursing is short and sharp and cannot entangle your opponent like a creeper, it can only be second-rate. If purely standard grammar is used, and multiple rhetorical transformations are not applied to the task, the cursing may go on interminably, but will have no real style. When boat people engage in a slanging match they acquit themselves well in all three respects and live up to their reputation. Say their boat was making its way along a narrow waterway, and up ahead a countryman's boat laden with firewood or some similar boat pulled out carelessly and it looked as if there might be a collision, the boatman would take the offensive and shout rudely, 'Are you blind? Bumping and barging all over the place, are you trying to get yourself killed?', or words to that effect. If there was an answer from the other boat, then the boatman would advance to the second stage, that of sustained wrangling. He would simply stop plying his oar, and curse his opponent up hill and down dale: after all, the fault was all on the other side, so his anger had to be given its head. However, they very rarely resorted to fisticuffs, nor would they resort to abusing a man for coiling his pigtail on his head or a woman for swinging her breasts. At this point you had to admire their rhetorical skill. I cannot now recall any examples, but when you listen to their discourse, it is bound to strike you that you have never thought words could be used in such a way, but only if they are used in such a way can they roll up in one the elements of resentment, venom, haughtiness, contempt, and such. I doubt if it would occur to the scholars who edit textbooks of human geography that the urban waterways of Suzhou could breed the proficiency in cursing that they do.

Because their oarsmanship is perfected in the city waterways, their strong point is caution and prudence: boats may fairly scrape each other, but never collide. When they get out of the city it is certainly true that they know how to tow a boat in a head wind and hoist a little sail in a following wind, but compared with the pilots of other boats they come nowhere. They only dare to tow the boat or hoist a sail when the wind is light. If a really strong wind blows up, they will cautiously and prudently tell you it is no go today. Take Stone Lake that I have to cross to go and tend my grave, for example. Although Mr Qu An's poem speaks of 'Wind in the heavens, torrents of rain,' something something, 'massed mountains rear and fall in front of me', actually it is not really a very big lake, and it has only one small squat hill beside it which couldn't be very steep because on the 18th of the eighth month by the lunar calendar every year a whole pack of shamanesses go up it to burn incense. As soon as the boatmen hear you say you want to go across Stone Lake they look up at the sky to see if there is any sign a wind might blow up. When they put out onto the lake, the tension shows on their faces, and all cheerful talk ceases. At the first sound of water lapping against the prow of the boat they warn each other in hushed voices: 'Waves! Waves!' One year when my family went to tend the graves, the wind blew up strong after ten o'clock; the boatman couldn't very well say he was turning back, but he absolutely refused to cross Stone Lake. As a result it was bad luck for our poor old legs: they had to walk about seven miles to get to the graves and back.

I now turn to the 'dang-dang boats' manned by people from Shaoxing. The boat is equipped with a small gong, and when the boat is leaving they strike it, 'dang-dang', as a signal; as they pass through towns on their route they strike it again, 'dang-dang, dang-dang', to summon passengers, hence the strange name. In my childhood there were no such boats in the Suzhou area; I couldn't say exactly when they were introduced. I personally did not get acquainted with them until I went to Luzhi to teach. The boats are moored outside the city, due to a conflict with the scheduled boat service, so it is said. The latter tried to put a block on the dang-dang boats because they were stealing its business. But the dang-dang boatmen are made of stern stuff, and they don't mind a fight if anyone stands in their way. Very likely there was some rough stuff, but anyway the scheduled service boatmen realized they were no match for those fellows from Shaoxing, so they had to be content with eyeing them disdainfully as they enjoyed the freedom of the waterways. Whether there was any business to do with registration and licensing I can't be sure, but the real fact was that the Shaoxing boatmen opened up a trade route for themselves by the strength of their right arms. We have a saying, 'Sparrows, beancurd, Shaoxing people', meaning that where there are sparrows and beancurd there are also Shaoxing people—which is everywhere. A comparison between the dang-dang boats and the scheduled service boats would go to show that the Shaoxing people are well cut out to win the struggle for survival: the fact that they are found everywhere like sparrows and beancurd is not without its significance. We will go into that later; first I will describe the structure of the dang-dang boats.

The dang-dang boat belongs to the family of the 'black awning boat'. It has a square prow, a turned-up stern, and an arched awning. There is only room for two people to sit in a row, which emphasizes the length of the boat. The sides of the boat are painted green, but the bilge is painted red, so that when the boat is lightly loaded a band of red is visible above the water line, making a strong contrast with the green. The awning is pure black. The rudder is either red or green: when not in use it is stuck up on the stern; the names of the town and villages on its route are scrawled on it, mostly in white. The boats are built of rough material, and they are put together in a make-do way: the purpose is served if the water does not actually gush into the boat. They are not bothered about having struts here and uprights there, like patches on a worn coat.

With other boats of ours we board them from the prow, but not the dang-dang boats. Normally we step onto their gunwale and edge into the cabin through a gap in the parted awning. This is because the cabin entrance up front is too small: to get in you have to bend low and squeeze through. It is much less fuss to board from the side. Given this reluctance of passengers to squeeze through the cabin entrance, the boatmen pile whatever goods they have for shipment there, which effectively blocks it up. But you have to be very careful when stepping on the gunwale. Everyone who has gone to Hangzhou knows about the instability of the rowboats on the West Lake; well, the dang-dang boats are not a great deal bigger than the West Lake rowboats, and their instability is of the same order. As the boat rocks towards you, you let your weight rest on the foot placed on the gunwale, and extend the other foot gently downwards so that it touches the flooring of the cabin. Once in the cabin you have to sit down, the seats consisting of thin and narrow boards on either side. These are set only about a foot higher than the flooring, which means your knees are thrust into prominence. If there is someone sitting opposite you, you are in a good position to have a 'knee to knee' confidential chat. You can support the small of your back against the awning; it is best not to straighten your trunk, because your head might bump against the roof of the awning and give you claustrophobia.

The first arrivals usually sit in the gap where the two sides of the arched awning are parted. Though this is the main thoroughfare, and they have to put up with the nuisance of frequently leaning sideways to let people pass, it is still a superior position, because they get the air, they can see the passing scene, and they can rest their arms in turn on the side of the boat to ease the cramp from sitting from a long period. But in a storm or in bitingly cold weather the flaps have to be drawn together, and so that position loses its advantage, and all passengers are equal, all sunk in an evil-smelling gloom.

Scarcely any of the boatmen who man the dang-dang boats are over forty, and they are all of sturdy physique. They don't know what it is to conserve their energy: they row like the devil from the word 'go'. Five men line the high stern, each in charge of one oar, or sweep, with one hand on the sweep handle and the other on the sweep rope. The sweeps are very long, and lighter than those on other boats. When the oarsman pushes out the sweep handle, the upper half of his body pitches outwards, as if he is going to fall into the water. Then when he drags the handle back again, he stoops on his heels, as if he is going to sit down. With five sweeps pulling energetically in the water like this, the boat is propelled forward at flying speed. Sometimes an extra oar is brought into play on the prow, the oarsman sitting with his back to the way the boat is going, and that of course increases the speed. The water plays a lively tune as it churns in the wake. While they row the boatmen sing snatches from Shaoxing opera, or joke with each other, their jokes being of the indecent sexual variety, or in the special style of Shaoxing humour. That helps them to forget their fatigue, and also relieves the passengers' boredom. They also like to compete with other boats. When they see another boat ahead which seems to be making speed, one of the boatmen will issue the order, 'Overtake!', and the others in immediate accord will redouble their efforts, their bodies stretching out horizontal for the push and nearly flat on their back on the pull, as if taken with a sudden fit of madness. When the boat ahead is duly overtaken, they hoot with laughter, congratulate themselves on their victory, and then resume their former speed.

Just because they row fast, people in a hurry prefer to take their boats. The journey to Luzhi, for instance, is a dozen miles; the scheduled service boats, which are also rowed, take six hours, while the dang-dang boats take only four. Even if you are not going to do anything in the two hours gained, you are still cooped up for less time, and besides the fare is the same: 140 cash or fourteen coppers (I am talking about fifteen years ago, it must be more now).

If there is a following wind, the dang-dang boats naturally hoist a sail. The sails are patched together from old clothes, old funeral hangings, flour sacks and whatnot, roughly square in shape. As the ship's hull is rather small, the sail looks disproportionately big. Its mast, located by the cabin door on the prow, is a surprisingly slender bamboo pole, which bends with the wind, and in a strong wind the sail billows out over one side of the boat. When that happens, the boat fairly races along, and the frothing sound of the water makes you think you are on a motor boat. But the timider passengers then get alarmed, because the boat is tipped to one side, with the lower side scraping the water. If the water is choppy you get spray coming into the cabin through the joins in the awning. Those sitting on the lower side find themselves forced backwards, and it is in all their minds that they will be the first in the water if the boat capsizes. Those sitting on the higher side have to exercise their muscles, stretching their legs out straight and clamping their feet to the floor; otherwise they would be ejected from their seat and end up in the lap of the passenger opposite.

Sometimes the wind blows across the boat. They still hoist their sail, but it is this moment blown out to the left, the next moment switches over to the right, with the result that the boat's course winds in and out. In those circumstances the boat is tipped now to this side, now to that, giving the passengers the impression of being on a seesaw. 'This is not the life for me,' some of them groan to themselves. For all that, the dang-dang boats very rarely have accidents. If the wind really turns nasty, the boatmen have drastic measures of their own. To illustrate, I was once on my way to Luzhi.

The wind was high, and the ballooning sail was nearly dipping into the water, but despite the bad weather the passengers were all in good spirits because of the extremely fast progress the boat was making. Then we got onto the Wusong River, which is very broad at that point. The boat steered to 'windward'. Suddenly there came hooting and howling some exceptionally fierce gusts of wind, and the sail, all wet and heavy, pulled one side of the boat out of the water. We passengers had no time even to exclaim in fright; we all clung to the awning or the seat planks for support. With a 'plop, plop', four of the boatmen jumped into the water and got a grip on the side of the boat that was tilted up, and stayed there until the boatman who had stayed on board lowered the sail. Then they climbed back on the stern and without changing their sopping wet clothes took up their sweeps and started rowing frantically.

Regarding the scheduled service boats, passengers and oarsman alike have a common philosophy, namely 'We'll get there in the end.' Since everyone will get there in the end, what's the hurry? It's not as if there is any desperately urgent business waiting to be done, so take it easy. Therefore you will see the boatmen sitting eyes closed, with a long-stemmed pipe in their mouth, from time to time remembering to draw on it; when that pipe is finished they slowly and deliberately twist together some strands of tobacco to refill the bowl, and smoke another pipe. In direct contrast to the dang-dang boatmen, very few of them are under forty. Not until they have had a good smoke do they get up, tidy the sail ropes, and brew tea for everyone. But that should not be taken as a sign that they are about to cast off, no, they still have to sit down and have a nice chin-wag. Only when the 'collector' whose job is to deliver letters and take things for people comes back to the boat is there is a little hope. Fortunately the passengers are in no rush: they turn up in ones or twos every ten minutes, or twenty-thirty minutes, and may get off the boat again to buy some snacks, or have a pot of hot tea, which will take another ten or fifteen minutes. Some people bring liquor, dried beancurd and peanuts with them, to last them their whole solitary journey. Others don't bring anything with them apart from an ever open mouth: before they have taken their seat they pick out a likely listener and start firing off. To arrive late is to them of no consequence, indeed not to arrive at all wouldn't matter either. People who are used to travelling by steamer or train should take a course in self-control before embarking on one of these boats, otherwise this cranky way of travelling will make them grumpy for at least three days.

The scheduled service boats are a lot bigger than the dang-dang boats. They are broad in the beam, and the cabins are square shaped and built of wood, not like the arched awnings of the dang-dang boats which only use reed matting. The stern shelter is also spacious, affording ample protection from rain and sun for the boatman. The front and middle cabins are the passenger area. In the front cabin you sit cross-legged; in the middle cabin there is a series of wooden planks placed crosswise, high enough for your legs to hang down when you are seated on them. But as the middle cabin is used for carrying goods too, the space below the planks is sometimes filled with bean cakes, rapeseed oil and stuff, so passengers have to sit with their feet tucked up.

The windows consist of square panels; to open the windows the whole panel has to be removed, otherwise they stay closed. Normally only one panel is opened on each side, which makes the air in the cabin somewhat fetid. If you get bored from sitting, a glance back at those old chaps rowing the boat from under the stern shelter will persuade you that your boredom is entirely trivial. The length of the arc between their push and pull is very small, no energy seems to be expended, and their eyes look unseeingly at the bank. Sustaining their position for who knows how many years and months, they have worn a footprint in the board they stand on. But they themselves do not seem to be bored: every day they follow the same old route, along which every blade of grass and every stone is familiar. When we compare our lives with theirs, we should not complain about a single boat trip being slow and tedious.

For a fast journey on the scheduled service boats you have to hope for a following wind. Their mast is a long thick pole erected between the front and middle cabins. The sail is vast, extending right to the top of the mast and supported by a large number of bamboo crosspieces. When the sail catches the wind the boat is propelled forward majestically; you have to concede they really look stylish then. A very strong wind will see the boat from Suzhou to Luzhi in as little as three and a half hours. Yet the passengers are after all of the 'we'll get there in the end' school of thought; though on such occasions they will vocally express their satisfaction with their good fortune, on the other hand they seem to object to the wind being strong and the boat fast, for they disembark with a disconsolate air. These boats suspend service when there is a head wind, unlike the dang-dang boats which pit human strength against any elements. When intending passengers get to the pier and see a lonesome boat tied up there with not a soul in sight, and conclude that the service is suspended, they turn back quite unperturbed. Since the wind will stop one day, the boat must leave one day. I who often have urgent mail for them to carry cannot be so philosophical: every time the school caretaker gives my letter back to me, saying that the boat is not leaving today, I have a whole day of restlessness to look forward to.

(1934)

My Own Patch of Green
天井裡的種植

Since we moved to Shanghai over ten years ago we have always lived in alley houses. Perhaps people in the interior don't know what alley houses are like. They are all on the same lines: the front boundary wall runs along the thoroughfare, and over the wall is an open space for common use; a number of houses make up a row; the passageway between the front and back row is called an 'alley'; a number of alleys together are called a certain 'village' or 'neighbourhood' after the landlord who owns the property. Inside the gate of each house is a well. Perhaps some people don't know what a well is. A well is a courtyard; however, the courtyards of the alley houses are very shallow: they can be crossed front to back in only three or four steps; laterally they are of the same breadth as the houses, which again is only five or six steps. Seen from the air, the name 'well' would seem peculiarly apt.

Immediately giving on to the well is the main living room. At the back of the living room a staircase rises transversely; it leads to the main bedroom upstairs and the back landing room. Due to the narrowness of the house, the staircase cannot reach the upstairs bedroom in one flight: it comes up against the wall, turns and ascends a further four or five steps before it reaches ceiling level. The 'landing room' is at the top of the first flight, so is lower than the main bedroom. Underneath the landing room is the kitchenette, and over it is the flat roof where clothes are dried—that is reached from the main bedroom by a different staircase. The landing room has got a bad name from writers in recent years as being a cramped and stuffy place to live in, but the layout of the alley houses is in fact quite admirable. As the saying goes, 'the sparrow may be small, but all its organs are complete': the alley houses come up to this economical standard.

If you live in an alley house you not only cannot plant stands of trees, you can't even plant a flower border, because the wells are all concreted over. If you want to enjoy flowers you have to grow them in pots. Normally the soil in the pots is used time and again, so its nutrients are soon used up, and there is nowhere you can get rich soil to replenish them. Hence the leaves and blooms of the pot plants are pathetically small and scrawny. Some families don't want to get their hands dirty, and at the same time can afford a small luxury, so they contract with a nursery to deliver new potted plants two or three times a month. In this way they have flowers all the year round to suit the season, with no bother to them. However, these people's interest is in not denying themselves a respectable level of decoration in their households; there is very little relation between their lives and the lives of plants. The state of the plants the nurseryman takes away shows that I do not malign them: if the leaves are not dry and yellow, the stems are bent and broken. Other people buy cut flowers from the market and put them in a vase. Not being sticklers for flower arrangement like the Japanese, they don't mind if their vases of flowers look like 'bundles of firewood' or 'magpie nests'. When the flowers die they are dumped in the rubbish bin, which is the end of the matter. Apart from 'we have flowers in our house too', it does not mean very much.

The pleasure we have in associating with plants is not at all confined to appreciating the flowers. If you look patiently at a lateral growing out or a leaf unfolding, there are constantly new configurations and colours and sheens to reward your observation. In autumn or winter at the gust of a west wind or a north wind, tree leaves fall with no show of reluctance, which seems all very dull. But if you look attentively you will see where the old leaf stem left the branch a tiny little protuberance: that is the germ of a new twig that will grow in spring.

The advent of spring can be predicted, therefore the sight of a bare branch need not make you feel deprived: you still have the expectation of a new greening next spring. Admittedly, such a thing is beneath the notice of connoisseurs. Their interest is in hunting down fine specimens of trees, and species varieties of flowers: common or garden kinds and hybrids do not merit a glance. But what does being a non-connoisseur 'amateur' matter if you can truly get enjoyment from flowering plants? That being said, there is no way you can truly get that enjoyment from buying cut flowers and sticking them in a vase, nor will getting the nurseryman to deliver a few potted plants every month do, because the time is too short—you cannot read the whole life history of a plant in them. Of course it is an improvement to cultivate pot plants yourself, but a plant in a pot is like a bird in a cage: it always looks hampered and sluggish, not itself. When all's said and done, planting in open ground is the only answer. Yet where do you get open ground? The wells of the alley houses are thick with concrete!

I often turned over in my mind the idea of getting rid of the concrete, and I shared this thought with other people. Those who had my welfare at heart came up with two objections. The first was, as it wasn't my property, it wasn't worth the trouble to prettify it with flowers and plants. The second was, I didn't know how long I would stay in this house, so was it sensible to plant a garden for my successors to look at? The first objection focused on expenditure, the second expressed concern over my getting no reward from my labours. I was not convinced by these considerations but they were both well meant, and I expressed my gratitude for them. Though I was not dissuaded, I did not take action right away. It was not until winter three years ago that I had the concrete on both sides of the well dug out, leaving only a path in the centre. Below the concrete there was a layer of rubble, which I had to get a workman to carry away in a wheelbarrow. He brought back earth from a field that was some distance away and tipped it in the hole that had been made. Four or five trips with the barrow brought the earth up level with the remaining concrete. At that point I bought a stock of plants, to wit two rose bushes, two wistarias, one red plum, and one peony rhizome. The roses and wistarias had shed their leaves, but little knobs of buds were already showing at the leaf base; the red plum was speckled with flower buds, some of which had already unfurled a petal or two; the peony rhizome was sending out pinkish shoots, like brush tips, which I found fascinating. To get them all off to a good start I bought a soybean cake from Jiangwan, dissolved it in water and spread it round the base of each plant. I had also heard that peonies needed rich fertilizer, so I first buried a pig's gut in the hole where I planted mine.

Less than two months later, the January 28th Japanese attack on the Chinese City took place. After the ceasefire I went back to pick up the pieces. The well was covered in a debris of bricks and lumber. Only a couple of branches of the plum tree protruded; some withered calyxes remained on them, but there was no sign of new leaves, so presumably it was dead. I was filled with anger and resentment; after that first glance I dismissed all thoughts of flowers and plants and such stuff from my mind.

On later reflection I decided my planting experiment really was uncalled for. It neither made another person's property pretty, nor gave my successors anything to look at. Apart from the consolation of having seen the plum halfway to flowering, I had got nothing whatever out of it. In the full sense of the words, it 'wasn't worth the trouble'—although the man who made that objection never envisaged what was actually to happen.

I moved house again last autumn. The new house was recommended by a friend. My fancy was taken the moment I walked through the outer gate, for the well of each house had only a concrete path across it, the rest being left as bare ground. No preliminary work would be needed. So after we moved in I decided to plant some things. A florist was introduced by a friend. I said I wanted a weeping willow, about as high as the upstairs balustrade. He said he could get hold of one; it would be delivered the next Sunday morning. When Sunday came all my family got up early, as if we were expecting a visitor. But the newspaper was delivered, and shopping completed at the local market, with no news of the weeping willow. We thought the florist must have taken pity on it and 'restored it to the wild', and began to resign ourselves to disappointment.

Suddenly the kids racing about in the alley started shouting 'The tree has come! The tree has come!' Three men carrying a leafy tree on their shoulders came to a halt at our door. I could tell before they set it upright that it was a poplar, not a weeping willow. Why didn't they bring a weeping willow? The willow was more laborious to plant and cost a lot more, etc. They gave me a lot of reasons. What did it matter, they argued, if the tree didn't hang down? It had the same vitality, and looked just as attractive. So I told them to plant it next to the door. It was in fact exactly as high as the upstairs balustrade. I paid the price of two dollars forty without haggling. Other people said it was too dear: in the country a poplar like that wouldn't fetch twenty cents. I didn't agree. Wasn't it worth such a small sum to pay for three men's labour to carry the tree all the way from Jiangwan, a distance of four or five miles, and to get a poplar with a big leafy crown? Even with ordinary commodities, it takes, for example, forty cents to buy a pair of socks, one dollar to buy three tins of cigarettes; leaving aside the matter of capital attracting profit, the price you pay is sure to be less than the enjoyment you get, because every article is the conversion of invaluable labour, while the price paid may be of dubious origin.

The poplar having been uprooted, three or four days after it was replanted the leaves turned yellow and hung down slackly, but the branches stayed green. Two weeks later, in late autumn, we had an unbroken spell of warm weather, which brought forth tender buds on the branches; that confirmed that we had nothing to worry about. Now we are at the end of the lunar year, and those buds have died in the cold west wind. But when the Qingming Festival comes round we will have a treeful of new foliage. By summer the dense leaves will shade our little well, taking the place of a summerhouse, which will accord with the economic principles of our household.

Besides the poplar I have planted an oleander, a green plum, a wistaria, a clump of rose bushes, a peony rhizome, and two shrubs whose name I do not know. That's not counting the little juniper that the previous tenant left. The well is small but my appetite is large. When these various things grow to their full size, they are bound to get uncomfortable with each other. I joke that I have set up an arena for a 'struggle for survival': it will be up to them to compete for 'natural selection'. That green plum has got a lot of flower buds on; tomorrow or the day after we will see some blossoms.

(1935)

Intellectuals
知識份子

Some historical researchers say that our traditional political system was 'Chinese style democracy'. Their proofs are: in our tradition, all government officials came from the civilian population; they were recruited by public examination according to quotas that embraced all regions; and new elements were admitted in batches every prescribed number of years. Hence it is clear that from early times our government was entirely constituted from the masses.

The word 'democracy' is not native to China, but came from the West. We need not examine the etymology of the word, as I believe everyone is roughly of the same opinion as to its meaning. I will simply say that we definitely cannot regard holding examinations to select a group of people to be officials as democracy, in the same way as we cannot regard a shop under sole ownership as a company organization because the owner employs a number of Zhangs and Lis as his hired help. In the traditional political system, to be an official was merely to be a hired help. Set over the hired help there was a boss, and that was the emperor. Whether it was in the glorious reigns of the Han and Tang, or in the feeble, declining years, of dynasties, the emperor 'treated the empire as his family estate'. When he ruled benignly, it was surely as an intelligent herdsman who allows his cows and sheep to graze well in order to get more milk from them. When he ruled cruelly, it was the behaviour of a prodigal son with an eye only to immediate pleasures and indulgences who does not shrink from ruining his patrimony, though it results in his own death and destruction. The idea that an emperor could 'make the empire common property', that is take the standpoint of the people at large and have their common interests at heart, is simply not imaginable. Our present notion of democracy, in contrast, is genuinely to 'make the empire common property', a company organization with every citizen a boss; it is entirely opposed to having one man as boss, with a bunch of assistants helping him to run his shop.

The historical researchers I mentioned are aware that it would be twisting the facts too much to equate China's traditional political system with our notion of democracy, and to hide their embarrassment have to resort to adding 'Chinese style', so as to fudge the issue. As to why they make this statement, if one wants to put it tactfully one could borrow Zhuang Zi's expression, 'the fog hasn't cleared from their minds'. To put it more directly, they want appointments, and to get appointments they are willing to contravene the clause in the Regulations for the Censorship of Books and Journals promulgated a few months ago which states 'It is not permitted to distort historical facts'.

However, we will let the historical researchers off the hook and turn our attention to holding office. From time immemorial holding office has been the vocation of the intellectual. Granted that by no means all officials have come from the ranks of the intellectuals, nevertheless it is a fact that the common aim of intellectuals has been to obtain office, or in other words find a boss, be his hired help, give him a hand. 'When Confucius went three months without a master he was anxious and fretful': you can see how eager he was to find a boss. Although someone like Confucius could not have had the notion of democracy as we conceive of it nowadays, because he lived in a different time, he still was mindful of the welfare of the common people, owing to his philosophy of benevolence. All the same, when he did find a boss who put his trust in him, he was inevitably placed in the position of a hired help, and had to look after the interests of his boss, or at least do nothing against his interests. And in the nature of things the boss's interests and the interests of the common people were in contradiction, that is to say the boss's interests could be served only at the expense of the common people's interests. Therefore 'to assist the sovereign to rule as well as Yao and Shun'[1] only became a dream of kind-hearted intellectuals. Whether those kings of high antiquity actually looked after the all-round interests of the common people, history offers no evidence. We only know that historians thought that after Yao and Shun there were no emperors who could compare with them. When the dream was not realized, there came the sighs of 'unused talent', there came the philosophy of 'come forth when employed, hide away when passed over'. The idea was, if I can't find a suitable boss, I am not prepared to be a hired help. Of course that didn't affect the boss in the least: he went his own sweet way, serving his interests at the expense of the common people's interests.

To be sure, it was not easy to be an official. To rise to become prime minister, with only one man above you and ten thousand men below you, was by any reckoning to reach the peak and summit of your career. Moreover, in the view of the historical researchers referred to above, the prime ministerial system was the best manifestation of 'Chinese-style democracy'. They maintain that prior to the Ming dynasty the prime minister was head of the government. The emperor's edicts had no force without the counter-signature of

---

[1] A quotation from Du Fu 杜甫, the Tang poet.

the prime minister. Hence the emperor could not be dictatorial. Yet if we look at the Han dynasty alone, there were numerous prime ministers who were sacked, killed or obliged to commit suicide. As a boss the emperor was very hard to serve: if remonstration went too far or flattery not far enough, offenders could easily find themselves in the dock. The saying that 'to be a companion to a monarch is like being a companion to a tiger' does not overstate the case. So when Shu Guang and Shu Ai obtained early retirement from the posts of tutor to Emperor Xuan of the Han dynasty, their wisdom was celebrated ever after. The fact that a certain person did not hold office in his life was worth recording in his biography, as if it was a remarkable feat. That is not to say that they had divined that the emperor's interests and the common people's interests were contradictory, and so disdained to be the emperor's assistants in defiance of the common people's interests, it is only to say they were shrewder than the average intellectual in being able to get out of the danger zone, or not get into the danger zone in the first place. Poems and compositions expressing aloofness mostly came about in this way. Songs written in the Mongol Yuan dynasty are filled with contempt for wealth and status, but their underlying message is that under foreign occupation it was more difficult than ever to be the emperor's hired help—or that you couldn't get a hired help's job if you tried.

No intellectual, it seems, has become emperor. Those down the ages who conquered the empire or usurped the throne were not intellectuals. That is because the intellectual had no real power: his prescribed role was that of the hired help. Given that role, even if he believed in the brotherhood of man, and pledged to work in the all-round interests of the common people, he had to ditch those ideas when he ran up against the obstacle of his boss. The Neo-Confucian Zhang Zai's four-clause doctrine was: 'Carry out the will of Heaven and Earth; fulfil the destiny of living beings; revive the teachings of former sages; establish the Great Harmony for all future generations.' Grand words to match grand ambitions. We will pass over the first three clauses and concentrate on the fourth. What is meant by Great Harmony? To our mind it should refer to all the common people enjoying a good life. 'The common people' is not an abstract notion: it means your Zhangs and Lis and countless other people of flesh and blood. 'A good life' is not an empty phrase: it means really and actually enjoying a reasonable level of material and spiritual life. Imagine, would the kind of Great Harmony which would entail the Zhangs and Lis and countless other people enjoying such a life be acceptable to the emperor and his hired help? If it were truly 'established', would there continue to be a place for the emperor and his hired help? It is obvious that the 'four clause doctrine' was only an incantation to occupy the lips and minds of the Neo-Confucian philosophers; the Great Harmony could never be established, and hardship remained the lot of the common people.

A hired help proved himself by assisting the emperor. If the emperor wanted a way cleared he helped clear a way; if heavy taxes were to be levied, he helped levy taxes; if the emperor wanted to promote the arts he turned out verses, and studied the classics and histories; if filial piety was to be the key to governing the empire, he was a strong advocate of filial piety. Such people were not necessarily given the highest rating, but in their own time they could be sure of achieving eminence and enjoying a life of luxury. However, all that had nothing to do with the all-round interests of the common people, because their interests simply did not enter into the equation: they were only there to assist the emperor. Take Sima Guang for instance. The Song emperor Shenzong accorded the study of history he compiled the title 'Comprehensive Mirror to Aid Governance'. Do not the words 'aid governance' show that this was a reference work for the emperor? Naturally Sima Guang was a good hired help. Then there is Wang Anshi. His radical New Policy could not be implemented, but he is regarded nowadays as a great politician. We will not dispute whether he was a great politician or not, we will only ask if in planning his New Policy he was calculating the benefit to the house of Song or thinking of the all-round interests of the common people. I would think he could only be said to have been a good hired help of Emperor Shenzong, and not to have represented any interests of the common people. If you wanted to be an official, either a good one or a bad one, you had only one choice and that was to take the side of the emperor. If you took the side of the emperor, of course you could not at the same time take the side of the common people. To make a somewhat sweeping statement, there has never been an official in our history who has taken the side of the common people.

Because a bunch of people were selected by examination to be officials and act as the hired help of the emperor, to say this was democracy would not deceive a child. Yet this is precisely the trick some people are trying to pull. I don't know how they could be so stupid.

That age has passed, the emperors have gone, the name of the state has changed to Republic, but judging by the spirit of the educational world, they are still intent on turning out a lot of hired hands, and looking at the majority of intellectuals, it is still the countenance of the hired hand one sees. Actually this is not a question of whether democracy can or cannot be realized or whether the common people can or cannot become the boss. When the time is ripe there will come a sea change; then what should be will be, what is to be done will be done. It will be the intellectuals who maintain the traditional spirit of the hired help and meet change with inertia who will find there is no niche for them to settle into.

(1944)

TRANSLATOR'S AFTERWORD

I have included this essay to show another side to Ye Shengtao and also because it borders on a different kind of essay, namely the *zawen* or polemical essay. As before, Ye's medium is plain words, but otherwise there are few identifying characteristics. Compositionally it is dominated by the well tried mechanism of the *zawen*, the hammering away at an opposition the author sets up in an attempt to prejudge the issue by nomenclature. Incidentally, I had trouble with the word I have rendered as 'hired help': the word in question, *huoji*, is used of shop assistants mainly, but also of other hired labour. I had to resist the temptation to translate it as 'flunky', although that was clearly the implication, because that would have been too prejudicial even for this essay. 'Assistants' on the other hand would have been too general. Intellectually the argument that the officials under the empire were 'hired help' is hardly more respectable than the argument that they were 'democrats' which the essay seeks to overturn. One has to allow for the fact, though, that in the warfare between the left and the right being waged at the time, weapons tended to be blunt.

One has to admire Ye Shengtao's prescience of the fate of Chinese intellectuals after the Communist victory, if that was the 'sea change' he foresaw. What he apparently did not foresee was that the intellectuals would be persuaded to become more docile servants of the new regime than they had been of any old one. It is also ironic that the prefix 'Chinese style' found new life in the People's Republic.

Feng Zikai 豐子愷 (1898-1975)

COMMENTARY

Feng Zikai was born and lived most of his life in Zhejiang province. His father, who died when Feng was nine, held the *juren* degree, comparable to Master of Arts. In 1914 Feng entered the Zhejiang Number One Teachers Training College in Hangchow. There he acquired two mentors for life: Xia Mianzun, who taught Chinese, and Li Shutong 李叔同, who taught music and fine art. On graduation in 1919 Feng joined with fellow graduates in setting up a training college for music, drawing and handicrafts. In 1921 he went to Japan for ten months, where he studied Western painting and music, and learned some Japanese and English. After his return to China he taught painting and music at a variety of schools and colleges, holding several posts simultaneously, as was common at that time. At two of the schools he was the colleague of his former teacher, Xia Mianzun, namely Chunhui Middle School, and Lida School, mentioned in Xia's essays 'White Horse Lake' and 'An Iron Mountain'.

The years from 1922 to 1933 were the busiest in Feng's life. His drawings, given the name 'cartoons' (*manhua*) by the editor, began to be published in the leading literary journal *Wenxue zhoubao* 文學週報 in 1925; they brought him immediate fame. He also started contributing essays to the journal in the same year. His first book of essays was published in 1931 under the title *Yuanyuan tang suibi* 緣緣堂隨筆(Essays from the House of Affinities). In this period Feng also wrote on Western musicology.

In 1933 Feng withdrew to his hometown of Shimenwan, where he had a house built to his own design, and devoted himself to writing and drawing. His cartoons of his children (often up to monkey business) with their perfectly apt legends done in his own inimitable calligraphy, are absolute classics. Feng had no equal in capturing these and other lighter moments in life. But this idyllic existence of his came to an end with the war launched by Japan in 1937. His house was destroyed in 1938, by which time he was on his way to the unoccupied interior. He stopped briefly in Guilin, and went on to Yishan in 1939, where he taught at Zhejiang University, which was in flight like himself. In 1942 he settled in Chongqing (Chungking) until the end of the war, selling his paintings for an income.

After the People's Republic was set up in 1949, Feng held a succession of posts in the cultural bureaucracy in Shanghai, for which recognition and reward he paid the price in the Cultural Revolution. He died three years after he was rehabilitated in 1972.

In his cartoons and in his essays Feng Zikai celebrated innocence: innocent pleasures, innocent absorption at work or leisure, natural and unselfconscious behaviour. When he carried his innocence abroad, however, he had no defence against the wicked world. That was where his other mentor, Li Shutong, came in. Li took the cloth of a Buddhist monk in 1918, and later attained eminence and a certain celebrity as Master Hongyi 弘一法師. Feng Zikai followed him into the Buddhist faith in 1927, adopting the religious name Yingxing 嬰行, 'The Performance of Infancy'. The fact of his conversion did not lead to his work being permeated with religiosity, far from it, but it is helpful for understanding some of his essays, particularly 'Autumn', translated here. In a more general and pervasive sense, too, his faith has its relevance for appreciating his essays, because if you put it together with his innocence, you have a kind of 'holy innocence'. Shorn of its unpleasant associations, 'holy innocent' may indeed describe the personality that his essays project. To take a leaf from the Buddhist book, it is as if the author, having lived a blameless life in some medieval rural community, had skipped a number of reincarnations, and been reborn straight into the 20th century. He finds he can love simple souls, but cannot cope with modern uncivilization. From our point of view as readers, the great boon from this is that his every experience is a discovery.

Eating Melon Seeds
吃瓜子

I have heard it said that all Chinese people qualify for a doctoral degree in three respects: using chopsticks, blowing on spills, and eating melon seeds.

Using chopsticks, blowing on spills and eating melon seeds are indeed skills of which Chinese people have unique mastery. The deftness and refinement with which they are practised can be astonishing. The masters of the chopsticks among us can use a pair of chopsticks to do the jobs of knives, saws, forks, ladles and such implements for scraping, raking, digging and picking, and more besides, all expertly. Those two sticks of bamboo are like parts of the body, extensions of the fingers, or like a pair of tentacles for food gathering. In action they resemble the tricks of the magicians; practice makes perfect, and the peak of perfection passes into the supernatural. Even we ourselves are awestruck, let alone Westerners.

As to the experts at blowing on spills, pride of place goes to the old gentlemen and ladies who cradle water pipes in their hands all day long. Their 'Let there be fire' is even easier than God's: they only need to blow lightly on the spill for the flame to come. To them the outlay of several dollars or even tens of dollars on the purchase of a lighter is quite unnecessary; a sheet of paper suffices. They roll the paper on their knees into a spill as and when required, stick it through the hole in the lid of a copper stove, pull it out and blow on it, and there the flame is. I remember from my childhood the book-keeper in our dye works demonstrating many special skills in spill blowing. I would hold a spill up level with his forehead, and he would push out his lower lip and blow air upwards; I held the spill level with his chest, and he pushed out his upper lip, and blew air downwards; I held the spill by his ear, and he blew air left or right out of the corner of his mouth; I put my hand over his mouth and he blew through his nose. The spill always caught fire after one or two blows. That will give some idea of the great attainments of the Chinese in the art of spill blowing. The pity is, since cigarettes and matches were imported into China and became popular, the 'national smoke' of the water pipe has fallen into neglect, and the 'national art' of spill blowing has gone into decline. Children who grew up in the cities actually don't learn how to blow, and some have even never seen a spill. Those who strive to preserve the national essence will look upon this as a worrisome phenomenon. In recent years quite a number of people have been striving to preserve the national essence. Chinese doctoring, Chinese medicine, Chinese boxing, Chinese music—all these have their advocates. Perhaps the national artefacts of water pipe and paper spill will in future find their advocates and be revived.

However, I think that the most progressive and highly developed of the three arts is eating melon seeds. The proof of this is the booming sales of 'king melon seeds' presently in the shops. According to those who take an interest in these things, melon seeds of the king variety have been marketed under multiple brand names in paper packets. The first to appear was 'created by scientific methods' by a certain big pharmacy; they were followed by a string of products of the Very Tasty Company, Scrumptious Company, and what have you. By now these packaged melon seeds are displayed on confectionery stalls even in the back of beyond, and do a roaring trade. From this we may deduce that the modern day Chinese are expert in the art of melon seed eating. I personally am very deficient in this line of country, to confess which is bad for Chinese prestige, but as we are among friends there is no harm in elaborating a little.

Feng Zikai

I have never voluntarily sought out or bought melon seeds. But on the urging of the host when I visit people's homes, or at banquets, or in Hangzhou's tea houses, when I see bowls of melon seeds ready placed on tables, I do pick them up and bite them. I have to choose carefully, picking out the larger, thicker, straighter and more evenly shaped melon seeds; these I place in my mouth, 'crack' between my molars, eject, and shell with my fingers. If I am fortunate enough to bite them in the right place, the two leaves of the shell split outwards without breaking the kernel, and the shelling is an easy job. If the pressure of the teeth is wrong, the two leaves of the shell fold in on the kernel and break off, which creates misery for me. The melon seed is broken in two horizontally, and the two halves of the kernel are forced tightly into the two leaves of the shell; like the Japanese hardbound books that come in very tight cardboard cases, they are very hard to extricate. I have now learned from Japanese people the way to extricate these hardbound books: you should not try to tug them out of the cardboard case forcibly, you should turn the open end of the case downwards, hold the case on either side, shake up and down, and the book will emerge from its shell by itself. However, this method is not applicable to the halves of a melon seed, on account of their smallness, so I can only shell them by picking at them with my finger-nails. When I am practising on the piano, I cut my finger-nails short, and fingertips as smooth as a monk's pate are simply not up to the job. I have to discard the seeds when no one is looking. At such times of acute distress I make up my mind to stop eating melon seeds. Yet after I give them up, I feel a kind of not-sweet and not-salty fragrance in my mouth which tempts me to go on. So despite myself I stretch out my hand to choose another seed, and commit it to my molars for biting. If I am out of luck and this seed is too dry and my bite too violent, the good and the bad perish together with a 'crack', my mouth is filled with little bits, and I am in a worse pickle than ever. All I can do is spit the saliva soaked fragments into the palm of my hand, make a careful choice, push aside the bits of shell, and lick up with my tongue the bits of kernel. But this choice is quite hard, because the inside of the bits of shell is also white, like the kernel, and I will mistake all the white as kernel, and lick it up and chew it; though its taste will not be as bad as the proverbial wax, it will still be like chewing grit. The bits of shell will embed themselves in the crevices between my teeth, and if there are no toothpicks handy they won't come out. When I am thus thwarted, I resolve to forsake melon seeds forthwith. The way I forsake them is mostly to rinse my mouth with tea and light a cigarette, or push the dish of melon seeds aside and shift my sitting position to face away from them, to express cessation of commerce with them. Nevertheless, after a few minutes of conversation with someone, without realizing what I am doing I stretch out my hand like them and feel in the bowl for a melon seed to bite. By the time I am aware I have broken my vow of abstention I have usually already cracked quite a few seeds. In this way, having eaten I have to abstain, and having abstained I have to eat; this endless cycle of eating and abstaining, abstaining and eating has caused me great distress, with the result that the mere thought of melon seeds now quite perturbs me.

Yet I notice that many other people are very well up in this skill. Of the three professional abilities of Chinese people, I would say the ability of cracking melon seeds is the most to be wondered at. One often sees idle young gentlemen with a cigarette between the fingers of one hand, and a handful of melon seeds in the other, in turn smoking and biting, biting and eating, eating and talking, talking and laughing: all very free and easy, truly 'a picture of nonchalance'! They have no need to pick and choose the melon seeds, or to shell them with their fingers. Once a melon seed is popped in their mouth, all it takes is 'crack', one bite, 'plop', one spit, and the whole shell is ejected and the eating proceeds apace. Their mouths are like very ingenious and sensitive machines: melon seeds are ceaselessly fed into them and they keep on going 'crack', 'plop', 'crack', 'plop' . . . entirely effortlessly, without ever needing to shut down.

Women and young ladies have a particularly attractive manner of cracking melon seeds. They hold the melon seed with their orchid-like fingers by its round sides, place it vertically between their front teeth, and bite its pointed ends. With a 'dik-dik', the points of the shell leaves split open to left and right. Then their hand nimbly changes direction and their head at the same time slightly inclines in support, so that the melon seed lies horizontally in the gap between the front teeth. The upper and lower front teeth press together to make the two leaves of the shell spring apart, then get a grip on the end of the kernel to pull it out, when it is eaten. In this manner of eating, not only is the crisp 'dik-dik' sound pleasing to the ear, the turn and poise of the hand and head is also very charming, indeed rather seductive. Even the discarded melon seed shells look pretty, lying there like so many orchids. So we may conclude that cracking melon seeds is an accomplishment of young Chinese gentlemen, and more especially a starring role of Chinese women and young ladies.

I have seen countless masters of the art of cracking melon seeds at banquets and in tea houses. And with the recent boom in sales of 'king melon seeds', young children of my nation have also acquired amazing skill in cracking melon seeds. Since my own ability is far inferior to that of children at home, I can only enjoy superiority in comparison with foreigners. I remember once sharing a cabin with a Japanese on a boat bound to Yokohama. Going through my luggage I discovered a tin of melon seeds a friend or relative had given me. To relieve the tedium of the voyage I opened it to share the contents with the Japanese. He had never eaten melon seeds in his life, so found these of rare interest. I brazenly pretended to be an old hand at the game, explained how they were eaten, and gave him a demonstration. My ancestors must have been watching over me, for the demonstration did not fail. But the attempt of the Japanese was really pitiful! He placed the melon seed correctly in his mouth, and bit it with a 'crack', but the bite went awry and the whole husk of the seed was saturated in his saliva, so that when he took it in his hand and tried to shell it, it slithered this way and that, eluding his grasp; finally it slipped onto the floor, beyond recovery. He swallowed his saliva and tried again. This time he took extreme care in the shelling, spreading the bits of melon seed on the cabin table, bending his head right over them, and prising the shell open intricately, as if he were repairing a watch. After a minute or two he had painfully extricated some pieces of kernel. He put them gravely in his mouth and chewed. When I asked him the taste he nodded his head and said repeatedly *Umai, umai*! (delicious!). I had to laugh. Putting those crumbs of kernel into his big mouth was like tossing a grain of rice into the sea: good for him if he could detect the taste of *umai*! But my laughing was not merely because of this comedy, it actually derived from my own pride and boastfulness. I thought to myself, you must admit this a skill peculiar to the Chinese: if someone as cack-handed as me could triumph over foreigners, think how well those countless experts of young gentlemen and ladies at home would do!

The person who thought of eating melon seeds was a veritable genius. There is no more effective way of 'killing time'. Apart from smoking opium there is nothing to rival it. The reason that it is most effective is that it meets three conditions: one, you don't get tired of eating; two, you can't get full from eating; three, you have to remove the husk.

The common expression for not getting tired of eating melon seeds is 'no stopping, no resting'. Because they have a kind of not-sweet and not-salty fragrance they can tempt you to keep on eating. You may decide to stop after the next one, but after you have chewed and swallowed it, a fragrance lingers in the mouth that makes you unable to resist feeling for another one in the dish or paper bag. It may be noticed of our eating habits that a consistent diet of sweet or salty things brings on satiety. Only non-sweet and non-salty things cannot be had enough of. That is the basis of the perpetual appeal of melon seeds. A friend much given to socializing told me an amusing anecdote relating to his habit of dipping into melon seeds. He once went with a friend to a playhouse, and after taking his seat saw an opened bag of melon seeds next to his teapot. He reached into the bag, fished out some seeds, and ate them as he watched the play. Having finished those he replenished his supply, and the process was repeated several times before he discovered that his neighbour, a stranger to him, was also dipping into the bag. Only then did he consider the ownership of this bag of melon seeds. He asked his friend quietly, 'Did you buy this bag of melon seeds?' The friend said 'No.' Realizing that he had unlawfully consumed another's refreshments, he apologized to his neighbour. The neighbour behaved handsomely, brushing the matter off with a laugh, and made him an honest man by inviting him formally to partake the melon seeds. All of which shows that melon seeds have an uncommon attraction for Chinese people: when they see melon seeds they eat them, and ask no questions.

The common expression for not getting full from eating melon seeds is 'you eat for three days and three nights, and grow a tip on a turd'. Because the thing is so insubstantial, there is no way you can fill your stomach, so even if you eat nonstop for three days and nights, it only amounts to a particle on the end of a turd when you excrete. This is a very important requirement for passing the time. If the bulk is large and it fills you straightaway, then it is of no use for killing time.

The aim is the opposite from that of food for famine relief. Food for famine relief aims to fill the stomach; food for passing the time aims not to fill the stomach. The ideal is to get taste without consuming substance, and to get hungrier the more you eat: just like the 'regurgitants' popular in the last days of the Roman Empire, you have a big nosh-up and after you are bloated and drunk, a course of melon seeds prepares you for another big nosh-up, and thus you can continue to kill time.

The need to remove the shell is another essential condition for food to pass the time. If there is no shell, the eating is too convenient, you are quickly satisfied, and the scope for passing the time is greatly reduced. You must remove the shell, and the performance of shelling must have sound and colour, to make it resemble an amusement rather than a chore. Otherwise it would not suit the life-style of the leisured classes, and they would not be able to continue to pass the time pleasurably.

After racking my brains to think of foodstuffs which fully meet the above requirements for killing time, there is only one in the world I can come up with, and that is melon seeds. That is why I said the person who discovered them was a veritable genius. And the Chinese, who enjoy melon seeds to the full, are truly wonderful exponents of the profession of killing time. Consider the roaring trade in melon seeds done by confectionery shops and southern food shops, consider the melon seed husks that cover the floors of teashops, wineshops and homes, and it is obvious that the amount of time killed amid the sound of 'crack, plop' and 'dik-dik' in the course of a year is staggering. If in future this profession expands further, I fear that the whole of China will go to extinction amid the sound of 'crack, plop' and 'dik-dik'.

I said to begin with that the sight of melon seeds perturbs me. At this point I am more perturbed than ever.

(1934)

Autumn
秋

It is now two years since my year of age carried the prefix 'thirty'. Never one to take things philosophically, I have felt the influence and intimations of this word in several ways. Though I am fully aware that in health and spirits I am in no way different from what I was at the age of twenty-nine, this notion of 'thirty' hangs over my head. It is like the opening of a parasol that casts one in dark shade, or like the tearing off of the page that marks the first day of autumn from the calendar: although the sun's power has not diminished, and the thermometer's reading has not dropped, one thinks of it only as fading strength or swan song, or as the prelude to frost and leaf-fall; from now on the natural world has shifted to the autumn season.

In truth my mood over the last two years has been of a kind to harmonize or blend with autumn. This is a change. In years gone by I only hankered after spring. I loved willows and swallows. Especially the young willow wands newly tinged with gosling yellow. I named my lodging 'Little Willow Hut', and did lots of paintings of willows and swallows, and also cut slender willow shoots and mounted them on cartridge paper as different styles of eyebrows, imagined the faces that would go with those eyebrows, and sketched in eyes, nose and mouth below them. At the first signs of spring in those days, around the end of the first month by the lunar calendar, when I saw tiny knobs breaking the smooth lines of the willow branches, with a suggestion of green that seemed to vanish close up, my heart was filled with delirious joy. But this joy immediately turned to anxiety, as if I was always telling myself: 'Spring has come! Don't let it go by! Quick, think how to entertain it, enjoy it, keep it with you for ever.' I had been genuinely moved by such lines as 'The golden hour, the beautiful scene, alas the ravages of time'; I took to heart the lesson of our forebears when they sighed over spring passing neglected. Now it was in my hands, I vowed it should not go by in vain! When the Qingming Festival, that time of deepest sorrowing for our forefathers, came round, my anxiety was intensified. I always wanted to make that day an occasion, so as to render fitting tribute to the season. I planned to write poems, do paintings, or go on a binge or an excursion. Although most of those plans were not carried out, or if carried out proved entirely fruitless, resulting adversely in drunken stupor, disturbances, and unhappy memories, yet I was never discouraged, and always felt spring was lovable.

To my mind spring was the only season. The other three were either the preparation for spring, or the interval when spring was awaited. I completely ignored their existence and meaning. I was especially indifferent to autumn, because summer succeeded spring, and I could see it as spring taken to excess; winter preceded spring, and so could be seen as making ready for spring; but autumn had no connection at all with spring, and so had no place in my mind.

In the two years since my year of age reached the start of autumn on life's calendar my mindset has had an entirely different orientation: it has become autumn too. But my state is different from what it was, I do not feel in autumn the extravagant joy and anxiety of former days. I just feel when autumn comes round that my state of mind is perfectly attuned to it. Not only has that joy and anxiety left me, I am often drawn by autumn wind, autumn rain, autumn colours and shades, into melting into the season, and losing for a time my own identity. What's more, my attitude to spring is not the indifference that I formerly felt for autumn. I now detest spring. Whenever the myriad signs of spring appear, and I see the beauty pageant of flowers, the bustle of bees and butterflies, and everywhere the mad rush of plants, insects and other things to multiply and procreate, it seems to me that nothing could better illustrate the vulgarity, greed, shamelessness and senselessness of this world. Particularly when in the first flush of spring I see the hint of green knobs on the willow branches, and the speckling of red petals on the peach trees, I find it both ridiculous and pathetic. I want to wake up a flower bud and tell it, 'So, you've come too to replay that old refrain! I've seen with my own eyes countless ancestors of yours being born like you, and striving each and every one to outdo the others in splendour; not one of them hasn't withered and turned to dust. What is the point of you too repeating that old refrain? Born into sin, what does the future hold? You'll drink and posture and play the flirt, and what you'll get for your trouble is being trampled and crushed and broken off, the same fate as all your ancestors suffered!'

To face facts, someone who has welcomed and seen off thirty-odd springs gets thoroughly fed up with the business of flowers: his senses are numbed, his passion is cooled. He will not be bewitched like a young virgin seeing the world for the first time by the magic of flowers, and praise them, sigh over them, take pity on them, mourn them. For of all things under the sun there is not one that escapes the law of flowering and fading, growing and decaying, living and dying, being and not being. Past history amply proves this point; we need not say more. Countless poets down the ages have written reams of verses, all alike, to express their sorrow at the passing of spring and their regret over the fading of flowers. This aping of each other is detestable. If I were to waste words myself on the subject of birth and ripening, death and extinction, it would be to say that birth and ripening are not worth mentioning; my praise goes to death and extinction. Compared with the greed, stupidity and spinelessness of the former, how modest, enlightened and dignified is the attitude of the latter! My preference for autumn over spring is based on that.

Natsume Suseki said this when he was thirty: 'Twenty years into life I learned the value of being alive; at twenty-five I learned that where there is light there must be darkness; now at thirty I know even better that where there is much light there is also much darkness, and when joy is abundant sorrow is also heavy.' I now deeply sympathize with this view. At the same time I feel that this is not the only facet of being thirty; a more particular one is the sense of death. When young people are thwarted in love they like to talk about death and dying, but that is only knowledge of the thing called death, not the sense of it. It is similar to not being able to sense what it is like to sit round a winter fire huddled in blankets when one is drinking iced drinks and fanning onself on a summer's day. Even we who have known thirty-odd changes of seasons could not in the recent heatwave get the sense of a nice crisp dawn. Things like crisp dawns, winter fires and huddling in blankets are just abstract data in the mind of people in the middle of summer: they merely know that such things lie in the future, but cannot experience the sensation of them. One has to wait for autumn, when the broiling sun has displayed its might and is gradually receding and flesh which has been swelled with sweat gradually draws in, when the wearing of unlined clothes inclines one to shiver and flannel is pleasant to the touch, for the knowledge of crisp dawns, winter fires and huddling in blankets to gradually enter the realm of experience and become sensation.

After my year of age reached the start of autumn, the most special state of mind it gave me was indeed this sensation of 'death'. How shallow were my thoughts prior to that! I believed that spring could be our constant companion, that man could stay forever young, and actually never thought of death. And I believed that the meaning of human life was only in living, and my own life was most meaningful; it seemed I couldn't die. Only now, with the benefit of the illumination of autumn rays, and under the benign influence of the spirit of death, have I comprehended that life's sweetness and bitterness, joys and sorrows are an old refrain that has been played billions of times under our skies, and are nothing to treasure. I seek only peaceful passage through and release from this life. To make a comparison, if a person suffers from madness, it is pointless to try to make anything of his confusion and delusions: one hopes only to rid him of his sickness.

As I lay down my pen, I see from my western window black clouds filling the sky, a flash of lightning on the horizon, and hear a faint rumble of thunder. A sudden shower of autumn rain mixed with hail pours down. Oh! So few days after the start of autumn, while the autumn mind is still young and green, it turns out that such discordance occurs: it scares me!

(1929)

Bombs in Yishan
宜山遇炸記

The first time Yishan was bombed would have been in the autumn of 1938, when I was in Guilin. It was said the target was Zhejiang University, and countless bombs were dropped. The university dormitories were out in Biaoying, a district which is criss-crossed by ditches, and the students knew what to do in air raids. By lying low in the ditches, they escaped without a single casualty. One student, however, was suffering from a mental illness; in his deranged condition, he refused to take cover, and stayed in a building that was bombed. The shock brought an immediate end to his symptoms, and he afterwards was restored to health and was able to resume classes. His story was often told at Zhejiang University, as a matter for celebration.

I encountered the second bombing, which took place in the summer of 1939. This time, though, it was anything but a matter for celebration. Quite a lot of people were killed near the bus station, quite a lot injured, and quite a lot more were frightened out of their wits. Ever afterwards I blanched at the sound of an iron wok lid being banged, or the hiss of steam from a kettle. I was such a bundle of nerves that when the old lady next door called her little boy Jingbao, I used to think she was shouting 'Jingbao' (Air raid warning!), and was poised to jump to my feet and run for cover. Now that it is over and I can lick my wounds, I still get angry at the thought of the vileness of the Japanese warlords. Thankfully, our final victory has been won, the Japanese have surrendered, and their warlords are being executed. And I have come through safe and sound. If I look back here on bygone days, it may actually help to lay some old ghosts and contribute to the festive mood.

We ran into trouble when we first arrived in Yishan. When the Zhejiang University bus carrying my own family of ten and a few other passengers, plus a load of baggage, got to the East Gate we were stopped by two policemen, who said an air raid alert was in force and we weren't allowed into the city. That explained why the gate was completely deserted. The driver immediately turned the bus round and drove back a mile or so, stopping under a big tree out in the country. We all got out and sat on some rocks in a gully. By then it was past noon, and stomachs were rumbling. Luckily we had a basket of *zongzi* to stave off our hunger.[1] It happened to be the Qingming holiday time, and though we were travelling we still kept to our old custom of making some 'Qingming zongzi' to take with us. So now all of us, that is my whole family of ten, the driver and the other passengers, tucked into the *zongzi* and sat around talking. The sun was shining, the breeze was gentle, the day was perfect. If we had been able to forget we were in Yishan taking cover from an air raid, and imagine we were picnicking by the West Lake in Hangzhou, that afternoon would have been pure bliss! The whole family mustered, from the two-year-old to the over seventies, out on a spring excursion, and a few friends along besides—how exhilarating, how civilized! Alas, the sad truth is that in this life we are sometimes obliged to make believe like that.

When we had finished the *zongzi* the sun was slanting in the sky, as if to tell us we could enter the city now. Thereupon we got back on the bus and headed back. This time we were indeed allowed to go through the East Gate. But no sooner had we alighted than a crowd of people started rushing in our direction. When we asked in alarm what was up, we discovered it was another air raid alert! Being newcomers we did not know the geography of the place, and had to

---

[1] *Zongzi* are little packets of sticky rice with meat and vegetable flavouring wrapped in bamboo leaves; they are normally eaten during the Dragon Boat Festival.

flee blindly in the wake of the crowd. Our children and old folk were not very mobile, so they made for the nearest cover of a thicket outside the East Gate. I fled with other people across the river and hid in a cave. The all clear did not sound till it was nearly dark. Fortunately when we got back to the bus we found the luggage was all still intact, and the rest of the family eventually straggled back, all accounted for. Then we had to find lodgings and somewhere to eat. We did not get to bed till late at night. We learned that there had been three alerts that day, those that we encountered being the second and third. We were also told that the thickets outside the East Gate concealed the station and the military command post. These would have been the prime targets for the bombers. Imagine, my family was hiding from an air raid right in the target area!

Our relationship with Yishan was measured in air raid alerts: we became acquainted in the middle of one and afterwards parted in one. In between we had alerts practically every day, and experienced one bombing.

To begin with we lived over the Kaiming Bookshop in town. Later on we could not put up with all the running about occasioned by the great number of air raid alerts, so we rented a small cottage some distance from the city, and the family moved out, leaving me and one small son in the Kaiming Bookshop. One day—it happened to be market day—I was idly gazing down from an upstairs window on the hawkers' pitches at the roadside when I saw a crepe fabric seller suddenly pack up his goods. The hawker on the neighbouring pitch, without inquiring into the reason why, did likewise. A third followed suit, then a fourth, and in no time all the hawkers along the street were packing up, telling each other 'It's an air raid!' They all made off helterskelter in search of safety. Quite befogged, I took my son downstairs to look for shelter myself. But once outside, I found everyone all smiles. In fact there was no air raid warning; it was only much ado about nothing. The alarm was sparked off, it transpired, by the fabric seller packing up early for reasons of his own. His movements were quite hasty and abrupt, which led the hawker next to him to think an air raid was coming, with the farcical consequences I have described. As the old saying goes, if three people say there is a tiger, there is a tiger. But behind the farce could be seen the real fear of air raids at that time. I found it impossible to settle down to anything in this jittery atmosphere, where people were afraid of their own shadows, so I took my son to join the rest of the family in the cottage in the country.

This thatched cottage was pitifully small: just three rooms, each ten feet square. We needed to buy two bunk beds to sleep the ten of us. The beds doubled as seats, the dining table doubled as a desk, without too much trouble. If you looked upon it as a boat rather than a house, it was in fact rather spacious. And there was the scenery as well: pavilion, terrace, escarpment, hills, stands of bamboo. These were originally the Dragon Ridge Gardens, and where we lived was originally the gardener's cottage. The escarpment was quite rugged, with lots of clefts and fissures. We hid in those clefts during the air raid alerts. At the first alarm we all stayed put, and waited for the emergency alert before taking cover in the clefts. But the enemy planes never came, and every time we returned peacefully to our little cottage. But later on, some days before the fall of Nanning, the neighbouring county was bombed and Yishan took fright. We ourselves came to think the rock clefts gave inadequate protection, and we ought to find a safer refuge. But inertia prevailed and we did nothing about it.

One day I fully intended to go out and look for a cave, but the weather was quite unsettled, alternating very oddly between sunshine and rain. Everyone said it was unlikely there would be an alert. My native indolence persuaded me to put off my expedition. Suddenly the alarm bell sounded. The people taking flight past our house seemed unusually panicky, and the changing of the bell was unusually ominous. On top of that, the emergency alert followed swiftly. I had to stop an acquaintance of mine to find out that reliable report had it that the enemy planes were especially active that day, and the chances were Yishan would be bombed.

Applying the test of air raid alerts to my family, they could be divided into two factions: the bold faction, namely my wife, my mother-in-law, and the youths over sixteen; and the timid faction, my older sister and the two girls. I could be said to be sandwiched in between, belonging to no faction; or you could say I was a fence-sitter, a misfit, or a member of both factions, because after a drink I belonged to the bold faction, but before I'd had a drink I belonged to the timid faction. That day the bold faction took cover in the nearby rock clefts. As I hadn't had a drink I joined the timid faction in going further afield.

Going further afield did not mean we had a safer objective in mind, it was just a belief akin to that of people who bought joss-sticks to worship the Buddha, namely, 'to fork out money is a virtue in itself'. Likewise we thought to go further afield must be a good thing in itself. We happened to fall in with some people we knew who were making resolutely for the open fields; they assured us there were caves up ahead. So we pushed on with our guides, getting bootfuls of water. Our cross-country trek ended in a spot where there really was a formation of towering rocks, and we hurriedly searched for the cave. These rocks were in the shape of a V laid out horizontal on the ground, allowing you to pass through the open end to the apex, but there was no cover overhead—actually it was no cave at all! Still, by this stage we could not move on elsewhere; if we were to die, we would die here.

Lots of men and women squeezed into the V. I crouched at the mouth of the V. Now able to take in the surroundings, I uttered an exclamation of dismay. In fact we were only a few hundred feet from the prime targets of the station and the sports field! It was a whole lot more dangerous here than among the rocks of the Dragon Ridge Garden. As I was getting all worked up I heard a heavy droning noise, and the people in the V shouted, 'The Jap bombers are coming!' whereupon they all ducked down and camouflaged themselves with the ferns that sprouted from the rocks. What was I to do, stuck outside the opening, with no protection at all? Suddenly I spotted on the outer slope of the V formation a slight depression overgrown with ferns. On the inspiration of desperation, I laid myself flat in the hollow underneath the ferns.

I lay still and watched the sky through the leaves of the ferns above me. A squadron of enemy bombers appeared in the distant sky heading towards me, the drone of their engines growing louder all the time. I thought to myself, there are only three possible outcomes today: one, I will get up and go home unharmed; two, I will be injured and be carried to hospital; three, I will be killed in this hollow. Any way, I had to take what came. I seemed to see one of those shakers used for drawing lots in front of me, with three spills in it: one marked 1, one marked 2, one marked 3. I stretched out my hand and drew one. . . .

As this thought was going through my mind, three bombers came up over my head. Suddenly they slowed and hovered. Then a black spherical object fell from the aircraft straight towards me. I could not bear to look, and covered my face, waiting for it to explode. First there came a whistling noise, followed by a 'crump'. The earth shook and the rocks shook. The blast lifted me from the ground. Yet I seemed not to have been injured. Peeping out, all I could see was a spreading pall of smoke, and the three planes circling over it. Another black spherical object fell from a plane, and a second whistled down from a different plane. The objects were right overhead. I covered my face with my hands, and heard 'crump', 'crump' all around me.

I pictured a bomb landing right in the middle of the V, going off bang, and all of us—men, women, young and old—blown to smithereens in a flash: an end like this would have been clean and straightforward, and would have put us out of our misery at least. But the latest bombs did not do that: they just demoralized us with their more powerful blasts. This proved the bombs were getting closer, and our danger was increasing. Suddenly I heard a woman howl from inside the V, followed by the sound of whimpering. I could not work out what was going on. Fortunately the enemy planes were moving on, the drone of their engines fading. We all began to breathe again. I got up, covered in dust, and crept over to the opening of the V. They were surprised to see me, not knowing where I had got to, or whether I was safe or not. Seeing them all unscathed, I asked why the howl. It turned out there was a wasp's nest in the V. One young woman had knocked against it, and had been stung, hence the howl and whimpering.

The enemy planes dropped a dozen or so bombs and, their blood lust satisfied, returned to base. Long afterwards the all clear sounded. We filed out of the V but could not see far for the dust and smoke, which still hung in the air. The girl who had been stung by the wasp set off home through the haze, her hand held to her swollen face. My terror had dissipated by the time I got home after my false alarm, but it had been replaced by a sense of grievance. This just wouldn't do! I hated to have my right to life controlled by the enemy! But what could I do about it? I was still pondering when my daughter came back and reported that numerous bombs had fallen around the station, on the sports field, by the river, and in the park; so many people had been killed and so many injured. One woman had been killed under a tree, her head half blown off while her body remained sitting erect. Lots of people had been carted off to the hospital shrieking and groaning. When I heard this report I realized how lucky we had been. It was clear the enemy had deliberately bombed the outskirts rather than the city centre, anticipating that the city would have been evacuated by the time they arrived. In that case our V had presented them with a nice target! I don't know what good deeds our little band had done to have saved us from harm. Thinking back on it now, perhaps that V foreshadowed the V that appeared on the night of 10 August 1945, the symbol of final victory.[2]

That night I could not contain my indignation. I felt that to kill people by 'air raid' was too unmanly. If there is honour among thieves, there is also an honourable way of killing. If we are both on level ground, and you come to kill me, I run. If I can't get away, I am killed by you. This kind of killing, simply in terms of killing, is fair enough, and one would die without complaint. But if they come to kill you from above and you have to get away from below, they are bound to have the upper hand, and you are bound to be on the losing end. The matter of dying was secondary, what was intolerable was the moral injustice and affront to one's feelings. I had to think of a way to render the killers from the air powerless against me and to save myself from further indignity.

The next day I had my solution. After breakfast I gathered together some fellow spirits from my family, and we set out for the hills, taking with us reading matter and victuals. We walked over a mile to the Nine Dragon Cliffs, sat in the entrance of a big cave, and read.

Having spent a carefree day, we returned at dusk. I was totally unaware of whether there had been an air raid or not. This style of life continued for over a month, during which time I was indeed free from further subjection to indignity. Nor was the city bombed again. But before long there came the news of the fall of Nanning. I had no choice but to take the refugee trail, carrying my sense of injustice along with me.

(1946)

---

[2] The actual date of the Japanese unconditional surrender was 14 August 1945; the signing of the documents of surrender took place on 3 September.

Yu Dafu 郁達夫 (1896–1945)

COMMENTARY

Yu Dafu was born in Fuyang, Zhejiang province. His father had been a teacher, a medical man and a local government clerk. He died when Yu Dafu was aged three. Yu had two older brothers and one older sister. As one of the essays that follows describes, this youngest son's schooling started with the traditional memorization of edifying texts and went on to modern subjects, including foreign languages.

In 1913 Yu Dafu was taken to Japan by his eldest brother. There he studied the secondary and high school curriculum, eventually gaining a place in the Economics Department of Tokyo University in 1919. According to his own account, he spent most of his time at university reading fiction, going to coffee bars to find girls, and drinking. By that time he read English, German and Japanese fluently. His preference in fiction was for Russian and German authors. Two novellas that he wrote in Japan, *Yinhuise de si* 銀灰色的死 (A silver-grey death) and *Chenlun* 沉淪 (Sinking) caused a great scandal when they were published in 1921 because of their Rousseau-esque confessions.

On his return to China in 1922 Yu Dafu was preoccupied with the Creation Society, which he had founded the previous year in Tokyo with Guo Moruo 郭沫若, Zhang Ziping 張資平 et al. Apart from brief spells teaching at universities in Peking, Wuchang and Guangzhou, most of his energy up to 1927 was spent on writing for and editing Creation Society magazines. By this time the Creation Society had converted from romanticism to revolution; personality and policy differences led to Yu Dafu's resignation. Moving to Hangzhou in 1933, Yu adopted the free-wheeling lifestyle of the traditional man of letters. When the war with Japan broke out in 1937 he did some propaganda work, then left for Singapore in 1938, where he edited newspaper supplements and wrote anti-Japanese articles. On the fall of Singapore in 1942 he fled to Sumatra and lived under an assumed name. He died after the Japanese surrender, apparently executed by the Japanese military police.

Yu Dafu thought that the essay's most desirable qualities were fine detail, freshness and true feeling. He disliked the English essay for being too philosophical, too unctuous, or too humorous. The subject matter best suited to display the qualities of style he valued was the description of nature, usually in the form of accounts of trips the author has made. Next were reminiscences, tales of encounters, and other things related to the author's life. This prescription was clearly very traditional, as was his preference for loose organization, and for inspiration over cogitation.

However, his weddedness to 'true feeling' went further than the traditional writer allowed himself to go. In his prose as in his fiction his frankness was taken to exceptional lengths; indeed critics are still in doubt as to whether some of his pieces should be regarded as factual or fictional. But whether the experiences he described were true or a projection of his fantasy, he was himself persuaded, and he persuaded others, that the *feelings* were true. Truthfulness, or sincerity, has always been regarded as a great literary virtue in China, possibly because social life required so much falsity. Other factors that contributed to his reputation were familiarity with classical poetry (his own classical poems are highly thought of), his knowledge of modern European literature, and the easy intimacy with which he addressed his readers. One can say without prejudice that his essays tend to be flimsy, but to his many readers that has been felt to be a virtue rather than a fault: they can relax and enjoy a pleasant read.

Village School and Academy
書塾與學堂

TRANSLATOR'S NOTE

As Yu Dafu himself is vague about dates in this episode from his autobiography, I should perhaps clarify. He was born in December 1896. He enrolled in his first primary school in 1902. Though his age was seven by Chinese reckoning, his real age was only five. He went on to enter the 'junior academy' in 1907, and graduated in 1910. The reason why the local people called the latter the 'foreign academy' was not that foreigners had any hand in running it, but that its curriculum was a modern one, along Western lines. Education generally was reformed in China following the abolition in 1903 of the imperial examinations based exclusively on the Chinese classics. The change in the curriculum explains the presence of adult pupils, who had to begin their education all over again. In fact the 'academy' was a junior school.

Prior to the establishment of the new public schools, elementary education was carried on in private family or village schools which had only one tutor. A wide range of ages was catered for, each pupil conning his lessons and being tested individually. In addition, each county had a Confucian Temple which served the educational functions of the local administration. It was common for the new public schools to be housed in those temples. Presumably the 'junior academy' that Yu Dafu writes about was built in the part of such a temple previously occupied by the cells where the candidates for the old degrees did their examinations.

The Chinese Essay

When we learned English in the old days, before China had textbooks of her own, we used a reader of the Nesfield's Grammar kind that an Englishman had written for Indian students. In this reader there was a lesson about how the Chinese went about studying. The illustration showed a bent-backed, bespectacled old gentleman with a pigtail, holding a pipe in his hand and listening to a pupil recite his lesson; the little fellow standing in front of him also had a long pigtail. For some unaccountable reason the content of this lesson made a deep impression on me: I can still repeat it more or less word for word. In describing the peculiar Chinese habits of learning it said: 'No matter whether reading out loud or to themselves, they always sway their bodies from side to side, swinging like the pendulum of a chiming clock.' The effect and pleasure of this swaying of the body while reading or reciting is probably not something that people who never attended the former Chinese village schools will be able to understand.

I cannot say exactly how old I was when I first went to the village school, but it must have been seven or eight or thereabouts. I just remember that late one winter night we were burning the New Year paper decorations, and I was already drowsy, rubbing my eyes and yawning away, when suddenly an old gentleman carrying a lantern called at the house and said he had come to take me through my first letters. I then offered incense at the altar with him, did my three genuflections and nine kowtows to Confucius' spirit tablet, got up and wrote a page of simple characters from a copybook after him, and read out four sentences from the *Three Character Classic*. In the spring of the new year there I was, my canvas satchel under my arm, my hair done in a pigtail secured with red thread, swaying from side to side, just like the little schoolboy in the English reader.

The thirty-odd years that have elapsed since then have soothed away all the pains suffered at that time; life in the village school, as I remember it now, was really very happy. As we had to sit at our desk from morning to dusk, the only exercise we got to help our digestion and tone up our muscles was waggling our bodies for all we were worth and chanting our texts at the top of our voices. We obtained temporary release from our prison when we relieved ourselves, consequently the lavatory became our playground. The naughtiest of us schoolboys was Chen Fang, the son of Mr Chen, the school inspector; the village school was in fact attached to the Confucian

Temple where the local education office was. Chen Fang asked to be excused twelve or thirteen times every morning without fail; this got too much for the teacher, who introduced a tally system, by which anyone who left the school to go to the lavatory had to carry a tally. As a result the malpractice of two pupils going to the toilet together and getting up to mischief was put a stop to, and fighting over the tally became the sole occasion for fun for the pupils.

Chen Fang was four years older than me, and he gave the lead to the other pupils. All the japes and pranks were instigated by him and carried out by his lieutenants and underlings, hence the teacher's retribution fell mostly on his head. Yet there were some cunning students who put the blame on him for things they did themselves: many a time he got a beating injustly. He knew his protestations would not be believed, and did no more on being punished in another's stead than bulge out his eyes, let fall some big tear drops, rub his head where it hurt, and forget it. Afterwards I went on to the new-style academy that was reformed from the then college, while Chen Fang moved away when his father lost his job. I have never met him again, nor will ever do so, because I seem to have heard someone in Hong Kong tell of his tragic death when the split between the Kuomintang and the Communists happened—exactly the same fate as befell Turgenev's Rudin.

From the village school to the academy! That change was greater and stranger to my tender mind than flying from the earth to the heaven. The strangest thing was that in size and age I was the littlest pupil in the whole school.

At that time the academy was the object of general admiration and curiosity. When some rows of old examination cells in the college were demolished and a birdcage-like Chinese-foreign building constructed, country people from as far as twenty miles away came in hordes to the town, carrying their provisions and umbrellas, to see the novelty. For the first six months after the school buildings were completed, the 'foreign academy' was the main talking point in town and village teashops and wineshops; and the academy students in their outlandish black twill uniforms seemed to be all-powerful head priests. People dared only give them sidelong glances, while they secretly preened themselves.

The head of this one and only junior academy of the upper grade in the county was an even more imposing personage. He used a blue sedan chair for his comings and goings, and was invited *de rigueur* to the county magistrate's dinners. On the fourth Saturday of every month when the county magistrate was due to supervise the afternoon composition class, the pupils were given a special ration of two meat-filled buns. Some of them who lived miles away in the country wrapped up these buns carefully and put them in their satchels to take home after class. When they got home they presented them to the local elders, not in imitation of the 'pure piety' of Ying Shukao who put aside some of the food Duke Yin gave him to take back to his mother, but because the buns were from the academy, and besides were the gift of the county magistrate; as such they could keep away evil spirits and confer wisdom.

Actually some of my classmates in the academy had passed the first degree examination under the old system, and were already around thirty years of age. They did not look too prepossessing in their uniform because of their round shoulders, but dressed in their gowns and mandarin jackets they had an imposing and dignified air as they swaggered off to their homes out of town.

At the end of my first year in the junior academy I scored an average of over eighty marks out of a hundred, and was unexpectedly promoted by the head and the county magistrate to two grades above my original class, along with four other pupils. This very normal occurrence actually caused some excitement in the county town, but led to a serious upset in my own family.

In the spring of the next year when school began again, our widowed mother managed to scrape together a few silver dollars for tuition fees and book fees. After she had paid them in I put to her an additional unreasonable request: I demanded that she buy me a pair of leather shoes. In my innocent eyes it would be the most splendid thing in the world to wear a pair of leather shoes to go with my uniform, and stride along with my chest out and my heels drumming on the paving stones. Having jumped a year, I would have to put on a show like that to be accepted by schoolmates who were half as old again as I was. My mother had already scraped the bottom of the barrel in getting together my school fees; naturally she hadn't got any spare two silver dollars to buy leather shoes for me. All she could do was screw up her nerve and take me along to the mainstreet shops that sold imported goods to see if she could get a pair on credit. In those days leather shoes were shipped in from Shanghai and sold on commission through the shops that handled foreign goods.

I trailed my mother in and out of one shop, two shops, three shops, from the bottom end of town to The Prosperity Store at the top end. The shop assistants were all alike very polite to us at first. They patted me on the head, and got out pair after pair of leather shoes to try for size. But at the mention of buying on credit they all turned their nose up, put on a cold smile, and said we'd have to ask the cashier. And each cashier in turn set his features forbiddingly, raised his voice an octave, and declared that no credit sales were allowed. In the last shop, The Prosperity Store, when we got the like heartless rejection I noticed that my mother was not only red in the face but her eyes were red-rimmed too. There was nothing for her but to turn away without a word and leave the shop. There being nothing I could say either, I followed her home.

When we reached home she sniffed back her tears and disappeared upstairs. After a long while she came down with a big bundle of clothes. I knew she was going to slip out of the back door and pawn the clothes for ready money. My heart broke. Weeping and wailing I got to the back door and held her back. I yelled out as if my life depended on it:

'Mother! Don't go, mother! I don't want them, I don't want to wear leather shoes! Those shopkeepers! Those terrible shopkeepers!'

Still holding her, I sank to my knees; for her part, she let out a wail and started crying. The noise of us weeping in unison alarmed the neighbours. Assuming I must have offended my mother, they descended on us to make the peace. The more they exhorted the more wretched I felt; the more my mother cried the more overwrought she became. In the end I made an abject apology, and was led away by my uncle to his house next door.

After that upset I never wore leather shoes, nor even wanted new clothes or instruments. It was also then that I started to study flat out, to rule out all but the poorest students as my friends, and to look with hatred on the rich and merchant class. Though I was only eleven or twelve at the time, because of this setback I started to act as if I had reached a ripe old age. This eccentricity of character is something I can do nothing about, even now.

The Winter Scene in Jiangnan
江南的冬景

TRANSLATOR'S NOTE

'Jiangnan' (literally: south of the Yangtze River) in this essay refers to the southern part of Jiangsu and Anhui and the northern part of Zhejiang province, along the lower reaches of the Yangtze, where Yu Dafu grew up. 'Jiangnan' is also used of the whole of southern China, and hence embraces Fujian and Guangdong provinces, but Yu Dafu is at pains to point out that is not his meaning.

The poem addressed to the bandits of the greenwood is by Li She 李涉. By honouring them with a poem, Li was allowed to pass unscathed.

Everyone who has spent winter in the north knows how nice it feels to sit round a stove brewing tea, or eating lamb hotpot, or shelling peanuts, or drinking white spirits.

And though the snow outside may be feet deep and the wind may boom like thunder, if the house has sunken stoves, heated brick beds and such amenities, the two or three months holed up indoors are a period of hibernation more agreeable than any other time of year. Let alone the old folk, even children who love to be active all cherish the winter, because there are lots of eats for them, like dried turnip, *yali* pears and other fruits, and boisterous celebrations to take part in, as on New Year's Eve, New Year's Day, and the Lantern Festival.

But it is a different state of affairs south of the Yangtze River. The trees, for one thing, are not stripped bare of leaves after the winter solstice. Wintery winds—from the northwest—blow only intermittently, making it cold for no more than one or two days. When the sky clears of clouds, and daybreak brings streets littered with leaves and a frost as white as cold cream on a black girl's face, the sun has only to fall on the house eaves for the birds to twitter again, the earth to steam again, and grandads to take the little ones out to the open lot in front of the house and sit with the sun on their backs chewing the rag and getting on with their outdoor lives. Who could say that the winter scene south of the Yangtze is not also very attractive?

I grew up in Jiangnan, and the impression of Jiangnan winters is deeply etched on my mind. Though as I approach middle age I have fallen in love with late autumn, believing it the most favourable season for reading and writing, I still think the winter scene in Jiangnan has a special feel about it that can match that of summer nights in the north: to put it in a modern way, a kind of clear and luminous ambience.

I have also been in Fujian and Guangdong in the winter. Warm isn't the word for it! Sometimes at the time of the lunar New Year you might have to put on your summer gown. When you go past country gardens you can still see over the fence a jungle of autumn flowers! It's true the temperature drops a few degrees after a storm, but a lined garment is all you'll ever need: fur gowns and padded jackets are definitely out. The climatic abnormality of the extreme south is not what I mean by winter in Jiangnan: it can only be called the eternal spring of the south, or the extension of spring or autumn.

Because the soil in Jiangnan is rich and moist, it retains heat and sustains plant life. Hence in the Jiangnan region, rush catkins stay firm until the winter solstice, and red leaves sometimes stay on the trees for more than three months. The tallow trees along the banks of the Qiantang River are another example: after the red leaves of autumn fall, the branches are still speckled with clusters of snow-white seeds; in a photograph you could easily mistake them for plum blossoms. Grass turns brown at the most, and always stays greenish at the roots; brush fires will not kill it, nor winter winds flatten it. If you go out of town for a walk on your own in winter and the weather is mild and the sky blue, you not only have no sense of blight and deadness, you even feel a mysterious vitality latent in your surroundings. The Jiangnan countryside is the best place for understanding what the poet meant by his famous line, 'If Winter comes, can Spring be far behind?'

Talking of country walks in winter, they are a special grace and favour bestowed by that season on the inhabitants of Jiangnan. Those who live in the frozen north will never have the chance of enjoying this simple pleasure in their whole lifetime. I do not know how winters in Germany compare with ours in Jiangsu and Zhejiang, but judging by the liking of many German writers for using the word '*Spaziergang*' in their compositions I would guess that that in southern Germany the seasons are about the same as ours in Jiangsu. The 19th century rustic poet Peter Rosegger (1843–1918), for example, includes the word for 'walks' in the titles of an exceptional number of his works, and the conditions he describes could well apply to the hill districts of our Jiangsu and Zhejiang.

Jiangnan is a region of rivers and tributaries, and bordering on the sea, abounds in lakes and marshes, hence the air is often humid. In winter you often get drizzling rain, and the winter scene of an out of the way village shrouded in drizzle conveys an inexpressible sense of pastoral peace. If you would just imagine, after the autumn harvest has been gathered in, a small hamlet of four or five homes on a river bank, their doors facing a long narrow bridge, their windows looking out on distant hills, amid thickets of natural forest trees; over this picture of a hibernal hamlet is sprinkled a layer of white rain as fine as powder, and a background is shaded in so faintly that you can hardly detect the ink: wouldn't you say this qualifies as pastoral peace? If you wish to add some features to the scene, then you can moor a little boat with a black awning before the dwellings, draw in some tipplers carousing in a thatched hut; then at sunset add a dash of amber to the sky, and paint a halo round the windows to represent the lamplight. Anyone coming upon a scene like this would feel liberated, released from petty cares, and finally forgetful of their own fortunes and their own mortality. No doubt we all recall the Tang poem that begins 'The dark rain sweeps the riverside village'. In this setting, the poet even treated the bandits of the greenwood politely: what was that due to, if not the enchantment of the Jiangnan scene in winter?

Mention of rain inevitably brings thoughts of snow. 'The evening draws in, the sky threatens snow, is there a cup to be had or no?' describes, of course, a snowy evening in Jiangnan. 'Plum trees' shadows on the cold shone path, the fragrance of wine in the snow-sprinkled village' brings together the 'three friends' of a winter's night, snow, moon and plum trees, and tells of flirting with the waitress in a wineshop. 'At the wicket gate the village dogs bark, the traveller returns on a night of wind and snow' describes a snowy night in Jiangnan when all is still. 'The village up ahead is deep in snow, last night a spray of plum blossoms opened'; and the next morning the village boys who like to romp in the snow like dogs come to report on the village happenings. Perhaps not all of the lines I have quoted were written in Jiangnan, and perhaps not all the poets who wrote them were from Jiangnan, but borrowing those lines puts the case in a nutshell, and they are infinitely more beautiful than the prose my clumsy pen can write.

In some years the Jiangnan region might see a winter without rain or snow, and just a slight fall of spring snow at the end of the first month or beginning of the second month of the lunar calendar. Last winter (1934) was like that, and I'm afraid this winter is sure to be like that. Reckoning by the solar terms, the coldest spell should be at the end of February 1936, and it should last seven or eight days at the most. These are what the country people call dry winters. They may be good for the wheat harvest, but they are bad for the population: a prolonged drought makes it easy for diptheria, influenza and other diseases to get a hold. But those willing to throw caution to the winds and enjoy the Jiangnan winter to the full will still welcome such years, because there are more mild and sunny days, and it follows that there are more opportunities for carefree country walks. Enthusiasts for what the Japanese call *Hikeng* and the Germans call *Spaziergang* look forward most to this kind of winter.

The weather outside my window is as fine as a late autumn day's. The crisp air, the cloudless sky, and the flood of sunlight tempt you out of doors. Very well, I must practise what I preach. I shall stop writing this tiresome essay, put up my pen, pick up my stick, and be off to the lakeside for a nice stroll!

(1935)

Zhu Ziqing 朱自清 (1898–1948)

COMMENTARY

Ever since the 1930s essays of Zhu Ziqing have featured in every Chinese school syllabus and every anthology of modern prose. We will consider below the reasons why he has appealed to everybody. First the facts of his life.

Zhu Ziqing was born in Donghai and grew up in Yangzhou, both in Jiangsu province. Both his grandfather and father were relatively minor government officials. On graduating from middle school in 1916, Zhu married the daughter of a doctor of Chinese medicine at his parents' behest. The marriage was a happy one, and produced six children. In the same year he was admitted to the preparatory division of Peking University and began on a degree in philosophy in 1917. Peking University was at the centre of the May Fourth Movement of 1919 which aimed to establish a new culture in the humanities and sciences. Zhu joined in the activities, and began writing 'new poetry' in the vernacular. It was as a poet that he made his name.

On taking his degree in 1920, Zhu Ziqing went with Yu Pingbo 俞平伯 to teach at the Zhejiang Number One Teachers' Training College in Hangzhou, from where Feng Zikai had graduated the previous year. Subsequently he taught Chinese at a number of other colleges and schools, and at the same time published his work, still mostly poetry, in magazines. In 1925 he was appointed to a post in the Department of Chinese Literature at Tsinghua University in Peking, where he rose to become Head of Department in 1932, and where he remained the rest of his life, apart from a year in London (1931–2) and the refugee years during the war, when the university joined with others to form the Southwestern United University in Kunming. Zhu returned to Peking in 1945, and died there from a gastric ulcer in 1948. During his academic career he produced books on classical and modern Chinese literature that are still widely read.

The *qing* element in Zhu Ziqing's name means 'clear', and the *bai* element in three of his pen-names means 'white'. Together, *qingbai* means moral purity. That is not a bad starting point from which to assess his oeuvre. Zhu Ziqing could be held up as the most successful product of the new culture movement, which, proceeding from humanism, sought to make a literature of decent but sensitive feelings accessible to all: a literature written in plain language by plainly human beings, as opposed to the literature of the past, which was written in an artificial language that conveyed only artificial feelings. Zhu Ziqing's writing, as all critics agree, expressed a personality that combined culture and refinement with honesty and sincerity.

Zhu's first published collection, *Zongji* 踪跡 (Tracks and Traces, 1924) contained mostly poetry; his second, *Beiying* 背影(View from the Rear, 1936) was all prose, as was his third collection, *Niwo* 你我(You and I, 1936). Some essays write bitterly of social and political issues, but those on personal and family matters and that describe a scene have had the greater appeal. The more contemplative pieces especially are carefully considered and crafted. No sentence is laborious, no sentence casual. It was the clearness of his sentence structure and of the progression of his thought that led, I think, his fellow writer Ye Shaojun to say that when the history of modern Chinese literature was written, Zhu Ziqing 'should get first mention for perfection of form and for the writing of the spoken word.' As for the latter, it is true that Zhu avoids words that are not in common use; even in his scenic descriptions he relies on reduplicating common adjectives (like *dandan de yun*, 'pale-pale clouds'), instead of calling on more abstruse, 'poetic' words. Yet Chinese readers hear a subtle melody coming through this plain and bare diction. Inevitably this 'melody' will be transformed or lost in translation; what one can descry is the organizational principle of leaving spaces between passages of controlled, precise, objective description for the escape of the poetry of the emotions.

As a last word on Zhu Ziqing's universal appeal, which had even ideologically hostile critics admitting to being moved, my impression is that it is bound up with the relationship between author and reader. Some writers place themselves in a position of superiority to the reader; Zhu manages to suggest that he is inferior to the reader, or at least is in need of the reader's support. It is as if he were a vulnerable younger brother making an unspoken appeal for understanding, or to younger readers a still vulnerable older brother sharing with them the pains and pleasures he has experienced.

The View from the Rear
背影

TRANSLATOR'S NOTE

This is a sentimental essay that probes the acceptable limits of sentimentality. The theme is universal and also peculiarly Chinese. At the time of writing, Zhu Ziqing had not seen his father for two years, and in a letter his father had spoken of his approaching death. It is natural in those circumstances, and more so of course on a parent's actual death, for a son or daughter to think fondly of the parent, to recall the parent's expressions of love and care, and to regret not having adequately returned the parent's love. Sorrow, self-reproach and guilt all demand expression at such times. This is the universal aspect. That there is a peculiarly Chinese aspect to it can be deduced from both the frequency with which the theme is taken up in essays, and the way the theme is handled. Starting from the assumption that the parent will not express parental love in words, the essayist picks out one or two acts that may pass notice because of their simplicity or routine or trivial nature yet actually are invested with deep significance—but only by implication. On the other hand, that implicitness is balanced by explicit voicing of emotion on the part of the writer, which may either punctuate the relatively flat narrative or be reserved till the end of the essay. Gui Youguang's essay on his mother may well have set a model for this minor genre.

Zhu Ziqing's essay shares with Gui Youguang's a quality highly prized by Chinese stylists, namely cleanness and bareness of language, unencumbered by figures of speech or rhetorical flourishes; this is associated with sincerity and depth of feeling. Though in 1925 there was a policy for practitioners of the new literature to write simply, no doubt Zhu Ziqing also chose to do so deliberately. His language is in fact so plain that a translator has to discipline himself to keep the level down to the comparable one of basic English. It is only with reference to his own emotions that the author rises above this level. His father's words and deeds are consistently represented in unremarkable words, in keeping with his reticence to articulate tender feelings.

This essay has maintained its place in Chinese school textbooks through thick and thin from soon after publication up to the present day. Apart from its appeal to national sensibilities, its success is due in no small measure to the artful choice of dominant image that serves as its title and is repeated several times in the body of the essay. Apart from his fatness, the father's physical characteristics are not described: all he has is a *beiying*, that is, a 'back view.' In that way he can stand for all fathers, who must at some time present their back to an observer. A 'back view' can also stand for leave-taking, as it does in the last paragraph, when the father's retreating figure disappears in the crowd. One aspect of the term that is lost in translation is its poetical associations: the *ying* element, variously used to mean 'shadow', 'silhouette', 'image', 'figure', 'reflection', 'shade', or 'trace', is widely used in poetic literature to capture fleeting impressions and sensations. A comparable word does not exist in English: 'back view' and 'rear view' are extremely prosaic. 'Silhouette' sounds more interesting, but unfortunately cannot apply in this piece, where the father's back is in full and plain view. I have had to resort to translating the term in different ways, but I hope the reader will remember that all references to rear views are *beiying* in the Chinese.

It has been two years and more since I saw my father. My most vivid memory of him is a view of him from the rear.

That winter my grandmother had died, and my father's job had come to an end; our troubles truly did not come singly then. I left Peking for Xuzhou, to accompany my father home for the funeral. When I saw the household things strewn about the yard, and thought too of my grandmother, I wept copiously. Father said: 'What has happened has happened, you shouldn't upset yourself. Heaven helps those who help themselves.'

When we got home, father paid back what was owed by means of selling and pawning things, and borrowed again to pay for the funeral. Those days at home were very gloomy, partly because of the funeral, partly because of father being out of work. Once the funeral was over, father decided to go to Nanjing to look for work, and as I was returning to Peking to study, we travelled together.

In Nanjing friends wanted to take us sight-seeing, and that detained us one day. The next morning I was to cross the river to Pukou, where I would take the afternoon train north. Father had already declared he would not see me off because he had too much to do; he arranged for a houseboy he knew at our hotel to go with me. He gave the houseboy his instructions in great detail, and repeated them over and again, but after all that still worried that the houseboy would prove unreliable, and could not finally make up his mind. Actually I was already twenty years old, and had made the trip to Peking two or three times, so it was no great matter. At last he decided to see me off himself. In reply to my protests that it wasn't necessary he just said, 'It's all right, I shouldn't leave it to them.'

We crossed the river and went into the railway station. While I bought my ticket he looked after the luggage. The luggage was too much for us to cope with; we needed to pay some porters to get it on the train. So he started haggling over a price with them.

At that time I thought myself very clever, and didn't quite approve of the way he spoke to them, so I butted in, but in the end he agreed on a price with them, and saw me onto the train. He chose a seat for me next to the carriage door, and I spread the Persian lamb overcoat he had had made for me over it. He told me to be careful on the journey, and told me to watch out at night in case I caught a chill. Then he instructed the car attendant to look after me well. I laughed to myself at his naivety: the only thing that mattered to them was money, it was a sheer waste of time to ask them to do a good turn! Besides, I was grown up. Couldn't I look

The Chinese Essay

after myself? Ah, when I look back now, I was really too clever for my own good!

I said, 'There is no need for you to wait around, dad.' He looked out of the window and said, 'I'll go and buy some oranges. Stay here, don't go away.' There were some hawkers waiting for customers behind the railings on the opposite platform. To get to that platform you had to jump down, cross the tracks, and climb up the other side. That would not be too easy for my father, seeing how fat he was. I volunteered to go myself, but he would have it his way. I watched him waddle over to the tracks, dressed in his black mandarin jacket and dark blue padded gown, with his black skullcap on his head. He slowly lowered himself down, which didn't prove too difficult. But climbing onto the other platform was a different matter. Supporting himself with both hands on the edge of the platform, he drew his feet up; then he inclined his body to the left and appeared to be making a strenuous effort. As I watched him from behind, my tears gushed out. I hurriedly wiped my face dry, afraid that he would see, afraid that others would see. When I looked up again he was already on his way back with an armful of bright red oranges. To cross the tracks he first placed the oranges on the ground, then slowly climbed down, then picked the oranges up again. I hurried to help him up when he got to my side of the track. He walked with me onto the train, plonked all the oranges down on my fur coat, and dusted himself off. Now seeming very relaxed, he said after a while, 'I'll be off, then. Write to me when you get there.' I watched him leave. After taking a few steps, he turned his head and saw me. He said, 'You'd better go in, there's no one looking after your things.' I waited until his retreating figure had been swallowed up in the throng before taking my seat. Then my tears came again.

In recent years, father and I have been on the move all the time, and our family fortunes have gone steadily downhill. He left home in his youth, stood on his own two feet, and did some great things. Being constantly reminded of his failure, he was of course unable to control his feelings; as his depression mounted, he naturally had to give vent to it. Trivial family matters made him fly into a temper. He came to treat me differently from the way he had in the past. But in these two years we have been parted, he has finally forgotten my faults, and is only concerned about my well-being, and my son's well-being. After I came north he wrote me a letter, in which he said, 'I have been reasonably well, it's just that my shoulder gives me a lot of pain, which makes it awkward for me even to eat with my chopsticks or write with my brush. Probably my final exit is not too far away.' When I read this I saw again, through glistening tears, that view from the rear of his fat shape, dressed in a long padded gown with a black mandarin jacket over it. Ah! When, I wonder, will we two be able to meet again?

Traces of Wenzhou
溫州的蹤跡

This is a very small horizontal scroll, just over a foot wide, painted by Ma Mengrong. In the left-hand top corner a long and flimsy green curtain is suspended at a slant; it occupies one third of the vertical and two thirds of the horizontal space. In the centre of the curtain is positioned a yellow hook, shaped like the spout of a teapot—this would be what they call a 'soft gold hook', I imagine. From the bend of the hook hangs a pair of tassels, stone grey in colour; their threads are somewhat awry, as if they are being pulled by a breeze. On the right is a full moon, which is shedding its pale bluish light over the whole of the surface of the painting. The moon is pure, soft and peaceful, like the face of a sleeping beauty. Sloping downward from the top edge of the curtain is a branch of a flowering crabapple. The luxuriant flowers and leaves are evenly spaced, there being five sprays along the length of the branch. Some are dense, some are sparse, but all are dainty and pleasing. The green leaves are so succulent that at a pinch the sap would flow; depending on how much moonlight they catch, there is a slight difference in their shade of green. The flowers are in full bloom, their red so gorgeous that it nearly brims over; the yellow stamens stand out sharply and brightly, the green background enhancing their attractiveness. The branch bends upwards like the raised arm of a fair maid. A pair of mynah birds sit on it, facing the curtain, with their backs to the moon. The one on the higher perch has its eyes half shut, as if, still hankering after something, it is reluctant to go to sleep. The one lower down is turned to face the other bird, and is already asleep, its head drawn in. The space below the curtain is empty, free of all trace of the brush.

We may wonder why, given the soft light of the full moon, and the lush and captivating beauty of the crabapple, these sweet birds perch together but dream separately. In the hush of night, why is the mynah on the higher part of the branch fighting to keep its eyes open? Whatever can it be waiting for? Is it loath to forsake the pale moon? Is it fascinated by the flimsy curtain? No, no, no. You must look for the answer below the curtain, you have to go behind the curtain—you have found the person who rolled up the curtain, haven't you? What charm and refinement, no wonder! We should have realized that the moon and the birds were not the only ones to be retiring. But so near and yet so far: how can I restrain myself? I call with all my might: will you come out from where you are?

This painting sets its scene so economically, its colours are so soft and vivid, that no one could not be struck by its brilliance. Though its canvas is tiny, its resonance is powerful enough to turn your bones to jelly. When I saw this painting I was transfixed, and could not tear myself away. Hence I have described my impressions in some detail in order to record the encounter, though I am a layman when it comes to painting, and the experts will laugh up their sleeves. Well, let them get on with it.

The Lotus Pond by Moonlight
荷塘月色

The last few days I have been quite troubled in my mind. Tonight as I sat in the yard enjoying the cool of evening I suddenly thought of the lotus pond I passed every day: it must surely look different now in the light of the full moon. The moon was mounting high in the sky, and the sounds of the children at play in the road outside had died away. Indoors my wife was putting our little Runer to sleep, drowsily humming a lullaby. I quietly slipped on my gown and went out, pulling the gate to behind me.

At the edge of the pond is a winding narrow cinder path. This path, being out of the way, is little used even in the daytime, and at night is all the more deserted. All around the pond grow many trees, lush and dense, while on one side of the path there are some willows, and other trees whose names are unknown to me. On moonless nights the path is overcast and gloomy, somewhat eerie. But tonight all was well, even though the moonlight was only dim.

I was the only person on the path, pacing along with my hands clasped behind my back. It was as if this domain belonged to me; and also as if I had transcended my normal self, had crossed into another dimension. I like excitement, and also like calm; I love to be in crowds, and also love to be on my own. On a night like this, alone in the all-pervading moonlight, one could think about everything, or about nothing, and so believe oneself to be a free man. One's daytime obligations, in terms of what one had to do and say, could be entirely ignored. This was the beauty of solitude. I resolved to make the best of this abundance of lotus and moonlight.

On the surface of the serpentine lotus pond all one could see was fields of leaves. The leaves stood high above the water, splayed out like the skirts of a tall slim ballerina. Here and there among the layers of leaves were sown shining white flowers, some blooming glamorously, some in shy bud, just like unstrung pearls, or stars against a blue sky. Their fresh fragrance wafted on the faint breeze, like snatches of song from some distant tower. At each breath of wind the leaves and flowers also gave a shiver, which passed over the entire breadth of the pond in a flash, like lightning. The leaves being so densely massed together, this gave the impression of an emerald wave. Beneath the leaves were channels of flowing water, but they were hidden from view, not even a hint being visible; but that only served to give the leaves more presence.

The moonbeams spilled placidly onto this expanse of leaves and flowers like living water. A thin mist floated up from the lotus pond. The leaves and flowers seemed to be washed in milk, and at the same time trapped in a dream of flimsy gauze. Although the moon was full, there was a veil of light cloud, which prevented it from shining brightly; but to me this was just right—we cannot do without deep sleep, admitted, but a quiet doze also has its pleasures. The moonlight was filtered through the trees, while the clumps of bushes on the high ground cast heavy irregular mottled shadows. The spare silhouettes of the arching willows appeared to be painted on the lotus leaves. The moonlight on the pond was not all smooth and even, but the rhythm of light and shade was harmonious, like a musical masterpiece played on a violin.

On all sides of the pond, near and far, high and low, were trees, the majority being willows. These trees ringed the pond like a fortress.

Only on the side where the path was were a few gaps left, as if on purpose for the moonlight. The trees were all of sombre hue, and at first sight looked like a bank of fog; but the grace of the willows could still be perceived. Above the crests of the trees a range of far hills could be dimly seen, but only in outline. A few gleams from street lights also leaked through the interstices of the trees, but they were wan and lifeless, eyes heavy with sleep. At this time the most animated of things were the thrumming of the cicadas in the trees and the croaking of the frogs in the water. But animation was their affair: it had nothing to do with me.

I suddenly bethought myself of the business of gathering lotuses. This was an old custom in the lower Yangtze region, apparently of very early origin, and most popular during the Six Dynasties. A rough idea of it can be got from poetry. I went on to recall these lines from 'Song of the Western Eyot':

> We gather lotus from the South Pond in autumn
> The lotus flowers are higher than a man's head
> We bend to get the lotus seeds up
> The lotus seeds are as green as water.

If those lotus gatherers had been here tonight, they would have been satisfied that the lotuses were 'higher than a man's head', but disappointed that there was not even a glimpse of flowing water. This led me to feel thoroughly nostalgic for the country south of the Yangtze. Absorbed in such thoughts, I suddenly raised my head, and found myself back at my own gate. I opened the door quietly and went in. Not a sound was to be heard. My wife had long since fallen asleep.

Liang Shih-ch'iu 梁實秋 (1902–1987)

COMMENTARY

Liang Shih-ch'iu's total literary output was of staggering proportions. Apart from numerous collections of essays and critical studies, he also translated the complete works of Shakespeare and compiled a substantial Chinese-English dictionary, to mention only the prominences. Even taking account of his long life, one must assume he was never stuck for a word or short of a thought. This fecundity, again one supposes, must have owed a great deal to his having entered deeply into his own Chinese culture and into the culture of the English-speaking world, beginning in his youth.

Liang was born in Peking, where his father was a senior officer in the police force. He went to the best schools, the most decisive for his future being Tsinghua College, a Chinese-American foundation, where he studied from 1915 to 1923. According to his later recollection, it was there he learned to write: his Chinese teacher taught him to cut out verbiage, and two American female teachers taught him how to structure a composition. Selected graduates from Tsinghua College went on to the USA for further study; Liang duly enrolled at Colorado College, then transferred to study at Harvard University, where he came under the influence of Irving Babbitt, and at Columbia University. On his return to China in 1926 he held posts at a succession of universities, the most eminent being head of the English Department at Peking University (1934–37, and again after the war 1946–49). In Chongqing during the war he worked for government educational and translation services, and also was editor of the literary supplement of the *Zhongyang ribao* 中央日報(Central Daily News). He moved to Taiwan in 1949, and served as Dean of Arts at Taiwan Normal University. On his retirement he completed his Shakespeare translations (in forty parts) and wrote a history of English literature, besides miscellaneous essays.

Liang Shih-ch'iu was embroiled in two major controversies in his career. The first was a few years after he returned from the USA. In 1927 he joined the Xinyue (Crescent Moon) association and acted as editor for its monthly magazine and its book series. This group with an Anglo-American bent was at odds with left-wing groups dominated by writers who had studied in Japan. Liang famously took on the formidable Lu Xun over the question of the class character of literature, Liang standing up for universal human values. Lu Xun's final description of Liang (in 1930) was 'a feeble capitalist running dog without a home'. With that label round his neck Liang was well advised to seek refuge in Taiwan in 1949, because in Communist China Lu Xun's word was law. The second controversy was sparked by Liang's announcement while he was literary editor for the *Central Daily News* that along with contributions to do with the war against Japan he also welcomed contributions that had nothing to do with the war. Sound patriots were outraged at that, and a storm broke over Liang's head. We may be glad that it did, because Liang retreated to a humble dwelling in the countryside, ironically named by him Quaint Cottage, and started writing his *Yashe Xiaopin* 雅舍小品(Little Essays from Quaint Cottage). Begun in 1940, they were not published as a book until 1949, in Taiwan. Two of the essays translated here are from that first collection (three more collections, written in Taiwan, followed).

It was immediately obvious to Liang's contemporaries that these were not 'Chinese' essays, and they still stand out half a century and many thousand more essayists later as uniquely alien to the Chinese 'spirit'. Their spirit is that of the early 20th century 'silver age' of Anglo-American essay writing. They are all topic-centred, and write with wit and often with drollery—and almost always with good will—of the human comedy. The author places himself well above the fray, and when he speaks of himself it is not as his personal subjective self, but as an actor in the play. His topics are homely things and human constants, absolutely 'nothing to do with the war'. Yet Liang's readers had no difficulty in relating to these essays as 'Chinese' too, for their matter was all the people and practices that made up their own society, and their language was all authentic Chinese, conspicuously in the classical expressions and the popular sayings, less obviously but equally certainly in its syntax. Such Chineseness of language was not all that common, as by the time Liang wrote the Chinese language had been strongly influenced by English.

The path that Liang trod in these humorous essays was of course a dangerous one. If the author strains to find humour in the everyday, he can easily part company with truthfulness and end up by just being silly. Liang rarely falls into this trap, and when he skirts it perilously near he rescues himself with a good turn of phrase. A common source of humour is the sneaking feelings that people will not normally admit to; these the humorist ferrets out and dilates on. An example from Liang's essay 'Gou'狗(Dogs) is the secret satisfaction that a dog owner feels when his dog scares the pants off a visitor, despite the profuse apologies he makes. What raises this observation above the mediocre is his analogy: the dog has proved that it is not like those functionaries who are just 'on the books' (*guaming chaishi*). His essays are full of unexpected but brilliantly apt expressions like that.

Although Liang's basic matter is all Chinese, he will illustrate his point by references to any part of the world and by quoting authors ancient and modern. That he was able to do so with ease and familiarity was thanks to an education that was rare in his time and is rare in ours. His predecessor as an

English-style essayist, Liang Yuchun (no relation) was extremely well read too, but his youthfulness (he died at the age of 26) would not submit to control. Liang Shih-ch'iu was over forty (the age at which one 'ceases to doubt', according to Confucius) when he started writing his *Yashe* essays, and his grip on the essay form is, in contrast, very evident.

Sickness
病

Lu Xun once conjured up the picture of a gent coughing up half a mouthful of blood while being helped onto his porch by two maidservants to look at the autumn begonias, pretending that this was a paradigm of high culture and refinement. In fact, while there are any number of things that are cultured and refined, illness is the great exception. One can understand that those who have not the good fortune to be able to view autumn begonias propped up by two maidservants might find that condition enviable, but to add the circumstance of 'coughing up half a mouthful of blood' seriously diminishes its enviability: I would not be surprised if marching off alone and unaided to a vegetable patch to look at turnips and cabbages might not be thought preferable.

I recently read an article that referred to pregnancy as a 'physiological abnormality'; to me it was the author who was 'psychologically abnormal'. The true form of physiological abnormality is illness. Just the sight of an invalid's face is hard enough for most people to stomach: as yellow as a notice of bereavement, or as green as a freshly unearthed ancient bronze; a layer of skin stretched over a skull, or just a flicker of an eyelid more than a mask. Illness is a change from normality, a necessary part of the process of changing from a living person to a dead person. Because illness is abnormal it is also ugly. They say that the picture of the Chinese Helen[1] clutching her heart and furrowing her brow is beautiful, but if

---

[1] The 'Chinese Helen' was Xi Shi 西施, a legendary beauty of the 5th century BC. There is a famous anecdote about her habitual frowning in *Zhuangzi*: 'The beautiful Hsi-shih [Xi Shi], troubled with heartburn, frowned at her neighbours. An ugly woman of the neighbourhood, seeing that Hsi-shih was beautiful, went home and likewise pounded her breast and frowned at her neighbours. But at the sight of her the rich men of the neighbourhood shut tight their gates and would not venture out,

the truth be told, that view is but a personal quirk; it may be safely discounted when one remembers the story of the man driven away from home because of his repulsive body odour who found a warm welcome at the seaside.

I once had a very long spell in hospital because I myself fell ill. I came to the conclusion that we Chinese men are extremely maladapted to staying in hospital. When he is in good health every man can be a little local despot. Servants, needless to say, are his hired slaves, his wife is only a slave who is provided with bed and board, and his parents are self-enlisted slaves. Accustomed as he is to living in the lap of luxury and having people at his beck and call, when one day his eminence finds himself subject to an indisposition and is carried off to hospital, he will not be content until he has moved his entire household (including the kitchen!) in with him. Once installed in the hospital, he acts as if he is in his own country villa, and has people running about buying watermelon, making lotus-root drinks, fetching water for him to wash, filling his thermos flask. Actually it would be more accurate to say the hospital is treated as a hotel rather than a home, principally on account of the noisiness. The fact that a patient in Ward 4 is about to peg out does not stop the visitors in Ward 5 from holding forth in loud voices; neither does the fact that the patient in Ward 6 has just swallowed a big dose of sedatives prevent the man in Ward 7 from hollering for his amah at the top of his lungs.

A hospital is the battlefield over which life and death fight for final victory; as such it will resound with groans and lamentations, shouts and jubilations—for human beings are not made of stone, and even a saint could not be expected to restrain himself in such circumstances. Those who get short shrift are those who thought a hospital was a place where they could recuperate in peace.

But there was one occasion when I found it in my heart to excuse the noise that came from the next ward. It was the middle of the night, and the voice was a woman's. First the bell rang, then came a call of 'Nurse!' Thereafter a ring, followed after an interval by a call, the tempo rising from largo to allegro, the tone becoming more and

---

while the poor men grabbed their wives and children by the hand and scampered off.' (*The Complete Works of Chuang Tzu*, Burton Watson, trans. [New York: Columbia University Press, 1968], p. 160)

more urgent, the pitch more and more shrill. Everyone in the hospital, apart from those resting in the mortuary, must have heard, but no one brought her what she wanted. The calls gradually turned to sobs, desperation gradually turned to entreaty, and by the time all the correct procedures had been followed and the thing had passed down the chain of command to finally reach her, its hour had passed, and it was of no more use.

The old-style notice of bereavement liked to use the phrase 'passed away at the end of his/her allotted span in the bosom of his/her family', not without reason. If you nurse an illness at home you may not get the best of treatment, but you won't be bothered by extraneous irritations. Supposing the illness were incurable and you had to slip this mortal coil, to do so in the bosom of your family is something that may justifiably be mentioned with pride, for it means the death would have been a comfortable one.

Serious illness may profoundly alter one's outlook on life. When I was at death's door, I was overcome by a sense that one could take nothing for granted in this life, and consequently took a more tolerant attitude toward everything. For instance, I normally made no allowances for one man I knew who drew a rice ration on false pretences, but when after several injections of heart stimulants I saw him blithely turn up again, I could not help softening toward him: it seemed to me he could after all be admitted to the human race. Lu Xun's last words were that he 'forgave no one, nor sought forgiveness from anyone'. This stand one can accept, but those of less than his great stature are likely when their strength ebbs to come to terms with humankind. After I had lain flat on my back for many days, I came to see everyone in a sympathetic light, and this old world of ours didn't seem such a bad place after all. However, when my temperature and pulse had nearly returned to normal, my old standards reasserted themselves and the scales fell from my eyes.

It is the weak who need sympathy. Sympathy extended at times of weakness is the kind most readily appreciated. If someone comes to visit you when you are so sick that you cannot feed yourself, that token of sympathy is taken in immediately, like gentle rain falling on parched ground. The invalid will be reassured that man can still reach out to man, that man acts more tenderly toward his fellow men than beasts do. However, to inquire after an invalid's state of health is an art: it is not the same as a journalist's interview, nor yet the same as offering condolences to the bereaved. My latest illness took a tortuous course, so much so that the story required half an hour to tell, or rather more if one used a Europeanized form of the Chinese language. Yet my visitors inquired with such earnestness and solicitude that I had no choice but to make a detailed report. When my repeat performances passed the thirty mark they began to pall, and I felt embarrassingly like those old professors who mount their podium year after year and put on the same record. My solution was to offer relatively extensive coverage to those visitors who had come a long way, and to stress the dangerousness of the illness, in order to persuade them that their journey had been really necessary and save them from disappointment; while local friends got a severely truncated version, with due apologies. Then there were those excessively warm-hearted people who would not leave until they had helped you in some way, or if they had to leave without helping you, felt very put out about it. To please them, I asked them to pour me a glass of water though I wasn't thirsty, putting on an act of appealing helplessness. Lastly there were the very straitlaced who, judging me about to depart this vale of tears, were induced to ponder on the eternal truths of the great religion, and assumed an ever more serious expression: they sat there wordless, plunged in deepest gloom. On these friends I will in future make the heaviest demands, for I realized that they not only could be relied upon to attend the sick, they were also the right people to hold a wake.

(1949)

Haircut
理髮

Having one's hair cut is not an enjoyable business. Anyone who has had a tooth out will feel a tremor at the sight of the barber's chair, because of its close resemblance to the dentist's. We don't expect the barber's chair to be of sandalwood inlaid with shell, or in Louis XIV style, but at least it shouldn't be so ugly—neither round nor square, and so stolid and rigid that when you lower yourself into it you think you are for the chop. The basket in which the itinerant barber carries the tools of his trade is even more alarming: sticking up from it is a little flagpole of the kind they used to dangle heads from.

Still, having one's hair cut is a necessary evil. 'The gentleman tidies his apparel, and has regard to his appearance: one does not have to have shaggy hair and a grimy face to be wise and virtuous.' This shows that having one's hair cut is all bound up with making a good impression. The Sikhs of India have never cut their hair or trimmed their beards, following the precept of 'guarding intact what one receives from one's parents'; accordingly every man jack of them has hair sprouting from all over his hair and face, and this being the rule, nothing is made of it. But in our society it will not do: if you have an unruly mop of hair, people will suspect you are in mourning for a parent, or have just been released from prison.

Whiskers are even more tiresome. If you let them grow, it does not matter if they are all straggly: any growth of hair around your mouth earns respect. To have your chin shaven so close that it takes on a bluish sheen is also all right—it also earns respect. The exception is a growth of a few centimetres, neither long nor short, and bristly like a hedgehog or a field of stubble: this really puts people off. I remember the bibulous monk Lu Zhishen's 'freshly sprouting whiskers, all spiky and uneven, were quite frightening': the blacksmith approached him with great caution; whereas the beard of Zhong Kui, the demon catcher, stuck out angrily like a spear. Since we do not aim to frighten people off, nor to crunch up demons, but do feel obliged to live up to the ideal of the gentleman, how can we not go to the hairdresser's regularly?

There is nothing about the barber to make one withold one's respect: he serves the public no less than the executioner and the butcher. Indeed he is more elevated than them, since he wears a suit, the mark of the upper class in China. If you become acquainted with an executioner, he will measure your neck for the best place to bring down the blade, simply from occupational habit. When you are seated, the barber rolls up his sleeves and likewise sizes up your head of hair without having any interest in its owner. A white cloth is thrown over you, not necessarily a very clean one: more often it is speckled like the 'tiger skin' paper calligraphers use. Then a band of cloth is drawn tight around your throat. Of course it is not life-threatening, yet it binds tight enough for you to know about it: if it were the barber's own neck, he would not use so much muscle.

In principle, hair is meant to be cut, but in practice a certain amount of pulling and yanking is involved too. The most suitable form of protest is to contract one's brows and make grimaces at the mirror, in the hope that the barber will see.

Placed as it is on top of the neck, the human head can turn relatively freely, yet there are some angles it cannot manage comfortably. The barber seems unwilling to take account of this limitation—he never seems to think the posture of your head is right, and is forever levering it this way and twisting it that way to suit the angle of his razor and scissors. I suspect barbers must all work out in the gym: otherwise how can you explain the strength of their wrists?

There is a good reason for a big mirror being set up in front of your chair. It is not for you to admire yourself in; the point is to tell you how the barber is disposing of your bonce, for there is no one who has no thought for his bonce. Yet our friends who wear glasses are under a handicap here, for once they remove them, everything is just a blur. They have to sit as rigid as zombies, especially when they catch the flash of cold steel. Another cause for regret is that they cannot pay due regard to their neighbours on either side. The customer stretched out on their left is being shaved, to the sound of a scythe shearing dry grass; they think it must be some hulking fellow, but not necessarily so: it might be a female customer. The customer to the right is being sprayed with perfume and rubbed with cold cream—almost certainly a great beauty; but not necessarily so: it might turn out to be a man. Just as well, then, not to look, for the sight may be extremely unsettling. To slump inert in your seat is the best solution.

The most pleasant of experiences at the barber's is the shampoo. The thick liquid soap dripping on your head reminds you of the Buddhist term for instilling wisdom—the richest cream being poured over your cranium. Then when his ten fingers scratch your head, it might not be as delightful as the attentions of the nymph Magu, yet they are as sharp as bird claws. The only thing that bothers you is that when your scalp is thoroughly tingling, that really itchy patch in the south-east corner has escaped the scratching altogether. When it comes to rinsing, you are almost sure to have your ears flooded, but considering that your customary ablutions are probably restricted to the heartland of the face, and the outposts on the far frontiers have to fend for themselves, for them now to get a thorough dowsing is in fact cause for celebration. On the other hand the hair-drier is no fun: at times it blows a cold wind, at others a warm front intrudes, making it unbearably hot. One thinks of it as a form of punishment.

The most testing thing is being shaved. When that incomparably sharp razor glides over your throat and eyelids and round your ears, all you can do is close your eyes and hold your breath and sweat it out. Robert Lynd wrote a piece called 'A Sermon on Shaving', in which he said:

> When the razor touches my face, I cannot suppress the thought, what if the barber suddenly went mad? Fortunately the barber has never gone mad, but I have met with danger of a similar sort. For example, a little French barber was shaving me during a rain storm, and he leapt a foot in the air when the lightning flashed. Then there was the drunken barber who felt for my face with his razor and missed it, like a boozer who reaches for something and catches empty air. At last the razor came to rest on my face, and he leaned on it to steady himself, but he used too much weight, and scraped off a patch of whiskers on my right jaw. As the razor still rested on my skin I didn't dare protest. Even a whisper might, I felt, unnerve him and cause him to lose his balance, in which case he might inadvertently sever my jugular vein. Then the razor was temporarily withdrawn from my face, no doubt with the intention of, as the French put it, *reculer pour mieux sauter*. Seizing my chance, I said in a nightmare voice, 'That will do, that will do, enough, thank you'.[2]

I can't pretend that such frightening experiences happen very often. Nevertheless, everyone will feel apprehensive if when they are being shaved they recall the joke of the comic monologue artist, to the effect that apprentice barbers practise on the fuzz-covered winter gourd; if they happen to be called away, they just clunk their razor down into the gourd. Later on, when they are qualified to serve the public, they are apt to mistake human heads for those same winter gourds.

Actually the dangers of being shaved are a secondary consideration. The most detestable thing is the utterly brazen way they feel over your face when the shaving is done. And you are obliged to tip them after that indignity!

---

[2] This quotation is back-translation from the Chinese, not the original English text.

Listening to Plays
聽戲

Listening to plays, not watching plays. Everybody in Peking used to say 'listening to', hardly ever 'watching' plays. The choice of word makes a big difference. The fact is, the singing was the main thing in our old plays. The formula was 'song and dance', but in reality there wasn't much dancing to be seen. I got a liking for listening to plays when I was young. Many's the time I have seen men sitting under the side gallery at a playhouse, sitting bolt upright against a pillar, with eyes shut, head wagging slightly, hand lightly marking the beat, concentrating with every nerve on the singer's rendition. When the singer hit a perfect note, it was to them like scratching an itch: a roar of 'bravo!' came from deep within them. If the singer hit a wrong note, they would equally forthrightly come out with a catcall. This was your true audience, it was they who maintained the standard of the plays' performance. Needless to say, they didn't keep their eyes shut all the time: sometimes they opened them.

Practically everyone who grew up in Peking liked to listen to plays, and I of course was no exception. To begin with I was afraid of going to the playhouses, because they were too crowded and the seats were too uncomfortable. I remember very clearly the Tasteful Teagarden I used to frequent: it was all long narrow benches and tables that were arranged end-on to, not facing, the stage, so that you had to twist your torso and swivel your neck to see what was going on on the stage. In the summer particularly, everyone stripped to the waist, but I was not in the habit of baring my back, and found it terribly embarrassing to reveal myself in the buff in public, but as soon as you took your seat there was a zealous waiter at your side ready to take your clothes and give you a tally in exchange. You looked round you then, and on all four sides there was screen after screen of flesh, so you had no choice but to divest yourself like the others. In front and behind, left and right, it was all flesh, milk white, lemon yellow and berry brown. It was like being surrounded by sides of meat in a cold store. (At that time the patrons of the playhouse were all men.) Though any appetite for carnality would have been satisfied, there was absolutely no pleasure in it. Plays lasted for four or five hours and if you needed to go to the lavatory in the middle you had to force a way through the phalanx of flesh, a way which immediately closed seamlessly after you; on your return you had to force open a passage all over again. So one looked upon going to the lavatory as a 'perilous path', except that there was only peril, no path.

Actually there was no cause for complaint about the theatre environment. Every kind of environment has its good reasons for existing in its own place and time. The playhouses were originally called tea gardens, and were meant for drinking tea and passing the time chatting; the plays on the stage were to begin with an ancillary entertainment. The hubbub of loud talk that went on there was quite understandable, seeing that it was originally a place of recreation where all and sundry met and mixed. Children could have a feast at the playhouses; needless to say there were peanuts and melon seeds, but there was also everything else they could imagine, like fruit-sticks, plum juice, oilcakes, junket, mushy pea cake, and so on. Grown-ups' jaws were not idle, either: set out on the tables were dried and fresh fruit, dim sum and the like. Food pedlars also shuttled back and forth crying their wares, both a boon and a nuisance. The waiters in charge of the hot towels used to throw rolls of them from one corner to the other, and I never saw them miss and hit anyone on the head. As an ardent playgoer friend of mine put it, this was a play beyond the play. Those perfumed towels could not be dispensed with, even though they were a most effective way of spreading germs.

You might ask, didn't such circumstances make watching plays just too uncomfortable? Granted, it was uncomfortable, but there was pleasure in it too. Letting your hair down has always been part of the Chinese character. In the playhouse everyone was free to do what they wanted: eat, drink, talk, shout, smoke, spit, (the little ones) cry, sneeze, yawn, wipe their face, strip off to the waist, get into a minor argument, row over a seat—nobody would think of interfering. Where else would you find such perfect conditions for letting yourself go? The Western theatre audience's practice of getting all dressed up and keeping as quiet as mice would have been sheer punishment to the Chinese playgoer!

Setting foot in a playhouse was to me in my youth like entering a different world. Of course I couldn't understand the singing, I could only appreciate the clowning and the battle scenes, especially where the warriors snatch each other's weapon. My favourites were the plays acted by Jiu Zhenfeng like *Hundred Herb Mountain* and *Sizhou City*.

They prompted me to buy some stage swords and spears and practise the exchange of weapons with my brother at home; surprisingly enough, we got one or two passes off pretty well. Still, we didn't attempt acrobatics like throwing yourself off piled-up tables, landing on your back and rebounding to your feet. Once when we were imitating Fan Zhongyu in the episode 'Jumping Out of the Chest' sending his shoe shooting up in the air so that it landed on his head, my brother in a moment of carelessness kicked his boot askew, and it landed with a crash on the glass window of our entrance hall. Apart from bringing down just retribution on our heads, this brought me to my senses before I became a fully-fledged play buff or play addict. When I was a little older and frequented playhouses again I had the luck to see a group of outstanding actors show their paces on the stage, people such as Chen Delin, Liu Hongsheng, Gong Yunfu, De Junru, Qiu Guixian, Mei Lanfang, Yang Xiaolou, Wang Changlin, Wang Fengqing, Wang Yaoqing, and Yu Shuyan. By and by I got to appreciate the real beauty of the opera, and felt the ordeal of sitting about for hours amid all that bedlam was a price worth paying. To hear one or two arias delivered with perfect tone and feeling was to make you drunk with their pitch and cadence, and cause the blood to flow freely and evenly through your veins. Friends who are deep in Western music might say this was bad taste on my part. I would have no answer; I would simply concede that this was the taste of our people, and that we were all contented with this taste. In all that bedlam a pretty high level of performance was needed to hold the attention of the audience. Normally there was nothing much worth seeing in the first part of the programme, but when the best acts on the bill came on, it only needed a famous actor to show himself for the house to fall so silent you could hear a pin drop. Any tipplers who stepped out of line were hissed quiet. To put up with a long spell of tedium in exchange for hearing a song that stirred your soul was a fair bargain. The saying 'the music lingered in the hall for three days without melting away' really describes what we felt.

Later on the old troupers withered on the bough and were replaced by a younger generation of actors. With them came cries for the improvement of the theatre, as if an art can be improved. I just know that after a certain number of years an art form gets old, feeble and dies, whereupon new shoots germinate; I never realized an art could still be improved after it has matured and worn out. The first reform was to lift the bar on female attendance. Now there was nothing wrong with that, but once women were admitted, the passages of doubtful propriety in the plays were largely excised, and in a certain sense this was thought to be a loss. The shape of the stage was changed from the three-sided raised stage jutting out into the audience to the proscenium arch kind; new playbooks came out, new melodies were introduced, and new costumes and props devised. I once saw Shang Xiaoyun play the *Milky Way Wedding*; this great big actor, got up in a skin-tight pink undergarment, pretended to bathe in the nude, and the audience joyfully applauded. I said to myself, 'It's the end, it's over. It's a different audience now!' The nature of the audience decides the nature of the play. It was now the few who went to listen to the play, the many who went to see a spectacle.

I left Peking long ago, and have lost touch with the theatre, but I did see some fine performances when I was young. When anyone mentions the 'old man' role, I see Yu Shuyan in my mind; in the warrior role I see Yang Xiaolou; the 'old woman' is Gong Yunfu; the divas are Wang Yaoqing and Mei Lanfang; the 'young man' is De Junru, the female warrior is Jiu Zhenfeng; the clown is Wang Changlin. . . . They set permanent standards for me, and it is easy for me to slip into thinking no one will ever compare with them. Our Chinese plays are like brush-written script: their champions champion on, but taking the broad picture into account, I'm afraid there is little hope of them regaining their past glory. The times have changed!

(1963)

Liang Yuchun 梁遇春 (1906–1932)

COMMENTARY

Liang Yuchun was given the nickname of 'the Chinese Elia', but it would be more fitting to call him the Chinese 'Citizen of the World'. Though he never set foot outside China in his short lifetime, he was more universalist, at least in his authorial persona, than any other writer of his age: that is to say, his interest was in humanity, not in his countrymen, except in that they were human too. To encounter his essays for the first time is to experience nothing less than shock at the ease with which he transcended national barriers and communed with the best of humanity in other lands. He felt he needed to, to stay human himself.

Comparatively little is recorded about Liang Yuchun's short life. Born in Fujian Province, his family background was a scholarly one. After secondary schooling in his home province, he went to Peking University in 1924 to study English. At that time the English Department had a galaxy of famous professors. The lively, liberal, youthful magazines edited by Peking University staff were also an encouragement to embryonic writers. Liang Yuchun contributed his first essay to one such magazine in 1926. By the time he graduated in 1928 he had had eight more published, including a startlingly perceptive appraisal of Charles Lamb, whom he regarded as the greatest of English essayists, hence the 'Chinese Elia' tag. While still an undergraduate he also completed *Yingguo xiaopinwen xuan* 英國小品文選(A selection of English essays, preface dated 1928), which was an annotated translation, with matching Chinese text, of ten examples from Addison to Robert Lynd.

Liang Yuchun was recruited immediately after graduation to teach the English essay at Ji'nan University, Shanghai. During his short stay there as a teaching assistant (July 1928–February 1930), he impressed his students with his 'Oxford English' and his Peking Chinese. He then returned to Peking to a job in the Peking University Library, which also entailed teaching some English language classes. While holding these jobs, Liang Yuchun continued with his essay writing and his translating; among many other things he translated Defoe's *Moll Flanders*. His first collection of essays, entitled *Chunlao ji* 春醪集(Spring wine) was published in 1930. His second collection, *Lei yu xiao* 淚與笑(Tears and laughter) was published in 1934—posthumously, for he died of scarlet fever in 1932, leaving behind his wife and baby son (his daughter also died of the fever).

With his death his country lost a rare intelligence, a sensitive and generous soul, and the most fluent writer of *baihua* (the vernacular language) in the whole of the Republican period (1912–1949). Those qualities are first-rate qualifications for an essayist, and indeed his work was immediately recognized as something special, but the curtailment of his career inevitably contributed to his subsequent relative neglect, which was compounded by the rapid politicization of Chinese literature: he was a 'citizen of the world' before his country was ready for him. However, his essays have been reprinted in Taiwan since the 1970s and in the People's Republic from the 1980s, and he is now firmly established in the modern canon.

By his own confession, Liang Yuchun was addicted to the English essay. He read the world's great novels with enjoyment, but once read they rested peacefully on his bookshelf, without being subjected to further 'violent perturbation' at his hands. Montaigne and the whole succession of English essayists were in contrast his constant companions. He found that the English essay told the truth, got behind appearances, and did battle with falsity and hypocrisy. In his own writing he followed suit. He also wrote on subjects well explored by English essayists ('vagabonds' for example), though in his own way. If in style his work resembles that of any English essayist, it is Hazlitt's rather than Lamb's: his words stream out seemingly under their own power: good, healthy, expressive words of the mother tongue. Like Hazlitt too, he was given to standing conventional assumptions on their head: so tears are preferable to laughter, the philosophy of death is more interesting than the philosophy of life, jovial people are not funny, and so on. On the other hand he could also write in the droll style of the English 'silver age', as on the pleasures of staying in bed.

In sharp contrast with the healthiness of Liang's language is the morbidity of his thoughts. Looking up from the bottom of the heap, first as a student, then as a lowly teacher, it is understandable that he should have been depressed by the pretence and pretentiousness of what he saw, but his pessimism was far more basic than that. In 'Yige "xinlike" de weixiao'—個「心力克」的微笑(A cynic's smile) he pointed out, 'to see through people's masks is common enough, but what is the good, when you discover that compared to their masks people's true visages are so boring, so dull, so little fun?'—and that was only for starters. Given this dim view of existence, we find that unlike his beloved Charles Lamb, the wise, kindly light leading his readers throught the dark vale, Liang offers only the analogy of 'a spark between the darkness before and the darkness after' to describe our universe. The great and glorious compensation is that when he blows upon that spark it burns with as pure a flame as one could hope to find in any literature.

I have translated less than is Liang Yuchun's due because other good translations of his essays have been published recently. They are Cathy Poon's 'Three Essays by Liang Yuchun' (*Renditions* No. 43, 1995) and Eva

Hung's 'The Priceless Moments of a Spring Morn' (in Lau and Goldblatt, *Columbia Anthology of Modern Chinese Literature*, 1995). By way of compensation, I add an excerpt from his half droll, half serious 'Mao gou' 貓狗(Cats and dogs). After saying how afraid he is of both animals, the cat because of its justifiable association with witches, he makes the association with the cities he knows:

> Shanghai is a dog. If you stand on the Bund and close your eyes, you can well imagine that it is a ferocious canine stretched out in front of you. Dogs can stand for the dark side of reality, and in Shanghai this darkness makes you take every step in fear and trembling, as if a rabid dog was really following you. Peking, on the other hand, is a cat: it stands for moral decay. Peking has a mustiness about it that makes you let everything slide, give up thinking, give up doing, just squat down and live out your days mindlessly. It really is as if a big cat has dyed its black mark on every soul, indelibly, for ever.

Other authors have expressed the same feelings, but none so imaginatively.

On the Road
途中

It is a nonchalant autumn day, with flurries of cold rain. I sit in the tram and see the assistants in the shops lining the route are almost all languidly talking, reading the paper, and drinking tea—especially drinking tea, because there is really a nip in the air today. There are some, too, just draped over the counter, looking at the weather. In sum the teeming streets of the foreign concession have suddenly taken on a relaxed and casual air. The towering commercial palaces all seem to have been transformed into small country huts, and the staff of assistants who normally are busy making money for the boss and buttering up the customers have actually become aware of the pleasures of affluence, and pass the time in idle badinage, just like the retired scholars of old. There are very few pedestrians in the streets, and even the foreign devils on the tram, on their way to the bank, are smoking their pipes and reading the adverts in their newspapers for something to do, with no sign of their usual irritability. That probably attests to the effectiveness of their raincoats!

At North Station I change to a bus going to the western country district. The autumn countryside has a special quality in the rain. You can't actually see the thin drizzle falling, you can only see the little raindrops turning up on the window panes, and the faint footprints of rain that skitter attractively across the surface of the river. Then there are the powdery raindrops that puff in through the broken pane and come to rest on my face. I feel like shivering, but the baptism of rainwater makes me wonderfully refreshed. Having long been caught up in the toils of mundane life, and habitually peering out on life through bleary eyes, it is rare for me to experience such freshness and clear-headedness. Looking again at the scenery, it has neither the delicate sheen of spring, which makes one feel it must soon pass, nor the dieback of winter, which suggests the end of the world is nigh; it is just quiet and patient. The fine haze of rain, now lifting, now closing, covers the land and enhances its beauty. I cannot help reciting to myself the line of the Song poet Jiang Baishi, my fellow countryman: how true it is that 'One of best things in life is the rain that heralds autumn.'

I suddenly recall her beetling her brows this morning and saying, 'Look at this weather, all wet and windy, and you've got to go such a long way. It's really too bad!' I have a little laugh to myself: it wouldn't occur to her that I am looking out of the bus window enjoying some nice scenery, would it? I guess she thinks I am feeling as miserable as sin, like a condemned man riding in his tumbril, when in fact I am enthusing over this spectacle of autumn grasses turning yellow, autumn leaves still on the trees. One should be grateful for all sympathy, even misdirected sympathy, so I let her go on pitying me as weary and stained from battling against the elements. Besides, if something disagreeable happens to me, and my displeasure unintentionally shows itself on my face, I can always blame it on the strain of my journey. In that way she doesn't have to keep probing until I tell her the truth, which will just add to her worries for nothing.

Actually I am very fond of taking to the road. At present my daily travel time is almost always over two hours. This has been going on for quite a few months, but I am not in the least fed up with it. Every day when I board the tram it is like starting a honeymoon journey. The people on the tram and the people on the street are mostly unacquainted with each other, so they don't put on false faces. There is no comparison with lecture halls, banquets, and government offices, where everyone is so intent on going through the prescribed motions. In parks, playhouses, amusement parks, and restaurants the visitors brim over with jollity, at least they pretend to, while in cemeteries, law courts, hospitals and druggists, the patrons all have deeply furrowed brows. Monotony prevails in both respects, and leaves us with a depressing sense of staleness. In contrast, people in the street and on buses and trams display a whole kaleidoscope of visages. You only need to sit on a tram and keep your eyes peeled for thirty minutes to discover on the faces of the people you see practically all the expressions of joy and sorrow in the human repertory, as well as every mood. You sit quietly in your seat getting on with your appraisal, and the other passengers are good enough to let you infer from their appearance and behaviour their life story and their present state of mind. The pedestrians outside enter your field of vision one after another, and you are quite free to observe them impudently, for they will not know you are doing so. What is more, they pass by in a steady stream, which means you can compare one with another. These ranks of ordinary people are a lot more interesting, I'm sure, than any carnival procession. Indeed the continuously renewed passage of pedestrians may be described as God's own carnival, and as such is of course far superior to the garish entertainments of our festivals.

Another thing is that our mental state while travelling is best adapted to detached observation, most receptive to external stimuli. We normally have some business in hand, either proper or improper, so our attention is inevitably concentrated on one object. It is only while travelling, particularly in the course of a long, familiar journey, that our mind is untrammelled, not preoccupied, and therefore occupied with everything. This is about the only opportunity we have in the midst of our rushing and scurrying to get a good eyeful of life in its true colours. Whichever way you look at it, then, travelling is our best chance to get to know life. The tram, bus, boat and pavement are as it were admission tickets to the grand exhibition of life. Sad to say, many people look on them as waste paper, and take their life's journey in vain.

An old saying of ours refers to 'reading ten thousand books, travelling ten thousand miles.' Of course, the bit about ten thousand miles means seeing famous mountains and majestic rivers and visiting great cities, but I prefer to put another interpretation on it. You can notch up your ten thousand miles by travelling the same stretch of road ten thousand times, and as long as you really use your eyes, I guarantee you will equally count as someone who has seen the world. The adage says 'The scholar can know the affairs of the world without leaving his gate.' Unfortunately the halls of learning of the scholars of old are closed to us, so we had better hit the road, and look about us!

Once we have a clear-sighted view of life, the accidence of reputation and fortune will be unable to disturb our inner serenity, and our souls will thereby gain eternal freedom, for many are the roads that lead to freedom, not just the one ordained by Mr Bertrand Russell. The people we have to fear are those who ponder questions with their face to a wall, not giving the road outside a glance: there is really nothing you can do with them, for they condemn themselves by their own inertia. Reading books is an indirect way of understanding life, taking the road is a direct way of understanding life. Truth is lost when committed to words, which is why I feel that the ten thousand books can be put aside unread, but the ten thousand miles require you to get up and go.

To understand nature there is no alternative to getting out and about, but I think that planned travel does not give you as close a feel for nature as ordinary walking about. The tourist is always intent on where he is going, and so is under pressure, which is surely not the right frame of mind if you are to receive the beauties of nature in your own good time. Furthermore, a scene is a living thing: it can by no means be reduced to a valley, a stream, a cave, or a cliff. Yet what tourists mostly see is indeed these dead scenes of nationwide fame, famous sights which everyone automatically praises, for some unknown reason. The tourists, stuck in the same groove, become new prisoners to a tradition of unchallengeable antiquity. Is it worth the trouble? you might well ask. They ought to realize that only the fine views that we ourselves discover have close attachments for us, can reach into our souls, and these fine sights are mostly come upon by accident, they cannot be had on demand. So it is that vistas of fields and cottages we might glimpse from the train window on a business trip can imprint themselves deeply on our heart, whereas the beauty spots we apply for sick leave to visit, at our own expense, only float like mist or smoke in our store of memories.

I took a trip to Hangzhou this spring and autumn, and every day I either sat in a rowing boat following the directions of the boatman, or was driven round the hills, respectfully obeying the orders of the driver. A slim little guidebook insidiously exerted supreme authority. When I had gone the round of all the famous sights and got back on the train for home, I felt relieved of a heavy burden. And when I resumed my quotidian mechanical existence, looking freely to left and right, no longer in fear of the boatman's, driver's or travelling companions' remonstrances, no longer obliged to see things that had to be seen, I was so happy I could have cried. The West Lake scenery has naturally dissolved, leaving not a rack behind. The trouble is, it dissolved too slowly. At first it still formed the backdrop to several nightmares of mine. Whenever I dreamed of our selfless driver leading us over the rugged rocks of Jewel Mountain or along the slippery stone path to Dragon Well, no matter how I pleaded with him he would always force me to go and see the roseate clouds of Roseate Cloud Cavern and the dragon's horn of Dragon Well. Thank the Lord, the West Lake no longer appears in my dreams.

As I said, many of the fine scenes that have meant most to me in my life have been got through the windows of the bus that goes to the western country district. I sit in the bus, being bumped up and down and jolted right and left, reading an interminable 18th-century novel. Sometimes I close the book and glance casually out at the weather, and suddenly get this impression of emerald green, fragrant flowers all over the place, and a cloudless sky of indescribable blue. Shocked awake to the coming of spring, my soul truly takes leave of my body and flies up to cloud nine. When next I look again, the good scenery is far behind us, and what is left of the journey is the mucky streets of Zhabei. The next day I pass the same spot again, and everything is as before, yet I can't help feeling that something is missing, something has changed. Thereupon that day's scene remains forever in my mind. Sweet things when looked on too long will cloy; genuinely fine scenes should fleet past like that, and never return. The worst thing about marriage is that you are together night and day; this turns all good things into bad things through overfamiliarity.

At other times, on madly hot summer days, in snowbound winters, I also come across unforeseen sights of unspeakable fascination: they are water to the dry fields of my heart. Soulmates are not hard to find: did not Lu You write 'There are no places where a tower does not catch the light of the moon'? To those who make themselves susceptible, taking the road is without doubt a short cut to understanding nature.

Well-meant Words
善言

Confucius' disciple Zengzi said, 'When man approaches death, his words are good and true.' Quite right. After spending their life in a complete muddle, people often do come out with a memorable saying on their deathbed, which strikes one as extremely wise and poetic. Goethe thought that the most wonderful sound in the world was the bawl of a new-born baby, but I think the ramblings of people as their end draws nigh are equally worth savouring. The other day I bought the posthumous works of Mr Liang Juchan, and reading the book at night, I saw that the last words of his Last Words were: 'It goes on, yet it's over.' When I closed the book and stopped reading I felt truly stopped, in my tracks.

When we see the way the universe goes ever onward, like 'the mighty Yangtze flowing day and night', we do think of it as never ending. Even if the universe were to be destroyed, that would only be a stage in its evolution. Yet when we look at the detail, there is nothing in the universe that does not pass away, never to return—the rosy cheeks of young maidens is hardly the sole example. It is commonly said that flowers will bloom again, while youth once gone is gone forever. But this year's carpet of pretty blooms thrusting up into the sun is definitely not last year's carpet of blooms. If on the grounds that this year's flowers make as good a display as last year's you can claim that last year's flowers enjoy eternal youth, then there is nothing to mope about, for at any given time there will be the same number of lads and lasses in the world.

In so many years' time the present universe will have changed beyond recognition, in which case will not this universe then have been extinguished? So-called growth is in fact extinction, because what has grown is no longer what it was. The ten-year-old me and the now me are as different as chalk and cheese, so I can say I was cut off in my boyhood. Our preachers like to go on about the end of the world, when in reality any day you care to mention is the end of the world. Our socially oriented sages, for their part, fully understand this principle, but only say with a smile, 'birth following on birth is what is called the Change', which shows how good we Chinese are at keeping people happy. Personally, I think it a much better idea to delve into the aspect of 'death following on death', and see what little amusement we can find there. Once we realize that we die every day, we won't see any point in going about the bothersome business of committing suicide, and we will have grown in character to be the equal of the egg-eating Zen master and the wine-swilling monk Lu Zhishen. How liberating that must be, to make a big sweeping bow to all the congregation of the faithful!

What I have said is not meant to encourage people to fold their arms and not get down to a job of work: in human history those with true accomplishments have all known their endeavours were in vain. Zhuge Liang's mind was too clear to harbour illusions, he was aware that he was playing a losing game, yet he was still willing to 'bend himself to the task, and go on till he dropped'. This is what is called 'having human stature'. If you feel there is nothing more worth doing than sitting still, then you may ponder paradoxes for a lifetime like a philosopher, and it is all right too even if you miss out on the meditating. That things should go on yet be over, be over yet go on, is the nature of the universe. Supposing we want to build a dream palace that suits our inclinations in this world of dreams and phantoms, the fact is that one day we will have to shift some bricks. The wise man finds contentment wherever he goes, precisely because he knows there is nothing he must stubbornly cling to, and yet the high priests still like to hold their strings of beads, otherwise they are straws blown in the wind.

Lu Li 陸蠡 (1908–1942)

COMMENTARY

Lu Li was born in a small town in the Tiantai mountains of Zhejiang province, a place untouched by the forces that were shaping the 20th century. His own family was well-to-do. His father could afford to send him to the best schools in Hangzhou for his secondary education: to the Christian Huilan Middle School in 1919 and the Zhijiang University Middle School (also Christian) in 1921. In 1926 he proceeded to Zhijiang University, which was set up by an American church mission, to read natural sciences, but he switched in 1928 to the new Labour University (Laodong Daxue) in Shanghai. The Labour University was founded by idealists to encourage the practical work ethic, which is probably what attracted Lu Li, but it disintegrated soon after he graduated in 1931. From 1931 to 1936 Lu Li taught in a middle school in Fujian province. In 1932 he married a younger cousin, Yuan Zhumei 袁珠美, who bore him a daughter. This wife died in 1936, whereupon he moved to Shanghai to work full-time for the Cultural Life (Wenhua Shenghuo) publishing house. His three books of prose, *Haixing* 海星(Sea stars, 1936), *Zhudao* 竹刀(Bamboo knife, 1938) and *Qiu lü ji* 囚綠集(Imprisoning greenery, 1940) were all published by Cultural Life. In addition he translated one novel by Lamartine (directly from the French) and two novels by Turgenev (basically from the English, but he learned a little Russian, too).

At the end of 1941 the Japanese took over the isolated International Settlement in Shanghai where Lu Li worked, and in 1942 they confiscated a truckful of books of the publishing house. Lu Li went to the police station to make representations, was detained, and was never heard of again. It was said that he obstinately refused to give the 'right' political answers, and died under interrogation. In fact his activities had all been legitimate.

Lu Li strikes me as the most profoundly and sincerely moral of all the writers included in this book. And I cannot think that his morality was unconnected with his Christian schooling. A Christian education in those days gave a very firm stiffening to the moral fibre, and filled the vacuum left by the degeneration of the morals of empire. In Lu Li's case he was said by friends to have had an uncompromising sense of right and wrong and a self-denying sense of duty. In his work the so evident sympathy for the weak and lowly, and occasionally the smiting of the ungodly, also have the true ring of Christianity, though he has no overt recourse to religion.

Lu Li's real-life personality concerns us less than his authorial persona. It is part of the essayist's creed that he should represent his views truly, but the personality of the author that comes through the words on the page is always a *projection* of the author's true self, adjusted to make the best stage lighting for the incident or matter he is to enact. In 'A Temple Lodging,' as in several other of his essays, the persona is the author as a young man, who still has all the purity of adolescence, and hopes and dreams of a life in which he can keep his goodness inviolate. He is therefore very ready to respond to goodness in others, especially where it is unexpected. It is most unexpected, as here, in those whom in Wordsworth's words, 'there were none to praise, and very few to love'. That is the moral core of the essay, and it exerted a powerful attraction for Lu's contemporary readers.

Equally important, however, are the fictional techniques that Lu Li brought to the 'essay' (he would have simply called it 'prose'). The reader often does not know what the essay is going to be about until the final stage. Lu Li sounds a preliminary note here and there, but goes off in different directions, describes scenery, introduces dialogue, tells tall stories, indulges in fantasies, before getting to the crucial encounter. Looking back from the end, however, one realizes that none of the foregoing has been irrelevant: it has all been adumbration for the main point, whether in creating the right atmosphere, or in leading from playful fantasy to impressive reality. In one of his best-known pieces, 'Bamboo Knife', there isn't even an 'I' narrator. It runs through a series of traveller's tales told to pull the leg of the locals to a concluding 'true' and sobering story of revenge. The reason I still include 'A Temple Lodging' as an essay is that though it is framed as a narrative, and has little or no general discussion, it is in fact as effective a treatment of the theme of homelessness as one could imagine.

A Temple Lodging
廟宿

'Only beggars and paupers sleep in disused temples and wayside kiosks, in doorways and on the sidewalk—or vagabonds, or homeless bankrupts, or footloose monks. Everyone who has his own dwelling, be it ever so humble, let alone those with a decent home to go to, should always go home to sleep, even if it is miles away and the time is the middle of the night. . . .' One summer's morning, before it was fully light, while I still lay in bed with my eyes closed, I heard my father loudly remonstrating in this fashion. Judging from his tone, he was extremely irate. Though he was not given to jesting, and had a somewhat severe demeanour, he rarely went as far as to give any of us a proper scolding. As long as we hadn't done anything really terrible, he pretended not to have seen or heard, and let us get on with it. I could not remember any previous occasion when he had rebuked anyone in such a loud and harsh voice.

His words had been addressed to my cousin. This cousin was a few years younger than me. More often than not he stayed with us, because he had lost both parents in childhood. It is said that a boy is closer to his maternal uncle than to the parents who bore him. And he was the only living offspring of my father's two sisters between them. When father spoke late at night of the decline of those two families' fortunes it was with a deep sigh. So my cousin was thoroughly pampered in our house. He was allowed to have his own way more than we were. In spring he went with the children of neighbours to kick shuttlecock, play ball and fly kites, and in summer went down to the river to catch fish and crickets, no restriction being put on him: the only concern was that he should eat well and play well and quickly grow big and strong. He was not to be worn and wearied with reading and writing. My father only had someone secretly keep an eye on him where there was some danger, on hillsides and riverbanks. As for us, though, we were often punished for taking part in those games, which caused us not a little resentment; however, we were older than him, so we didn't make an issue of it.

My cousin's behaviour was even more unbridled in his own home: there he was a real bundle of mischief. His house was only a mile away from ours, and as he came and went between the two, he was sometimes lost track of. On the morning we referred to he hammered on our door as dawn was breaking, demanding to be let in. He was hardly through the door before he panted: 'Uncle, do you know where we spent the night last night? Yesterday evening I went with my mates down to the sandbank to catch crickets, and we stayed there right till it got dark and the Seven Sisters were nearly up in the sky, so we had a sleep in a roadside tea kiosk, and I came back here as soon as it got light.' He sounded quite pleased with himself, and evidently expected his uncle to commend him, to praise his valour. Instead he got a dressing down. At the time I felt truly sorry for him. He had been in so high spirits, and then had a bucket of cold water poured over him: he wouldn't have known where to put his face! There is no telling what my cousin felt inside, whether it was regret, injustice or resentment, but judging by the fact that he never afterwards spent the night outside, he probably concluded on reflection that there was some good sense in what his uncle had said.

Having overheard this lesson being read, I was more wary than ever of overstepping the mark myself, although in the course of time I grew dissatisfied with the narrowness of the world I lived in. I grew to dislike the rooms and passages within our four walls; I hated that dull, overfamiliar room I slept in every night, and all its furnishings: that old wardrobe carved with characters in seal script and ancient bronze script that I couldn't read; that wooden chest with raggedly torn red paper sealing slips round its lock; that 'squirrel stealing the grapes' carved on my bed headboard and outlined in green, with a grape eternally held between the squirrel's teeth, and never reaching its belly; on the front of the fascia board were incised various carvings: on the right a fellow wearing the cap of a top graduate forever riding a horse, followed by two retainers, one always holding up an umbrella, the other always carrying a box of gifts; on the other side was a beautiful girl sitting in a carriage, with a white face, red lips, and gold-coloured clothes, and behind her two maidservants holding fans; and many other carvings besides, like 'Blissful Harmony', 'Magpie with Plum Blossom in its Beak', etc. I was sick of them all. Those trappings that never changed could not satisfy my curiosity, that little nook could not contain my ecumenical youthful ambitions, I wanted to break out of those confines, fly to a new place I could not yet name—no, just to get out of the prison of that house would have done me!

I imagined to myself, if I could spend the night sleeping on the grass down by the riverside, with nothing to obstruct my view, I could look for miles around. There would be flowers growing all over in the grass: red ones, white ones, violet ones, cross-shaped, bell-shaped, butterfly-shaped . . . all bent low with the weight of the dew. Shooting stars would fall from the sky like rain: reddy-gold, orange-yellow, greenish-blue, big ones, little ones, round ones, five-pointed ones; I would fill my pockets with them, full to bursting. Then when I got home I would decorate the inside of my mosquito net with them, in ones and twos, all bright and shining . . . then when mother came with her horsetail whisk at bed time to open the net and drive away the mosquitoes, she would get a big surprise, and say 'Oo, where did you catch all these fireflies? Dirty things! . . .' And then I would laugh myself silly, and when I got my breath again would say: 'These are stars, don't you see? I picked them up by the riverside. You'll let me stay out again?' I would take hold of her skirt and turn round and round her as if circling round a millstone, and she wouldn't get angry.

I also had a vision of the polar explorers I had seen in a picture book, who were said to eat the flesh of polar bears and sleep in bags sewn together from polar bear skins. . . . I greatly admired the inventor of those sleeping bags: if I had a sleeping bag, I could leave that old house and go somewhere new. In the daytime I would feed on wild fruits along my way, and in the evening sleep in my bag, with my head poking out. I wouldn't be cold, as my bag would be windproof, and I could sleep where I pleased, not having to find soft grass. . . . I dreamt such dreams tirelessly, but in fact never once spent a night away from home. I did sometimes accompany my mother to an out of the way water mill to have rice hulled and ground, but however late it was when we finished, we always went back home to sleep.

Occasionally I went to an untended temple to play. In the corners the walls were often blackened by the smoke of fires, or heaps of straw would be on the ground. My older companions told me this was where beggars slept, and the fires had been lit either to fend off the cold or to cook food they had begged from people or stolen from fields. The floor of the temple was usually made of flagstones or tamped earth, so you could imagine how cold and damp it was. There was normally no door to the temple: if there had been one originally, it would have been taken down by them and chopped up for firewood. The nooks and crannies of these temples were draughty in winter and plagued by mosquitoes in summer: definitely not places you would choose to sleep in. I thought father was right when he said that if you had a home you should go back to it to sleep. Once I noticed that some thick wooden stakes had been nailed to the platform underneath the altar table that stood before the image of the Bodhisattva. 'That's to stop the beggars napping under the altar table,' I thought. 'Does that mean the Bodhisattva is not fond of paupers?' Homeless people were really in trouble if the gods they turned to wouldn't give them protection.

I passed my childhood peacefully under the wing of my parents, knowing nothing of the hardships and afflictions of the world outside. As I recall, the first time I realized that the journey of life was not at all as lovely as I had imagined, was in the summer of my eighteenth year.

The Chinese Essay

That summer I was returning from K. On my journey I fell sick, from what cause I know not. It was not mild sickness: I was feverish, my head ached, and my limbs had no strength. Fortunately I was approaching the riverport of X, and would soon be on my home ground. My ears also heard the familiar sounds of my native dialect. I knew that I would not come to grief in these parts, so my anxiety was relieved. I still had some sixty miles to go from X, all of it through mountain country intersected by rivers. To travel by boat upriver would take four or five days. There were no buses (since then the stupendous task of driving a road through the mountains has been completed, and the route is open to motor vehicles); neither were there horses or mules for hire. True, there were sedan chairs, but they were both expensive and uncomfortable, so I followed my regular custom, which was to walk upstream and take a boat downstream. I handed my baggage over to a small forwarding company, and stepped out on my own on the road to home, my umbrella over my shoulder.

At mealtime on the second afternoon I reached a place called Longhairs Ridge. It derived its name from a battle with the long-haired Taiping rebels: the scattering of the longhairs by the local inhabitants is recorded on a stone tablet set up on the ridge. The ridge was not all that high, but it was very steep. A wave of dizziness overcame me when I arrived at its foot, and I felt drained of strength. 'Let me rest a while,' I thought. There were no dwellings thereabout, but some fifty paces from the road there was a temple under a big maple tree. A group of porters were sitting in the temple, cooling off; they had placed their loads in the shade of the tree. A pedlar had set up a candy stall in front of the temple, and was rattling his drum, as usual, to attract customers; it was in fact the sound of his drum that had attracted my attention to the temple. I slipped inside, and sat on the platform under the altar table—thankfully there were no stakes on the platform, which was a tribute to the liberality of the country people. Some wax candles were lit in front of the altar, and smoke was curling up from the incense burner, which told me that the temple was not untended, as I had thought. A refreshing scent wafted over on the breeze. Looking up I saw that honeysuckle had climbed all over the screen wall in front of the temple entrance; most of the blossoms had already fallen. 'It's a pity I'm too far from home, otherwise I could pick the flowers and sell them to the pharmacy!' So thinking I leaned back on the table legs, dozing and recouping my strength.

Time passed, and the porters departed one after the other. The sun had already climbed over the ridge, and its gigantic shadow was thrown over the temple. The flat farmland in the distance was still bathed in sunlight, but this band of sunlight gradually retreated under the advance of the ridge's shadow, getting narrower and farther away as it did so. The candy pedlar and I were the only ones left in the temple. Finally, with a rattle of his drum and an enquiring look at me, the pedlar left. The drum and the look seemed to be meant to tell me, 'It's getting dark, you'd better be on your way!'

I would say my habit is not to think at one minute what the next minute will bring. So I lingered a while after the pedlar had gone, sitting there motionless. The departure of the men had bequeathed a quietness to the temple. Now that the noise of humankind was stilled, the birds flew down from the roof ridge and gathered on the wall, and made their own noise with their chattering. Dusk had fallen when I stood up. A wave of dizziness passed down through me from my head, forcing me back on my heels. I staggered, and could not hold my ground. I sat down again. I felt my forehead. It was burning hot, but there was no sign of perspiration. I realized that I was shivering, too. 'I've taken ill. This time it's serious.' I leaned back against the table legs, as before.

In the present stillness, the dusk gradually settled like silt that had been suspended in a turbid current. With the setting of the sun, the dispersal of the people, the return of the birds to the woods, the cessation of the world of motion, the dusk began to filter down. As with the precipitation of silt, it had its clear divisions: the heavier, coarser particles filtered into the valleys and foothills, making those places dark first; the higher levels increased in lightness, until at the very top it was almost clear and transparent. Since my temple was situated in the foothills, the dusk there was of course thickest and densest; half-way up the ridge it was twilight; on the top of the ridge and on the peaks of the distant mountains it was still luminous and transparent. A solitary eagle circled high in the sky, there where the dusk should have been thinnest. Perhaps sunlight reflected down by the white clouds still shone on its back. The eagle was blessed, for it was the last to be drawn into darkness. I, for my part, at the foot of the altar table in the ancient temple, was caught in its trap.

By and by the crescent moon became visible in the western sky, a golden hook against the black curtain of night. It would have been possible for me to have scrambled over the ridge by the faint light of the moon, and to have got to the lodging house by the ferry crossing two miles further on. But I had missed my chance: I didn't have the strength now to take the first step.

When I considered that the temple was really not very dirty, and how pleasant the scent was of the honeysuckle growing on the wall, I got to wondering how it would be if I slept that night under the altar table, as I was not in a fit state to walk on. I thought: 'Perhaps in the middle of the night, like those weird and fanciful stories say, I will hear the mountain spirits whisper that in a certain place there is a pot of gold and a pot of silver! . . . Ah, I understand how those stories come about. Probably someone like me—no, someone poorer and more wretched than me—who very likely has had a little bit of education—likes to daydream, and thinks himself hard done by—has also slept under the altar table of a deserted temple—not because he was ill, though—has spun these stories to while away the lonely hours of the long night and satisfy the lust for gold that "makes the strongest man succumb". On meeting people he would say: 'Listen to this! One day I was passing through—note "passing through"—some place. It got dark, and I couldn't find a lodging, so I put up in a ruined temple. Late at night—mm, around midnight—I heard the sound of someone whispering. I couldn't believe anyone would turn up at that hour! I decided it must be evildoers—not that I would turn anybody in for the reward. I held my breath and listened, and listened. At first the sound was muffled, but the last words I heard absolutely clearly. They said that not far away, by the roots of a big lacquer tree—yes, a fearsome lacquer tree—three feet below the surface, there were two square stone slabs, and under the slabs were two big pots; the one on the left was a pot of gold, the one on the right was a pot of silver. No one dared to approach within twenty feet of the lacquer tree. If they went nearer, their head and face would swell up in a hideous manner . . . but if they made a brew of green beansprouts and washed their face and smeared their body with it, and rushed over to the tree and started digging with a duck-bill mattock . . . then they could get the buried treasure without the slightest trouble. . . .'

Our pauper would have told the story of this eerie encounter wherever he went, at first for a joke, then more seriously with every telling, till finally he would be ready to swear that he had heard the voices with his own ears. Those told the story would certainly have objected, 'In that case, why didn't you take the chance to get rich yourself?' 'Because, don't you see, I just didn't have the money to buy green beansprouts to make the brew!' Then he would laugh, and the teller and the listeners would all be content.

With such musing, I took off my cloth shoes, intending to use them for a pillow. Though this was the first time I had slept in a temple, I was not afraid. Tomorrow I would feel better, and would be on my way before daybreak. I could make it home in one go. . . .

Suddenly I felt my heart sink. I remembered my father's rebuke to my cousin. I reflected that his words were very weighty. Did he rebuke him purposefully loudly, so that I would hear? Did he foresee that one day I would find myself in a predicament away from home, and not wishing to order me directly to follow the rule of 'departing late and lodging early', did he seek to warn me by adopting that angry tone? Father knew that I was cautious by nature, so he hardly ever tried to drum anything into me, but from time to time he did inject words of caution in his conversation, which always impressed themselves on my mind. If when I reached home he were to examine my countenance as usual, and ask solicitously 'Where did you stay last night?', would I confess tearfully, 'Er, . . . I was unwell, and couldn't travel. I stayed the night in a temple at the foot of Longhairs Ridge, by myself. . . . ', or should I for the first time tell a lie? What would father think of my story? . . . All parents toil to make a home for their children, no matter whether it is big or small, poor or rich, in the hope that the children will never be reduced to vagrancy, yet despite that how many souls in reality have to sojourn in the wild, and in deserted temples!

Gripped by pain, I banished the fantasies I had just played with, and stood up. Making use of all the support I could find, I made my way out of the temple. That dark and gloomy ridge that lay across my path was in effect an insuperable barrier. 'Who takes pity on him who has lost his way'! The fugitive memory of that ancient saying depressed me. The sickle moon had hidden itself behind the ridge, thickening the ridge's gloom. As there was clearly no prospect of continuing on my journey, I returned to my seat below the altar table. I slumped back in fatigue, then got up again.

'Uh? Are you on your way from X? What are you doing sitting there in the dark?'

This question was asked by a middle-aged woman who had come into the temple with a basket of incense sticks. She looked closely at my face, evidently surprised to see me. The way she inspected me made me extremely embarrassed.

'Are you young X?'

To be so unexpectedly addressed by my childhood name took me aback. My instinct was to deny it, but I was lost for words.

'You don't remember me. Well, that's only to be expected, it's been ten years now. I'm your distant cousin; XX is my elder brother's name. I used to live no more than a hundred yards away from you. I carried you about when you were little.'

She hastily introduced herself. There was no question of her eyes deceiving her.

I knew the name of this elder cousin, and I also knew her fate. It was true that I hardly left her side when I was little. She carried me, or led me by the hand, to gather wild fruits. I remember her weaving a beard out of very tough grass that grew by the river, and hanging it over my ears. At the Dragon Boat Festival she made me a sachet to hang round my neck. And I sometimes went to sleep in her arms. Once she put on a big pair of gloves, and made me cry with fright in the dark—that I recall distinctly, as by then I was older. She did not seem at all distressed at leaving me when she got married: on the day of her departure, while I clung onto her all in tears, she just smiled sweetly, making no effort to conceal her happiness. Afterwards, I heard some news of her, all of it very saddening, but as it was only gossip I couldn't place great faith in it. As to how she happened to encounter me in this place at this time, I could only put that down to a surprise sprung by fate.

Seeing that I gave no answer to her question, she doubtless concluded that I was not resting in the temple by choice, and did not pursue the matter. Instead she proposed hospitably: 'As it's dark now, you can come and spend the night in my place. Sorry it's a bit dirty.'

Not taking no for an answer, she bustled me over to her home. Actually it wasn't a home, it was a side-room on the left of the temple. I hadn't noticed it before, as I had entered the temple from the right. There was only a bed and a cooking stove—no chickens, cat, dog; no children, no old folk. It wasn't much of a home.

I sat on the bed and confirmed that I was her younger cousin. She asked eagerly: 'Why didn't you hire a sedan chair? You're studying in the big city, you're really lucky. You're what they call the cream of the cream.'

When I went on to ask her questions, her words flowed like a torrent. She poured out the woes of her lifetime. While in the past I had always gone to her for sympathy when I felt hard done by, to pour out one's woes to a younger cousin was just not done, but she had to, as there was no other soul she could tell. She told how she had been rejected by her husband, rejected by her own brothers, rejected by her neighbourhood elders, how she had lost her darling son, how she had ended up alone and friendless. She was only about thirty years of age, but she looked an old forty. She also recounted how she had come to the temple, and said that every morning and evening she replenished the joss sticks on the altar, collected the candles that had not burned out, and so on. The temple got two sacks of grain a year as rent from its land, and she managed on that, together with the income from the small donations from worshippers.

'You rely on this one and that one, when you should rely on the Bodhisattva.' Fearful of the unreliability of people and able to turn only to a god for help, that was the depressing fatalism she uttered.

At that point she broke off and asked me, 'But why were you sitting there so late at night?'

'I'm not well,' I replied simply.

Hearing I was unwell, she abandoned the rest of her story and hurried to light the stove. Then she got a bundle of herbs from a corner—that medicinal plant something like peppermint was widely used in our district—and put it in a pot to brew while she straightened out her bed and insisted I lie down. From somewhere else she found a packet of brown sugar and stirred it into the mixture, which she then brought over to me, piping hot, at the same time apologizing: 'It will taste a bit bitter, I haven't enough sugar.'

As she was bringing the brew to me, I saw in her gait and the way she carried the bowl the same person I had known more than ten years before. I was familiar with her every little mannerism. I felt consoled, I felt happy. The sense of all the family comforts I associated with her restored role of elder cousin made me forget that I was out in the wilds. She said I should stop talking and go to sleep. For herself, she spread an old felt blanket on the floor in front of the bed. Under this tender loving care I drifted off to sleep.

When I was leaving the next morning she pulled and patted my clothes into place, as had been her habit in the past. When I looked back from halfway up the ridge, she was still standing outside the temple, lost in thought. Back home I drew a veil over the incident, saying I was unwell, and didn't feel like talking.

On my next journey from home, I took the boat downstream and did not pass that temple. I returned by a different route, again bypassing it. Subsequent trips were also made by boat. Two years ago when I purposely took a roundabout route to call on her, she was no longer there. It was another woman living in the sideroom. She had no idea where my cousin had gone to. Nor could I discover her whereabouts from enquiries at home.

'Those who stay in disused temples and wayside kiosks are in peril,' I found myself thinking.

'Everyone who has his own dwelling should always go home, even if it is miles away, and the time is the middle of the night. . . .' My father's words kept ringing in my ears. Suppose it were hundreds of miles, with many rivers to cross in between? Then for sure they would be beyond parents' care.

Yang Jiang 楊絳 (1911–)

COMMENTARY

Yang Jiang is as highly thought of for what she is as for what she writes. The two, of course, are inseparable, as it is only through her writing that the public knows her; nevertheless a benign circle has formed, whereby a very good impression of her person is got from her writing (though she never praises herself), and that good impression is fed into further reading of her work, which does not fail to reinforce the good impression of her person.... In short, people have come to look upon her as one of the very best of her generation. And I have to say, rightly so.

Yang Jiang was fortunate in having a very enlightened and highly principled man, Yang Yinhang 楊蔭杭(1878–1945), as her father. He had studied in Japan and the USA. During his career as a law officer under the Republic he was twice removed from his position for prosecuting important personages. Apart from setting an example to Yang Jiang, his fourth daughter, he gave her every encouragement to develop her own mind and interests. It was not to suit her interests, however, that she chose to take a degree in politics at Dongwu University in Suzhou, more out of a sense of what she 'ought' to do. After taking her BA degree in 1932, she relinquished 'ought' for 'like', and went to study foreign languages in the graduate school of Tsinghua University, having already taught herself some French. Spanish, her other main foreign language, if we exclude English, was also self-taught.

At Tsinghua Yang Jiang became friendly with Qian Zhongshu 錢鍾書, a young man from her hometown of Wuxi who was to become one of China's most learned men. They married in 1935, and departed for England, where they both studied at Oxford University. A further year was spent in Paris before they returned to China in 1938, where they both taught at various universities. In Japanese-occupied Shanghai Qian Zhongshu wrote his famed novel *Weicheng* 圍城(City Besieged), while Yang Jiang turned her creative talents to writing for the theatre. The Chinese spoken drama (as opposed to the traditional opera) had its heyday during the war; Yang Jiang had two comedies performed in Shanghai, and a tragedy published but not performed in 1946.

In 1953 both husband and wife were appointed as 'researchers' at the Institute of Literature in what later became the Chinese Academy of Social Sciences, where they remained for the rest of their careers. Yang Jiang soon found that literary criticism brought unlooked for consequences, and so applied herself exclusively to translation, until the death of Mao Zedong and the fall of the Gang of Four led to the lifting of most ideological controls. Her most notable translations were Lesage's *Gil Blas* (1956) and Cervantes' *Don Quixote*, published after a long delay in 1978. For *Don Quixote* she was awarded a medal by King Carlos of Spain.

Yang Jiang's best known original work is undoubtedly *Ganxiao liu ji* 幹校六記 (Six Episodes from Life in Cadre School, 1981), for it has been translated into all the world's major languages. This is her account of life in the rural commune to which she and other members of her institute were sent during the Cultural Revolution to engage in manual labour and 'learn from the poor peasants'. Lunatic and in many ways cruel though the exercise was (Yang-Qian and their cohort were sixty and over), Yang Jiang emphasizes the kindness she discovered and the good humour that sustained her and her fellow 'students'. Most of her best prose writing is in fact in the mode of reminiscence.

It does not seem accidental that Yang Jiang should have translated *Gil Blas* and *Don Quixote*, for the spirit of mischief that pervades both novels is present in her own nature. An aspiration to chivalry is there too, though in her circumstances it could rarely find expression. It is perhaps the 'unsocialized' personality of the author that readers most appreciate, by which I mean that amply qualified though she is to sit at any high table, her sympathies lie with Sancho Panza, who preferred to sit with his bread and onion in his corner. As for her style of writing, it is generally praised as clean, honest and succinct, intimate but not gossipy. The impression of 'cleanness' probably derives from her following the classical practice of connection by juxtaposition, thus dispensing with messy conjunctions (like 'thus'). Being a great reader, she naturally and inevitably is frequently reminded of things in books, but because such associations are natural to her they are acceptable to the reader. One of the great attractions of her style is indeed the literary phrase or reference that crops up unexpectedly, but in case that gives the wrong impression, the same applies to expressions from the demotic language or from her local dialect. Unfortunately, none of that may be evident in the translations, which have to resemble English, to a degree.

The Art of Listening
聽話的藝術

If there is an art of speaking, it follows that there is an art of listening. Speaking is creative, listening is critical. The aim of speaking is expression; the aim of listening is understanding and appreciation. Those who are not good at speaking are normally good at listening, like the critics despised by poets and authors down the ages: they themselves cannot create, or have failed in the attempt, and so hey presto they turn into master critics, in the same way as robbers down on their luck became thief-takers. The minor English poet [William] Shenstone said: 'A poet that fails in writing becomes often a morose critic; the weak and insipid white wine makes at length excellent vinegar.' Here, however, you will not find severe judgements or sharp attacks; I seek only to understand and appreciate. If what I write has to be classed as criticism, it is only the criticism of the romantic-impressionist school.

Listening consists of three steps: listening with your ears, understanding and appreciating. In listening we cannot exercise the free choice we can in reading. If the words are disagreeable, we cannot snap the lips of the speaker shut as we would snap shut the covers of a book and be done with it. We can 'turn a deaf ear', and deal with it like any beastly nuisance: 'put up the shutters, make no response', and pass the interval day-dreaming or meditating. Yet this method has its drawbacks: for instance, a troublemaker can make use of the weakling behind the shutters according to the principle 'silence implies consent'.

Perhaps to ostentatiously not listen would suit better. There once was a teacher who instructed his son how to behave: 'In the presence of visitors you may not hum a song, snap your fingers or tap your feet—that behaviour signifies disregard.' But there is no harm in resorting occasionally to that behaviour, then while the other person is distracted, change the topic. Of course, to show one's temper in listening without causing offence requires a high level of art, but to knead oneself into a sponge to maximize one's capacity to absorb requires even higher self-cultivation, because as we listen our own ego is liable to suddenly pop its head out like a jack-in-the-box and shout, 'Put a sock in it!'

Not even constant training and discipline will make it obedient, I fear—barring one circumstance, which is that our aim is not to understand and appreciate, but something else. The 19th century English poet Sir Henry Taylor, who was also an able administrator, said in *The Statesman*, his book about the secret of success: 'No siren has ever charmed the ear of the listener, as the listening ear has charmed the heart of the siren.' Successful people have no doubt long known that secret. What is more, many 'sirens' imagine themselves to be the good girl in the fairy story who only had to open her mouth for pearls and gems to be rolling all over the place, too many for straining ears to cope with: they had to be collected on uplifted trays. When the pearls of words were reverently inlaid in notebooks, the 'good girl' would be sure to bestow yet greater largesse.

There is no need to listen seriously to this kind of person's words, in fact it is better not to listen at all; to look absorbed and attentive is enough. Nor does one need to understand: it is quite sufficient to assume an expression of pleasure and admiration. If one has heard and understood, and is afraid of letting one's true feelings be seen, it will do to put on the expression of a dumb cow, for the siren's heart is easily satisfied.

In listening to people talk, the best plan is to follow the example of Tao Yuanming and 'not try to understand too deeply'. To insert a lot of detailed annotation would be too tedious. However, one still needs to understand the general drift. To dismiss someone's talk out of hand before getting the real point, and think all talk is boasting, flattery, lies and gossip, is to forget that talk is essentially an art, not a daily necessity like fuel, rice, oil and salt. To blame someone's talk for being untruthful is the same as blaming a novel for not being constructed on fact, or a painting for not being as accurate as a photograph. The function of talk can be compared to clothing: on the one hand it conceals the body; on the other it reveals and accentuates certain parts of the body. We would never think of censuring clothes for concealing the truth or distorting facts. On the contrary, people would think it scandalous if we went about without a stitch on. Are we to believe that a person's self is naturally more beautiful than a person's body?

Everyone knows that the truth of a work of art does not refer to correspondence with fact. Aristotle pointed out long ago that poetic truth is not historical truth. Natural born poets are probably more numerous than natural born historians (here I use the word 'poet' in its original Greek sense of 'creator'), and the most common form of creation is making talk. Confucius claimed to 'pass on, not create', but in practice did the contrary! Still, when we see a play, listen to a story or enjoy the works of art, we only look for poetic truth: we are well aware they are false, but are happy to take them as true, a state Coleridge described as 'willing suspense of disbelief'. Quite the opposite is the case with listening: 'poetic truth' cannot satisfy us, we long to know the facts of a matter. We can call this state of mind, *pace* Coleridge, 'unwilling suspense of belief'. At the same time we invariably use Aristotle's principle of 'the inevitable and probable' to deduce what the real truth is. To give some simple examples, if a woman complains 'Oh, this hair of mine is impossible! I wish I'd been born bald!', who would credit it? The 'inevitable and probable' would lead one to deduce that she is very conscious that she has a nice head of hair. Or if somebody says, 'Such-and-such a person is trying to get me to go and help him out, but such-and-such an organization won't let me go. It has really put me on the spot,' what that probably means is that he is trying to find an opening with someone, and his present job with the organization is in peril, but his manoeuvring has not yet succeeded, so he genuinely is in a fix. If a bigshot makes a statement on behalf of an organization he heads quashing a rumour, we will exclaim, in accordance with the 'inevitable and probable' principle, 'Ah! It looks as if there is really something in it!' If a person blows his own trumpet, he must have a sense of his own inadequacy; very possibly he comes to believe what he repeats, and so manages to fool himself. If a person flatters you to your face, then you have to resist your natural inclination and 'unwillingly suspend belief': he is of course doing his social duty, and saying what the other party expects; that is, he has perceived the way you like to think of yourself. If a person too enthusiastically praises someone not worthy of praise in his absence, it may be the cleverest form of flattery, made in the hope that it will get back to the person so praised and prove more gratifying than direct compliments; or it may be the same tactic the teacher mentioned above recommended to his son for dealing with rivals—exaggerated praise can give rise to distaste; or the aim may be to denigrate one person by praising another.

If in our listening we pursue this line of examining every word, we will overreach ourselves, and leave nothing to enjoy. It does no good to be too shrewd. Though everyone talks, good talkers are as rare as other artists. Apt words and clever phrases only make us admire the art of the author, whereas clumsy words make us like the author himself.

The higher the art of the talker, the more we tend towards 'unwilling suspense of belief': it makes us suspicious, even nervous. Clumsy words are like the fig leaves Adam and Eve used to cover their private parts: they just signify their sense of shame, and their desire to conceal their ugliness from the angels. The dissembling of children, for instance, when they try to talk an adult into giving them something to eat, and pretending curiosity ask 'What is that? Can you eat it?': they make you laugh, but also win your affection. Or when someone as small as a frog blows himself up as big as an ox: we can't help sympathizing, and wishing that he had indeed been endowed with the size of an ox, so that he could save himself all that effort. Maladroit flattery at least shows that the speaker means well. Plain abuse of others often merely serves the purpose of showing how virtuous one is oneself, and is not particularly malicious. High principled behaviour and lofty character elicit respect, but it is a person's weakness that make them lovable. A famous wit once said, 'If you want to be loved, don't parade your virtues, parade your faults.' And added: 'It is human nature not to forgive those who do not need to be forgiven.' The element of human nature is helpful for understanding the psychology of the listener. We admire clever words, yet it is the inarticulate person who gets our sympathy and affection. No doubt talking is the art of ordinary humans, but the talker is the creation of god.

(1940s)

Cloak of Invisibility
隱身衣

Sometimes my husband and I amuse ourselves with make-believe.

'If you had the choice of some magical power, what would you want?'

We both wanted a cloak of invisibility: with one for each of us we could go on rambles together. Our idea was only to see the world free from restraints, not to do any mischief. But if we warmed to our game we could easily get up to naughty tricks, in which case people would become aware of our presence and we would have to beat a hasty retreat.

'Oh dear, we would have to have winged feet too!'

'And a protective charm!'

The more we went into the implications, the more our requirements became, so we decided a cloak of invisibility wasn't such a good idea after all.

As a matter of fact, as long as you don't plan to do anything that society forbids, there is no need of a magical power: you can find a cloak of invisibility in the mundane world. It is just that ordinarily people do not prize it, indeed they are even afraid to put it on, in case like a wet shirt they won't be able to take it off. That is because the material is made from humbleness. If a person's station is humble, he or she will be looked at but not seen, or seen but ignored.

I remember that in our anecdotal literature there is a story about a man who returns home in a dream to the family he has sorely missed, but his family cannot see him. He opens his mouth and speaks, but his family does not hear him either. When the family gathers round the table to eat, he joyfully goes to take his place, but there is no seat for him. People of humble status are like this disembodied spectre, and will have the same feelings. If others have no regard for you, naturally they will look at you but not see you; if to their mind you are of no consequence, they will ignore you however wide open their eyes are. Your 'self' will feel neglected or slighted or insulted, but the other person will not know you are there. Though you exist in the human world, it will be as if you have not yet taken human form, have not yet been born. Would not a lifetime like that be no life at all? So if you claimed that a cloak of invisibility of this kind was very comfortable, and freed you from all troubles and cares, your listeners would only think you were consoling yourself for your inferiority, preaching 'sour grapes'.

You can see that the average person is not reconciled to being overlooked from the multitude of phrases we have for superiority: people aspire to be 'a man above other men', to be 'the pick of the bunch', to be 'head and shoulders over others', to be 'in the limelight', to 'burst upon the scene', to be 'top-notch', to 'stand out', and so on and so on. They complain despondently or rage violently, with the sole aim of one day ridding themselves of their cloak of invisibility, so that they can appear in public and show what they are made of.

English speakers have a phrase for society: the snake pit. Each of the teeming mass of snakes desperately sticks up its head, stretches out its body and shoves the other snakes aside or pushes them down; one snake's head after another breaks the surface and goes under again; one snake's body after another arches up and is pressed down; snakes tails are knotted into balls, indistinguishable and inextricable.

The thrashing and fighting never stops: if you're up I'm down, if you live I die. So if you can't stick your head above the ruck, you are buried for life. If you can get your head out, you are like the foam and spume that sit on the crest of the ocean waves, you shine and glow in the light of the sun and moon. In other words, the man of mettle gets his just reward. Given that life is short, the brief moment on the crest of the waves can still be the mark of a life's achievements, and be something to be proud of. Who would be a good-for-nothing? Who would want to be always grovelling at people's feet?

Yet the truth is, some of god's creatures are beautiful, some are not; some are talented, some not. It takes ten thousand skeletons to make a braided general. How can your ordinary footsoldiers all become famous heroes? There are those who sit in sedan chairs, there are those who bear the chairs; there are the host and guest at dinners, there are the servants who bring the tea and food; at the table someone sits in the place of honour, others sit below the salt. In the kitchen there is the chef with his ladle, the scullery maids with their coals. Natural endowment is also unequal: how can everybody be on the same footing?

People also differ in their inclinations. Mrs Wang in chapter 26 of *Rulin waishi* (The Scholars) rhapsodizes over the magnificent wedding banquet Squire Sun put on, where she sat in the place of honour and had a maid at either side to part her veil of pearls as big as peas and allow her to get her mouth to her cup of honeyed tea. Sancho Panza, on the other hand, in chapter 11 of *Don Quixote*, declines to sit at the banqueting table, preferring to eat his bread and onion in his own corner without any pretension to refinement or good manners. Some people aspire to sit on high perches, others prefer to 'creep along close to the ground'. Every man to his taste; you can't force your own on others.

If someone has a particular idea of himself, you can't get him to change it. Supposing he would rather 'creep along close to the ground', you have to let him get on with it. If someone has an ambition that is not realized, he himself can't change fate. Our mediocre brethren, for example, might take it into their heads to be 'a man above other men', but how can that be done? There is an old saying: 'To want to be top dog is to look for trouble.' The higher a monkey climbs, the more unappetizing a spectacle its bare red bottom presents. To be in a hurry to rid oneself of the 'cloak of invisibility' will lead to making an exhibition of oneself if all that one is wearing underneath is 'the emperor's new clothes'. A lot of people possessed of a modicum of talent waste the energy of a lifetime striving for superiority, only to achieve nothing: all totally pointless.

The sentiment 'He is just a man, the same as I am' can be found in our Chinese history, and the Westerners have a similiar saying. The sense is only to encourage people to make the best of their opportunities, and not give up on themselves. A Spanish proverb says, 'A man is what he does.' That is, a person's worth is not decided by rank or birth, but by achievement. We might add a rider: suit the purpose to the material. A turnip should endeavour to be a good juicy, crunchy turnip; a cabbage should endeavour to be a good round, firm-hearted cabbage. Turnips and cabbages are everyday vegetables; they don't pretend to be the fine fruits laid out on temple altars. At home the children have a rhyme to the effect that the shepherd's purse in bloom outdoes the peony, but that could hardly be. I have seen a tiny blue flower among the grass, and have often wondered whether it is what the Westerners call a 'forget-me-not', on account of it being too small to attract notice. But to my way of thinking wild flowers and vegetables put out their flowers to repay the kindness of sun and dew, not in the hope that people will 'forget me not'. As the poem says, 'Flowers and plants have their own properties; they do not ask for lovely ladies to pick them.'

I am fond of Su Dongpo's line 'Ten thousand people like a sea, one self hidden', and also admire Zhuang Zi's idea of 'sinking into the ground'. Society may be a 'snake pit', but birds still fly over the 'snake pit', and beside the 'snake pit' there are also fish swimming in their pond. In all ages, past and present, people have avoided the 'snake pit' and 'hidden themselves' or 'sunk into the ground'. They disappear in the crowd like water drops in the bosom of the sea, like tiny wild flowers concealed in the grass, not seeking 'forget me not', not seeking to 'outdo the peony', but enjoying their ease, and content with their place. If you don't try to climb high you have no fear of falling, and have no need to elbow others aside or do them down; you can preserve your innocence, fulfil your nature, and apply your mind to doing what you can do.

Moreover, under the cover of a cloak of invisibility there are other gains to be made, which cannot be snatched from you. Su Dongpo said, 'The bright moon over the mountains, the fresh breeze over the water' 'are inexhaustible treasures the Creator has provided'; these one can enjoy at one's pleasure. But apart from the Creator's treasures, there are also the things created by our fellow human beings. Manners and mores are more fascinating than bright moons and fresh breezes: they can be read like a book or watched like a play. Descriptions in books, performances in plays, are in the end only works of art, however lifelike they might be. Manners and mores are unthinking and artless, and frequently go beyond rhyme and reason, taking startlingly or frighteningly original forms; so they make a deeper impression, and give more peculiar pleasure. It is the humble person who is best placed to see the true face of manners and mores, as opposed to artistic performances directed at an audience.

However, all this is wasted breath. I doubt if those eager to rid themselves of their cloak of invisibility will take any notice, or if those who were unaware that there was such a thing as a cloak of invisibility in the mundane world will open their eyes now they do know. To be fair, cloaks of invisibility, whether supernatural or natural, do have their drawbacks—and not minor drawbacks, at that.

The science-fiction novel of the Englishman H. G. Wells, *The Invisible Man*, tells of a man achieving invisibility by scientific means. But after becoming invisible he has a really hard time. For example, he can't wear clothes in cold weather, or if he does he has to stay at home: if he goes out he has to go naked, because someone wearing clothes, shoes, hat and gloves but without a face running about the streets is sure to cause uproar and fear of witchcraft and sorcery. He has to cover his face completely: the top by pulling down the brim of his hat, the bottom by muffling it in his scarf, the middle by putting on dark glasses and wrapping his nose and cheeks in bandages and sticking on plasters. What a to-do to conceal the fact that he was invisible!

Of course, this was the invention of short-sighted science, and is far inferior to the magical cloak of invisibility. The latter can be taken off at any time, and can be worn over ordinary clothes. However, the body of flesh and blood below the cloak is only mortal stuff; it cannot stand extreme cold or heat, and is susceptible to injury. Let alone assault with knife or spear, scalding with water and searing with fire, even knocks from bricks and wood, or trampling from heavy feet, are more than it can bear. So if one has no spell to effect instant evasion, one can only guarantee one's safety by developing an adamantine body like the Buddhist saints.

There are similar drawbacks to the mundane cloak of invisibility. The soul in the house of flesh cannot be impervious to the blowing hot and cold of snobbery, and cannot suffer knocks. It is idle to talk of making yourself invulnerable to cuts and burns. Yet if you do not have that invulnerability, the very advantage of being able to see the true face of manners and mores turns against you, and you are liable to explode with anger, or be stabbed in the heart; you will certainly not be in the mood to sit back and enjoy the spectacle like a good play. What's more, it won't be like a play performed to entertain an audience that you can choose not to watch. If the Limping Devil (*le diable boiteux*) that the French novelist Lesage created invited me to join him on his nocturnal excursions and offered to lift off the roofs of houses to let me see what was going on inside, I would certainly turn his offer down. Do you have to be an eyewitness to get worldly wisdom? Through being an eyewitness do you necessarily get worldly wisdom? Life is too short! If you think you have seen all that life has to offer on the basis of your own experience, and congratulate yourself on your superior insights, you will have people laughing up their sleeves at you, because mundane cloaks of invisibility, unlike the magical kind, are available everywhere, and are worn by very large numbers of people. Can they all be blind?

Still, when all's said and done, cloaks of invisibility are better than the emperor's new clothes.

(1984)

He Qifang 何其芳 (1912–1979)

COMMENTARY

He Qifang's really distinctive essays, written in his thirties, were so much the creation of his emotional life, and his emotional life was so much the creation of his childhood experiences, that some account of the latter must be given. The following picture is pieced together from his own essays.

He Qifang was born in a mouldering country mansion in the district of Wanxian, in the eastern part of Sichuan province. The family, ruled over by He's grandfather, appears to have been still quite wealthy, but those were unruly times, and wealth was an attraction for bandits, and soldiers-cum-bandits, so the grandfather built a fort on a nearby cliff with five other families, and there He Qifang lived, he says, for five to six years, practically cut off from the outside world. The situation got so bad at one point that the family moved for their safety to the neighbouring province for a couple of years. For his education He went to a private school, where the curriculum was as feudal as the beliefs and customs of the local people, who doubted that the Republic would last. He Qifang speaks of no childhood pleasures; in fact he seems to have been thoroughly unhappy: 'ignored at home, friendless at school'. Far more than the average child he lived in a world of his own, created out of stories in books and embroidered with his own imaginings. The dream-like atmosphere of his early essays, which played a large part in their success with the reading public, is obviously attributable to his solitary childhood.

At the age of fourteen, He went to a modern middle school in the county town, and in 1930, after a year in Shanghai, went to Tsinghua University in Peking. In 1931 he transferred to Peking University, where he read philosophy. On graduating in 1935 he became a schoolteacher. In 1938 he went from Sichuan to the Red Army base in Yenan, along with Sha Ding 沙汀 and Bian Zhilin 卞之琳, where he joined the Chinese Communist Party. As a faithful upholder of the thought of Chairman Mao he rose through the ranks, and in the People's Republic became a guardian of orthodoxy in the literary sphere. His posts included the headship of the Institute of Literature of the Chinese Academy of Social Sciences, and the editorship of the leading organs of literary criticism. Being one of the big guns in the cultural hierarchy, He was persecuted in the Cultural Revolution. He died of stomach cancer soon after the fall of the Gang of Four.

He Qifang began his literary career as a poet. The volume of poems written by He, Bian Zhilin and Li Guangtian 李廣田 entitled *Hanyuan ji* 漢園集 (The Han Garden, 1936) attracted considerable attention. His prose compositions evolved out of his poetry. His first volume of prose poems and essays, *Huameng lu* 畫夢錄(Painted Dreams) was crowned with success: it won the *Dagong bao* prize for prose in 1936. Other collections of poetry and prose followed.

There can be no doubt that as a prose writer He Qifang excelled as a painter of mood and scene. His attempts to be more rational fail due to lack of intellectual control. His best mood-and-scene essays were published in *Painted Dreams*, and the best of those is 'Elegy', translated below. Lin Fei 林非 has described the *Painted Dream* pieces as 'broken threads of spider web floating in the air'. If that is a weakness, He has in the case of 'Elegy' converted it to a strength, in that the floating fantasies, identified as such, are interwoven and contrasted with bare, harsh reality. Uniquely in this piece He openly declares his web-spinning by providing footnotes that tell where he has 'borrowed' passages from. The chief source is literature in Romance languages, principally French and Spanish (the Spanish poet referred to at the end, incidentally, is said by Bonnie McDougall to be Azorin). Otherwise, he confesses the fact when depictions of his short-lived aunts are the product of his imagination. Yet his having to fill the vacuum with his imagination underscores the seclusion in which his aunts passed their days, invisible even to their little nephew. They die, too, out of sight and nearly out of mind. The way that He Qifang introduces romance, discards romance, and recreates romance, with the aid of the hypnotic repetition of phrases shared by illusion and reality, is I think unparalleled in modern Chinese prose.

Elegy
哀歌

. . . Like songs women sing in fogbound lands, she sings an age-old legend full of sadness and love, that tells of the misfortune of a princess who is shut up in a tower by her father, because she fell in love.[1]

Adeline or Sylvie.[2] Aurelia or Lola.[3] French girls' names are soft and musical; they make you think of slender figures, slender fingers. Spanish girls' names? Shining, mysterious, big black circles of eyes. I cannot but feel a tinge of resentment against our ancient country.

---

[1] Author's note: I remembered this opening from a French novel. There are no quotation marks, because I borrow the sense.

[2] Author's note: These two French girls' names are chosen at random.

[3] Author's note: These two Spanish girls' names are chosen at random.

When I had to choose names for the sisters in this elegy, I thought and thought, and in the end made them three nameless sisters. And, why did I see a black shadow, feel a slight chill? Because I remembered the lonely times of childhood?

Thirty years ago. Twenty years ago. Still today, probably. Country girls are still shut up in their women's quarters, waiting for 'the command of their parents, the mediation of the matchmaker'. In Europe, though girls are sometimes shut up in convents, and not allowed home or to enter society until a certain age, yet there is a difference from our own ancient customs. Now our city girls have a vague new notion of love. We have already seen some bold rebels come to grief. But I am more moved by the fate of those girls who belong to the past, who while away their lonely time without expectations, in silence, with a smile hovering on their wasted rosy lips.

We have no way of imagining our grandmother's youth or our mother's youth, because even imagination needs the support of personal recall. Our sisters, like ourselves, have come to a fork in the road, and cannot tell what might lie ahead. Most on our mind are our young and beautiful aunts, and their life fading away in their cloister. Ah, we have seen their white faces appear at their upstairs window that opens onto the distant mountains, the blue sky and the white clouds, and linger long. And then seen their long slender fingers, with nails dyed red with the juice of the balsam flower, slowly close the shutters at dusk. Or they have sat on low stools in the light from the window, heads bowed over their embroidery—a pillow case or a door curtain—concentrating on the tedious work of completing their own trousseau. Their trousseau already fills several chests. Beside the new chests are some old ones, that contain their mother's and grandmother's trousseaus. The foot-wide sleeves trimmed with a broad band of lace are in the style of their grandmother's time. The narrow sleeves trimmed with little satin roundels are in the style of their mother's time. Both are long out of fashion. When they open those chests they may break into happy but tearful laughter.

Let us stop our imagining. My memories of those aunts are extremely simple. Of the oldest aunt and the second aunt I only remember that the former was slender and sickly; I can no longer recall any difference in their features. As to happy or tearful laughter, I never heard any. But I did see their flower garden: limpid—a muzzy sort of limpidity. Stone steps, clay tubs, all kinds of plants, to which I cannot give their proper names. In those days, if I had been left alone among the orchids trailing down like ribbons and the fronds of evergreens and palm trees hanging loose like unkempt hair, I would have howled as if lost in the depths of a forest. Yet I did rather like the pond in their garden. And the three-storey pavilion that you don't often see in the provinces. Many times the sight of it excited my childish mind, giving rise to many fancies, but still I dared not go along that gloomy garden path to climb up it. Did my aunts often go along that gloomy garden path and run up the winding staircase to get a distant view? Did they often lean over the stone balustrade that surrounded the pond, and peer down at the water and the water plants? I never saw them do so. Their home and our home was in an old mansion. The long stone steps before the entrance hall that formed the dividing line, and the inner courtyard, and that high wall which sent back echoes, all presented a threat, a sign. And so the doleful news of the death of the slender, sickly aunt came to us across those long steps.

Let us leave that big bare old mansion. A residence that is entering into dotage, just like a person entering into dotage, takes on an eccentric, baffling character. We had moved to a newly built fort. Our quarters were next to my aunt's quarters. All day long we heard the sound of stone-breaking from the back of the fort. The sound of men at work. We were building a watchtower and making a water cistern. In the opinion of my grandfather, in the opinion of his worm-eaten block-printed books or yellowing hand-copied books, no work should have been carried out that year in that direction because, according to the books, it would break the 'three taboos'. My grandfather was a very learned man. He knew a lot of strange lore, which he firmly believed. If anyone wishes to challenge that ancient mysterious lore, let them go and debate with him. So in the middle of the night he burned incense and recited a kind of spell to forestall the evil consequences. Night after night he recited. The puzzling thing was, the exorcism was not effective. First, a stonemason fell down the back of the cliff; then two deaths followed one after the other: those of my uncle's three year old daughter and of my second aunt.

My memory of my third aunt is longer, but still simple. Head bent, tracing patterns in front of the window of the little turret; opening a chest with a big bunch of keys, smiling a melancholy smile as she talked to herself; sitting playing cards with the old folk in the lamplight; a yawn. Confined in that fort with my long and monotonous childhood.

A stone fort perched high on a cliff must call up associations with French or Italian castles inhabited by debilitated nobles and blond or chestnut haired damsels who lift their vibrating voices to the sky to sing of ancient legends full of love and heartache. Away in the distance from a tall church belfry comes floating the deep and resonant tolling of bells that seem to have woken from a dream. But our fort was full of barrenness of sound. In the morning and at noon, a few long cock crows. The dark shadow thrown by the eaves crept up the outer wall, very slowly, finally climbed over and fell on the fields at the foot of the cliff. Then sunset. That was a very accurate chronometer, which told me when I should run down from the watchtower to begin my morning lessons, or noonday lessons, studying those ancient, enigmatic books that our grandfather and father had studied before us in their own childhood. And my third aunt was perhaps sitting the while before the windows of the little turret, concentrating on the tedious work of completing her trousseau. She had long ago been betrothed, in accordance with 'the command of her parents, the mediation of the matchmakers'.

Vanity of vanities, all is vanity. Everything bears out that motto on King David's ring. When we are sad it makes us happy; when we are happy it makes us sad.[4] We had passed long and monotonous months and years in foreign parts, we had some memories of other residences and other damsels. Damsels just escaped from country villages, leaning over the rails of steamboats in passage, the river breeze blowing their short hair; or damsels taken travelling abroad, and now come back with vague new notions. What thoughts did their eyes, their slightly knitted brows, give rise to in us? Did they make us think of those young and beautiful aunts of ours? We had been away from home for three, four, five years. After the long fatigue of journeying we had returned to our native place. A fine sunny day. We were amazed that the woods, streams, roads had not changed. We got to the door of our house. The door creaked with age. We went into the

---

[4] Author's note: I seem to recall these three sentences from a story of Chekhov.

parlour. The worn lacquer chairs were still placed at either side of the long table. On the table there still stood a crackle-glazed long-necked vase. The vase was quite empty, as it had always been. We could not make out if we had blundered into the past dimension, or if everything there existed outside of time. At length we saw some silver strands in our mother's hair.

From her excited, disjointed and longwinded gossip we gathered that some of the old folk had found final release from their chronic illnesses, and some people in their prime had departed this world through misadventure. It was in these perplexing yet moving circumstances that I heard the last news of my third aunt: she had got married, then died. Died, then been forgotten. But when her silhouette appears in our mind, it is as a Spanish prosewriter has said: We see a garden, a village copse, and low trees laden with dust, and lanterns hung on posts blown sideways by winter gales. . . .

(1935)

Ch'i Chun 琦君 (1917–)

COMMENTARY

It is perhaps significant that Ch'i Chun's (Qijun in *pinyin*) authorial name is a personal name, without a surname. She is the kind of writer who invites her readers to enter into a personal relationship, to see her as an older friend or relative, but without being sloppy about it.

Born Pan Xizhen 潘希真 in Yongjia county, Zhejiang province, she lost both her parents in infancy and was brought up by her paternal uncle and aunt. They treated her as their own child, hence when Ch'i Chun wrote in later years about her family, as in the essay translated here, and many others, her aunt features as 'mother'. Ch'i Chun's uncle/father was a military man of high rank and high culture, her aunt/mother a homely country woman; the one gave her the benefit of a good education in classical literature, the other taught her to be plain and honest. When Ch'i Chun was twelve the family moved to Hangzhou, where she went to secondary school and university. At Zhijiang University, where she read Chinese, she greatly admired her professor Xia Chengtao 夏承燾, who was also a noted lyrical poet. He taught her that both in literature and life the supreme virtue was absolute sincerity, allied with composure.

On graduation Ch'i Chun taught at secondary schools for a few years. After the war ended she joined the Ministry of Justice as a civil servant, and continued in that career when the ministry moved to Taiwan in 1949. She retired in 1969, by which time she had published ten books of essays, short stories and children's stories. She then taught at different universities in Taiwan before taking up residence in the USA, where she still lives. Her books now number around thirty.

Ch'i Chun writes mostly about the people in her life, including her present family and acquaintances, but most affectingly of those she grew up with on the mainland. Critics have ascribed to her the quality of *tongxin*, a kind of childlike truthfulness or pureness of heart. She has herself confessed that tears fill her eyes every time she thinks of family, teachers and friends from the past. To the depth of feeling is joined vividness of recall. So Ch'i Chun's chief strength is in the literature of nostalgia, written in the spirit of human decency (biased towards Confucian values) and faintly Buddhist compassion. Even the people who do bad things are forgiven in the end. Her great popularity may in part be due, as has been suggested, to a widespread regret in the population at large for the loss of warmth and intimacy in human relationships and particularly for the erosion of the Chinese way of life. In Ch'i Chun's pages those things are commemorated and perpetuated.

Remembrance of the past deeply imbues classical Chinese poetry, in which

Ch'i Chun is well versed. Chinese critics claim that the language of classical poetry, especially the song lyrics (*ci*), is the bedrock of Ch'i Chun's language. It is true that classical poems often employ very plain and direct language, as Ch'i Chun does, but if there is any inheritance it is in the preservation of native rhythms. Her style is more obviously related to that of traditional vernacular novels, which used the good healthy language of the people. But in underlying sentiment there is of course a connection, as indeed there is with classical Chinese prose. Readers may wish to compare Ch'i Chun's 'Chignon' with Gui Youguang's pieces on his mother, translated above. Gui's language was pure classical prose, which is very compact and laconic, whereas Ch'i Chun composes in modern Chinese, which is expansive, but the similarity in sentiment and approach is striking. Whether Gui's 'blank spaces' or Ch'i Chun's ample detail is more affective I leave it to the reader to judge.

Chignon
髻

When my mother was young, she combed her 'silken tresses' into a long, thick braid, which in the daytime she wound spiral-fashion to form a pointed chignon high on the back of her head, and at night let down to hang down her back. I used to sleep close at her shoulder, my finger curled round the end of her braid, my nostrils filled with the scent of Twin Sisters hair tonic and the stale smell of hair grease. The unpleasantness of the smell was compensated by the sense of security that mother's nearness gave me, and I soon fell into a sound sleep.

Once and only once a year, on the seventh day of the seventh month, did my mother push the boat out and give her hair a thorough wash. The rule with country people was that hair could not be washed on ordinary days. If it was, the dirty water would flow down to the underworld, where the King of Hell would bottle it up for you to drink after you died. Only the water from hair washed on the Double Seventh flowed harmlessly away to the Eastern Seas. Consequently on the Double Seventh the women in all households, great and small, spent the better half of the day with their hair spread loose. Some women with their hair falling down their backs were as beautiful as story-book goddesses, but others were as ugly as witches. A great-aunt of mine was a case in point. Short and wrinkled, she had lost most of her hair, but she used charcoal to black out her temples in a square, and then working back, blackened the whole of her bark-like pate. After she washed her hair, all the charcoal was gone, exposing a pate that was one half completely bald; a little tail of hair clung to the back of her head. This fluttered behind her as she tottered about the kitchen helping my mother with the cooking. I didn't even dare look in her direction.

By contrast, my mother's soft, glistening black hair fell on her shoulders like a sheet of satin. A current of air would from time to time blow a lock of short hair across her milky-white cheeks; narrowing her eyes, she would push it back into place with the back of her hand, only for it to float free again the next minute. She was short-sighted, and when she screwed up her eyes she looked particularly pretty. I thought to myself, if father were at home to see her black and shining head of hair, he would be sure to go out and buy her a pair of glittering diamond hair pins. Mother would certainly wear them a while to please him, but would soon take them off out of embarrassment. Then it would not be long before that pair of hair pins became my hair ornaments for when I dressed up as a bride.

Father did come back soon afterwards. He did not buy a pair of diamond hair pins, he brought a concubine with him. Her skin was smooth and white, and her cloud-like hair was even blacker and more shiny than mother's. Her side tresses were puffed out like two cicada wings to half cover her ears, and at the back were drawn together in a huge 'horizontal S' chignon, just like a bat settled on the back of her head. She presented mother with a pair of jadeite ear pendants. Mother just put them away in a drawer; she never wore them, or let me play with them. I think she probably thought they were too nice to wear.

After we moved to Hangzhou mother no longer needed to look after the cooking, and father expected her to entertain guests. Her pointed spiral of a chignon really did not go down well, so father insisted that she changed her hair style. Mother asked her friend Aunt Zhang to dress her hair to make an 'abalone bun'. In those days the 'abalone bun' was a hairstyle for old ladies. Since mother was only in her early thirties it was odd to adopt an old ladies' fashion. My father's concubine sniggered when she saw it, and my father's look was black. I asked her on the quiet, 'Mother, why don't you do your hair in a horizontal S too, and wear the jadeite ear drops that auntie gave you?' Mother pulled a long face and said, 'Your mother is a country woman. It wouldn't be right for her to do her hair in one of those modern styles or wear such fancy ear drops.'

Auntie, that is my father's concubine, never confined the washing of her hair to the Double Seventh, in fact she washed it several times a month. After washing, a little maidservant fanned it lightly with a big pink feather fan, separating the wispy strands and making them float out in a way that induced a kind of languor in anyone watching. My father sat on a sandalwood couch, puffing at his hookah; he frequently turned his head to look at her, his eyes lighting up when he did so. Auntie dabbed on her Three Flowers hair oil, sending out a cloud of perfume, and then sat up straight before her mirror to wind her hair into her glossy 'S' chignon. I stood watching, spellbound. Auntie handed me a bottle of her Three Flowers hair oil and told me to give it to mother. But my mother put it on top of the wardrobe, saying, 'The smell of those new hair oils turns my stomach.'

My mother could not always call upon Aunt Zhang to do her hair. When she dressed it herself, her 'abalone bun' was bunched up tightly, not far removed in appearance from her former spiral hairdo. Even I thought it ugly, never mind my father. In time auntie engaged a Mrs Liu to be her hairdresser. Mrs Liu had a bright red skewer stuck through her hair. A pair of big feet supported her dumpy body, and walking made her puff and pant. She came at ten o'clock every morning. She arranged auntie's hair in all kinds of styles of chignon, like 'phoenix', 'feather fan', 'two-hearts-as-one', 'swallow-tail', and so on, always ringing the changes. The styles set off auntie's smooth, clear skin and her svelte, 'water snake' figure, bringing even more delight to father's eyes.

Mrs Liu urged mother, 'Madam, you really should do your hair more in fashion, too.' My mother shook her head, pursed her thick lips, and went off without saying a word. Not long afterwards she engaged a Mrs Chen as hairdresser on Aunt Zhang's recommendation. Mrs Chen was older than Mrs Liu. She had a large, flat, sallow face, and two gleaming gold teeth projecting over her lip. You could tell at first glance that she was a gossip. While she did mother's hair she jabbered on about old Mr Zhao's eldest daughter-in-law and Chief of Staff Li's third concubine. Mother sat there like a sphinx, not making any response, though I found it all quite fascinating. Sometimes Mrs Liu and Mrs Chen came together, and mother and auntie sat back to back on the porch having their hair dressed at the same time. Auntie and Mrs Liu laughed and talked together, but mother, for her part, only closed her eyes and conserved her energies. Mrs Chen's interest flagged, and she soon stopped coming, though not before I clearly heard her say to Mrs Liu: 'What does an old fossil of a country wife like her want a hairdresser for?' I was so angry I cried, but I did not dare to tell mother.

After that I did my mother's hair myself, standing on a low stool. I combed it into the simplest 'abalone bun' shape. I stood on tiptoe and looked at mother in the mirror. Her face was not as plump and glowing with health as it had been when she bustled about her kitchen in the country. Her eyes looked fixedly at her own reflection in the mirror, as if glazed; they no longer screwed up in a smile. As I held my mother's hair in my hand, combing out one tress after another, I realized that my little boxwood comb could not disentangle the knots of her distress—for the sound of father and auntie enjoying each other's company filtered constantly along the passage.

After I grew up and went away to school, I sometimes did my mother's hair when I came home in the holidays. Every time it passed through my hands, it felt thinner and thinner. When I recalled how in my childhood her jet-black hair cascaded over her shoulders every year on the Double Seventh, and how happy she looked then, pain clawed at my heart. But the clouds lifted from my mother's brow when I came home, and she often smiled, which shows that the bond between mother and daughter makes for the greatest happiness.

While I was studying in Shanghai I received a letter from my mother saying she was suffering from rheumatism and could not lift her arms. Even the simplest spiral-shaped chignon was now unmanageable, so she had to cut short the few sparse strands of hair that remained to her. I sat reading the letter by the window of my dormitory in the pale moonlight, shedding desolate tears. I felt the chill of the late autumn wind, and put the woolly cardigan my mother had knitted for me round my shoulders, which made me as warm as toast again. I had to face it, though: my mother was old, but I could not be always at her side to see to her needs. She had cut off her sparse strands of hair, but no scissors could cut the threads of care ravelled in her heart!

Shortly afterwards, auntie came to Shanghai on business, bringing mother's photograph. In the three years I had been away, mother's hair had turned silver. I stared at the photograph, my mind distracted by anxieties I could not share with auntie. She seemed to understand how much I missed mother, for she launched upon a long and wordy account of mother's present circumstances. Her heart was none too good, and what with her rheumatism too, she could not get about nearly as much as she used to. I listened with bowed head, thinking it was she who had made my mother's life miserable, but my hatred for her had all gone. The reason was that after my father died mother and auntie surprisingly became companions dependent on each other in their misfortune, and mother had long ago ceased to resent her.

I looked closely at auntie again. She was wearing a grey quilted gown, and had a white flower in her hair. At the back of her head her hair was no longer done in an eye-catching 'phoenix' chignon or 'two-hearts-as-one' chignon of yester-year, but in the simplest of banana curls. She wore no make-up on her face. I thought she looked altogether sad and lonely, and could not resist a surge of deep sympathy for her. She was not like my mother who was glad to hide herself away; she had enjoyed a glamorous life with my father for nearly twenty years. When one day her support was removed, her sense of emptiness and loss must have been even greater than my mother's.

After coming to Taiwan, auntie was my only family. We lived together a good many years. In the long gallery of our Japanese-style house I watched her sit by the window and do her hair. She pummelled her shoulder with her fist, saying, 'My hand is so stiff! I really am old.' Yes, she was old now, too. Her black hair, once like a cloud, was falling out; only a handful remained, and that was streaked with white. Those days in Hangzhou, when she sat back to back with mother having her hair done, not a word passing between them, so fresh in memory, were long gone. In our life on earth, what is love? What is hate? My mother had been dead many years, auntie had entered upon old age, and now that her feet were at last set on that same path that leads we know not where, her hours were lonelier than anyone's.

Absorbed in such thoughts, I remembered her beautiful 'S' chignon, and said to her, 'Let me give you a new hairdo.' She smiled sorrowfully: 'What do I want to look fashionable for? That's for you young people.'

Could I stay young for ever? Ten years have passed in a flash since she said those words, and my youth has been left behind me. I have already lost interest in our loves and hates, greeds and obsessions. Mother goes further from me with each passing day, auntie's ashes lie in a cold monastery. What in the end is there that is permanent? What is there that is worth taking to heart?

(1969)

Eileen Chang 張愛玲 (1920–1995)

COMMENTARY

To distinguish Eileen Chang (Zhang Ailing) from the other writers chosen for this anthology, I am tempted to describe her as a 'city slicker'. She seems in retrospect to represent better than anyone else the Shanghai sophisticates of the 1930s and 40s who had grown up speaking English or French along with Chinese, knew the ways of the world, and were nobody's fools. Culturally they sought entertainment rather than edification, going to see Hollywood and Shanghai films, local Chinese opera and teahouse performances, and reading light literature, fashion magazines and tabloid newspapers. They tended to see themselves as Shanghainese first and Chinese second, which was only reasonable, as they had more in common with the International Settlement than with the Chinese hinterland. The fact that Eileen Chang was 'Eileen' before she was 'Ailing' is quite significant.

If there was a common Shanghai culture, there was little commonality in the life histories of the Shanghainese, as the city had drawn entrepreneurs from all over, and those citizens created their own opportunities. Eileen Chang's family had already accumulated its wealth by the time she was born. Her father made a quite thorough job of dissipating it. Since her mother disappeared to France for long periods, Eileen led anything but a sheltered life in her childhood. By the time she reached university age, the Second World War had started, so she chose to go to the University of Hong Kong to read English, but then Hong Kong was overrun and she returned to Shanghai. It was in Japanese-occupied Shanghai that she began writing for middle-brow magazines. Her short stories quickly made her one of Shanghai's most popular writers. Despite her youth she produced in the remaining few years of the war a remarkably mature and brilliantly written stream of fiction; her works from this period are now regarded as classics of modern Chinese literature.

Eileen Chang remained in China for two years after the Communist victory. She then decamped to Hong Kong, where she published two anti-Communist novels, *The Rice-sprout Song* and *Naked Earth* (1954). She later went to the USA where she married and was widowed. The last years of her life before her death in 1995 were spent in total seclusion.

Eileen Chang was not a dedicated essayist. She wrote to earn money and to amuse herself. She does not seem to have taken too much trouble with her essays—she skips a lot from one thing to another—but they are far from superficial: given her acute intelligence and keen eye they hardly could be. The reason why her observations are so refreshing is that she pays no dues and takes no prisoners. She takes no heed of what she should say (the besetting sin of her compatriots) or whom she should placate, she just writes down exactly what she thinks. Mercifully that does not result in cynicism but in engaging honesty. Eileen Chang drew great advantage from not being a man and not being an intellectual. Men, in her time at least, felt they had roles to play and intellectuals have positions to defend. As a young woman without prejudices, Eileen Chang saw things in their primary colours.

The following essay on Chinese religion was originally written for foreigners', as her own prefatory statement confesses. It has nevertheless been included in a number of recent selections of her work as an authentic and worthy 'Chinese' essay, probably for the reason she gives, that putting things in simple terms as for a school primer sometimes helps to clarify matters. Where—indeed whether—the original, presumably English, version was published has so far not been established. The Chinese text is at seventeen pages too long to translate in its entirety, but as it is not very cohesive, excerptation does no great injury.

The Religion of the Chinese
中國人的宗教

On the surface the Chinese have no religion to speak of. The intellectual class of Chinese have for many years been atheists. The influence of Buddhism on Chinese philosophy is another question, but Buddhism has left very little trace on the education of ordinary people. The fact that Chinese literature is full of sadness is due to lack of belief in anything. It takes pleasure only in material details (hence *The Golden Lotus* and *Dream of the Red Chamber* set out the menus of whole banquets in exact particular and with unflagging interest for no other reason than fondness), because the details are normally pleasant, satisfying and absorbing, while the main theme is always gloomy. All general observation of human life points to emptiness.

People in all countries of the world have a similar feeling. Where the Chinese differ is in that this feeling of 'vanity of vanities, all is vanity' always seems to be a new discovery, and stops there. One Chinese after another sees the flower petals carried away on the stream and promptly sheds tears into the wind, sighs at the moon, senses the transitoriness of life, but that is that: they do not think about what follows. Extinction is inevitable, yet they do not for that reason lose heart, despair, go off the rails, indulge in gluttony and debauch—which apparently is the logical reaction of Europeans, like those of the Renaissance who once they ceased to believe in eternal life after death gave themselves up to pleasure and devilry, and generally raised Cain.

Educated Chinese people do not think they are heading anywhere as year after year of their life passes, nor do they think that mankind is heading anywhere as generation after generation passes. So what meaning is there in living? Meaning or no meaning, living is living: it doesn't matter very much what we do with ourselves, but a better life is a happier one, so for the sake of one's own enjoyment, the wise thing is to behave oneself. Apart from that, caution dictates that a blank space should be left—not that one should blunder in and stir up white mists of mystical possibility, but that one should rein back from the brink and put an absolute stop to all thought. In similar fashion, Chinese paintings are strictly required to leave a blank space at the top; without it the painting loses balance. The trickiest thing in both art and life is to know when to call a halt. The Chinese pride themselves most on this virtue of restraint.

Needless to say, the lower classes could hardly survive in this dreary rarefied atmosphere. Their religion is an amalgam of unrelated superstitions—astrology, fox-spirits, vegetarianism. Ancestor worship appears to be the only concept that upper and lower class people have in common, albeit that to intellectuals it serves a purely emotional function, showing reverence for the dead, without any religious significance.

However, further investigation reveals a common religious background for everybody. The only difference is that educated people are tempted to believe in it but won't confess it, while ignorant people confess it but don't much believe in it. The greater part of this hazy psychological backdrop is Buddhism mixed with Taoism and the demonology of latter-day Taoism; which having marinated in Chinese brains for a number of years is quite unlike the original Buddhism. The superstitions of the lower classes are fragments taken from this broad structure—the structure itself, one might add, has rarely been inspected as a whole, probably because of its overfamiliarity. Since the lower-class superstitions are a part of a systematic world view, they do not qualify as superstitions.

Can this world view be classed as a religion? The Chinese peasant will be more reluctant to give a positive answer the more you press him. At most he will say, 'There must be ghosts and spirits, mustn't there? Not that I have seen any.' As to the intellectuals, they will say that they don't believe, and won't actually be lying, but their thought and behaviour have been secretly dyed with the colours of the religious background, because they would like to believe even though they don't. The truth is that religion is mostly wish-fulfilment. Let us now look at the wishes of the Chinese people.

The Chinese have a Taoist heaven and a Buddhist hell. On death all souls go to hell to receive judgement, so in contrast to the Christian subterranean fiery pits, where only bad people go to suffer for their sins, our underworld is a comparatively well ventilated place. By rights 'The Shades' ought to be in everlasting twilight, but sometimes they are like a perfectly normal city, the focus of interest for tourists being the eighteen levels of dungeons. When living souls escape through an aperture and drift down to hell, it is quite routine for deceased relatives and friends whom they meet there to take them around sight-seeing.

There are lots of different legends about the form of ghosts. The more academic theory is that ghosts are no more than undispersed breaths of air, that is, gaseous: on which basis it is deduced that to look at they are grey or black silhouettes, and being vulnerable to draughts, in the course of time are gradually worn away, hence the saying 'New ghosts are big, old ghosts are little.' But in the imagination of the masses ghosts incline to the photographic model, so when a ghost reveals itself it is always the dead spit of the dead person.

The underworld police arrest the soul of the departed and take it before the court. The King of Hell presides over the highest court. His subordinate officials are chosen from the most capable of ghosts. Prisoners who performed great acts of charity in their lifetime are immediately released, and ascend to heaven via a golden staircase. Sinners detained in hell are subject to all kinds of punishments in accordance with their sins. For example, corrupt officials have large amounts of molten copper poured down their throats.

Middling people all go to get reborn. Their situation and fortunes in the next life all depend on how they behaved in the previous life. A good man is born into a wealthy family. If he was not entirely blameless he is born into a wealthy family as a female—females have a much harder time than males. If he was not formerly of good character, he is born into the lower classes or as an inferior kind of animal. Butchers become pigs. Undischarged debtors become beasts of burden, and work for their creditors.

Before leaving hell, ghosts drink an opiate which makes them forget their previous life. They are driven onto a huge cogged wheel, and when they climb to the top and look down in panic, they are pushed from behind by a ghost gaoler and fall—fall into the hands of the midwife. The idea of reincarnation is found in all oriental countries, but is nowhere visualized as clearly and concretely as in China. Children with bruise marks on their bottom are assumed to have been given a kick by the ghost gaoler because they were scared to make the jump. As the mother rocks and pats her child, she chides: 'Were you so unwilling to come?'

Retribution for sins may be in hell, in the life to come, or indeed in the present life—an unfilial son's own son is unfilial, a mistress who whips her slavegirls gets a festering skin disease on her back. This punishment may be carried out simultaneously in the mundane world and the underworld. A man once went down to hell to look around and saw a lady he knew being whipped; he assumed she must have died. Returning to the land of the living, he discovered she was still alive, only she had weals on her back.

The legal procedures for arrest and trial are not always followed to the letter. In plenty of cases, where someone has maliciously caused the death of another person, the court may set aside all formalities and allow the victim to personally arrest the evildoer. After the ghost possesses him, the evildoer speaks in the voice of the deceased, exposing his own secret, and then commits suicide. A more straightforward and no-frills method is striking dead by thunderbolt, though that is applicable to only the most heinous crimes. The thunder god burns the name of the crime on the back of the evildoer. Samples of 'thunder writing' have been collected and published as a book.

Because of its lack of constancy, the administration of underworld justice allows latitude for much guesswork and interpretation. Thus the Chinese theory of inexorable retribution is invulnerable to criticism: it is easy to find evidence to support it, but absolutely impossible to find evidence to disprove it.

The Chinese nether world is like an open book: there is no mystery attached to it. The law there is an exact replica of the law in the developed stage of Chinese civilization. Only because it is based on human nature, the officers of the underworld sometimes make mistakes. Before the soul of the departed descends to hell, it normally has to undergo a preliminary hearing in the temple of the local god. The temple of the local god is the district court for the nether world, and the post of the local god is invariably filled by some deceased high official (as Lin Daiyu's father Lin Ruhai became the local god in *The Sequel to the Dream of the Red Chamber*); that being so, there is the possibility of them being bribed. Though the high court of hell is comparatively fair and just, its clerks often make mistakes with their registers, and have someone hauled in before his allowed span on earth has come to an end. When the mistake is confirmed after a lot of ups and downs, he can only be restored to life by dint of 'borrowing a (freshly dead) corpse', because his original corpse is by then beyond reclaim.

・・・・・・

Though its jade buildings, flowers and plants convey a sense of hygienic blankness that is close to 'non-action', that is the only Taoist colouring to our Taoist heaven. The rest of the picture is all based on our historical tradition. The Jade Emperor directly rules over countless fairy palaces and indirectly rules over the human world and the underworld. In relation to the Buddha in the West and the Guanyin Bodhisattva in the Purple Bamboo Grove, and various other deities who have their own realms, his role is that of feudal lord. Talented females on earth who die young are qualified to be chosen as palace attendants. If one of these celestial maidens carelessly breaks a flower vase, or laughs out loud when curtsying to her master, or is caught flirting, then she is banished to the mundane world, falls in love and suffers hardships, in the process supplying material for folktales. Such an interruption of heaven's eternal bliss does not seem to be very disagreeable.

The division of labour is taken to extremes in the administration of heaven: there is for example a god for scholars, a god for soldiers, a god of wealth, a god of longevity. Down on earth every city has a city god, every village a village god, every home two door gods and one hearth god, every lake and river has a dragon god. In addition there are sundry immortals without portfolio.

Although the dimensions of the Chinese heaven are imposing, it pales in comparison with the Chinese hell. Its lines lack definition, because unlike hell it ultimately has little relevance to the mass of humanity. But even though Chinese people put no store by heaven, they can believe in it whenever it suits them. Their faculty of idealization is amazingly sturdy. To give a secular example, on the radio two lovers in a Shaoxing opera were saying goodbye with a thousand exhortations and a tearful series of 'Beloved!', 'Dear one!' As the strings were tuning up for the song the announcer butted in with a plug for the programme's sponsor! 'For immediate delivery to the Wang residence, 3rd Floor No. 13 Cihou North Estate, Annan Rd.—One bottle of Dettling.' Yet the dramatic tension was not broken at all.

In view of this Chinese insensitivity to anticlimax, Chinese religion is impervious to any blasphemy. 'Jade Emperor' is another name for a wife, especially a shrewish wife; the distinction between reverence and mockery is not very clear. In the pantheon of gods there is the Queen Mother; when she first appeared in Chinese myths she was as ugly as sin, but afterwards she was dressed up to be a fine upstanding old lady. Together with Magu, one of the Eight Immortals, she decorates birthday feasts for old people, though not as an object of faith. All the same the Chinese do not object to them consorting on equal terms with the All-merciful Guanyin. Foreigners could not imagine Father Christmas mixing with God.

'Spiritual salvation' for the Chinese differs with the individual. People who are satisfied with an endless succession of mundane lives feel no need for 'salvation' at all: as long as they conduct themselves in a reasonable manner, they will not do the kind of great wrong which will exclude them from further life.

Those who see real life as suffering and hope to create a more tolerable environment mostly adopt the Buddhist mode: silence, solitariness, immobility. Chinese people of this persuasion can roughly be divided into two camps.

The more pacific among the faithful—retired officials, old ladies, widows, neglected wives—shut themselves up in a little room and copy out scriptures that they do not aspire to understand. Being divorced from the world, they have no opportunity to sin, and so achieve a negative goodness which earns them a better environment in the next life and a greater share of worldly enjoyment. But complete divorcement from the world is not usually possible, so they have to make substantial concessions. Vegetarianism, for instance, not only eliminates the sin of taking life, but if pushed to the extreme of not eating cooked food also has positive value: if they eat only fruit for the whole of their life, there should come a day when they grow white fur all over their body and change into a divine monkey, free to gambol off on its own business. In fact, however, Chinese vegetarians hanker so much after meat that they have invented 'mock chicken' and 'mock ham'. Better still, they have invented a regime of 'fancy abstinence', which entails abstaining from meat on the first and fifteenth of the month or on such days as the Bodhisattva's birthday. Pious Chinese live on the borderline between the religious and the mundane, putting one foot over it then drawing it back again, believing that a clerk in the underworld will faithfully record every fraction of an inch of withdrawal.

As for energetic young people, they go into temporary retreat to seek for knowledge and power, so that when they return they can rid good citizens of their oppressors, and reform society. They sit motionless for hours on end, their minds empty of thoughts. At dawn and midnight they do deep-breathing exercises, drawing in the essences of the sun and moon to assist the accretion of a superhuman 'invincible power'. Physical exercise always carries a subtle moral overtone to the Chinese, being associated with preparing oneself for a high calling and 'refining one's mettle'. The skill of the boxer and the inner peace of the recluse are analogous and complementary.

Fighting one's way with one's fists right to the kingdom of heaven is the central theme of Chinese adventure novels. China has novels on a par with Western boy-scout stories, and their readers include lots of adults as well as students and apprentices. Before the knight-errant takes it upon himself to 'carry out the will of heaven' he goes into the mountains to learn boxing, swordsmanship and military strategy. The notion that to improve the world you first have to cut yourself off from the world is very deep-rooted, even among people who don't read martial-arts novels.

Some people are not satisfied with mere improvements to reality; they want to go higher. The majority of them would rather become an immortal than a deity, because the title of deity is normally a reward for distinguished services: that is, you really have to put yourself out to get it in the first place, and afterwards when you become an official in the celestial kingdom you are loaded down with duties. A clean and honest magistrate automatically becomes a deity after he dies if his community erects a temple to him. Particularly pure and virtuous women often have their own temple, too, but whether they continue to enjoy the support and sustenance of the local people depends on them taking responsibility for the grain harvest, the weather, and answering private prayers.

• • • • • •

Immortals, who don't have to worry about where their next meal is coming from, pass their time in simple pleasures, like playing chess, drinking wine, and travelling. They exist in another time dimension: to them one day is equivalent to a thousand years on earth. This doesn't seem to be of much benefit; it merely makes them more apathetic than we are.

• • • • • •

Although immortals are happy in their entirely carefree enjoyment of their riches, they have no opportunity in their irresponsible life to practise their social skills, and such skills, however painfully they have to be learned, are still the strong point of the Chinese, which they would not willingly give up. Hence the Chinese attitude to the 'blessed isles' is irresolute: half wanting, half detesting.

Actually the Chinese heaven is superfluous. Hell is good enough for most people. Provided their conduct is not too bad, they can look forward to a limitless succession of similar lives, in which they work out predestiny and unknowingly sow the seeds of future relationships, conclude old feuds and incur new enmities—cause and effect are woven closely together, like a mat made of thin bamboo strips; you get dizzy trying to pick out the pattern. The Chinese are very fond of this aspect of life, and once they take a liking to something they can't have enough of it, as has always been the case. The film *A Fine Example to Posterity* has been adapted as a Peking opera; the novel *Autumn Begonia* has been adapted as a modern play, a Shaoxing opera, a comedy, a recitative with string accompaniment, and a Shanghai ballad: the same audience faithfully goes to see it time and time again. Chinese musical compositions, whether named 'The Wild Goose Lands on the Sandbar' or 'Autumn in the Han Palace', always repeat the same tune again and again, complacently chewing and savouring, with no climaxes and no endings—when they are finished they start again, using a different title.

● ● ● ● ● ●

When modern Chinese films and literature present positive goodness, the goodness is always suggestive of Christian missionaries, which shows how Christianity has influenced Chinese life. The model Chinese are seen smiling calmly, being bravely cheerful, wearing the fashions of two years ago, addressing wives as 'mater'; the women knit, the children play '101 Best Tunes' on the piano. Female authors very quickly grasped the sentimental value of the church bells ringing for vespers and of kneeling in prayer by one's bed. Stories in popular magazines often feature heroines establishing orphanages in memory of their departed loved one. These stories are worthy of attention, because they represent the flights of imagination of the average educated wife and mother.

Pupils in missionary schools, being of an impressionable age, get used to associating hymns and church with solemnity, discipline and youthful idealism. This attitude can persist into adulthood, even if they are never baptised. Youthful revolutionaries are hostile to established religion, but they are not opposed to Christianity, because Christianity brought hospitals and chemistry laboratories along with it.

The film *A Charitable Passage Across the Sea of Humanity* features a married couple. The husband pours his money and energy into the stock exchange, while the wife serves the people as a doctor. In her spare time she joyfully helps the children conduct chemistry experiments in the cellar. *A Charitable Passage* is the one and only Chinese film that has a sustained display of virtue, kept up for over twenty minutes on end. Most Chinese films afford only a fleeting glimpse of goodness, to serve as a contrast to darkness.

In ancient China all positive good derived from human relationships. The highest ideal of Confucian government was no more than providing enough food and good public order to allow kinship and friendship room for expression. In recent history the Chinese suddenly came to see that the family was the dregs of feudalism, fathers were diabolical tyrants, mothers were good-natured fools, fashionable wives were playthings, rustic wives were live offerings on a sacrificial altar. All basic relationships having been subjected to repeated attacks of this kind. The Chinese have become as inhibited and suspicious as Westerners, which is very tough on them, as apart from personal relationships they have no other beliefs.

Therefore it is not surprising that modern Chinese find it so difficult to describe goodness. When novels and plays have their heroes and heroines find their way out of the labyrinth and set out for the sunlit uplands, they come to an abrupt end—critics may castigate and berate them all they like, they still have to end there.

......

But the greatest obstacle to Chinese people being converted to Christianity is rather that the life to come that it depicts does not appeal to Chinese tastes. We can leave aside the old-style Christian heaven, where there is perpetual playing of golden harps and singing to the glory of God. The more progressive view of the earth as a kind of moral gymnasium where we limber up in order to go on to display our prowess in a nebulous other world, is also unacceptable to the self-satisfied and conservative Chinese, who regard human life as the centre of the universe. As for saying that a human life is but an ephemeral bubble in the tidal flow of the Great Self, such a promise of eternal life without individuality is not very meaningful either. Christianity gives us very little comfort, so our native folklore can still stand up to the high-pressure proselytizing of Roman Catholic and Protestant Christianity, though it has not counter-attacked, though it hasn't the support of big capital, has no propaganda literature, no splendid peaceful sets, not even a bible—for since almost nobody understands the Buddhist sutras, it is as if they do not exist.

A Beating
打人

I saw a policeman hitting someone on the Bund, for no reason, simply because he felt like it. It was a boy of fifteen or sixteen, quite neatly dressed, in padded jacket and trousers, with a belt around his waist. I did not see clearly what the policeman was whipping him with—it seemed to be the long loop attached to the end of his truncheon. Down came his arm, *thwack!*, time after time, driving the boy up against a wall. The boy did not try to run away, though he could have. He looked up at him, screwing up his eyes, in the way country people squint against the glare of the sun in the open fields, and there was even the hint of a smile on his face. It had all happened too suddenly: people without stage experience often lag behind in adjusting their expression.

I have never had a strong sense of justice. If I don't want to see something I can shut it out. But this time I couldn't help it, I kept looking round at them. I felt choked. With every blow my heart contracted. When he had finished his beating, the policeman sauntered over in my direction. I fixed him with a venomous stare, only sorry that I could not look real daggers. I hoped I could express my utter contempt and anger, the kind of disgust one feels for a leper. But he was only aware he was the object of attention, and smugly tightened his belt. He was a northerner with a long face and a big mouth, not at all bad looking in fact.

He walked over to the door of the public lavatory, and laid hold of a shabby looking man in a long gown who happened to be standing there. He did not set about him straight away, he just glared at him as he fingered his truncheon. Torn between panic and indignation, the man actually came out with a witticism: 'Is it because I was going for a crap?'

Probably because of my lack of ideological training, I forgot all about the class revolution, and in my anger wished I were a high official, or else the First Lady, so that I could have stepped up to the policeman and boxed his ears.

In the novels of Li Hanqiu,[1] written in the early years of the Republic, there would have come at this juncture the intervention of a public-spirited Western missionary or the concubine of the Chief of Police (the confidante of the heroine, the old flame of the hero). Momentary naivety is excusable, but systematic naivety is really not a good thing.

---

[1] Li Hanqiu 李涵秋(1874–1923) was a schoolmaster, journalist and popular novelist.

Wang Ting-chün 王鼎鈞 (1925–)

COMMENTARY

When Japan invaded China in 1937, the walled town in Linyi county, Shandong province, where Wang Ting-chün (Wang Dingjun) lived, soon came under the control of the Japanese army. As a teenager Wang joined a guerrilla unit which operated in the countryside. Military operations took him far over northern China. In 1949 he joined the exodus to Taiwan, and began a career of teaching, broadcasting, journalism and playwriting. He wrote a large number of short plays for radio, edited a newspaper supplement, wrote regular newspaper columns, and compiled guides to writing for inexperienced authors. Collections of his essays and newspaper commentaries became best-sellers. He now lives in New York, but continues to publish in Taiwan.

Wang Ting-chün is one of the few 'virile' essayists in Taiwan. His writing is fluid, non-academic, and—for want of a better word—natural. He was one of the first to apply the techniques of fiction to prose compositions. Very likely it was his experience with the mass media, especially with radio drama, that made him seek to energize and electrify the essay form so as to hold the casual reader's attention and persuade him that what he was reading came from the workshop of life, not from the playground of the mind. The essays that follow are examples of what he has done in that way.

'Footprints' spools out a string of thoughts in an uninterrupted monologue. To make the monologue corporeal, so to speak, it is addressed to a 'you', not an abstract reader, so paralleling in prose Browning's breakout in verse to 'dramatic monologues'. Moreover, the 'you' is specific: supposedly the speaker's one-time sweetheart, now wife. And the 'you' is given presence and some passive participation by being chided for having a bad memory. The speaker's thoughts seem to have been occasioned by the 'homegoing' (*huan xiang*) concession allowed by the Taiwan government to residents of Taiwan to make private visits to see their relatives on the mainland. In keeping with the 'dramatic' character of the essay, that is not mentioned till well into the text. While I am about explanation, I should clarify one reference in the essay that might escape other readers as it escaped me initially; it is, unexpectedly, to the Old Testament. The rainbow seen over the Qinling mountains during the Sino-Japanese war is a reminder of God's covenant with mankind after the Flood: 'I do set my bow in the cloud, and it shall be for a token of the covenant between me and the earth' (Genesis 9:13). Here the rainbow stands for the hope for peace and a new and better order.

'The Last Word in Beauty and Ugliness' affects a different voice, and is still more dramatic in casting. In fact the demarcation line between prose and fiction is blurred to the extent that this piece has been included in anthologies of fiction. It is presented as a tale told to other tellers of tales, and thus may be construed as distancing the author from responsibility for its truth to fact. The historical fact, indeed, is that the 'empress' whose beauty most impressed the speaker as a young soldier could not have been an empress at all, as none of the wives of Henry Puyi 溥儀, the puppet emperor set up by the Japanese in Manchuria, escaped to Peking after the war. At most she could have been a lady-in-waiting. Nevertheless, since Wang himself classifies the piece as 'prose', not fiction, we must assume that it is his own experience that he writes of, and that he must have believed at the time that the 'empress' was an empress. The naive and artless tone adopted for the narrator suggests that he was so credulous, and the last paragraph underlines the possibility that he may have been deluded. Rather than explain all that in words, the author has chosen to 'stage' the explanation by suggestion. Perhaps a more basic qualification for essay status is that the piece does do what the title portends, namely to say what are the extremes of beauty and ugliness that the author has met with, rather than to tell a story with an outcome. Though the 'empress' may not have been genuine, she still may have been extremely beautiful, and her apparently tragic circumstances would no doubt have enhanced her beauty; the eunuch may have been conniving in a deception, but his self-exposure would still have been extremely repulsive. Readers cannot complain that their expectations have not been met.

The Last Word in Beauty and Ugliness
最美和最醜

So everyone tells a story about the most beautiful and the ugliest thing they have come across, fine. You have all told your stories, now it's my turn. The night is late, you are tired out, the fire in our room is nearly out, and the dew outside is starting to turn to frost.

I don't feel like telling a story, but I have to. You may not feel like listening, but you have to. The pact we made binds us like a rope, and we can't wriggle out of it. You took up too much time with your stories; in the few minutes that are left for me, I have to make mine short and sweet, and get you to admit when it's over that it's not only truly a story about the last word in beauty and ugliness, but also the best.

At the same time this story is the last word in truthfulness—I saw

The Chinese Essay

it all with my own eyes, heard it all with my own ears, just as you are seeing and hearing me now. If anyone doesn't believe me, they can look at the ring on my wife's finger. You've all seen that ring, with the shining pearl set in it. The story I'm about to tell says how I came by that pearl.

That pearl was originally worn on the finger of an empress. Have you ever seen an empress? I have. We are talking about Peking, after the victory over Japan. Her husband was the Emperor of Manchuria, and you all know how he ended up. She got out in the confusion, and skipped to Peking, where she settled down, because that's where she'd come from. Ah! This takes us back twenty-five years, no, twenty-seven years. We'd just got demobbed, and we went back to Peking, thinking ourselves young heroes, and qualified to lavish our affections. We regularly over-tipped the waiters in restaurants, gave handfuls of coins to beggars, and bought loads of things we didn't need so as not to disappoint the shop girls. We often went to see the empress, out of sympathy because she'd fallen on hard times. We wouldn't admit it was to satisfy our own curiosity.

It was really a big thing, when you think about it, to still be able to see an empress in 1945. It was like suddenly discovering when you have grown up a toy you'd played with as a boy, still in perfect condition. Like an archaeologist seeing a 4,000-year-old bronze vessel that has just been dug up. Like primitive African masks and models being displayed in a skyscraper, the kind of place that most represents modern civilization. The novelty, the dare, the joy, the sense of superiority, the excitement! Imagine! Let's go and see the empress! Go and see the empress! Say you proposed today that we should go and see the world-champion junior baseball team, your call wouldn't be more ringing than ours, more chipper, more cocky.

That empress was twenty-two years old, and believe me she was beautiful. In the last twenty years I've knocked about a bit, covered 4,000 kilometres, I've gone from boom towns to quaint old cities, from the most decadent places to places where they know everything there is to know about nutrition and cosmetics, but I've never seen a girl prettier than her. Being an empress, she couldn't very well go and live with her poverty-stricken dad and mum and brothers and sisters, she had to have a place of her own. She thought so, and her dad and mum thought so too. The 'palace' that she rented temporarily was very small and ramshackle. It only had one bed, one table and two benches, besides an antique red lacquer chest with gold tracing. When we went we sat on the benches. Her policy was neither to receive anybody nor to refuse anybody entry. She simply sat on the edge of the bed, very upright, with her eyes cast down and one hand resting on the chest, not looking, not listening, not speaking, not moving. Apart from for eating, sleeping and other necessary functions, she sat like that all day long, ignoring what went on outside, and even what went on inside.

Despite the fact that she was more silent than the sea, more upright than a mountain, us crowd of young single men still often went to see her. It only needed one of us to say he was going to see the empress for the rest to troop along too, without raising any objections. And every week there were one or two who did say that. We crowded into her little room, laughing and chatting among ourselves; in fact as time went on we even took along our own beer and pickled pork and stuffed ourselves at her table. She seemed not to see us, and we pretended not to see her.

We gradually got to know a lot of things. We learned that the empress had vowed never to remarry. She had taken a bag of jewels with her when she escaped from the palace. She was selling the jewels to support herself. She had sworn an oath in blood to her parents and to Heaven and Earth to kill herself when the jewels ran out. She ate very little and spent very little, in effect spinning out her life as long as possible. By and by we also found out that though the empress's situation was wretched, she still had a eunuch to wait on her. This eunuch had fled across the border from Manchuria, and hearing there was an empress in Peking, had hurried along to report to her. He had found a place to stay out of town, and came into town every morning, to this dark and stuffy room, to wish the empress good morning. Then he cleaned the room from end to end, and shopped and cooked for the empress. When he had prepared her meal, on no account would he stay and eat himself: not a shred of vegetable or a grain of rice would pass his lips. He went back to his thatched shack in the outskirts to nibble on his cold and hard corn bread.

We then had another thing to amuse us—go and see the eunuch.

The eunuch was bent over with age. The first thing we noticed about him was his bald crown ringed with whispy white hair; then the puffy bags under his eyes, his missing teeth, the yellowed whites of his eyes. His manner was quite the opposite to the empress's; he invited us in extremely courteously, but the ceiling was too low and we came out again and talked to him outside where we could stand upright. We were most eager to learn how a eunuch became a eunuch, but he wouldn't talk about that subject. No matter in what roundabout way we approached it, we always got back the reply, 'Why harp on the past, sir? That's of no interest at all.'

While we kept on getting nowhere, the eunuch had some new visitors, one man bringing along three others. Obviously the chap in the lead was a guide, and the rest were sightseers. The eunuch invited them extremely politely and smoothly to enter his shack. Seeing how dirty, cramped and dark it was inside, one sightseer hesitated in the doorway, but eventually made up his mind to enter after his companions. The eunuch closed the door, shutting us out. The guide also stayed outside. He lit a cigarette, and asked us if we had seen it.

Seen what?

Didn't you come to see the eunuch?

Yes, we had already seen him.

How did you know he was here? And how much did you pay?

Pay? We hadn't paid a cent.

How come? How is he going to eat if you don't pay? To be frank, how am I going to eat?

I didn't know what the guide was on about, so I tried to pin him down. Did those three chaps come to see the eunuch? Yes. You brought them? Yes. They pay to see the eunuch? Of course. What do they pay for? The guide was taken by surprise. He asked me in return, if it wasn't for money, who would drop their trousers and let people have a look-see? Thereupon he glanced at the tightly closed door and grumbled to himself: those blighters are taking their time, aren't they? Getting a proper eyeful!

Then he turned back to us and said: I'll bet you haven't had a look. I'll bet you don't know how to go about it. If you're willing to put your hand into your pocket, you can leave it to me. He told us straight, if you don't have a look you'll regret it, this is the only opportunity you'll ever have. There won't be any more eunuchs to see after this one, not for love nor money.

Seeing we made no response, he tried the hard sell: this is your genuine eunuch, lots of foreigners come to see him, and afterwards say how worthwhile it was, how glad they were they came. True, it doesn't come free, but it's money well spent.

So at last we understood what he meant by coming to see the eunuch. At the same time we understood what those three people were doing inside with the white-haired eunuch. We had found out how the guide and the eunuch lived. It was really too vile, it was the vilest story I had ever heard. That great revelation left me dumbfounded. None of us responded, not knowing what to say. We were still lost for words when the door opened. While the eunuch refastened his waist sash, the sightseers opened their wallets. The eunuch bowed and saw his customers out with the utmost courtesy. His manner had all the poise and smoothness of the best trained assistants in some old-established Peking shop.

I looked closely for some sign of shame in the eunuch's expression, but there was none. Every afternoon he waited here for business to come to him, and every following morning he went in all sincerity to where the empress lived to do his habitual duty. He was heard to say that were it not for the empress he would long ago have died. That might well have been true. He had found a reason to keep on living, found it in the empress's little room: as long as he could serve her his life was worthwhile. Since he had a justification for living, he had a justification for his means of staying alive. He did not let us see his distress: in his eyes we weren't fit to, even though we could be allowed, on payment, to see his mutilation. It was he who sold the empress's jewels. Whenever the empress ran out of money she would hand him a piece of jewelry, and he would shuffle out with back bent, and after ages and ages would shuffle back with back bent, and present the money with both hands, his body all of a tremble. As he watched the empress take the money, lock it in the chest, take her seat on the edge of the bed and rest her hand on the lid of the chest, the tears fell from his eyes.

Then he knelt before the empress, pressed his face to the ground, and cried his heart out. The empress's neighbours regularly heard him wailing. Every time he sold a piece of jewelry he would wail. Only the empress witnessed his grief, though the empress very likely did not rightly understand how great his grief was, nor how deep it was.

Afterwards I left Peking. The beauty and ugliness remained deeply impressed on my heart. When I met people who had come from Peking, I enquired about the empress and the eunuch, wanting to know if their lifestyle had changed. Oddly enough, those people could tell you all the trifles and trivialities of Peking, but they hadn't heard of the empress and eunuch. There was no way I could explain that, because in my mind they were illustrious personages, their weight pressed nightly on my chest, making me cry out in my dreams. Could it be that those two people only existed for me? . . .

Later on the world split into two, and no one would come from Peking any more, no more news would come of the empress. So this story of the last word in beauty and the last word in ugliness hasn't got a sequel.

Footprints
腳印

Homesickness is aesthetics, not economics. You don't look for rewards when you pine for home, nor do you need to compete with others. My homesickness is romantic, verging on decadent, and is as mild as suffering from a cold.

You may remember the tale that when someone dies, his ghost has to collect all the footprints he left during his lifetime. To carry out that task his ghost has to retread every step he has ever taken. Those footprints are imprinted indelibly on boats and vehicles, on bridges and roads, in streets and alleys. Even though bridges may have collapsed, boats sunk, roads been resurfaced with tarmacadam, and river banks made into dams, the ghost only has to turn up for the footprints to reappear.

Imagine us having to retrieve our own footprints from under layers of yellow leaves in that dense forest, in the same way as we gathered nuts when we were young. Picture the flower market as bright as day in the lamplight, the long avenue a sea of bobbing heads, and us parting a wall of legs to pick up footprints, as we retrieved shoes that had come off in the crush in days gone by. Think of that lake! One day we will have to crack the mirror surface, tear the shadows cast by clouds, go down to the bed to collect footprints, as we collected pebbles in times past. In the public square where people could sing and dance and skip and jump, your footprints would not be complete, mostly only a toe or a heel. Outside your gate, outside your window, the wall of your backyard, within the compass of your lamplight within the compass of your *wutong* trees' shade, my footprints were imposed one layer on another, spring summer autumn winter, a thousand, ten thousand layers. If one day they were all to resurface, they would pile higher than the roof of your house.

Sometimes I get emotional when I think of this tale, sometimes I am sceptical. Granted that I don't have to worry how many footprints my back and shoulder could bear, just as I don't have to speculate how many angels could stand on the head of a pin, but how can this tale be reconciled with other tales? When the Day of Judgement comes, won't there be ox-headed and horse-faced lictors from the underworld waiting with their token of office and their iron chains for the soul to leave the body? Trial and sentence follows immediately, so the soul will have no time to go and collect footprints; afterwards it drinks the soup of forgetfulness, and is reborn in the world, so it will be unable to go and collect footsteps. How could a ghost be so high-minded, so do-as-you-please, so individualistic? Very well, if the ancient saints and worthies took it upon themselves to create myths, modern saints and worthies may revise myths. We have to take apart that close-knit narrative structure and admit new fictions.

To my mind the plot of the footprint-collecting story is somewhat over-complicated and goes beyond common knowledge. If it were me, I would like if possible to collect your footprints as well as mine and make a proper job of it. If collecting footprints were just a person's last whim, or a lot of people voluntarily forsook the practice, then if need be there might emerge an occupation, an agency for collecting footprints. In my case, what I would want retrieved would not be limited to footprints. Those songs—all around in the places where we sang there are the notes we threw out: the songs are frozen there waiting for us to go and breathe on them to sound again. Those tears—in the places where we cried, the hot tears turned to molten metal, flowed back down our throats, set as iron in the heart and soul: when we return to those old haunts the iron will melt and revert to tears again, old tears like vintage wine. The people are scattered, the tears are scattered, the songs are scattered, the footprints are scattered. Would that I could sort them and tidy them and put them away, like carefully pouring fine wine into a jade wine cup.

Perhaps the important things should be seen to while we live, as we cannot tell what awaits after death. Perhaps the story of collecting footprints is just to remind the wanderer in his declining years to make a retrospective journey. We are taken in by false appearances, behind us lies the truth. And if we retrace the course of our life, the terminus of our journey is of course our birthplace.

Can youth be restored? Apparently not, because the experiments of all alchemists have failed. But there is a secret formula that can be tried, which is the journey that goes by the name of collecting footprints. This journey is in the opposite direction to the former one, it can be carried out in reverse sequence, so time can seem to flow backwards. In my case, if I stood on the banks of the Yangtze River and remembered the celebrities crossing south in shoals, I would feel I was twenty. If I sat where the river runs dry, and looked at a rainbow against gathering clouds, looked at the covenant God made with the Chinese in the Qinling Mountains, and watched how the rainbow adorned the mountains to match the colours of the imperial palace, I was fifteen. If I stood barefoot on the spot where I first saw ants fight and chicken fly up into trees, and let the feel of the mud pass through the soles of my feet to the top of my head, I was only six.

Of course, we are talking about feelings, not about fact. Fact is in the eyes of customs officials, and on your passport. The fact is that visiting old haunts is like returning as a semi-ghost—unrecognized, you are asked politely where you hail from. But sometimes feelings are what you are after, and you forget about facts; feelings may deceive one, yet though one wastes away one does not regret it. I feel I am a written word, deleted by a critic, and restored by a rhetorician. I feel my tight-fitting vest has been pulled to pieces—comfortable, but cold too. I feel like a sliced sausage that at the last cut of the knife hopes it will make a good meal.

Have I left footprints behind me? How is it that in my green youth, between fifteen and twenty, I felt I was mounting the clouds and riding the mists, my feet never touching the ground? The men of old had a saying that reading a book should give you the feeling of being knocked over the head; I feel the same way about 'homegoing'. For forty years we didn't hear a dicky bird, then all of sudden you couldn't get away from homegoing, homegoing, homegoing—do you remember? One of our country wiseacres told a story about two travellers meeting in an inn. They got round to boasting about the high buildings in their respective hometowns. One of them said, we have a building at home, and on the roof of the building there was a sparrow's nest, with some eggs in it. One day, somehow or other the nest came to pieces. On the way down the eggs hatched, the little sparrows broke out of the shell, and before they reached the ground their wings hardened and they could fly. So none of those sparrows fell to their death. They swooped low over the ground, and then shot up into the sky. Just imagine how high that building is.

I hope you still remember that story. You've forgotten too many things. Forgotten stories, forgotten songs, forgotten place names and people's names. How could you? Those stories, those songs, those place names and people's names should coexist with our souls, coexist with our characters. It puzzles me what you apply your memory to.

... The traveller said, just imagine how high that building in our hometown is. The other traveller laughed, and without turning a hair replied, we have a tall building at home too. Once a young girl fell from the top, and by the time she got to the ground she was already an old lady. How do you think our building compares with yours?

Long ago I felt the call of distant places. I had a yearning to see such high buildings, and didn't care how hard or how long the journey might be. Now I think the high buildings are not in some far-off place, they are our home. If I ever went home, the feeling might come to me that I had fallen from that building in my youth, and had become an old man on touching the ground. So quick, so simple, so straightforward! None of the pains of growing up, of shrinking small, none of the expectations and disillusionments, none of life's long runs long tests long songs long years of fretting long nights of weeping would have had time or had the chance to happen. 'Myself of now and myself of yore, only the blink of an eye between us', no leisure to get worked up about anything. This would have to be the great release, the great relief, this is the great sundering, the great renouncement, the great separation, the great abandonment, and also the great end and beginning. I am afraid I would not even be able to roll around on the ground, for the air would buoy me up.

Yu Kwang-chung 余光中 (1928–)

COMMENTARY

Fate seemed at first to treat Yu Kwang-chung (Yu Guangzhong) unkindly, but being uprooted in his youth by war and revolution in fact turned out to be his making. Born in Nanjing in 1928, he had to flee with his family in 1937 before the Japanese invading forces, and after returning to Nanjing in 1947 he again fled before the Communist advance in the civil war. His family settled in Taiwan in 1950. It was there that opportunities opened up that would have been denied in China. Having been among the first batch of students to graduate in foreign languages from the National Taiwan University (1952), Yu began his career as a university teacher in 1956, and in 1958 made the first of several extended visits to the USA, latterly to teach—not English but Chinese. Again it was to teach Chinese that he went to the Chinese University of Hong Kong (1974–85), by which time he had made a name for himself as a poet. His first book of poetry was published in 1952; by now the total is over a dozen. To begin with a modernist, his loyalty shifted over the years to the Chinese poetic tradition, aiming to preserve continuity in internal values rather than outer form.

Yu Kwang-chung's first book of essays was published in 1963, and a steady stream has followed. What distinguishes Yu's essays from those of his contemporaries who have had the American experience is his wit and his working of words and phrases. Probably his best essay, 'Listen to That Cold Rain'聽聽那冷雨, demonstrates the latter skill chiefly, exploiting auditory effects and the pictorial qualities of Chinese characters to such an extent that any translation would be a pale imitation. I have chosen instead two essays where wit is predominant. It will be immediately obvious that there is a family resemblance between these essays, particularly the first, and the wartime essays of Liang Shih-ch'iu, both ultimately deriving from the Anglo-American 'light' familiar essay. Like Liang's, Yu's command of Chinese and English literature and language is extensive, and quotations and allusions, often cleverly twisted into a new aptness, abound. Of the two, Yu is the more conscious rhetorician, as may be expected from a poet (much of his cleverness in that regard is regrettably submerged in translation). A certain amount of posing and self-caricature is inherent in the genre, but again a difference is noticeable between the two essayists, in that the 'I' character in Liang tends towards the typical (he could be anybody), while in Yu the 'I' tends towards the personal (he could only be Yu Kwang-chung). The trend in recent decades has indeed been towards personalization in essay writing, especially in Taiwan, encouraged apparently by readers who prefer gossip to anything thought-provoking. However, Yu Kwang-chung does not betray his intelligence.

Thus Friends Absent Speak*
尺素寸心

To get letters from friends, especially airmail letters from overseas that bear the stamp of exotic climes, is unquestionably one of life's greatest pleasures, provided, that is, that they do not call for a reply. Answering letters is a heavy price to pay for the enjoyment of reading letters. The inevitable consequence of tardiness or infrequency in answering letters is a corresponding reduction in, and ultimate cessation of, the pleasure of receiving letters, in which case friendship is prematurely broken off, until the day in sackcloth and ashes you summon up the willpower to put pen to paper again. Through this dilly-dallying the pleasure of receiving letters has turned to the misery of owing letters. I am an old lag in this respect: practically every one of the friends I have made in my comings and goings can recite from my crime sheet. W.H. Auden once admitted that he was in the habit of shelving important letters, preferring instead to curl up with a detective novel; while Oscar Wilde remarked to Henley: 'I have known men come to London full of bright prospects and seen them complete wrecks in a few months through a habit of answering letters.' Clearly Wilde's view was that to enjoy life one should renounce the bad habit of answering letters. So I am not the only one to be faint-hearted in that regard.

If it is conceded that replying to letters is to be dreaded, on the other hand not replying to letters is by no means a matter of unalloyed bliss. Normally a hundred or so letters are stacked on my bookshelf, of diverse maturity of debt outstanding, the longest being over a year. That kind of pressure is more than an ordinary sinner can bear. A stack of unanswered letters battens on me like a bevy of plaintive ghosts and plays havoc with my smitten conscience. In

---

*Since the Chinese title 'Chi su cun xin' (A root of plain silk, an inch of heart) is untranslatable, I have substituted the quotation from John Donne's 'To Sir Henry Wotton'.

principle the letters are there for replying to. I can swear in all honesty that I have never while of sound mind determined not to answer people's letters. The problem is a technical one. Suppose I had a whole summer night at my disposal: should I first answer the letter that was sent eighteen months ago, or that one that was sent seven months ago? After such a long delay even the expiry date for apology and self-recrimination would surely have passed? In your friends' eyes you have already stepped beyond the pale, are of no account. On the grapevine your reputation is 'that impossible fellow'.

Actually even if you screw up all your moral courage and settle down at your desk to pay off your letter debt come what may, the thing is easier said than done. Old epistles and new missives are jumbled up together and stuffed in drawers or strewn on shelves; some have been answered, some not. As the poet was told about the recluse he was looking for: 'I know he's in these mountains, but in this mist I can't tell where.' The time and energy you would spend to find the letter you have decided to answer would be several times that needed to write the reply itself. If you went on to anticipate that your friend's reaction to receiving your letter would be less 'surprised by joy' than 'resentment rekindled', then your marrow would turn to water, and your debt would never be cleared.

To leave letters unanswered is not equivalent to forgetting friends, no more than it is conceivable that debtors can forget their creditors. At the bottom of such disquietude, at the end of your nightmares, there forever lurks the shadowy presence of this friend with his angry frown and baleful looks: no, you can never forget him. Those who you really put out of your mind, and do so without qualm, are those friends who have already been replied to.

I once held forth to the poet Chou Meng-tieh in this wise: 'You must immediately acknowledge new publications friends send you. After the usual thanks and congratulations you can conclude with the sentence "I will get down at once to a close and reverential perusal." If you delay these congratulatory letters for a week or a month, then you are in trouble, because by that time you would be under an obligation to have read the book and could not get away with these general compliments.' Meng-tieh was quite overcome. Unfortunately I have never followed my own advice and must have lost many friends as a consequence. But I do remember sending in a fit of enthusiasm a new book of my own to some friends. One of them took a couple of months to send a note of thanks, explaining that his wife, his daughter and his wife's colleagues had all been desperate to read this great work, and he was still waiting his turn, which showed how fascinating the book was, etc. To this day I don't know whether to believe this story of his, but if he was lying one has to own that his was a stroke of genius.

It is said that the late Dr Hu Shi not only responded to all requests, he even personally answered letters from schoolchildren asking for advice. On top of that he wrote his famous diary, never missing a day. To write letters is to be considerate to others; to keep a diary is to be considerate to oneself. That such an *éminence grise* could after his intellectual labours be so thorough and methodical on both counts leaves one lost in admiration. As for me, having already confessed myself unable to cope on the epistolary front, diaries would be a sheer luxury.

I am inclined to think that few of my contemporaries can hope to emulate the natural and easy-flowing style of the older generation of writers and scholars in their exchange of letters. Mr Liang Shih-ch'iu, for example, is burdened with great fame, and because of his many connections naturally has a great deal of correspondence to deal with, but in the more than twenty years I have known him he has always replied promptly to my letters. Moreover, his own are unfailingly witty and written in an elegant hand, revealing a different side of him to the joviality that characterizes our *tête-à-têtes*. Given my fear of writing letters, I can't say I correspond with him very frequently. I also have to bear in mind the fact that he stated in one of his *Cottager's Essays* that there are eleven kinds of letters that he does not keep—no doubt mine are number eight on the list. As far as I know his most frequent correspondent is Chen Zhifen. When Chen was young he was always exchanging letters with celebrated writers like Hu Shi and Shen Congwen, and he built up a voluminous collection of famous men's autographs. Mr Liang has humorously called him a 'man of letters': perhaps by now his own turn has come to have his letters collected.

My friends fall into four schools on the basis of their letter style. The first school's letters are shot off like telegrams: just a few lines, maybe twenty or thirty scribbled words, with the momentum of a blitzkrieg. The trouble is that the recipient has to spend a lot more time puzzling out and deciphering the message than it took the sender's pen to gallop across the paper. Peng Ko, Joseph S.M. Lau, and Pai Hsien-yung are representative of this school. The second school writes letters like a young lady embroiders flowers, finely drawn, the characters handsomely formed, a true study in calm and unhurriedness. As for content, apart from their practical function they express the writer's feelings and have an engaging tone that it is a pleasure to listen to. Stephen Soong and C. T. Hsia can be said to typify this school, especially C. T. Hsia: how comes it that a great scholar writes such copybook tiny characters, and always uses economical aerogrammes? The third school comes between the first two and follows the golden mean: their letters are neither tepid nor fiery, their pace is well modulated, and they are written in big bold characters, open and candid in mien. Yen Yuan-shu, Wang Wen-hsing, Ho Huai-shuo, Yang Mu, Lo Men are all 'exemplary characters'. One might mention especially Ho Huai-shuo for the wide sweep of his discussion, while Yang Mu spaces his characters far apart and leaves large gaps between lines, at the same time indulging his liking for parchment-gauge notepaper: his cavalier disregard for postage puts the rest of our gallant band in the shade. The fourth school employs the writing brush and covers the page with loops and whorls, the form of the characters being somewhere between the running and the 'grass'; these are the celebrities who scorn to conform. Lo Ching is of their number.

Of course those who put on the most style are Liu Kuo-sung and Kao Hsin-chiang: they don't write letters at all, they simply telephone from the other end of the earth.

(1967)

My Four Hypothetical Enemies
我的四個假想敵

After taking in Hong Kong the common entrance exam for students overseas, my second daughter Youshan was given her first choice of Foreign Languages at Taiwan University. This news relieved me of the worry that all my four daughters would marry Cantonese boys.

Of course, I have no prejudice against Cantonese boys. In my six years in Hong Kong I have had quite a number of nice Cantonese young men in my class who won my approval as their teacher, but if you ask me whether I would be content to see my daughters all carried off by those 'dishy' and 'smart' young fellows, the answer is 'no'. The question of whom my daughters should marry then arises. To put it lightly, they will marry of their own free will; to put it arcanely, they will marry the person they are meant for. It is pointless for a father to anticipate what he might gain or lose. Moreover, it is the mother who is normally the communications hub in such matters; in the natural course of events she becomes the daughters' confidential adviser, even their confidential comrade-in-arms—the adversary being not the boyfriends, but the father. By the time the father wakes up, he is already under attack from front and rear, and has little chance of turning the tables.

In a father's eyes, a daughter is most lovable up to the age of ten, because she then belongs wholly to him. In a boyfriend's eyes, her most lovable age is after she has reached seventeen, for she is then like a student in the graduating class, her thoughts directed wholly to the outside world. There is an inherent contradiction between father and boyfriend. To a father, there is nothing more perfect than a daughter in her tender years; her only fault is that she will grow up. You could fast-freeze her into a state of suspended animation, but I fear that would be illegal, and sooner or later her boyfriend would ride up on a white horse or a motor bike and wake her with a kiss.

I didn't resort to freezing them like they are supposed to do for space travellers, I allowed time to press and harry, and month to succeed month. When I rubbed my eyes again, somehow or other my four daughters had grown up, one after another, and the gate to the old fairy tale had slammed to, barring all return. My four daughters, in order of seniority, are called Shanshan, Youshan, Peishan and Jishan. As they all have the element 'coral' (*shan*) in their names, they could space out to form a coral reef. When Shanshan was twelve, I remember Peishan, who was not yet nine, announcing to our guests, 'I say, you probably don't know my eldest sister is a young woman now!' The adults present were much amused.

Some time ago now, the Peishan who had provoked amusement was herself, along with our youngest, Jishan, also tapped by the magic wand of time and dubbed a 'young woman'. In the shadows there are four 'young men' on the prowl. Though they come on tiptoe and holding their breath, I feel four pairs of eyes behind me, burning and boring like those of all bad boys bent on mischief. They are waiting for the right moment to step out into the open, affect a benign smile, and call me father-in-law. I will naturally ignore them: fancy thinking they could get away with that! I am like a fruit tree, enduring as the universe, that has stood here many years, taking its share of wind and frost and rain and dew, and in return is now laden with fruit, too heavy a crop for it to bear. And you, whippersnappers who chance to pass by, have the effrontery to put out your hand and pick my fruit! Serves you right if you trip over my ground roots and come a cropper!

Yet the most annoying thing is the way the fruit on the tree actually falls into the passer-by's hand of its own volition. The tree blames the passer-by for presuming to pick the fruit, while the passer-by claims that the fruit just happened to fall, and he merely caught it. In these affairs there always has to be collusion from within for an attack from outside to succeed. When I got married myself, in the beginning, wasn't there a young woman who 'opened the door and bowed the burglar in'? It is quite true, as they say, that a castle is most easily taken from the inside. But that was then, this is now. A pedestrian crossing the road detests cars; the same person driving a car detests pedestrians. Now it is my turn to be a driver.

For a good many years now I have been accustomed to keep company with five females. It has seemed just in the nature of things that the bathroom should be filled with the smell of scented soap and perfumes, that the sofa should be littered with satchels and hair curlers and that no one should contest my monopoly of the wine at the dinner table. I have also got used to referring facetiously to my dwelling as 'the girl students' dormitory'. As the warden of 'the girl students' dormitory', I naturally do not welcome strange male guests, especially those with dark designs. But the girl students in my charge, the first three in particular, are showing signs of 'instability', which makes me recall the line of Yeats:

'Things fall apart; the centre cannot hold.'

My four hypothetical enemies, be they tall or short, fat or thin, students of medicine or of literature, will emerge in their true colours from the mists of my foreboding, and come forward one after another, and circuitously and deviously in faltering words, or straight to the point, brazenly and impudently, either way will desire to take his loved one, that is my daughter, if you please, out of the house and off my hands. The unseen enemy is most to be feared, the more so because I am out in the light, he is in darkness, and besides, is hand in glove with a 'traitor in my midst'! There is really no way of forestalling him. I can only blame myself for not acting in good time and refrigerating my four daughters long ago, so that time could not abduct them and society could not pollute them. Now they are all grown up, and cannot turn back; my four hypothetical enemies, those four sneaky underground workers, are now fully fledged too, and no power can stop them.

It is best to get the first blow in: I should have resolved this matter while my four hypothetical enemies were still wrapped in swaddling clothes. At least the American poet Ogden Nash advises me so. In an ingenious poem titled 'Song to Be Sung by the Father of Infant Female Children' he says he has been beset by anxiety since the birth of his daughter Jill. Somewhere a male child is also growing up; though he now hasn't a thought in his head, and his mouth is blowing bubbles, he is destined one day to wrest his daughter Jill from her father. So whenever the father sees a male child in his pram in a park, he turns pale and thinks 'Is *he* the one?' As he broods, murder springs to mind ('My dreams, I fear, are infanticiddle'). He wants to open the infant's safety pins and pepper his talcum powder, salt his milk and sand his spinach, and lastly throw an elegant alligator into his perambulator to play with, all to force him to struggle through fire and water to harry somebody else's daughter. So you see, there is a precedent for the poet to take his future son-in-law as a hypothetical enemy.

Yet, too late, all too late. It was a strategic error not to have been resolute in the beginning and taken exceptional measures, like those in Nash's poem. The present situation can be described in a sentence commonly seen in the history books: 'The bandits have penetrated our defences!' Previously the posters and cuttings on my daughters' walls and under the glass top of their desks were pictures of the Beatles, Joan Baez, and David Cassidy; now it is photos of boyfriends all over the place. To put it mildly, the invading forces have captured a beachhead, and the war is as good as lost. When I was young, such photographs were classed as top secret: if they weren't hidden in one's pillow, to lend close support to dreams, then they were concealed between the leaves of a book in some deep recess, to be taken out occasionally and gazed at raptly. It was unthinkable that they should be on open display twenty-four hours a day.

I have no documentation on when the first batch of suspicious looking hypothetical enemies invaded the Yu residence on Hsiamen Street in Taipei. I only remember that after we moved to Hong Kong six years ago, the army at our gate was succeeded by a lot of Cantonese-speaking youths. As to the details of the campaign, I would have to ask the female generals who were nominally defending the citadel: being the 'dopey monarch', I was kept in the dark. I just remember the enemy artillery first directed its fire at our letter box; in time I was able to guess who was writing those letters addressed in a slovenly hand. Then the fire was directed at our telephone. The 'point of impact' was behind my desk, which turned my writer's corner into their battlefield. I must have suffered from concussion a dozen times a night. The Cantonese language having as many as nine tones, I found it difficult to work out the enemy's deployment. Now I have come back to Hsiamen Street with Youshan, it is my wife's turn to fend off the Cantonese troops; at my end I only have to watch out for Taiwan braves, which is a lot lighter job.

Attacks on the letter box are minor annoyances, no more than silent films of warfare. As a matter of fact I would prefer it if tender-hearted youths really got down to writing love letters, for at least they would be getting practice in composition, and the Chinese language could be saved from extinction in this age of audio-visual education. No, the frightening thing is the telephone. That repeated ringing of alarm bells extends the battlefield from the outside letterbox to the heartland of the study: the silent film becomes stereophonic sound, with the hypothetical enemies firing live rounds. Even more frightening is that the hypothetical enemies really have stormed into the citadel and have become real enemies of flesh and blood, no longer playthings of the imagination. It is like a military exercise getting halfway through, then suddenly changing into a real war.

The real enemy is visible. Under the ministrations of a certain daughter, he occupies one corner of the sofa, and the two start twittering together, or exchanging confidences in fits and starts; even when they merely gaze at each other tenderly, the atmosphere is stifling: no one in the house can breathe. The sisters get as far from the action as they can. The departure from normality is only too apparent. If by chance the enemy stays to dinner, the atmosphere is even more strained. Postures are taken up, as if for a photo-call. The dinner table is usually as noisy as a duckpond; now the four sisters seem to be acting in a dumb show. The very chopsticks and spoons appear to have got news of the occasion, for they suddenly behave with extreme caution. I am fully aware that this overweening youth might not be destined to be my son-in-law (who can tell where my darling daughter has got to in her course of transmutations?), nevertheless a wraith of hostility enters unbidden and clouds my spirit. I know too that my daughter will one day surely fall from the vine like a ripe melon and be carted off, but I hope it will not be by the self-important puppy in front of me.

I need hardly say that my four daughters can be obstreperous, and at such times in my anger I can't wait for my four hypothetical enemies to appear and carry them all off. But if that really were to come about, I would rue the day. I can imagine that the two occasions in life that make for the greatest sense of emptiness are when one retires, and after one's youngest child finally gets married. Stephen Soong once said to me, 'I envy you for having all your daughters with you!' I wonder. I don't feel I am to be envied at all, at least at present. Perhaps that will be true in the future when my youngest, Jishan, has gone off on her honeymoon with my hypothetical enemy, and I will sit on the empty sofa with my wife, turning the pages of the photo album that preserves their childhood, and remembering how it once was—the big event of a tour with all six of us in one car, or the festivity of a dinner party, with everyone enjoying the bright lights. There are lots of things in life that have to be past, like the wake of a boat, before you think them beautiful. I found myself again hoping that my four hypothetical enemies, those four blundering young tyros, would have the door shut in their face a few more times, and postpone their appearance.

In a poem of his, Yuan Mei compares giving birth to a daughter to being awarded a pass degree as a consolation for failing honours. This donnish remark is quite clever, though it betrays the feudal prejudice in favour of male issue. Adopting Yuan Mei's way of putting it, I got four pass degrees in a row, which is a pretty high score. Now that the four Yu girls are four little women, and my four hypothetical enemies are watching and waiting, if I were to be asked what requirements I had for a son-in-law, I would be temporarily stumped for an answer. After lengthy reflection I might say: 'Well, you know, on high there is the marriage register of the Old Man Under the Moon which nobody can tamper with, as Wei Gu found out; down here there are two lovers who have plighted their troth, and as the *Book of Changes* says, "When two hearts beat as one, their power is enough to cut through metal." What cause do I have to go against Heaven and offend man by putting my oar in? Besides, the "till death do us part" business is an impenetrable mystery: there is no way to predict it in advance, and no way to retract a false move after the event. Even a super computer of the 21st century would, I suspect, be unable to work out probability for it. So the best thing would be to make a show of liberality, pretend to be laid-back, win the fair name of enlightened father, and when the time comes take along my personal seal and preside over the wedding.'

My imagined questioner would just laugh, and ask me accusingly, 'What do you mean, "pretend to be laid-back"? Anyone can see you're anything but laid-back.'

Of course it is true I am not laid back: if I was I wouldn't be their father. The problem of race, for example, is very bothersome. Suppose a daughter were to lose her senses and fall in love with a shoulder shrugging, hand spreading, gum chewing young oddball, what should I do? Rationally speaking I would want to treat all sons-in-law equally, and be a tolerant and generous citizen of the world. But emotionally, tolerance does not extend to approving of a laddie with arms as hairy as a monkey's carrying my daughter over the threshold. To be sure, we no longer live in times when 'strengthening Chinese defences against the barbarians' is desirable, but to allow a simple family to expand into a miniature United Nations would be going too far. At this point my imagined questioner would laugh again, and would ask me if I had heard that children of mixed blood were brighter than average. I would say: 'Yes, I have, but I don't aspire to bouncing a genius of a half-caste grandson on my knee. I don't want a boy-genius calling me "Grandpa" in English, I want him to call me "Waigong" in Chinese.'

My questioner would not let it go at that: 'What about provincial origins then?'

'They don't matter,' I would say. 'I am the fruit of a marriage between Jiangsu and Fujian myself, and I didn't turn out badly, did I?

When my mother first wrote home to Wujin from Fujian to say a local person had proposed to her, her family were all of a dither. 'So far away!' they said, 'How could she marry a southern barbarian?' Later on my mother's family found out that, apart from the language barrier, this southern barbarian in-law passed muster. In recent years Cantonese boys have been plugging away ceaselessly, putting a great deal of pressure on my family. If one day Canton and Fujian became allies through marriage, it wouldn't surprise me. And if a Taiwanese lad tried very hard to get into my good books, I wouldn't particularly stand in his way—as long as his interest was not in discussing literature with me. As for boys from other provinces, from Heilongjiang to Yunnan, speaking all kinds of dialects, I would welcome them if my daughters did.'

'What about education?'

'Any field would be all right. And he needn't be a scholar, either. Scholars usually don't make good sons-in-law, and even less do they make good husbands. My one condition would be that his Chinese would have to be very good. If his Chinese was bad, the contagion would spread to my grandson!'

Another laugh. 'Would looks be important?' he would persist.

This time it would be my turn to laugh: 'You've really lost touch with reality! That would be for my daughter to attend to: don't ask me to worry about it!'

Suddenly I would hear the doorbell ring, interrupting my obtuse questioner. When I got up and opened the door, a mop of long hair would tell me another hypothetical enemy had come to raid the Yu house.

(1980)

Zongpu 宗璞 (1928-)

COMMENTARY

Zongpu (Feng Zongpu 馮宗璞) is the daughter of the philosopher Feng Youlan 馮有蘭 (1895–1990), who taught at Tsinghua University and later at Peking University. During the war against Japan, Tsinghua University was incorporated in the Southwest United University, and Zongpu spent the years 1938–1946 in Kunming. After returning to Peking she entered university and graduated from the Foreign Languages Department of Tsinghua University in 1951. Her subsequent employment included staff work for Zhongguo Wenlian, a national body set up to organize literature and the arts, and editorial work for *Wenyi bao* 文藝報 (The Literary Gazette) and *Shijie wenxue* 世界文學 (World Literature). In 1981 she was transferred to the Foreign Literature Research Institute of the Academy of Social Sciences, where she is still a research fellow.

Zongpu began writing seriously in 1956, while working for Zhongguo Wenlian. She wrote chiefly short stories, but also some children's literature and essays. Although she joined the Communist Party in 1956, and tried to remould her ideology, she found it increasingly difficult to write to rule, and gave up writing entirely from 1963 to 1978. Since 1978 her published fiction has been awarded several prizes. Starting in 1979 she has experimented with different narrative modes: her first-hand knowledge of Western literature has enabled her to be something of a pace-setter at home.

I have preferred the following essay about the Yuanmingyuan over others of Zongpu because the place has a fascination that foreigners can share. The Yuanmingyuan was the original summer palace of the Manchu emperors. Sited north of the city in what was once open countryside, it is now across the road from Peking University. In the 1740s the Qianlong 乾隆 emperor had a set of gardens, fountains and stone buildings built to make a miniature Versailles along the northern boundary of the park. His designers and engineers were an Italian and a French Jesuit priest who were employed at the time at the Qing court. Engravings of the buildings and gardens in their original state show those 'Western Mansions' to have been a minor wonder of the world: fairy palaces of elaborately carved stone, and intricately constructed waterworks. Now only scattered ruins remain. In 1860 an Anglo-French expeditionary force pillaged and set fire to the Yuanmingyuan to take revenge for the torture and death of some of its emissaries. Further destruction was done by the eight-nation force that invaded Peking to relieve the siege of the foreign legations by the Boxers in 1900. After that the Qing court more or less abandoned the Yuanmingyuan, and city dignitaries and local people made off with most of the stonework. The remains are today as

Zongpu described in 1979, except that some tidying up has been done.

Some explanation of the essay itself is called for. On her 1979 visit which occasioned the essay, Zongpu was accompanied by a young man who had been disillusioned by the Cultural Revolution. She thinks of the first time she came to the Yuanmingyuan, thirty years previously, with fellow students from Tsinghua University. Their generation, in contrast, had been highly idealistic: to them the ruins stood only for national humiliation, and should be made over, as indeed they hoped to see the whole world made over; and they all wanted to do their bit to create a proud future for their country. That setting may not be very apparent.

The wistaria at the end of the essay is part of Zongpu's private imagery. Its cascade of flowers is associated with the sparkling flow of living waters, an emblem of animation.

The '*liu* . . . *liu* . . .' sound that the wind seems to make in the ruins means 'stay'. Unfortunately, neither 'stay' nor any of its synonyms in English sounds anything like a wind, so '*liu*' had to be retained, and here explained.

The Call of the Ruins
廢墟的召喚

The declining winter sun shone weakly on the fields. The outline of a sickle moon had been visible over the Tsinghua Observatory since soon after noon. As I followed the recently made tarmacadam path, to my left were furrowed fields, their soil dry and apparently brick-hard, spotted here and there with fragments of stone slabs and tablets. On my right was what had been in summer a lotus pond, now merely a leftover of winter desolation. When I skirted the hill covered with bare trees and the great vista of ruins lay revealed to my sight, I had as always a strange feeling, as if history had run backwards and I was in the time of ancient Greece and Rome. It would have been fitting too if the lissome figures of the fabled concubines of ill-fated ancient Chinese emperors could have been glimpsed flitting like phantoms among the litter of stones and jungle of grass. Because of the remarkable 'stability' of Chinese society, the continuity of the tradition was preserved unbroken for thousands of years, right up to the Dowager Empress Cixi.

This stretch of ruins is part of the Garden of Eternal Spring, one of the three gardens that make up the Yuanmingyuan. Looking from east to west, there are the remains of a rounded terrace, an oblong temple, a now unrecognizable court, and the square bases of little kiosks. These were all once buildings in the occidental style, and so were popularly known as the Western Mansions. In this overgrown wasteland, the ruins of this group of buildings are just like a string of capsized ships in the process of sinking, with the rank weeds as algae and the stones strewn about as pockets of foam in the turbid sea. Over thirty years ago, when I came here for the first time, I thought, surely they will have sunk by the next time I come? They ought to yield the space they occupy, so that a new everything could be constructed. But every time I came again, they were still moored there in the open fields. The broken columns of the Temple of the Far Seas were still standing starkly under a grey-blue sky, looking quite forlorn and forsaken. The arched stone gate of the Great Water Wonder was still curling its waves. The stone screens of the Water Wonder Throne still exhibited their weapons and armour, the chiselling as sharp and virile as ever. But the stone waves did not swell, the carved weapons were forever immobilized. Those ruins that had been subjected to unspeakable insults lay peacefully in their berths, for all the world as if nothing worth mentioning had happened.

Like the stone carvings, time was here brought to a halt, frozen. Architects say that architecture is frozen music. In that case, what are the ruins of architecture? Frozen history? Take the stone ornament like a hemispherical vessel in front of (or perhaps beside) the Palace of Calm Seas. When I was young I had my photograph taken sitting in it along with some friends. Now that stone 'bowl' was as it ever was, while I of course no longer had the energy to climb onto it. But this made me glad, because the change in me was nothing but the working of natural law. I had not, after all, been frozen into immobility. . . .

I could only gaze disheartened on this vista of frozen history. There had originally been two big fountains in the empty space between the Great Water Wonder and the Water Wonder Throne—I imagine that the name of 'wonder' was given because the beauty of the play of waters reached its acme in the fountains. Off to the west could be seen a huge block, tapering towards the bottom, like a section of an inverted pyramid. Standing silently under this 'pyramid', you felt how small man was, how large the world was, how long history was. . . .

A big stone tortoise by the path still crouched impassively. The stone stele that should have stood erect on its back lay toppled over on the mound. Perhaps the tortoise was longing to shoulder the stele and carry out its appointed task. The wind whistled through the copse on the other side of the path, rising and falling, plaintive and sorrowful. The wind seemed to float the sound '*liu* . . . *liu* . . .' over from the ruins.

I turned round in surprise. The stone columns of the Lookout on the Other World shone white against the gathering dusk, and a gap in the heap of stone blocks was like a mouth that was trying to speak to me. To tell me of the great fire here that had lit up the sky? To tell me how time should be measured here? Or did you want to tell me your yearnings, your expectations?

The wind blew across the ruins again, as before making the sound of '*liu* . . . *liu* . . .'. I suddenly realized: it was a summons! Summoning people to stay and remake this frozen history. The ruins did not want to remain stranded there forever.

Yet hadn't I already striven for that? How fiercely we had disputed, the little group of us, beside this very stone tortoise. How fervently we had argued, how passionate were our beliefs! Given that the life of the individual is an insignificant concept in comparison with mankind, everyone has their reasons for taking a different view of what can be done with it. I just thought, the ancient state of Chu long ago became Hubei province, but the glory of the *Songs of Chu* of Qu Yuan would shine on the world till the end of time, wouldn't it?

There came the racket of cawing over head. I looked up to see a huge flock of jackdaws, lit by the setting sun, swoop over the copse of bare trees and disappear into the western sky that was already suffused with pink. Under their wings the sunset clouds were putting on their most spectacular show. The Western Hills were daubed with a layer of subdued red, making their outlines clear in the haze. There was a bluish tinge to the red which gave it a solidity in keeping with the tangible chill in the air.

The scene was familiar to me. I automatically closed my eyes.

'We should give this heap of ruins over to the mist and sunset.' The youth at my side was talking to himself. After an interval of over thirty years I started arguing again with young people. I didn't blame them— how could I? I spoke hesitantly, without the courage of my convictions. 'You should stay! Just because they are ruins, they need every one of you.'

'The meanest person may be called to account, you mean.' He was a bright young man: he expressed clearly the thought I had put into faltering words. 'But how should each of us give an account of himself? How can the environment be improved, so as to allow each one of us to give an account of himself?' He smiled, his smile half cynical, half helpless.

I suddenly gained the courage of my convictions: 'Isn't that "how" just what we have to think about?'

He did not reply, and I stopped speaking to watch the kaleidoscopic changes of the sunset. Wandering back, we came to the pond. The water had turned to ice; lotus stems stuck up through the ice; the stems glowed like shot silk. The sun was sinking into the hollows of the distant hills, its rays flushing the hill crests on the horizon a fiery red. Some bare trees on the bank were so placed as to form a picture frame for the setting sun. Yet by then the soft red Western Hills had all taken on a bluish-black hue, fresh and sleek as if just emerged from a dowsing of rain; they seemed to have nothing to do with the dusk, but still they emitted a faint glow, which, reflected on the ice outside the picture frame, made one think of cold moonlight.

There was a rustling in the grass beside the trees. Someone was there painting. He was mixing colours on his palette: loading and spreading, spreading and reloading, as if he would never capture those extraordinary colours on paper.

'He's not a painter,' the young man commented, 'he just likes this scene. . . . '

The broken bridge rearing up in front of us was the only relic of a bridge in the whole of the Yuanmingyuan. From a distance it looked like a jumble of stones, but from up close the structure of the bridge was still whole. The hump of the bridge was high, and only a small part of its deck remained; however, there was now no more than a trickle of water under the bridge, so one could step across it without using the bridge.

'Maybe I could think about the summons of the ruins.' The young man suddenly smiled. His smile was still half cynical, half helpless.

We continued to watch the sunset. The fiery ball sank out of sight, leaving the distant hills clothed in purple bands of different intensity. The dense bands were like wine, the pale bands like a dream. The in-between bands reminded me of the wistaria in spring. That sunset tapestry spread across the sky could have done with more wistaria petals!

I seem to have heard they are going to restore the Yuanmingyuan. I wonder if they can leave part of the ruins? Preferably around the Temple of the Far Seas, or just that broken bridge would do.

Why? So that people can stand and mull over this span of frozen history, so that they can remember the summons of the ruins.

Koarnhak Tarn 陳冠學 (1934–)

COMMENTARY

In obedience to the author's own wish, I have given precedence above to the Taiwanese spelling of this author's name. Chen Guanxue is how his name is written according to the Mandarin pronunciation. The reason why he should wish to be thought of first and foremost as a native of Taiwan will become clear from reading the two linked essays that follow.

Koarnhak Tarn grew up in farming country in Pingtung county in the south-west of Taiwan. In 1952 he went to Taipei to study for a degree in Chinese at Taiwan Normal University, after which he taught in middle school and junior college, and went on to be an editor in a publishing house. In the 1970s he published his own books on the Taoist philosopher Zhuang Zi and an edition of the Confucian *Analects*. In the 1980s he wrote on the history and language of Taiwan. To date he has published four books of essays.

The regret for the loss of the countryside under the pressure of population and the mechanization of agriculture is a universal theme. Koarnhak Tarn expresses it with rare passion, backed by intimate knowledge and insight. Those who are tired of, or disheartened by, the theme universally will still find much fascinating local detail here, and a new slant informed by the philosophy of Taoism.

The Countryside of the Past
昔日的田園

When I lived in the city I longed for the present countryside; when I went back to the present countryside I longed for the old countryside. The old countryside was the habitat of my youth; on top of that, it was positively idyllic in comparison to the city and the countryside of today. Simply by virtue of the association with youth, of being the realm of one's youth, there is ample ground for cherishing its memory; but with every step it recedes the more reason there is to think of it as a measure of perfection for the new age!

I turned my back on the old countryside in the autumn of 1952, to seek an education, never knowing that I would be away for all of twenty years. When I came back in the spring of 1972 the old countryside was no more. As I went all round looking, smelling and listening, I wanted to lie down and weep for the old countryside. But

I was past the age when I could indulge myself with such childish abandon. So for the last ten years walls of sadness and nostalgia have been building up in my heart.

Living in the present countryside, I often have daydreams in which I catch glimpses of the countryside as it used to be, half wild and half cultivated, the one interspersed with the other. Now just because one's body size only requires a bed space six feet long by three feet wide, you should not make beds of only those proportions. There must be room to spare for you to get pleasure and relief from anything. The thing one misses most about the countryside of old is that the untouched wilderness used to stretch out among the ploughed fields, giving room to spare. In this wild, grasses were free to grow rank, or thin scrub to cover the surface; it was home and feeding ground to birds, rodents, snakes and rabbits, moths, butterflies, bees and scorpions; village boys used it for grazing their sheep and cattle and as their playground to sport in; village men and women used it as a reserve for firewood and kindling, and a nursery for medicinal herbs. It was a place that the eye could rove over, the ear could delight in, that you could take from for your needs or leave to its own fruitful purposes. It gave you an infinite feeling of spaciousness and ease. As Lao Zi said, 'From things' substance you may derive benefit, from things' insubstance you may derive utility.' Ah, how one longs for the countryside of old!

Apart from being bound up with the virgin wilderness that brimmed with the vitality and exuberance of a nature still whole, the countryside of old left its ploughed fields fallow in winter (for the sugar cane fields the fallow period was the beginning of the lunar year). Every year after the end of the autumn rains, grass was allowed to take over the fields and make whatever use it could of the little moisture that remained. Like all poor relations, its diet was meagre and its circumstances straitened, but as it had been given the gift of life on this earth, it put on the best show it could. Consequently, once every year the unity of the fields and the wild was restored: as far as the eye could see, the whole landscape was a continuum of browns and greens, as if the clock had been set back to the prehistoric age. To look upon it was to be stirred at the core of one's being by a sense of the primitive, and get a taste of the potency of primordial chaos. At this time the farmers took advantage of the slack season to repair their farm implements, re-thatch their houses, make odds and ends for the home, or fashion for themselves a long-stemmed pipe of bamboo. The farmers' wives quietly went about neatly patching old clothes that there had been no time to repair properly before, or making new clothes for the family, or else trimming the edges of the straw sleeping-mats and refurbishing the bedding. If they still had time on their hands they would spend it sizing up the local young men and women to work out who would make a good match.

Since there was so much wasteland in the countryside, the field paths were naturally very wide. In the old days there was enough room to drive an oxcart around the borders of the fields; that is, they occupied a space roughly equal in width to a car lane on the modern roads. These boundary ridges or field borders were actually part of the wasteland, so the grass was allowed to grow shoulder-high on them: the farmers never gave them a thought. Under the grass cover the ground was honeycombed with rat runs, which were often deeper and broader than the ruts left by the oxcarts. The boys used to set rat traps in these runs: they placed them at intervals after sunset, and made their way home in the dark, full of hope. At break of day they found a bamboo pole suitable for carrying the traps back with, and chased excitedly through the morning dew back to the runs. Normally they could expect to catch one or two big rats, and if they were lucky four or five, with a snake as a bonus. The boys were timid and superstitious too: if they found a snake they would throw the whole trap away. But if there was a man with them he would be delighted: he would take the snake home, boil it with shreds of ginger, throw in some rat meat, and mix in a cup of rice wine; the brew was given the fancy name of 'hill tiger duelling hill dragon', and the neighbours invited in for a bowl of it. Those border paths were my favourite haunt as a boy.

After the fields and the wild had been back together for a season, spring came round again. The first thunder of the year roused the creatures from their hibernation, the spring rain pelted down, and the countryside, hearing the thunder and drinking in the rain, woke up. Thereupon the farmers one and all streamed out into the fields, driving their oxen and shouldering their ploughs, husband and wife loaded down with gear. Their songs resounded through the vales and hills. Bamboo hats bobbed about in the undergrowth, oxen plodded along crisscrossing ridges. Cows lowed to their calves, boys chased calves, calves chased boys, brindled dogs and black dogs were in and out of everything. The countryside was just like a painting, just like a poem, just like heaven on earth.

In those days the motive power in the countryside was entirely physical strength, that is, the strength of oxen and of humans. The resources needed to supply these two kinds of energy came from the countryside itself: the oxen ate grass, the humans ate yams. Self-sufficient, self-renewing, these resources never ran out, never ran short. The waste products from these energy sources were in turn wholly beneficial to the countryside: the human and bovine manure was returned to the land, so endlessly renewing its material. With this in view, every homestead had its compost heap for organic waste; this compost heap formed a triad with the sun and the rainclouds: they were the farmers' 'three treasures'.

Every family had at least two or three oxen, and some had as many as a dozen. The custom was to attach a harness over the head of the ox, from which two rows of brass bells hung down, one on either side; every time the ox shook its head the bells tinkled pleasantly. In the busy season practically all the oxen, like the humans, went down into the fields, forming a long procession out in the morning and back in the evening. As they spread out into the fields like a babbling stream dividing on its downward course, and returned to the village like rivulets merging and pouring into pools and gullies, the sound of the bells flooded over the countryside, and became its theme song.

In the slack season the oxen were all handed over to the herdboys to take out to graze. Crowds of boys drove the oxen onto the wasteland. Once the oxen started feeding the boys would play games like house, hide-and-seek, wrestling or cricket fighting, and would not band together to drive the oxen back until noon or dusk. Sometimes they threw themselves into their play with such a will that they covered themselves in dirt from head to toe, and when they remembered their oxen, they were nowhere to be seen, nor could they be found for the seeking. Then the boys knew they were in for it; they had to brace themselves for a whipping when they got home. Generally speaking there were two possibilities: either the oxen had eaten their fill and made their own way back; or they had strayed from the wasteland into the cultivated fields in search of food, and were led back by the owner of the field. Whichever was the case, one thing was certain: the boys' little bottoms would feel the lash of the whip. The afternoon or the day after the herdboy got his drubbing, he would exact repayment from the oxen's backsides when he drove them out again; and the manner in which he taught them to behave themselves was the exact replica of the way he had been taught by his dad. This was the rule everybody accepted: when you make a mistake you have to take your punishment; when you take on a debt you have to repay it.

The herdboys played a big role in the old countryside: though they were only little mites, that should not obscure the fact that they were fully-fledged keepers of livestock!

Given then that the young boys took on such important responsibilities in country life, what about the girls? They may have been only five or six years old, and knee-high to a grasshopper, but they were still given responsibility for important tasks. As everybody had their hands full in the busy season, the little girls were charged with looking after the house. They had to dust and clean the furniture, the cooking range and the bedmats, and sweep up inside and outside. In preparation for the noon and evening meal they had to squat down in front of the fire and boil a big pot of yam and rice mash; this had to be constantly pressed down and new ingredients added until the pot was full. And in cold weather they had to heat up a cauldron of water. When their fathers or grandfathers felt like celebrating, they might have to make a long trek to the shop in the next village to buy a pot of rice wine and perhaps a salted fish to take back and fry. These little girls went out by themselves in storms that turned the day into night and in winds that cut like a knife, along narrow paths that wound through grass that grew higher than their heads, and with a stony surface as rough as the back of a hedgehog under their feet. Such a rigorous upbringing in childhood ensured that these young girls would become good wives and mothers, able to bear all the burdens and strain that life imposed on them.

If even the little children had to work for their keep, the hard grind of the adults can be easily pictured. At the onset of the spring rain after the New Year they sowed their sesame and peanuts. When their shoots broke the surface, the sesame had to be thinned, gaps in the peanuts filled and after that came the ploughing and the hoeing. The crop was ready for harvesting in a hundred days. The sesame was left standing, and the seeds gathered when the pods opened in the midday sun. There was no time for delay, all hands had to be out in the field at noon, either after a hasty lunch or no lunch at all. As they worked under the broiling sun, with the earth underfoot baking hot, the heat was sometimes so intense that people came down with dysentery. The peanuts grew underground, so the plant was lifted whole, but stray pods invariably broke off, and these had to be dug out with the fingers; from this digging the women developed index fingers as hard as those of the martial arts experts. Then the summer came in in giant strides, and with it the hurry to plant yams, and sugar cane as a catch crop. The summer deluged the countryside with a superabundance of sunshine and a sufficiency of rain. The yams, sugar cane and wheat were given their head, and sprang up even faster than Jack's magic bean stalk. At which sight the farmers' faces cracked in a smile.

The farmer's life was hard, it is true, but they were growing their own crops, and they did not begrudge their toil. Besides, they did not have to toil all the year round. You would be very much mistaken if you thought they collapsed in a heap after their day's labour. The typical farmer had a big supper, then took a bench out into the yard to enjoy the cool of the evening. Some played and sang to the two-stringed fiddle, some to the balloon lute, either by themselves or in concert; or else the youngsters chased fireflies round the edge of the yard while the grown men pitted their strength outside. The oldsters, for their part, smoked their long pipes under the eaves, and talked of many things, while the women sat sewing and mending by the light of the oil lamp, entertained by the talk outside. Everyone was full of life, and at peace with themselves. The life they led had been arrived at as a result of thousands of years' experience, and then maintained for further thousands of years; it was the healthiest kind that man could enjoy, one that was in perfect balance. A rough idea of how healthy and balanced their life was can be got from the pattern of the settlements in the old rural era.

Just like the birds and the beasts of the countryside which preferred to make their nests and lairs in the thick of the green woods, the farming folk chose to build their houses in dense copses—a few thatched huts, which in effect were no different from the nests and lairs, except for being somewhat larger. Though the houses were hidden away, their plots ranged from 1,800 square feet to 6,000 square feet, and there were gaps between them. If need be, they could shout across to their neighbours; otherwise the chickens and dogs maintained regular voice contact. Birds moved in alongside, field mice joined their community, swallows and sparrows made their homes in the eaves, buzzing insects shared their rooms. Breezes came in through their doors, moon and stars looked in through their windows. Cocks supervised the dawns and dogs looked after the dusks. What the biologists call symbiosis extended in the old countryside even to the inanimate things of nature. A better scheme of things could not have been devised!

Autumn arrived before the farmers could look round, and the yams and the corn were harvested. Stripped of its greenery, the countryside prepared to enjoy the fresh coolness of the new season. The shrikes timed their arrival to coincide with the bareness of the soil, and the visibility of the grubs: the valleys were alive with their screeching. The crickets also opened up the entrances to their holes and sang all night in front and back yard, indeed up hill and down dale. This was in fact the season when the countryside was at its liveliest; one's ears were filled from waking to sleeping with the noise of the shrikes in the daytime and the noise of crickets after dark. Every square foot of the soil had its choristers singing for all they were worth. It was then that the boys came into their own. You would see them in the buff, setting off after shrike with their pole traps, hook traps and basket traps, and the next minute they would be carrying big tins of water to flush the crickets out of their holes round the village.

It is no exaggeration to say that the countryside was a boy's paradise. From one year's end to the other they had sports to amuse them. When the yams were harvested the boys went ahead of the plough to look out for quail nests. It was their privilege to keep whatever young birds or eggs they found in the nests; and it was taken for granted that any bird nest in the trees came within their domain. No one was as fleet and nimble as them at getting to the mountain guavas and wild grapes, either. When they had nothing else to work off their energy on, they got together to hunt out a snake and pound it to pulp; and if a house shrew strayed across their path it would die the death of a thousand cuts. On the other hand, when chicks were hatched they would take the part of guardian angels, threatening the eagles that circled overhead with stones. In hot weather hordes of them would plunge into the weir pond to bathe in its cold spring-water, then on some slight provocation might chase each other stark naked into the village—everybody else being under orders to look the other way. They really revelled in their authority. The boys got up to endless tricks. There was a kind of grass called goose grass that grew in the middle of the tracks, so tough that even oxen could not uproot it; the boys used to tie its ends together, to trip up the oxen. This shows how mischievous they were. Being out in the sun all day, they were burnt as black as goblins: in truth, they were the spirits of the countryside.

All those who lived in the countryside of old had their joys, it was just that the boys had the lion's share. For every picul of pleasures, the boys took eight pecks, leaving two pecks for the rest to divide among themselves. For instance, when the farmers ploughed the fields, especially when they were working the canefields to earth up the stems, it would often happen that they had hardly set the blade of the plough in the soil and gone many rods before there was a whirring of wings and a hen pheasant would fly up from beside the ox's feet. In an instant the farmer had let go of the plough and dived to snatched his prize. Or else he would catch a glimpse of something white and gleaming, which would turn out to be a nest of pheasant eggs; there might be as many as twenty, each as big as the eggs of the chickens they kept at home. In the old countryside pheasants were everywhere: they were as many as the prairie chicken in America that we see in the nature films. Just wandering around you would be bound to run across pheasant cocks with their bright red cheeks and dazzling plumage. Wild rabbits were common, too; from time to time the farmers would take a brace for the pot.

To gather mushrooms and fungi after the rains was the women's pleasure; some would go farther afield to net shrimps and loaches.

The highest gratification for the farming families was to reap what they had not sown. When all is said and done, the farmers' pleasures were all related to the basic matter of production. Pure pleasures that transcended production, let alone enjoyments, were very few for them.

The farming families had to wait till the autumn harvest was in and the rains over every year before they could enjoy all together one or two pure pleasures. The vagabond company of players known as 'roving angels' arrived in the sunset glow and set up their props in whoever's yard was convenient. The women were dressed up like opera singers, and always sang the same old favourite arias. The men girt up their loins and put on a few bouts of boxing. After two or three hours they sold their nostrums, packed up and left, and the villagers dispersed and returned home contented.

The next time the villagers heard the sound of a proper band would not be until the New Year Festival.

It was as uncommon for the farming families to gorge themselves on fish or meat or sweet things as it was for them to see a show. They grew sugar cane themselves, but the children only got to eat something sweet twice a year: once was at the winter solstice, in the form of rice balls, and the second was at New Year, as sticky rice cakes and little doughnuts. Otherwise the children had to wait for sweet stuff until somebody's daughter got engaged to be married, when every house got its share of 'big biscuits' to celebrate. By rights the Mid-Autumn Festival was another time when there should have been sweet food, but to lay out good money on buying mooncakes went against the grain of the farmers' plain life. The fifteenth of the eighth month was the birthday of the village god. It was said that the god was partial to old sow's meat. The children, thanks to the god's bounty, were allowed to partake, but what they got was old skin and scrag that seemed to date from the Bronze Age: it defied mastication, and could only be swallowed whole.

At the Grave-Sweeping Festival they ate spring rolls, and at the Dragon Boat Festival the leaf-wrapped sticky rice patties. The seventh month, the Month of the Ghosts, saw the most feasting: on the first of the month the gate to ghostland was opened, and every house made sacrifices to the ghosts, which meant there was something to eat; on the fifteenth, the Festival of the Ghosts, the big service was held, which meant there was a lot to eat; on the twenty-ninth or thirtieth there was the service to see off the ghosts, which meant there was something to eat again. Three feasts in one month was a very kind gift of the ghosts. After that the next chance of a slap-up meal was not until New Year's Eve, when the children got little packets of coins as well. New Year's Eve was in fact a day in heaven for old and young alike. Apart from these festival times, women also got something special to eat in the month after they gave birth, and their menfolk occasionally invented their own excuses.

Looked at in this way, the farming folk truly had a hard life. Indeed, there was a saying popular among them, to the effect that the best things in life were 'every sitting after dusk on the 29th, every year eighteen springs', which meant to enjoy at every meal the fare of New Year's Eve, and every year to be eighteen years old.

But the farming folk were right to treat themselves harshly, because pleasure and enjoyment can only sap one's spirit, and make a slum of life.

Actually, the farming folk lived better than anyone else; the countryside gave them a life of the highest quality.

The countryside gave the farming folk a blue sky and green sward; therein were their dwelling and their work place. At any time they could expand their chest and feast their eyes. The bright sun, the gentle night, work and rest, everything had its time, there was a time for everything. The singing of birds, the flitting of butterflies, the ever-present sight and smell of flowers on the roadside and round the houses; how could these fail to lift one's spirit? The trees reached towards the sky, serene and relaxed, grass and herb sprang up everywhere under foot: how could the life-spark not be fanned into flame? Given the freshness of the air, the sweet water of the springs, the wholesomeness and true flavour of the local produce, how could the blood not circulate freely and the sinews not be supple? And if you throw in the simple nature of the farmer, self-denying and deliberately slow, you have to admire him as the original natural man.

The life of the farmer of old was perfected by a millennium of trial and error. The fact that it was followed unchanged for thousands of years shows that there was no room for improvement, that it was the ideal life for mankind. Still it might be asked, was the old countryside really so kind to the farmer, was there not the slightest fault that could be found with it? The answer is no. However, there are some matters that need to be explained, otherwise there might be some misunderstanding.

The law of the countryside, derived from practical experience, was this: integration meant survival, isolation meant death. Hence the ecology had to be in balance. If this law was enforced with a rod of iron in the old countryside, it was not out of cruelty, as it might appear, but with good reason. From day to day, from season to season, a balance was struck: if there were billions of insects, there were millions of birds to keep them down; if there were millions of rodents, there were thousands of eagles and snakes to keep them within limits. The imperative was that each species should gain that portion that would enable it to survive. Accordingly, the farmer too claimed his portion of existence. As long as the farmer sowed his seeds at the right time, the countryside itself would look after everything else: the sunshine, the rain, the pest control—none of these did he have to worry about. But the farmer got no more than his due portion. Since the countryside had provided him with a life of the highest quality, it could not offer the largesse of luxury and wealth. If he got more than his rightful due, it would only bring about his eventual destruction; this was what the countryside knew perfectly well from experience. So the countryside kept to its iron law, which it applied unswervingly. The farming folk, for their part, had developed long ago a plain and undemanding character, they accepted what fate sent them, were content to coexist with the rest of creation, and did not expect more than fair measure.

Although the countryside usually maintained a balance, total precision, getting it exactly right, was out of the question. Just as the agricultural calendar provided for an intercalary month every four years, so when the operations of the old countryside periodically produced a surplus it used drought and flood, pest and virus to mop up the excess. Unless one thinks the thing through, one might mistakenly jump to the conclusion that the countryside was barbarously cruel. After this adjustment the countryside completely regained its balance, and the farming folk were guaranteed the continuance of their superior way of life.

How one misses it, the countryside of old!

(1983)

Today's Countryside
今日的田園

Nietzsche has written that Zarathustra came down from the mountain to announce that God was dead. Actually God may not be dead, and even if God is dead, as long as the world survives, and as long as the laws which hold the world together remain in force, all of creation can carry on as before. But if today we announced the death of natural man, we would be talking about him being dead and in his coffin. To say that natural man is dead is to signal the end of an ideal world. More than 2,000 years ago the Jews declared that the first man and woman had been expelled from the Garden of Eden because Eve ate of the fruit of knowledge, but it seems they were anticipating, because they were talking about mankind bringing misfortune upon its own head as a result of its quest for knowledge, while the Garden of Eden continued to exist. Actually, as along as Eden continued to exist, man had not been expelled. Not until the day came when man destroyed Eden by his own hand did he really lose his paradise.

When I came back after twenty years away, I discovered that the old countryside was gone. It was an unfamiliar landscape that met my eyes: only the ridge of hills to the east and a few old neighbours—some varieties of birds that had been spared, and the dry stony soil—testified to the fact that this was where the old countryside had been.

The tracts of wilderness had disappeared from the landscape, as had the broad field borders crisscrossed by rat runs. Most of the borders had been ploughed up along with the scrub; only small strips had been left standing to form boundary ridges roughly a foot wide. A very few had been preserved as paths for carting produce. That 'room to spare' feeling of luxuriance and expansiveness was no longer there, nor could one smell that primeval air that penetrated to the depths of one's being. I had longed to see again those brown and green colours, to touch again the boulders with which the wilderness was strewn, to walk again the open heath, to seek out again those original denizens of the plain, ever active in between the baking earth and the scorching sun—the feathered birds and the winged insects; but all had vanished without trace.

Some orchards had appeared on the flatland. The oxen were far fewer than before, and not a herdboy was to be seen. Looking at the distant spot where I knew my own village was, I could not see the trees that should have marked it. As it turned out, the village trees had all been cut down to build more houses when the population increased and brothers set up separate homes for themselves. Only the odd sparrow perched on a roof, in depressing contrast to the abundant numbers I remembered: the place was as dismal as if it had been visited by a plague. Happily, there were still a few swallows swooping over the village. The sky at least did not seem to have changed.

On the way home I had already detected something wrong about the air—a faint smell of pesticide. And all along the way I heard the sound of motors, engines, vehicles. Sitting at home, these noises came from all directions. Electricity had been laid on in all the houses, and the village had underground water storage tanks. Now that the drinking water did not come from the springs, a lot of carrying was saved, only when the electricity failed there was not a drop to drink. There were no chimneys left, as all the houses used gas. There was no use for all the dead wood, and no place to put it. The compost heaps were done away with, for several reasons; first, there was not enough room for houses, let alone making compost; second, the plastic bags and packaging could not be broken down by bacteria and microbes, and were a great nuisance in among the compost; third, notions of hygiene made the farmers think that a compost heap next to the house was not nice. So the dustcarts were always coming and going, playing their chimes to the tune of 'The Maiden's Prayer'.

Radios and televisions broadcast a succession of songs and operas day and night; the shops were full of sweets and biscuits, soft drinks and tins of fruit; the meat vendors came sounding their horns every day, and two fishmongers called daily too. People sold green vegetables, which the farmers no longer grew themselves. To all appearances it really was 'every sitting after dusk on the 29th' just like New Year every day of the week. But it was very hard to say whether this was an improvement in the standard of living or a deterioration in the quality of life.

The night was no longer soft and gentle, for electric light made it as bright as day. The farming folk slept later. Chickens had become scarce, so one no longer heard the waves of crowing spread from coop to coop in the night; at most there was the odd isolated crow. As the cocks could find no rivals to fight, they turned their attentions to people, pecking the children's backsides and the grown-ups' ankles. They went round creating havoc, for all the world as if the devil had got into them.

No one looked after the cats: they crouched in every corner. The dogs had been stolen: there was hardly one to be seen. As a result no dogs barked in the daytime, while the cats squalled all night. It made you think the world was upside down.

The character of the villagers had changed, too. The fallow season had been abolished, the underground water reserves were drawn on all the year round, the farmers flogged the earth to make it produce two golden eggs a day. The extra income they got from flogging the earth was used to build showy houses, spent on audio-visual entertainments, and competition in extravagant pleasures: plainness and simplicity had gone out of the window.

Now ten years have passed since I returned, and the countryside has undergone another radical change. The flatlands have all been enclosed as orchards, so cutting off one's line of sight and hampering one's movements. Now country people only have the roads to walk along, and the countryside has shrunk as far as it can go. If the orchards had formed whole plantations, a great forest of fruit trees, the effect would have been the same as living in some high woodland, and 'the defeat of the morning would turn into the victory of the evening', so there would have been no net loss. But every patch of orchard was surrounded by barbed wire, and, with the paths practically obliterated, one was totally boxed in.

In this situation oxen served no purpose, besides which there was no grass for them to graze. Apart from one or two old farmers who had grown up with oxen and kept one for old time's sake, the rest had stopped using them. The continuous tinkling of oxbells that used to be so intoxicating was gone from the land, as was the lowing sound peculiar to that beast.

Since the oxen were no more, how could there be herdboys? The herdboys had long since been sent to school, the younger ones to primary school, the older ones to public middle schools. As there was no tradition of 'book learning' at home, the great majority did not take to study, and with the herdboy heredity from their ancestors pulsing in their veins, it was a trial for them to be chained to a desk in a schoolroom. They did not take to study, but they did take to waywardness: half of them have become problem youths. When they grow up they will be a serious force for social unrest. It is all very sad.

When the girls leave school they flood into the cities to work in light industry. Thanks to the cheap female labour that every farming household has contributed, Taiwan has grown prosperous. But the girls who were born to live on green sward under blue skies, breathing fresh air and steeped in peace and tranquillity, have become inhuman cogs in machines. They are shut up from morn till night in factories, and lay waste their youth in fetid air and deafening noise.

I cannot help but feel revulsion when I see country folk eat chicken fattened for the table. It is now over twenty years since I have tasted chicken myself. If I were to have a yen for it again it would only be for the domestic fowl of the old countryside, which were the only chicken worth eating.

Nor can I bear to see country people eating so-called 'young white cabbage' that grows one or two feet high. Aside from the indigenous young white cabbage of the old countryside, is there any other kind worthy of the name?

I cannot abide either the oversized peanuts, the big pods of peas, and the yams as big as your head that country people eat now. I pine for the button peanuts, the small pods of Holland peas, and the double-skinned yams.

The eggs in the old days were wholly nutritious; now they are not only lacking in nutrient but are actually toxic. Everything else is the same.

All my life I have liked grass. Without grass there is no soil, no higher vegetable life, no animals, and no mankind. In the present countryside you don't see any grass, except on the road verges: herbicide comes down in a thick fog at regular intervals to poison it. Fortunately a few blades survived in my yard. In rainy weather I let it prosper according to the workings of nature; in dry spells I watered it morning and evening. Just as I had hoped, I soon had a patch of emerald green. The grass attracted butterflies and moths to lay eggs, which hatched into caterpillars, which in turn attracted the small birds that had nothing to feed on otherwise. They kept the owner of the yard company all the day long. The emerald grass, the flitting butterflies, the climbing and swooping of the birds, the sweet bird song and background murmur that filled my ears: the rewards of these things far exceeded the labour of my regular watering. Later I discovered that the birds were actually imitating the butterflies and moths, and were building nests in the trees round the yard. I counted the grass wagtail, the black-billed tit and the moss bird, besides grackles, blue flycatchers and sparrows. One morning I sat quietly for two hours, and discovered to my surprise that one bird call came every second, which was a higher frequency than for the old countryside. But I had collected *all* the birdlife in one place! It was a matter for lamentation, not rejoicing.

After the villagers became fruit farmers, they were confident that their sprays could cope with the pests, and looked upon birds as not only useless but also harmful. So they strung nets up all round their orchards. At fruiting time this is excusable, but after the fruits were finished, the nets were still left up. The orchard keepers neglected to inspect the nets, so the birds that were caught in them died in them, were blown by the wind and baked by the sun, decomposed and dried. Of small birds one could pick out the grass wagtail and the moss bird; of medium-sized birds, grackles, and the black drongo: of big birds the speckled pigeon, the green pigeon, and so on. Not one variety of local bird was spared. No wonder my yard was regarded as a sanctuary by the little birds.

By the end of June the local variety of lemon trees have borne their crop, and at the beginning of July the old leaves are shed, forming a thick carpet underneath, and they start to put out new leafbuds. I was surprised to see swarms of honey bees and wild bees round the tender buds. I thought at first that the buds might have a scent of nectar about them, which possibly misled them, but on closer inspection I discovered the bees were buzzing round the buds and sucking busily, then rubbing their back legs together vigorously: clearly they were acting as if they were brushing pollen. Only then did the truth dawn on me. By that time of year the fruit trees had long ceased to blossom, and the bees were going to be short of food anyway, but if there had been tracts of wilderness with flowering plants, they could have just about scraped through. As it was they were driven to seek sustenance from the buds of lemon trees: clearly they were hungry enough to eat anything. This sight lasted for some days, until the young leaves turned green. The original law of balance in the share of resources had broken down; the small birds and the bees were the first to suffer as a result. Without the birds the countryside is bleak and cheerless. Without the bees, butterflies and moths, some plants have no means of pollination; the awful consequences we can only await with trepidation.

Once I saw a colony of bees swarming round a drain. I was so shocked that I composed this homely poem to myself:

> Pristine beings of the floral realm,
> Before your kind meets its doom
> You descend to such sorry depths!

> Fate has decreed your end to be cruel,
> No pleas will move hearts of stone.
> Then die, then die,
> Pristine beings of the floral realm!
> That grasping two-legged beast
> Is also fast nearing his end!

Whenever I hear 'The Maiden's Prayer' I feel unclean. Whichever way you look at it, there is no excuse for treating the saint as a buffoon. Now that they use maidenly purity as a call sign for collecting garbage, is it any wonder that molestation of young girls is all the time increasing? Because I refuse to bow to this form of defilement, and to please myself too, I started up a new compost heap after I came back. In this way I can avoid participating in befouling the world, and suit my own convenience: I can clean up and tip out my rubbish whenever I feel like it. One day I saw a butterfly on my compost heap. The rain had stopped, and the slanting rays of the sun that came through the branches of the trees had a soft golden touch to them. The air sparkled with moisture. Of itself it was a beautiful enough sight—even the mucky compost heap looked quite beautiful in the sunlight and moist air. I was unprepared for the appearance of the butterfly, and another pang of sadness went through me. I could not help murmuring:

> Pristine beings, oh die oh die!
> There is no place left in this world for you.

But when you come to think of it, if there is no place for other creatures left, can the farming folk survive on their own? The quality of their life has gone into decline; in fact it has not simply declined, but dramatically declined, fallen to zero, or even below zero. Consider the functions grass performs: it preserves the soil, it makes the organic matter that is the most important constituent of soil, that aerates the soil, nurtures the germs, moulds and other forms of microbes and insect life that serve to effect chemical changes to the soil; then it is the breeding ground for insects that carry pollen, and the feeding ground for the birds that control the population of insects; thirdly, it is food for animals. The relentless ploughing up of the grassland, the blind destruction of grass in the fields, has set in motion a serial progression of ecological exhaustion. On top of that, the continual application of pesticides and the liberal spreading of chemical fertilizers have resulted in the total extinction of some of the pollinating insects and the outright death of the soil. Yet despite all this use of pesticides and chemical fertilizers, the original pests have not in all cases been destroyed; instead there has been a rampant proliferation of harmful insects, bacteria, microbes and viruses that are resistant to the poisons, and the physiology of the crops has been damaged, leading to the weakening of their resilience and the destruction of their natural immunity. Fatal diseases that were unheard of in the countryside of old have broken out in the wake of all these artificial measures, and have got out of control. All this is hastening the imminent end of the modern countryside. Already in America, and in our own Taiwan, agricultural land is abandoned, and this dead land will surely proliferate like cancer cells, until the modern countryside follows the old countryside to perdition.

Even if the soil does not die, and the pollinators survive, the farming folk themselves are still headed for destruction. Previously, in the age of the old countryside, tropical diseases regulated human labour productivity, so that a balance was struck between production and consumption; tuberculosis regulated the human life span, so that a balance was struck between births and deaths. Nowadays there are no tropical diseases or tuberculosis in the villages, but illness caused by poisoning is roaring ahead: live births are increasing, but the death rate is higher still. The villagers put their head on the block for the city-dwellers: for a mere pittance of compensation, the city-dwellers make the villagers breathe 99% of the pesticides, while they keep very far away, and consume only a 1% trace of the poison. Even the iron constitution of the farmers has to give way, break down and fail. If by good luck they escape with their lives, the next generation will take off to the cities, every man jack of them; with no one left to carry on the inheritance, the fate of the villages is still sealed.

How depressing it is, the countryside of today!

(1983)

Huang Chunming 黃春明 (1939–)

COMMENTARY

Huang Chunming is first and foremost a novelist. Perhaps for that reason, his occasional essays have something special about them.

He is a native Taiwanese, born in a small town in Yilan county in the northeast of Taiwan, in the middle of farming country. His father was a shopkeeper. His mother died at the age of 24, having produced five children, of whom Huang Chunming was the oldest (then aged seven). The children were then looked after by their grandmother. Huang Chunming seems to have been an unruly child; he certainly got into a lot of fights, and must hold the record among our authors for the number of times he was expelled from school. Eventually he managed to graduate from teacher's training college, and taught for three years in a primary school before doing his military service. Afterwards he worked for the Yilan radio station, then moved to Taipei where he kept changing jobs. Mostly he worked for advertising agencies, until in 1973 he found employment making children's programmes for television. In 1976 he went to the USA for a year to join the writers' workshop at Iowa University. He still lives in Taiwan.

Huang Chunming's humble background, his peregrinations, and the variety of his employment, equipped him with a knowledge of life at ground level in Taiwan that was unrivalled among the ranks of published authors when he joined them. His first collection of short stories came out in 1969, and it was followed by four more in the 1970s. He was soon recognized as the outstanding exponent of 'native soil' literature. His subject was the theretofore unsung heroes of ordinary life, mostly people just scraping a living, in time-honoured (and dishonoured) ways. His stories were uplifting, though unsentimentalized and often sad.

Huang Chunming came late to writing essays. The two examples that follow come from a collection published in 1989. He explains in his preface that he was scared off prose writing in middle school by a perspicacious teacher who pointed out that his essays were full of pretentious phrases that obscured any meaning he might have intended. Having learned to write from the heart for his fiction, he was ready to have another go at essays. His writing certainly strikes one as fresh, free of the mannerisms and know-how that practice brings. It is also unsophisticated and not always clearly expressed. Yet somehow Huang Chunming makes his shortcomings into virtues, and on the altogether positive side he clearly excels in bringing scenes to life, as one would expect from a talented writer of fiction. In the last analysis, what made me choose his work in preference to that of currently more highly esteemed essayists was that he writes of things important to him, and writes to make a difference.

We Can't Bring Back the Past
往事只能回味

Recently I lived for a spell in the south.

One day on a country road I was shocked to see an old friend's new face. But this shock did not conform to past experience. Normally we experience shock in this way: first we give a nervous start, then our heart thumps fast, and finally we get a hold of ourselves. If the person who caused the shock is a stranger, naturally we are displeased. If we know him, at most we will curse him while he enjoys his joke. However, what startled me this time was actually an old friend putting on a new face. The old friend was not a person, but an old trade, 'driving Brother Hog'.

The said 'driving Brother Hog' is the business of keeping a breeding boar for the express purpose of responding to requests from people who keep sows to have them served. In Taiwan everyone called this line of business 'driving Brother Hog'. Because in the past practically all farming people in Taiwan kept pigs, some more, some fewer, and some kept sows for breeding, the trade of driving Brother Hog spontaneously arose to meet a need. Everyone who grew up in the country in the old days has seen the old men in their black cotton smocks, wearing a bamboo hat, driving along a boar, with a water ladle in one hand and a bamboo whip in the other. The most remarkable thing about these boars was the huge shiny scrotum tucked between their hind legs. Only a boar equipped with such a large-scale scrotum would merit the fraternal appellation of Brother Hog which we gave him. Actually the scrotums of all Brother Hogs grew too big for their boots, so to speak: it was not a question of tucking in between the hind legs, in fact they forced the two hind legs apart, obliging the legs to splay out as they walked, and take every step cautiously; no jerkiness in rhythm was tolerable. Consequently the fat bottom over the scrotum was forced to wobble from side to side so extravagantly that the situation seemed precarious.

If the old man behind was not in a hurry, he let the pig waddle along at its own slow pace; otherwise he drove it along with cuts of his little whip. In hot weather the scrotum was a drag on Brother Hog, and when they passed a stream the old man would dip his ladle in and water it. By and by, the scene we have described came like the oxcart to typify the living backdrop to rural life in Taiwan. Mr Lan Yinding, the water colourist famous for his paintings of the Taiwan countryside, has painted 'driving Brother Hog', as I recall. And Mr Yang Yingfeng has also published a picture of it in the *Bumper Harvest* magazine. Otherwise, if anyone whose stock of impressions of the Taiwan countryside goes back to then wants to check it out, they need only close their eyes for a little path to appear in their mind and an old man trot out along with Brother Hog. They will even be able to tell if they are starting out to do their business or if they are on their way home after concluding it. If starting out, Brother Hog's step will be vigorous, and he will be drooling at the mouth. There is an expression in Taiwan, 'Brother Hog dripping saliva' that is used of men getting overexcited when they talk about women. If on the other hand they see Brother Hog being driven along with cuts of the whip, then he is sure to be on his way home, having transacted his business. Funnily enough, the very same thing applies to men.

The trade of 'driving Brother Hog' must go back a long way. In the society in which it features, the daily speech of the common folk has taken up some sayings that relate to it. Say, for example, that someone knows for sure that a certain business proposition will at best be much ado about nothing and no money can be made out of it, yet his friend is set on it out of wishful thinking, then he might issue the warning, 'You won't listen to good advice, but I'm telling you that in the end all you can look forward to is getting fun out of driving Brother Hog.' The explanation is that the trade of driving Brother Hog doesn't pay. Firstly, the energy of Brother Hog is limited. If he were to do one bit of business each day for a whole month, he himself would have the appetite for it, but the old man who is his drover wouldn't approve: if Brother Hog died from exhaustion, he would starve to death. Secondly, in those days one transaction would bring in less than 100 dollars, and one transaction meant a successful impregnation, which often entailed several trips back and forth. The old man's daily meals, plus a bottle of rice wine in the evenings, wouldn't have cost very much; the main thing was feeding Brother Hog's huge appetite, and buying tonics to maintain his potency. That cleaned the old man out. But to say he got nothing out of it wouldn't be true either. He always officiated over Brother Hog's mating, which gave him a ringside seat at displays of porcine sexual prowess, indeed he had to lend a hand himself. This would have been an unfailing source of interest all year long, and would have had its own satisfaction. 'Getting fun out of driving Brother Hog' captures the living truth, no less.

Vocabulary relating to driving Brother Hog extends in the Taiwanese language beyond popular sayings to riddles. When I was little my grandad made up riddles for us to guess. One that we couldn't guess went, 'He wears a black cassock, and tramps for miles to find a wife.' That rhymes in Taiwanese. The answer was supposed to be an animal. Because of our age we didn't understand the connection between mating and married couples, so couldn't guess that it was the black Brother Hog who wore a cassock, and instead of acting properly like a monk, tired himself out walking miles to find a wife. When Grandad explained the riddle I got my first inkling that people also had to copulate in order to produce children.

......

In present-day society where the sexes mix freely, it is not very difficult for a man and woman to be evenly matched. In the closed society of the past where the sexes were separated, to still make an even match was quite an art. How did they manage it? There used to be a saying, 'If you don't do a turn as go-between in this life, in the next one you'll be driving Brother Hog.' Almost all marriages in the past were brought about by go-betweens. But they couldn't rely solely on the service of professional matchmakers. Even granted a very nimble pair of legs, they could not get around to act for all the men and women who were ready for marriage. What is more, with their slippery tongues they made a cripple out to be the opera character who poses with one foot raised and a pock-marked woman to be the moon goddess *au naturel*. As a result many parents were left regretting their children's unhappy marriages to their dying day. So they relied on the moral obligation of relatives and friends to share the work of matchmaking. In this way the stockpile of work hoarded by a small number of professional go-betweens got to be cleared. Then again, relatives and friends were a lot more reliable than professional go-betweens. They played an important role in the marriage system of the old society. There are things in life where to activate a third party is not easy: one has to resort to inducements, or threats, or connections. The amateur matchmakers of that time were the product of those three pressures working in concert. They were either relatives or friends of the principals: that was the connections function. If the matchmaking was successful and led to a union, there was a 'thank you' present to be had, which might be quite considerable, and was perfectly legal. If the bride later bore a male child, another 'thank you' was presented. That was the inducement. And the threat? That was as quoted: 'If you don't do a turn as go-between in this life, in the next one you'll be driving Brother Hog.' A nicer threat could hardly be imagined.

Returning, then, to the matter of 'driving Brother Hog', we can see from the formulation as a threat what the social status of that trade was—leaving aside how many people believed in reincarnation. In the traditional order, following behind officials, farmers, artisans and merchants, there were barbers, bandsmen and actors, but drovers of Brother Hog came still lower down. With very few exceptions those who drove Brother Hog were old gaffers who were all alone in the world.

The march of time is merciless. Anyone who stands in its way is crushed, though like the drovers of Brother Hog they might have no one to turn to. At the same time as Taiwan developed industrially and the economy took off, the livelihood of the old gaffers who drove Brother Hog was all but cut off by the Commission on Rural Reconstruction. Unquestionably, the Commission made a positive contribution in general to Taiwan's agriculture. As far as pig rearing was concerned, it not only introduced new concepts and techniques, it also imported new breeds, and raised productivity and profits. As part of the plan it put its whole weight behind artificial insemination. This posed an immediate threat to the survival of the traditional trade of 'driving Brother Hog'. For the old drovers, necessity was the mother of invention: overnight they came up with the theory of warm sperm to break the siege of artificial insemination. Up in arms, they addressed the farmers in this fashion:

'This artificial insemination is an invention of the devil! Everything in the world is as God made it, how can we go against nature? Let's leave aside doing right by people, and just talk about the facts of the matter. If you want to breed pigs properly, the sperm has got to squirt into the sow's belly while it is still warm, otherwise it's useless. What do you think the boar grows such a long prick for, if not for that? It's certainly not for peeing, because the sow doesn't have a prick yet manages all right. Everything works as nature intended. Men don't know what they're doing. That misbegotten artificial insemination of theirs, what it is is putting warm sperm into a cold test-tube, and all the warmth evaporates. Any halfwit could tell them that that cold sperm can't compare with our Brother Hog's warm sperm. . . .'

It was on the strength of this cold sperm versus warm sperm argument that the old gaffers cut an escape route through the enemy lines.

In the foregoing I have spilled a lot of ink to fill out the picture, because I wanted you to get to know the voice and face of this old friend. Though we haven't seen him for a good many years, our impression of him is still very vivid. When that day I met him on a country road in the south, I felt a thrill of pleasure, but also a sense of shock at seeing his new face. He no longer is an old gaffer, and Brother Hog is no longer driven in the old sense. The drover is a healthy young man, and he drives a one-and-a-half ton truck loaded with six different breeds of pig to drum up custom. Placards hang from both sides of the truck naming the six breeds of Brother Hog: Berkshire, Yorkshire, American Landrace, Maryland No. 1, and the native Taoyuan and Meinong. The truck is driven very slowly, not out of fear of jolting the pigs, but because it is parading round the streets to advertise its wares, and if it is driven fast people may not have time to take in the message, and women who keep pigs will not dare to shout after it 'Hog man!' The young people have come up with the new idea of broadcasting recorded music through a loudspeaker. The first song I heard then was 'Meilan I Love You'. Each Brother Hog on the back of the truck appeared nonplussed, as if he was overwhelmed by this unaccustomed stardom. The truck passed me, and as it receded into the distance the first song ended and the second song took its place: 'We Can't Bring Back the Past'. I suddenly found myself laughing: Mr Liu Jiachang had unknowingly written two good songs for Brother Hog and Sister Sow.

The truck disappeared from view, but you could still hear its sound. I could hardly believe what my eyes had just seen. A sense of nostalgia had germinated in my heart, and that had set my mind turning over impressions of the past. As I stood there disoriented, saying a silent goodbye to the truckful of Brother Hogs, I saw just at the point I lost sight of it a hazy image of an old gaffer approaching, driving Brother Hog. When my mind cleared, I realized that the iron heel of rapid social change had left the old drovers of Brother Hog trodden in its wake. The sayings, aphorisms and riddles connected with driving Brother Hog had also lost touch with present-day life. In time to come no one would know those figures of speech which had once enriched and vitalized the language. Of course, today will give rise to today's vocabulary, but at the present time, apart from scarifying new words like environmental pollution, nuclear war, energy crisis, and so on, how many vivid expressions have come into the language of our daily lives? I say to myself:

'Didn't that song get it right? We can't bring back the past.'

(1974)

Waiting for a Flower's Name
等待一朵花的名字

A title like this that suggests something very poetic or picturesque would normally belong to the style we associate with sentimental women writers. If they used this kind of title it would not only be consistent, it would also immediately attract a lot of young readers by virtue of the combination of title and pen-name, and would achieve the desired sensory effect. But when I use the title I have trouble reconciling myself to it, first of all: it is out of keeping, it doesn't seem right. Yet bearing in mind the story I am about to tell, no other title would be as fitting as 'Waiting For a Flower's Name'. Supposing I go ahead with it, I will still have the jitters, fearing that the reader on seeing a non-female author's name with the title will say, 'Yuck, a weirdo! How revolting!' I don't think such worries of mine are neurotic. They are quite well founded, because in my own reading I often come to such snap judgements, which lie somewhere between prankishness and malice. The fact that this title can be used by some but not by others shows that there is still striking inequality between the sexes. As a male author, I protest. Come what may, I have to use this title.

The fact is this: I really did wait somewhere for a flower's name. That day I went back to the house I had left empty in the Yilan countryside after typhoon Gerald was over, and on the way stopped by the dyke at Lanyang where the Muddy River runs into the sea, which I was going to use as the location for a story. It was dusk when

I got there, and not many people were on the footpath along the top of the dyke. I let my eye wander over the scene. Inadvertently my gaze was drawn to a wild flower beside the path. I took the few steps up to it, stooped down and examined it closely. It was more fascinating on near view than from a distance, but I would not venture to describe its fascination, because the quality that drew one to it was like the vital spark that a painting, however lifelike, cannot capture. I would have kept on looking at it indefinitely if my legs had not become so numb from stooping I thought I would never be able to stand up straight again. Similar flowers were scattered across the slope of this stretch of the dyke. The flower was creamy-white, medium sized, and grew from a vine. As well as taking pleasure in its beauty, I also felt put out. I could give a name to the weeds that grew alongside it, like horsewhip, thunderball, ox-tether, scabby-head, and so on. That flower was the only thing I was unfamiliar with, and I was impatient to get the answer. Before long some secondary school boys came along on their bicycles. I stopped them and asked. None of them knew.

'Do you come from around here?'

'Yes, we all come from around here.'

While I was about it I asked them the names of the other wild plants. They still could not identify the plants native to their locality, despite them all coming from farming families thereabouts. As they rode off with their bulging satchels on their backs, I gazed after them, feeling the gloom of close of day.

Then a young man who looked like a civil servant came by. He also was local, he also did not know the flower's name. I asked him if he had seen this kind of flower before. He said he thought he had. He answered my questions without checking his stride, obviously none too keen to engage in conversation with me. I thanked him in conclusion. He turned his head to look at me when he had got some distance away, unable to figure me out.

After another interval a young lady on a bicycle came along from the land side. She was dressed quite fashionably. When I accosted her she did not get off her bike, she just slowed her speed to such a degree that it needed some skill for her to keep her balance. But when she took in that I wanted to know the name of the flower in front of us, she bent forward and gave a mighty thrust to her pedal, sending her bike shooting forward. While I stood nonplussed, she twisted her head to look at me with an expression of disgust, and at the same time uttered an exclamation like 'Don't give me that stuff, you *** !' The first bit I heard distinctly, but I didn't catch what sort of person I was supposed to be. I didn't understand how I had offended her, or why she should get angry and give me a mouthful. Looking around, I saw that it was nearly dark, and the place was deserted. That gave me the clue to the young woman's reaction. She obviously thought I was some kind of pervert, and she had been subjected to sexual harassment. It was quite understandable. Of course I knew why I wanted to ask the wild flower's name, but her best guess was that I was up to no good.

I was not willing to accept failure to find out that flower's name. In my imagination such a beautiful flower should have a correspondingly beautiful name. My curiosity made me resolve to stay till the sun went down, even if no one else came along to ask.

At last I saw two silhouettes approaching from the sea side. It was a grandmother carrying a chock-full plastic bag and a six- or seven-year-old boy walking unwillingly behind her. I heard her scold the child:

'. . . I'm not going to take you out again. A big lad like you, I ought to complain about you not giving me a piggy-back. Fancy you wanting me to give you one!' She came up to me as she was speaking, and noticed me watching them. She added, 'Look, the gentleman is laughing. Get on with you, run on ahead and tell them we're back.'

'Is that your grandson, ma'am?'

'That's right, my third son's boy. As obstinate as a mule.'

She stopped, and while waiting for the boy to catch up, asked me: 'Are you looking for somebody?'

'No, ma'am, I wanted to ask . . .'

'It's late. Why don't you come and rest your feet at our house? It's just below the dyke there.' She paid no attention to my words.

She turned back to the child and hurried him up: 'If you don't look lively the water bogies will come and get you.'

The boy looked at the flood water tossing and churning on the inner side of the dyke; keeping to the outer edge, he hurried past his grandmother and went on ahead.

'That little mule-head, he's not afraid of anything, except bogies.'

'Excuse me, ma'am, do you mind telling me what this flower is called?' Blocking her path, I pointed to the ground.

'Oh! Now then, that's called a trash flower.'

No doubt she couldn't see properly. I stooped down and cradled the flower in my hand.

'No, I mean this flower.'

'That's right, it's a trash flower,' she replied with complete conviction.

I still wasn't willing to credit it.

'Well, what did it use to be called?'

'Ever since I was a little girl it's been called a trash flower. I don't know about before that.'

'What is this flower used for?' I asked, thinking that such a beautiful flower must have some value.

'What use? No use. The vine it grows from is all prickly. When we see it growing in the garden or over the fence we get someone to root it up.'

I was so surprised I was lost for words.

The boy was already thirty or forty metres distant by this time. He turned round and urged his grandmother to hurry up.

'My grandson is calling me. Come, come and have a meal with us. We live just over there.' She was moving off as she spoke.

'Pardon, ma'am, did you always live here?'

'Sure. I've always lived at East Creek. Don't worry, come and have a bite with us. . . .' She stopped to reply, her tone sincere.

'That's very kind of you, but I won't trouble you.'

The setting sun hit the hilltop, just as the small silhouettes of grandmother and grandson stepped onto the horizontal line where the sky touched the sea. I was so moved by the spectacle that I turned my head from east to west several times to take it in. Then the sun went down, and the people could not be seen.

I had waited for the name of a flower. Its name was 'trash flower'. This totally unexpected answer, and the sudden remove from the one extreme of wishful thinking to the other extreme of sober reality, rooted me to that dark wasteland spot. I smoked some more cigarettes and fell to ruminating.

It wasn't necessary to go back to the old lady's childhood; even the rural society of Taiwan's recent past was innocent of such terms as 'fashion', 'leisure activities', 'sophistication'. The ordinary folk at the grass roots still spoke of diligence as being 'tough', going away to find work was called 'begging for food' or 'looking for a grubstake', making an effort was 'busting a gut'. It is not hard to deduce from the vocabulary of daily life the living conditions of the time: it really wasn't easy to keep body and soul together. So in every family as soon as labour potential matured it was invested in agricultural production. On the overall production line, whoever's work ability was high—who could carry the heaviest load, who could cut the rice stalks fastest—was top dog; whoever's work ability was low was a loser. Anyone who loafed about, did not engage in production, and lived off the backs of others, was called 'trash'. That beautiful flower was called a 'trash flower' for the same kind of reason, no doubt.

Having reached that conclusion, it suddenly came to me what that girl wearing fashionable clothes had said when she swore at me before dusk fell. The words I hadn't heard clearly I could now fill in: 'Don't give me that stuff, you piece of trash!' Could it be that my curiosity and liking for that flower, to put it bluntly, tarred me with the same brush?

Engrossed in thought, I finished my few remaining cigarettes and flicked the last butt away. The glowing red arc spent itself in the invisible stream. 'Waiting for a flower's name' was really no romantic story, was it?

(1987)

Yu Qiuyu 余秋雨 (1946–)

COMMENTARY

Yu Qiuyu went to secondary school and university in Shanghai, and he stayed on at his university to teach, but his home was in Yuyao in Zhejiang province. He therefore is well qualified to write on 'Shanghai people', having been among them for so long, yet not being one of them.

Yu's first publications were academic works that arose out of his career interests—three books on the history and theory of drama (1983–85), and one on artistic creativity (1987). They won him prizes. The essays of broader interest that he contributed to the leading Shanghai literary journal *Shouhuo* 收穫(Harvest) were a by-product of his academic career, in that they originated in trips he made to confer and lecture in China and abroad. These essays were published under the title *Wenhua kulü* 文化苦旅(Stressful Cultural Journeying) in 1992. Another collection, *Shan ju biji* 山居筆記(Notes Made while Living in the Hills) followed in 1995. They won their author more prizes, and a very admiring broad readership, not only in China itself but also in Taiwan, Hong Kong and Singapore. His essays were praised as unprecedented in their breadth, penetration, display of learning and wealth of experience, and for being infused with a kind of personal poetry: in other words for combining the virtues of the scholarly essay with those of *belles-lettres*. They mostly included personal history, in the traditional Chinese travelogue manner—that is, what he did and whom he met in a place—but their chief purpose was to draw together local threads of national cultural history, and express his feelings on the subject. In the words of his own preface to *Wenhua kulü*, his scenery was not natural scenery, but cultural scenery.

The wave of exceptional popularity and praise that Yu Qiuyu's essays were greeted with was followed by a spate of criticism. The targets of criticism were that he got out of his depth expatiating on historical matters about which he had scraped together only a smattering of knowledge; that he was inclined to emotionalize like a romantic novelist; that he fictionalized events in the past; that he wrote opinion as fact; that cultural conservation made him blind to real progress. Though there is some truth in those criticisms, his popularity has hardly been dented. The reasons are not hard to find.

The first is that his essays filled a historical want. In mainland China the Marxist-Leninist orthodoxy that had for most people's lifetimes expunged all alternatives had become a hollow shell by the 1980s. Apart from knowing that they now had to make money, people were told they should be patriotic, but they did not know what they had to be proud of: to coin a useful phrase, they did not know 'where they were coming from'. Yu Qiuyu's essays peopled that void: they said the landscape was full of living history, which was theirs, and which they should claim. Outside mainland China the sense of Chinese cultural identity had been mostly lost too, eroded by foreign modern ways. There too there was a thirst to be satisfied.

At the same time, Yu Qiuyu was not a propagandist; he clearly wrote from personal conviction and passion. He was and is, however, a natural showman. Even his detractors concede his eloquence and ability to dramatize. Furthermore, to substantial content he added substantial length, some of his essays being thirty-five pages long.

Given the desirability of including one of Yu's 'think pieces', as think pieces are otherwise very rare, their length was to me an embarrassment. With due apologies to the author, abridgement was the only answer: better that than nothing. Again, subject matter presented a difficulty, as I wanted to avoid footnoting.

'Shanghai People' recommended itself as being relatively self-contained. All that needs to be explained about it is the trouble Shanghai was in after the Communist victory in 1949. Although the International Settlement had been of great use to the Communist Party in opposition, affording its members protection from Chinese law, and the city produced great wealth for the country, Shanghai had also been the scene of the infamous massacre of left-wing activists in April 1927, and gangster organizations were very powerful there. Its capitalist business practices were of course anathema anyway. Hence after Liberation the Shanghainese were regarded as delinquents, and kept on a short leash. That accounts for their sense of disorientation described in the essay. Ironically, the reputation of Shanghai was later blackened on the other side, as in the late 1960s and early 70s it became the stronghold of the fanatically Maoist 'Gang of Four'.

Shanghai People
上海人

......

From a modern geographical perspective, Shanghai is a good proposition. Beijing is a typical Chinese capital city: with the Great Wall at its back, it sits facing south, stately and secure. Shanghai is just the opposite: its face is turned east, confronting the vast Pacific Ocean, and behind it is the mighty Yangtze that links together the whole of China from west to east. To a self-sufficient China, Shanghai was out on a limb, and inconsequential; but in the contemporary world of open access, it is in a commanding position, where all streams converge.

If the Pacific didn't matter much to China, Shanghai wouldn't matter much either. You can't expect interesting things of a tightly sealed door. On the contrary, a door might let in strong winds from outside, or the noise of some commotion at the portal, to disturb the peace of the householder. We had the natural granaries of central China and the Sichuan basin, whereas Shanghai had hardly any rice to offer; we had countless fresh-water waterways, whereas Shanghai's salt water, however much there was of it, was undrinkable; we had our sacred mountains to anchor our religion and our beauty spots, whereas Shanghai could not boast even a decent promontory; we had broad public highways crisscrossing all our regions, whereas to get to Shanghai you had to take a roundabout byway; our state glories in its ancient history, whereas Shanghai is too young even to qualify as a county.... What did this people who had grown up dependent on the Yellow River want with a Shanghai tucked away on the sea coast?

From the beginning Shanghai was not very much in tune with, or compatible with, the awesome dignity of Chinese civilization.

Shanghai had to wait till the 19th century for an employee of the British East India Company called Lindsay to state its importance on the new world map in a report to his government; it then became one of the five Treaty Ports established by the terms of the Treaty of Nanjing. Shanghai was opened up by the British navy in 1842. Change was rapid thereafter. Western civilization swept in along with its detritus, and hapless China gambled more and more heavily on the place. In a very short time there was created an uproar which could be heard from every corner of the globe.

The descendants of Xu Guangqi[1] were both psychologically prepared for and surprised by the uproar that overwhelmed them. On the one hand there was an invasion of colonizers, adventurers, upstarts, gangsters, hooligans, prostitutes and triads; on the other hand there was a forgathering of colleges, hospitals, post offices, banks, trams, scholars, poets and scientists. Against the background of the sound of steam whistles on the Huangpu River, the nightly flashing of the neon lights, Western suits and leather shoes jostling

---

[1] The Ming dynasty court official from Shanghai who was baptised a Christian by the Jesuits, and learned their mathematics.

with long gowns and mandarin jackets, the babel of Chinese dialects and European languages, and the comings and goings, there was constant turnover, things replacing each other with the highest frequency. This society was a newly invented monstrosity, but more exactly it was a nexus and a thoroughfare: different torrents collided here, and out of the turbulence huge waves were raised.

Any historian, confronted with this place, would feel his head swim if he had to think of a way to define it. You could say it was the breeding ground of the Chinese nation's shame in modern times, but if a nation that has survived into modern times never exposes itself to the impact of modernity, isn't that shameful too? You could also say it was the starting point of China's transition to modernity, but which nation's step in the transition to modernity has been as hasty, panicky, nervous and chaotic as Shanghai's? Then again you might say that it was a city culture that arose in opposition to rural culture, but where is there a city culture that has from the first been coveted, divided, surrounded and enveloped by a pervasive rural force, as Shanghai's has?

In a word, it is a gigantic paradox. When you concentrate on its filth, it will put on a show of dazzling brightness; when you do reverence to its great power, it will turn round and show you its back wall, pitted and scarred.

Yet within this paradoxical structure an ecology and a mindset gradually took shape that was at odds with contemporary China as a whole. In the early years of this century numbers of new-style revolutionaries and thinkers were put on the wanted list by the feudal dynasty, and Shanghai with its foreign concessions became a refuge for them. The important thing here was that feudal tradition and Western values came into direct conflict in Shanghai over the question of pursuit and sanctuary. The Shanghainese read their newspapers every day, worked things out for themselves, and began to understand that by international standards many legal principles that China had followed since ages past were perverted and unreasonable. So from a succession of actual cases that made the news in main streets and back alleys, the Shanghainese got a vague idea of the proper implications of the notions of democracy, humanism, freedom, rule of law, political prisoners, maximum penalties, and so on, and acquired a heartfelt contempt for the feudal traditions that could not stand up to comparison. That contempt was not the fruit of armchair philosophizing but the common-sense option that actual experience and observation pointed to, hence it gained extremely widespread currency and became habitual in this city.

At the same time as these cases were coming up, an event of more symbolic significance occurred. The Shanghai gentry and bureaucrats joined together in vigorously campaigning for the demolition of the walls of the old city, because they clearly impeded the flow of traffic and the operations of commerce. In their petitions they repeatedly asserted that the demolition of the walls would be proof of the 'social enlightment of the citizens'. Of course some people objected, but after much argument, the Shanghainese finally removed their city walls, and became a community unusually free from the confinements of feudal tradition.

Later on a revolution that originated in the countryside changed the history of Shanghai. Shanghai became a lot more subdued. One batch of Shanghainese went away. The majority who were left were required to fall into step with the interior, and to take up economic responsibility for it. Shanghai faced about, calmed its nerves, and took up the role of obedient eldest son. Just like Juexin in Ba Jin's novel, *Family*, it shouldered a heavy burden: there could be no more escapades. Forget about the siren sea wind at the city's back, the machines in the workshops were thundering, the rush hour trams were full to the roof, everybody was tired, Shanghai at night became deserted. Village cadres from the interior were drafted in to Shanghai to put a final cap on the exuberance that gave people the wrong ideas. In order to prepare for the war that was supposed to be coming from the Pacific, large numbers of factories were relocated to mountainous regions in the interior. The more remote and rugged the terrain, the more likely it was that a Shanghai factory would be there. The simple mountain folk laughed at the workers behind their backs: 'Huh! Shanghainese!'

In recent years, the Shanghainese have begun to feel unsettled again. People from Guangzhou, Shenzhen and Wenzhou have descended on Shanghai, their purses bulging. The Shanghainese have glared at them, but kept their distance. They feel a degree of inferiority, yet have not entirely lost their self-respect. They think to themselves: if we Shanghainese really stood up, the boot would be on the other foot. They may just be consoling themselves; I pass it on for what it's worth.

Perhaps there is some justification in the self-consolation of the Shanghainese. The Shanghai culture is first and foremost a quality of the mind and spirit. It cannot be reduced to a matter of economics.

The most notable feature of the Shanghai moral temperament is toleration, based on personal freedom. To the Shanghainese toleration is not a policy or a promise but an instinct.

・・・・・・・

Shanghai people do not normally find fault with the lifestyle of others, as long as it does not intrude on themselves. Compared with people in other places, they mix very little with their neighbours in apartment blocks and staff quarters. If several families are forced to share a kitchen or toilet, friction and rows are very common, however, because each family is jealous of its independence and freedom. Hence the tolerance of the Shanghainese is not expressed as deference, but as 'minding your own business'. In the moral sense, deference is a virtue, but in the deeper cultural sense 'minding your own business' is perhaps closer to the modern view of tolerance. To acknowledge the reasonableness of the right of separate existence of different modes of life, to concede that each may go its own way without interference, has more far-reaching significance than exercising the deference attained to by strenuous moral discipline. Why should one want to be deferential? Because there is a single choice: if not you, then me; if I don't defer to you, I have to contest with you. This is the basic lifestyle and moral starting point where a uniform order is in force. Why can you 'mind your own business'? Because the choice is multiple: you go your way, I go my way; nobody will swallow up anybody else. This is a non-aggression pact built on the premise of a pluralistic world.

・・・・・・・

In the Shanghai vernacular there is the ultimate rhetorical question: 'What's it to you?' If a girl's dress attracts comment from colleagues when she is working in another place, she might address the criticism in her reply, with 'What's wrong with the skirt being a bit short?' or 'I wear jeans because it saves trouble', or something of the sort, but among girls in Shanghai the question resolves itself very simply: that is a private matter, and even if the clothes make her look a freak it doesn't concern anybody else. Thus a 'What's it to you?' cuts short all argument. The tone of this utterance may be indignant, or it may be piqued, but the message is the same.

In the cultural and academic sphere, the scholars who are best attuned to the Shanghai mentality are not keen on 'reviewing questions' with others, or on making ripostes to others' 'reviews'. There is a multitude of paths in the cultural and academic spheres; if everyone takes a different path, occasionally getting distant sight of each other, that is good enough: why should you want to keep in step? In recent years we have heard of several so-called 'north-south disputes', 'disputes between the Shanghai school and Beijing school', but these disputes have mostly been the brainchildren of the northerners. Even if Shanghai people are 'reviewed', they rarely counter-attack; they stubbornly stick to their own opinion. When they meet objections, a little voice inside them says 'What's it to you?'

......

Another feature of the Shanghai temperament is astute calculation of practical advantage. Perhaps this is a throwback to Xu Guangqi's mathematical achievements, perhaps it is a competence shaped by a rapidly changing environment, but in any case the Shanghainese have always been interested in provable benefits, and have no patience with doddering and slow-wittedness.

In scientific research and management and trading, the Shanghainese are not very adventurous, but they rarely miscalculate. Every unit in the country has its thorny problems. In general they find it pays to recruit Shanghainese to handle them. That is no secret anywhere.

Unfortunately, in practice there are not nowadays many jobs requiring the use of brainpower that are given to Shanghainese, so their talent spills over, and their ability for astute calculation is used in the wrong place, which has resulted in a big fault in the character of the Shanghainese.

Shanghai people don't like lavish banquets; they don't like going around with visiting friends for days on end to show how loyal their friendship is; they don't like listening to big lectures, and are not given to long speeches themselves; cultural salons would not get off the ground in Shanghai, because the participants would work out that the loss in time spent would not be worth the gain; when they go away on business, the Shanghainese are not keen on staying in luxury hotels, even if they are qualified to do so, because there are no real benefits to be gained. . . . There is nothing wrong with any of these things, and if the astuteness of the Shanghainese was confined to this level, they would not be thought objectionable.

However, you can find at every turn in this city the wasteful use of sharp wits. Quite a few people who want to get to a distant part of the city will spend a lot of time working out which bus routes, and when they have to change buses, which bus fares, are most economical: even a difference of a few cents is taken seriously. It may happen that another passenger on the bus will confidently propose an even more economical route; the precision over the itinerary is comparable to that of a military strategist selecting a line of attack. Even more saddening is the fact that such discussions on buses often attract mass participation. Shanghai may very well be the top of the league for the incidence of rows over the sharing of water rates and gas bills in communal staff quarters.

Perhaps all this could be attributed to poverty, but while they argue a foreign cigarette dangles from their lips, the cost of which would doubly offset the disputed sum.

This Shanghai tendency to haggle can, I find, be put down in great part to protecting and expressing personal astuteness. Intelligence can constitute a life force which constantly demands to be discharged, even if the object is extremely petty. Only in its discharge does a person get a sense of his strength. For the poor old Shanghainese a high IQ has become a cross to bear. Excluded from getting into calculus, from drawing up designs, from operating production lines, from the front line of commercial competition, what are they to do? Take part in quiz games? They are too old for that. Go in for gambling? Bad for the reputation and the finances. They can only expend their wits on these trifling and inconsequential matters; though they may get het up if they take them seriously, it still counts as a diversion.

Actually, brains and eloquence like theirs ought to be put to use in the verbal battles in foreign trade negotiations.

Another feature of the Shanghai character is its aspiration to an open culture, which derives from its history of international contacts.

Compared with the rest of the Chinese people, Shanghainese take a relatively balanced approach to international society. They have never looked down on foreigners in their hearts, hence they are not likely to fear foreigners, or show them excessive respect. In the main they have a high regard for foreign ways, but temperamentally they are averse to fawning on foreigners.

······

We may be sure that this is closely related to the city's history. The old generation of rickshaw men could all speak a few words of English, but such a humble class as they still dared to take the foreigners on in the May 30th disturbances. All along there have been foreign nationals living in the backstreets of Shanghai, and they mix wholly naturally with long-standing neighbours. The salespersons in Shanghai shops take foreign customers in their stride; they are even able to estimate the purchasing power of foreign customers, and make suggestions as to what they should buy.

In a lot of northern cities they refer to foreigners as 'foreign chums'. This amusing expression, which is neither respectful nor contemptuous, seems to be familiar but is actually distancing; there is no chance of it taking root in Shanghai. In Shanghai parlance, very few people, apart from children, lump foreigners together as 'foreigners'. Assuming their nationality is known, they are called specifically Americans, English, Germans, Japanese. This signifies that even the ordinary townspeople feel a certain closeness to foreigners.

In the present day all Shanghainese, regardless of their degree, cherish the hope of sending their children abroad to study. To go to Japan and support their study by doing odd jobs is a choice made by young people themselves when they run out of alternatives. Heads of families do not favour this course; they hope their children will be able to go to university in America in a right and proper manner. An international field of vision is here becoming pervasive.

Even before China opened up, in fact, the Shanghainese nursed a secret desire for international culture in the education of their children, no matter whether it could be satisfied or not. Shanghai middle schools continued to place weight on English, though it was hardly used in those days, and no parents were in favour of dropping it. The Shanghainese demanded that their children learn to play the piano or sing after school, but at the same time were not at all eager for them to be recruited into the army entertainment corps, which then had a glamorous image.

∴∴∴

In the upheavals of the Cultural Revolution it seemed that everything was extinguished, but occasionally foreign classical music delegations quietly showed up. The newspapers gave them no publicity, but there was an immediate rush on the box office, and people fought for tickets. Where had all those fans of foreign music been hiding? When the concerts were performed the audience was all respectably dressed, and in orderliness and manners conformed entirely to international conventions, so upholding the prestige of Shanghai. A few years ago countless Shanghai people queued up all night in the biting wind for a Beethoven symphony concert. Two years ago my college tested the water by putting on the 'theatre of the absurd' play *Waiting for Godot*. By normal standards this play is to all appearances as dry as dust, and indeed it played to poor houses in many cities abroad, but to our surprise the Shanghai audience sat through it, without catcalls, without comment, and without cheers either. There were doubtless quite a lot of people who were completely baffled by it, but they knew it was a world-famed play that ought to be seen. If they didn't understand it, that was quite to be expected: it wasn't the fault of the play, and it wasn't their fault either. Night after night audiences came and went, quiet and composed.

There is no point in pretending that there is the same pursuit of international culture at the lower levels of Shanghai society, but long immersion in the life of this city breeds a respect for culture in general. The doctrine that 'education is useless' had its day in Shanghai, but the situation was rather different from elsewhere. The great majority of parents could not accept the idea that a child able to benefit from further study should voluntarily quit school; the doctrine that 'education is useless' was applied only to children who were really no good academically, as a sop to conscience, and as an excuse to neighbours. Even in the turmoil of the Cultural Revolution, the last cohort of university students to graduate before the Cultural Revolution remained the most sought-after marriage partners, despite the fact that their salaries were then very low, their prospects nil, and their appearance unprepossessing. In certain historical circumstances and social environments, this respect for culture is blind to material benefit. The fact that the Shanghainese, who are very alive to material benefit, can in this respect disregard it, seems to me one of the big ways they differ from the Cantonese, close kin though they may be in many other ways.

······

The character of the Shanghainese has been structured to a great extent by over 100 years of excessive prosperity and turbulence. In the first part of this century the world was their oyster, but it has to be admitted that they did not at that time boss the city. For a long time the Shanghainese held the position of servants, staff, and assistants: it was foreigners and other Chinese who stood in the first line, accepting the pleasures and risks of enterprise. The bulk of the Shanghainese occupied the second line, observing, comparing, following, advising, worrying, congratulating themselves, tasting over and over the pleasures and risks of the second line. The few Shanghainese who broke through into the first line left Shanghai if they were successful. Though the Shanghainese were well informed, and could cope very well in the modern competitive society, they lacked the daring to take their fate in their own hands, and hadn't the self-confidence to let their individuality shine forth.

Right up to the present day, even the pick of the Shanghai bunch are best fitted to work as senior functionaries of multinational enterprises; few if any will become empire-building chief executives of companies. The Shanghainese have far more circumspection than drive, far more adaptability than creativity. They have the poise of top people, but not the bearing of top generals. They have the field of vision to encompass the world, but not the strength of character to bestride the world.

Thus the Shanghainese are always expecting. As they set their sights high, whatever comes will not satisfy their expectations, so they have to resort to grumbling, but grumbling is as far as they go. What restricts them is their functionary mentality.

Not having the courage to be front runners, not having the toughness to command the heights, Shanghai people's astuteness has faint-heartedness as its fellow. They don't laugh uproariously, they don't go in for the kill, they don't strike out into the hills on their own, they don't fight last-ditch battles. Even in their recreations they don't let themselves go; they are chary, they are wishy-washy. Even in their courting they lack romantic colour.

The ugliness of the Shanghainese is an extension of this. Having lost life's grand design, intelligence has become their own personal plaything. From those of high education who have taken on the polish of the salon, we only hear a spate of witticisms; we cannot find the surge of flood tides. Those of low education dispense their wit without regard to the occasion, commonly descending to the snide and hurtful. At one degree worse, they descend to philistinism and hooliganism, and become the dregs that are a nuisance on the downtown streets. The Shanghainese don't have a very pleasant time, but since they haven't a feeling for life, they haven't a sense of tragedy;

and since they haven't a sense of tragedy, they have no acceptance of eminence and greatness. They claim to have a bent for comedy, but comedy is all it is: they cannot rise to true humour, because they do not possess the breadth of mind and waywardness that is essential to humour. Consequently they are bereft of profound sadness and profound gladness: the two great fundamentals in the experience of life are but faint shadows.

· · · · · · ·

Even that self-esteem which get's everyone else's back up is simply the blind defence by the Shanghainese of their way of life and way of thinking: devolving on petty things, it does not amount to a style. Truly strong people also have a share of self-esteem, but their confidence in their own ability makes them generous and open-minded; they would not look critically on others merely out of infatuation with their own lifestyle, speech and manners.

To sum up, the character of the Shanghainese may be ingeniously constructed, but it lacks the bubbling hot springs of vitality. Hence the city has lost the power to scald anyone, lost its bounding exuberance.

Sad to say, the barbs thrown at the Shanghainese often stem from a more backward set of priorities. The Shanghainese are criticized for their worship of foreign ways, for being opinionated, unorthodox and heretical; they are required to revert to simplicity and guilelessness, return to the fold, reforge the links of unity. Shanghai people, who breathe the salt air of the sea, have responded somewhat obstinately to this. There has been no instant confession of sins. They prefer to hold out for a while longer, rather than comply hastily. There is a chance that out of the present perplexity and uncertainty there may emerge a generation that one could be proud of.

The desirable development of the Shanghai character would be towards more freedom, more sturdiness, more ardour, more grandeur. Its supports would be the ocean, the world, the future. So far this kind of character has not been collectively embodied in any Chinese city.

If this city forever remains a crowded market of functionaries, if it remains a nursery for overseas Chinese, it will dim and fade from the future world map. History has never given any status to appendages.

If people can find temporal meaning in geographical space, they can easily understand that China in losing Shanghai lost a generation. The loss of Shanghai culture was a tragedy for the whole nation.

Zhang Xingjian 張行健 (1959–)

COMMENTARY

Zhang Xingjian grew up in a village on the loess plateau of Shanxi province, near to the town of Linfen. In his youth he worked the land. In 1983 he gained a place in the Shanxi Institute of Education, and started writing for local literary magazines. After graduating in 1986 he worked in the educational service of the district of Linfen. He is a very prolific author, having published to date in provincial and national magazines over twenty novellas, over fifty short stories, and some hundred essays. He regards himself very much as the son of his native soil, and is proud of the robust qualities that the harsh life of the plateau has bred in Shanxi people. He is now a member of the Chinese Writers' Association.

The following essay is significant as a demonstration of a kind of rhetoric that developed in the revolutionary years of communist China. In its pure form, attained to in the Cultural Revolution (1966–76), it was fascinating but repellent, because of its monstrosity. In a dilute form, as here, its energy can be channelled to a proper literary end, and produce something special.

I can give an idea of what that pure rhetoric was by recounting an experience. In 1976, just before the Cultural Revolution was to end—though no one knew it at the time—I was a member of a foreign delegation that visited a museum of revolutionary history in China. The guide who explained the exhibits was a small young woman who in between speeches conversed in a perfectly normal and relaxed manner. But when she went into her speeches she lifted herself on to her toes and her chest swelled out like a bullfrog's; her words swooped from peak to peak, and nearly took the plaster off the walls with their reverberation. The speeches were a mixture of rhapsody, rant, and rodomontade. At the end of each speech she deflated, and returned to normal.

From that legacy Zhang Xingjian has drawn vigour, exuberance and robust masculinity. Applied by the right person to the right subject, these can be excellent qualities, and are the more to be prized because of their present paucity. Few subjects could be more fitting for those qualities than the bare loess plain of northern China, made famous by Chen Kaige's film *The Yellow Earth*. To the legacy Zhang has added his own figures of speech and his own rhythms—most noticeably in his unpunctuated strings of words. 'Goodwives' (I'm afraid there isn't a good English word for *poniangmen*) is principally a celebration, rather than an essay, but it comes into our orbit because his rainbows are not suspended high in the sky, but come right down to the ground.

The 'Song of the Simple Life' 擊壤歌 mentioned in the first paragraph is an agricultural work song ascribed to the 3rd millennium BC. It celebrates the self-sufficient life of the farmer.

Goodwives
婆娘們

Our home soil grows all the cereals, grew the 'Song of the Simple Life', grew the ancient legends, and also grows a tribe of goodwives every bit as wild as men.

The climate is hard, the language of those who survive in this climate is also hard. A fine and sturdy name, goodwife. When red-veiled maidens, to the joyous blowing of horns and the din of exploding firecrackers, step with either foreboding or light heart across their man's threshold, the same as their grandmothers, mothers and aunts did before them, then that is the end of the carefree days of their girlhood, then they lose the protective shade of the two great trees of their former home, then they inherit that weighty, solid, resounding title, then they take up a life that like the name is as heavy as a mountain. . . .

The women who have become goodwives expertly measure up their own husbands with women's eyes, whether they have married of their own choice, or left it all to their parents to arrange, or to cement an alliance between two families by exchange of brides, and after the fierceness of the storm and the transport of the soul, or the terror the frenzy the pain and madness of that unforgettable night, when everything is as quiet and peaceful as a windless and dustless coppice on top of a loess rise, they wipe away two glistening tears of pleasure or pain and seriously weigh and ponder the life that lies ahead of them.

Under their mother-in-law's kindly eye, or perhaps even gimlet-sharp surveillance, they begin sewing stitching mending weaving steaming buns and sponges making preserves and vinegar. Only at this point do they discover that the little knacks they learned before marriage, like stitching together inner soles for their sweetheart and rolling out noodles for their old dad, were pitifully few and paltry, and, red-faced and ashamed, get down to learning the real skills of running a home.

With every day their belly swells, the boldness of the goodwives increases. As the root of hope for the clan and the asset on which women pride themselves grows and expands inside, they dare to choose pretty patterns, allow themselves food fads, and waddle next door like ducks and sit on the edge of the brick bed or on the steps with other goodwives and enumerate their mother-in-law's faults, complain about their father-in-law's failings, and do not forget to express scant regard for their husband's younger sister(s). . . . One day, at dusk or at dawn, a series of agonizing shrieks will suspend the hearts of a small peasant family from the roof-beams; no need to spend money, no need to go to hospital, she can manage stretched out on her own brick bed with the country midwife her mother-in-law called for her. The dishevelled goodwife, wracked with pain, curses heaven curses earth curses her own cruel husband; she has none of the pretence of her pampered city sisters. Beads of sweat roll down her forehead, willpower and tenacity are exuded from between her tightly clenched teeth . . . a bawl announces the arrival of a brand-new life. The prop and support for this generation has sprung forth; there has sprung forth the future of the clan and the status of the goodwife. From this time forth she will shed the bashfulness of her maiden days, and think nothing of pulling open her jacket in the street and stuffing a snow-white breast in the baby's mouth, think nothing of opening her mouth and letting rip with full-throated laughter; think nothing of using vulgar language to repay in kind the vulgarity of men. . . .

Goodwives understand menstruation but don't make allowance for menstrual periods. On their bodies is always written the words 'up and doing': even if their bones are weary and their tempers frayed, they still have to go out to the fields as usual, and act as their man's right hand, picking bean sprouts planting sweet potatoes dibbling maize transplanting sorghum gathering cotton. The blood-red flowers from those six or seven days are used to dye the magnificent sunset glow of evening. When the men get to work with their seed drills, they harness themselves between the drill's shafts like a donkey, bend their waist to make a beautiful pictograph, thrust their sturdy round haunches high in the air, to make a rich and productive 'family managed' field or a loess hillside that her man may plough and sow.

Yet they get beaten up by their men. Usually it is because they gave their father-in-law a dusty answer, lost their temper with their mother-in-law, or got in a row with their sisters-in-law over who should get the three fine plates or the two blue-flower-patterned bowls when the family property is divided up. They are not going to put up with their man raining blows upon them. Red and puffy about the eyes, they tie up their bundles, retread the path that they take only on high days and holidays, and spill out their grievances tearfully to their own parents. Thus their grievances are reduced by half. The other half evaporates over the next two days. On the third day they lean against their parents' doorpost, stitching a shoe sole for their old dad and at the same time keeping an eye on the little path that leads into the hills. They miss the real and substantial little home that belongs to them. If the chickens are not properly fed they will go elsewhere to peck and lay their eggs; if the pig is not fed regularly it will definitely not be ready for selling by the end of the year; the kids will always be thinking of their mother; that 'cruel beast' can't cook so he'll eat and drink whatever he can get his hands on and he's got stomach trouble too hasn't he . . . the swelling round their eyes subsides under the chafing of anxiety . . . finally three black dots appear on the path leading to the hills. The one skipping and jumping in front is their son, the one in the middle with the date-red blanket draped over it and with a bell hanging from its neck is their little long-haired donkey, the figure bringing up the rear that they would know anywhere is, yes, their man. Their mouth shapes the curse of 'gallows bird', but flags fly in their heart, and their face breaks into a black peony of a smile. . . .

Goodwives know how to love the land and know even better how to love their man, that love being based on that home of hustle and bustle, noise and clamour. They have another world, tender and intimate. On countless nights they use their rough fingers to scratch their man's itchy places, use gentle zephyrs and fine rain to dispel their man's weariness, make a bed of their broad bosom to let their man dream in vivid detail a sweet yet frenzied dream, and afterwards go forth together to meet the morrow of unbroken aching toil.

Goodwives are the makers of threnodies in the villages. Whenever an older member of a neighbouring family passes away, the goodwives, their face a mask of grief, place themselves out of beholden duty before the bier and keen their sad and moving music. Very often they enter into the part and unbosom themselves of genuine emotion; tears and snot run together to form little white streams. They lament the hardness of existence, weep over unhappy fate weep for others weep for themselves, create a mournful atmosphere with their weeping, create a simple and honest way of life with their weeping, and by a tradition of weeping over many years create a deeply sad funeral culture.

Goodwives have a full measure of motherly love and respect for their parents-in-law. They will not eat an egg for the whole of a year if they can squeeze out from the gaps between their teeth the few coppers to pay their son's school fees. They will sew more patches on their own patched clothes if by doing so they can make their man presentable in company. With the passage of time and when passing time lengthens the furrows on their brow and their son has a young goodwife too, the goodwives more thoroughly understand how to treat their own mother-in-law and daughter-in-law, how they themselves should be daughter-in-law to their mother-in-law and mother-in-law to their daughter-in-law. The double role pushes the goodwives to an intersection in family history, from where with a little less impudence and a little more gravity they can, together with their man, steer their little family boat more steadily as it launches into the wave-tossed open sea of the future.

To be without a man is gloom without the sun, to be without a woman is drought without rain. Life on our home soil needs sunshine needs radiance needs still more the moisturing of rain. It was because the loess plain and the men of the loess plain had been scared by the drought of rain and the drought of women that they gave birth to strings of lusty and dashing or plaintive and beguiling folksongs and lovesongs which gave voice to the hope and expectation of unmarried men to continue their blood line. In their wonderful vision, the goodwives make their appearance, treading the hilltops treading the horizon treading the melodies of the yellow earth; they perform the harmonies of the pots-and-pans symphony, they broadcast the euphonies of the pigs-and-fowls chorus, they give play to the arts of the Goddess of Weavers to weave the long cataract of life; shouldering their son and leading their daughter, they set out on the beaten path to the far beyond that their forebears took before them, set out for the sunlit zone they have dreamed of.

When the spring breezes come to the loess plain, the dark ruddy faces of the goodwives, windblown suntanned rainsoaked, spring to life like the wheat seedlings, become animated, glowing, comely. They hum tunes from Shanxi opera or Shaanxi opera, and sometimes croon the most tuneful popular songs. After much hesitation and spying out of the land, they at last take their courage in their hands and exchange their baggy cotton trousers for jeans or sweatpants to outline the peaks and valleys of their anatomy, and in this outfit go to the market in town where they buy books for sons, knick-knacks for women and a bottle of pervadingly fragrant toilet water. They might consult their men over buying a black and white television with the money they got from selling sheep, so that they can all see something of the outside world. . . . When the summer wind calls, its tongues divide the goodwives' ranks, part of them leaving behind or temporarily leaving the loess plain they hate like hell and love like mad, and go into the town or into the city to push a barrow selling ice lollies or fix up a little cookshop against a wall and as they stretch the noodles and fry the dough sticks, they stretch out their own female values and fry up a brand-new life. . . .

The goodwives stand on the fertile soil of this new life and face the male wind battering them from all sides. . . .

Goodwives, the goodwives of our home soil.

(1991)

References

Sources

The classical prose selection consists almost entirely of anthology pieces; they had to be so in order to represent the classical heritage. It follows that the original texts can be found in numerous Chinese collections, old and new. To get a good overview, I used two big anthologies of recent date, namely *Gudai sanwen jianshang cidian* 古代散文鑑賞辭典, ed. Wang Bin 王彬 (Beijing: Nongcun duwu chubanshe, 1987), and *Zhongguo guwen jianshang cidian* 中國古文鑑賞辭典, ed. Wu Gongzheng 吳功正(Nanjing: Jiangsu wenyi chubanshe, 1987).

Both of these attach an 'appreciation' to each text. For detailed notes and explanations I found most helpful the *Zhongguo lidai sanwen zuojia xuanji* 中國歷代散文作家選集, published jointly by Joint Publishing (Hong Kong) and Shanghai guji chubanshe, each volume of which has a different editor. The only classical prose item not to be found in anthologies is the excerpt from Li Yu's *Pleasant Diversions*; for that I used *Yiqing sishu* 怡情四書, ed. Xue You 薛友(Hubei: Hubei cishu chubanshe, 1997).

There are also numerous general anthologies for the modern essay. The bulkiest known to me is, for the period up to 1949, *Xiandai sanwen jianshang cidian* 現代散文鑑賞辭典, ed. Wang Bin (Beijing: Nongcun duwu chubanshe, 1988); like its companion volume above, it affords a useful overview. The works of individual authors are nowadays relatively easy to find. Some of their original books have been reprinted; more often, Complete Works and variously assorted Selected Works have been published. Thanks to the virtual abandonment of ideological governance in this field in China and Taiwan in the last two decades, publishers in both places, and in Hong Kong also, have left very few gaps in the ranks of essayists here represented. There would be little point in listing source texts for the majority of my selections, as they will be found in titles like 'Selected Prose' or 'Complete Prose' under the author's name in any library catalogue: publishers and dates will vary, but the text will be the same. I therefore list below only those that may take some effort to find because the authors published many books of essays, or because 'Selected Works' do not abound.

Lu Xun
    Three summer pests (*Huagai ji* 華蓋集)
    The evolution of the male sex (*Zhun fengyue tan* 准風月談)

Ah Jin (*Qiejieting zawen erji* 且介亭雜文二集)
  Confucius in modern China (*Qiejieting zawen erji*)
Zhou Zuoren
  Relentless rain (*Yutian de shu* 雨天的書)
  Reading in the lavatory (*Kuzhu zaji* 苦竹雜記)
  On 'passing the itch' (*Bingzhu houtan* 秉燭後談)
  The ageing of ghosts (*Yedu chao* 夜讀抄)
  In praise of mutes (*Kanyun ji* 看雲集)
Liang Shih-ch'iu
  Sickness (*Yashe xiaopin chuji* 雅舍小品初集)
  Haircut (*Yashe xiaopin chuji*)
  Listening to plays (*Qiushi zawen* 秋室雜文)
Koarnhak Tarn
  The countryside of the past (*Tianyuan zhiqiu* 田園之秋 and *Fangcao* 訪草)
  Today's countryside (*Tianyuan zhiqiu* and *Fangcao*)
Zhang Xingjian
  Goodwives (*Jiushi niandai sanwen xuan* 九十年代散文選, ed. Chen Xianfa 陳先法, 1991)

Translations and Studies

There are a great number of books in Chinese on both classical and modern prose, and countless periodical articles. A list of just those I have read or consulted over the years would be very long, and would not suit the nature of this publication. I confine myself to the mention of only one, which offers a good survey of Chinese prose from the earliest days to the present, and contains references to specialized studies. It is *Zhongguo sanwen shigang* 中國散文史綱, ed., Liu Yan 劉衍 (Changsha: Hunan jiaoyu chubanshe, 1994).

In English there is no similar work. From the beginning, Chinese prose has been translated rather than surveyed, and that only sparsely. Tribute should be paid to H. A. Giles as a pioneer in the field. His *Gems of Chinese Literature: Prose*, first published in the 1880s, consisted of a selection of translated pieces from the year dot up to his time, tacked together by brief notes. It is still a good read, but as he was working before the advent of modern sinology, it is not very reliable. Sad to say, the later masters of Chinese-English translation paid little attention to essays. Arthur Waley, Burton Watson, David Hawkes, Angus Graham and Cyril Birch translated the odd piece only incidentally or as a contribution to general anthologies of Chinese literature.

References

To list now those general anthologies which put together provide a fair sprinkling of classical essays, they are:

Cyril Birch, comp. and ed., *Anthology of Chinese Literature* (New York: Grove Press, 1965).
Victor Mair, ed., *The Columbia Anthology of Traditional Chinese Literature* (New York: Columbia Press, 1994).
Stephen Owen, ed. and trans., *An Anthology of Chinese Literature: Beginnings to 1911* (New York: W.W. Norton, 1996).

Restricted anthologies devoted to classical prose include a double issue of *Renditions*, published by the Research Centre for Translation, Chinese University of Hong Kong, entitled 'Classical Prose' (Nos. 33 & 34, 1990), and another double issue on 'Classical Letters' (Nos. 41 & 42, 1994). In addition, a Renditions Book by Liu Shih-shun entitled *Chinese Classical Prose: The Eight Masters of the T'ang-Sung Period* was published in 1979.

A few other anthologies-cum-studies restricted by period or subject matter have been published elsewhere. The contributions of Lin Yutang (1895–1976) certainly deserve mention. In his day Lin's English-language books had far more readers than any sinologist's. His *The Importance of Understanding* (Freeport, New York: Books for Libraries Press, 1960) was a patchwork of translations of familiar prose of the late Ming and Qing dynasties, unexplored territory at the time. More recently, Richard Strassberg has published *Inscribed Landscapes: Travel Writing from Imperial China* (Berkeley: University of California Press, 1994), and most recently Yang Ye has brought out *Vignettes from the Late Ming: a hsiao-p'in Anthology* (Seattle: University of Washington Press, 1999).

A handy guide to individual classical authors is William Nienhauser's *The Indiana Companion to Traditional Chinese Literature* (Bloomington, Indiana: Indiana University Press, 1986). As for monographs on authors, their slant is rarely towards prose compositions. For general interest it is worth listing some that relate to the writers here translated, as follows:

Tao Yuanming
    James Robert Hightower, trans., *The Poetry of T'ao Ch'ien* (Oxford: Clarendon, 1970).
    Roland Fang, *Gleanings from Tao Yuan-ming* (Hong Kong: Commercial Press, 1980).

Liu Zongyuan
    William Nienhauser, et al., *Liu Tsung-yuan* (New York: Twayne, 1973).

Ouyang Xiu
> Ronald Egan, *The Literary Works of Ou-yang Hsiu* (Cambridge: Cambridge University Press, 1984).

Su Shi
> Ronald Egan, *Word, Image and Deed in the Life of Su Shih* (Cambridge, Mass.: Council on East Asian Studies, Harvard-Yenching Institute, 1994).

Yuan Hongdao
> Jonathan Chaves, trans., *Pilgrim of the Clouds* (New York: Weatherhill, 1978).
> Chou Chih-p'ing, *Yuan Hung-tao and the Kung-an School* (Cambridge: Cambridge University Press, 1988).

Li Yu
> Patrick Hanan, *The Invention of Li Yu* (Cambridge, Mass.: Harvard University Press, 1988).

Yuan Mei
> Arthur Waley, *Yuan Mei: Eighteenth Century Chinese Poet* (Stanford: Stanford University Press, 1956).

As for modern essays, some may be found translated in *The Columbia Anthology of Modern Chinese Literature* (New York: Columbia University Press, 1995), edited by Joseph Lau and Howard Goldblatt. Cumulatively, the greatest numbers have appeared in *Renditions* over the years, if we leave aside the Beijing publication *Chinese Literature*. Again I list the few books I know of that relate to the authors here translated, with apologies for overlooking any:

Lu Xun
> Yang Hsien-yi and Gladys Yang, trans., *Selected Works of Lu Hsun* (4 vols), (Beijing: Foreign Languages Press, 1956–1960).
> Leo Ou-fan Lee, ed., *Lu Xun and His Legacy* (Berkeley: University of California Press, 1985).
> ———, *Voices from the Iron House: A Study of Lu Xun.* (Bloomington and Indianapolis, Indiana University Press, 1987).

Zhou Zuoren
> David Pollard, *A Chinese Look at Literature: the Literary Values of Chou Tso-jen in Relation to the Tradition* (Berkeley: University of California Press, 1973).

Yang Jiang
> Howard Goldblatt, trans., *Six Chapters from My Life 'Downunder'* (Hong Kong: Chinese University Press, 1983).

He Qifang
> Bonnie McDougall, ed. and trans., *Paths in Dreams* (St. Lucia, Queensland: University of Queensland Press, 1976).

GPSR Authorized Representative: Easy Access System Europe, Mustamäe tee 50, 10621 Tallinn, Estonia, gpsr.requests@easproject.com

www.ingramcontent.com/pod-product-compliance
Lightning Source LLC
Chambersburg PA
CBHW031542300426
44111CB00006BA/140